THE NECESSITY OF FREEDOM IN HEGEL'S TURN BETWEEN LOGIC AND HISTORY

The Necessity of Freedom in Hegel's Turn Between Logic and History

EDITED BY
EMILIA ANGELOVA

UNIVERSITY OF TORONTO PRESS
Toronto Buffalo London

© University of Toronto Press 2026
Toronto Buffalo London
utppublishing.com
Printed in Canada

ISBN (cloth 978-1-4875-6430-8)   ISBN 978-1-4875-6432-2 (EPUB)
                                   ISBN 978-1-4875-6431-5 (PDF)

Library and Archives Canada Cataloguing in Publication

Title: The necessity of freedom in Hegel's turn between logic and history /
    edited by Emilia Angelova.
Names: Angelova, Emilia, editor.
Description: Includes bibliographical references and index.
Identifiers: Canadiana (print) 20250325764 | Canadiana (ebook) 20250325810 |
    ISBN 9781487564308 (cloth) | ISBN 9781487564322 (EPUB) |
    ISBN 9781487564315 (PDF)
Subjects: LCSH: Hegel, Georg Wilhelm Friedrich, 1770-1831—Criticism and
    interpretation. | LCSH: Liberty—Philosophy. | LCSH: Logic, Modern. |
    LCSH: History—Philosophy. | LCSH: Political science—Philosophy. |
    LCSH: Phenomenology. | LCSH: Aesthetics.
Classification: LCC B2948 .N43 2025 | DDC 193—dc23

Cover design: John Beadle
Cover image: Envato

The manufacturer's authorised representative in the EU for product safety
is Mare Nostrum Group B.V., Mauritskade 21D, 1091 GC Amsterdam, The
Netherlands. Email: gpsr@mare-nostrum.co.uk

We wish to acknowledge the land on which the University of Toronto Press
operates. This land is the traditional territory of the Wendat, the Anishnaabeg,
the Haudenosaunee, the Métis, and the Mississaugas of the Credit First Nation.

University of Toronto Press acknowledges the financial support of the
Government of Canada, the Canada Council for the Arts, and the Ontario Arts
Council, an agency of the Government of Ontario, for its publishing activities.

Canada Council for the Arts · Conseil des Arts du Canada

Ontario Arts Council · Conseil des Arts de l'Ontario
an Ontario government agency
un organisme du gouvernement de l'Ontario

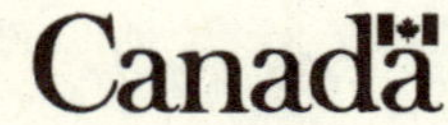 

Funded by the Government of Canada · Financé par le gouvernement du Canada

Canada

MIX
Paper | Supporting responsible forestry
FSC® C103567

Contents

Editor's Acknowledgments

This collection was intended in part as celebrating the legacy of Hegel's *magnum opus* of the *Philosophy of Right*. I thank for their loyalty all the contributors to this volume, most of whom are leading scholars in today's significant revival of a systematic reading of Hegel. To read Hegel systematically is to approach the normativity of the concept as retroactively grounding the practical nexus between logic and history, and as well, understanding as intrinsic to this nexus the philosophy of right and the phenomenology of spirit, bringing closer together the early and the mature works. I thank John Burbidge, Constantin Boundas, and Elaine Stavro for sharing scholarship, advice, friendship, and wonderful support in the early stages at Trent University, where the project germinated. I thank the Department of Philosophy, Concordia University, for giving me further support in teaching and research. I thank the fabulous graduate and undergraduate students in my seminars on *The Phenomenology of Spirit* for letting me expand the horizon of interpreting Hegel. My deepest indebtedness is to Rebecca Comay, for her supervision of my own doctoral work and many years of unconditional support. This work would not have been possible without my partner and colleague, philosopher David Morris, whose love and care give me energy every day.

The success of this volume was made possible through the patient and steady professional advice of the series editor at the University of Toronto Press, Len Husband. I thank Len and two anonymous reviewers, whose constructive and penetrating comments early on proved transformative in making this volume a better work on Hegel.

Editor's Introduction

EMILIA ANGELOVA, CONCORDIA UNIVERSITY

Hegel's philosophical position is unique in the tradition of German Idealism in that it takes freedom to be a necessity that permeates and grounds philosophy as a system. This necessity is not, however, merely abstract or theoretical; indeed, his *Philosophy of Right*[1] proceeds as a theory of the existence of freedom *as* "right" in history. This leads to a remarkable, consequent feature of his system: that the generation of historical meaning is shaped by the actualization of the logic of the concept, which actualization is his topic in the *Science of Logic*.[2] For Hegel, then, the generation of historical meaning integrally involves logical activity. This particular connection between history, freedom, and logic has received renewed attention from scholars in recent years, especially through new results about Hegel's *Philosophy of Right*. The theory of normativity proposed in this work posits the existence of freedom and its validity, as right, as necessary to the shaping and becoming of ethical, moral, practical, and political life. New scholarship adds that for Hegel, this theory of freedom's becoming actual is a process that integrally involves the self-actualizing of the concept from out of the essence of ground. That is, freedom in its practical life shapes itself according to the logic of the concept and philosophical foundation as ground.

Through close textual studies the present collection illuminates the sources of this connection between logic and history and draws out implications for how we understand the practical life of the social world as a whole. The contributions work in the intersections between philosophy of right, logic, phenomenology, history, and aesthetics to demonstrate this realization.

This introduction has a twofold purpose. First, for those new to these points about Hegel, it provides context for and an initiation into this connection between logic and history. It does so through a discussion anchored in the work of a key scholar in this area, namely Stephen Houlgate, whose work has been influential in opening up connections across Hegel's works, and especially between the *Philosophy of Right*, the *Science of Logic*, and the *Phenomenology of Spirit*.[3] Second, for scholars who are familiar with these points, it synthesizes them anew, around Houlgate's work, so as to provide an overview of unifying themes and efforts of the collection, and to organize various scholarly results around this core.

In terms of general introduction, Hegel's *Philosophy of Right* has not always been read together with the *Science of Logic*. The last two decades have yielded new approaches that understand the normativity of freedom through both freedom and history, foregrounding the meaning of action and transforming received orthodoxy about Hegel's philosophy of the subject and political rationality. The last ten years specifically have yielded increasingly anti-metaphysical interpretations of the system, integrating the philosophy of nature without a rupture into the philosophy of spirit.[4] More recent readers of Hegel, such as Terry Pinkard, Karen Ng, and James Kreines, form the latest wave in the revival of interest in a systematic interpretation.[5]

The present collection emerges from the systematic approaches that developed more robustly in the first decade by focusing more squarely on the logic and philosophy of spirit taken together, and brings back to its rational justification the foundation on which rests Hegel's most salient thinking connecting *Philosophy of Right* to the *Logic*. The interest in the systematic interpretation of freedom and history on normative conditions not accidentally began with Stephen Houlgate's emphasis that "presuppositionless thinking"[6] is the philosophical foundation of the method as found at the beginning of the *Science of Logic*. In the first place, this radical interpretation broaches the view that not just epistemic normativity, but a deeper ontological normativity underpins the structure of thought informing Hegel's mature critique of morality onwards of 1816. Just two decades ago, Houlgate leaned into the system of Hegel linking specifically the ideas from these two magisterial works. In the second place, the mature critique does not simply decree a justification from out of the method of logic, how the normative dimension of freedom, which Hegel understood as "external sphere of right," stands against Kant's "formalism of right."

That is, Hegel conducts a systematic deduction of the speculative idea of the philosophy of right while he is precisely not fixing reality in a pre-conceived idea. The method gains in value only through the process of self-actualization of which the individual in turn must find itself as having become a part. The individual takes on an active life as subject and as part of the rationality of the "whole," by way of establishing itself as foundation, yet never as "first" and origin but always retroactively, as coming to presence in a return to, its own having been. Self-grounding and retroaction are the modes of production of the concept's coming to presence, the self understood as method. The method of Hegel unfolds from immanent ground. It roots the system in a capacity for self-preservation and change as well, since it is simultaneously bound up with a dynamics of powers that the self is unable to supersede except through objective analysis, a struggle of internalization to resolve the antagonism of its surrounds, living through contradiction, crossing over to being with, and for the other. In making what is foreign to the self into its own coherent centre and driving force, Hegel posits that separating of the self from itself and transformation of being for itself through being with the other is the origin of the concept, and that by its own nature the concept is the idea of a political rationality as a self-beginning.

Put otherwise, Hegel's addressee is the scientific mind that approaches the reality of its world, not by demagogy or doxa but by objective analysis of experience, obtained through reflection on concrete, historically situated subjects as citizens of a modern society. The subject who finds itself thrust into a world appearing rife with contingency and immediacy is naturally inclined to understand itself and its world, socio-political events as atomic, independent occurrences unrelated to a past, or any sort of unfolding of a rational order. Hegel not simply rejects the atomistic individual, but his method of the dialectic articulates the demand that the task equally lies with motivating that subject's interest in the rationality of the political. These concretely embodied conditions of the life of the subject not in isolation but within a social group lead Hegel to the mature critique. It is subsequent to articulating the demand for motivating interest in the rationality of the political that the *Philosophy of Right* provides an argumentation of rationality in systematic form.

What, more specifically, marks out the systematicity view? Presupposed ontologically as lying at the foundation of rationality in the notorious couplet "the real is rational, the rational is real," Hegel's freedom is not an extant entity but a self-beginning as principle. The mature critique of morality in this way demands argumentation of rationality in systematic form wherein freedom is a self-determination of the truth and essence of ground grasped *as* form: immanence, necessity, and retrogressive grounding all articulate this form's self-actualizing rationality. In this regard, Houlgate's pioneering work on the presuppositionless thinking at the foundation of the beginning of ground, then, inspires recent interpretations of the normativity of freedom wherein the method takes on the systematicity view predominantly in the direction of incompletion and new beginnings, making room for new things. I articulate three major ways to underscore how this alters understanding, specifically, the contributions to method from the mature critique.

First, the *magnum opus* of the *Philosophy of Right* famously begins with the emergence of will from out of something external, impulse [*Trieb*], the centre of Hegel's mature critique of Kant's ethics, what is Abstract Right. The method, proceeding as a self-actualizing idea transposed into the philosophical foundations of the *Logic* advances a novel understanding of the major argumentation of Hegel's transition from the Ethicality into Morality account. Scholars in this approach of normativity from systematic foundations include Kevin Thompson,[7] and specifically working from the value of method in this account, this approach is represented in Angelica Nuzzo,[8] Paul Redding,[9] and others. Among divergent approaches, we distinguish the kind defended in Houlgate from those centring on the role of freedom not ontologically, but as confined to Hegel's "ethics," what, for example, governs Allen W. Wood,[10] and Beatrice Longuenesse,[11] among others. A third way into this is through robust normative accounts of action and agency combining the systematicity and ethics approaches, for example, in Christopher Yeomans.[12] Finally, an initial approach deriving from the sociality of reason, and connecting to the ethics approaches tied to normative discourse ethics began through the 1990s and still strong today with Terry Pinkard,[13] and Axel Honneth,[14] to mention two of its founders.

In terms of scholarship, normativity was first developed by R. Pippin's influential 1990s account[15] of the idealism of Hegel and the satisfactions of Self-Consciousness, deriving from the 1806 *Phenomenology of Spirit*, to which I return below. Normativity played a role in informing the last two decades of approaches by deepening the concept from Self-consciousness, experience, intersubjective dialectic of recognition, the social groups of master and slave. An apt distinction that sets these apart from Houlgate's novel approach to the method of the *Logic* concerns how the question of origins becomes a question of presuppositionless beginnings, and this opens up for new inquiry Hegel's system.

What are the salient traits that prominently feature in the inquiry that opens up? To begin with, by 1820, the mature critique grows out of the idea of ground as non-founded ground, in the system of the *Science of Logic*. Hegel's first division in the *Philosophy of Right* is Abstract Right, beginning with the objectivity of Ethicality: a subject overwhelmed by contradictory, because self-external, impulses. The inner structure of the subject derives its unity from the speculative idea of the identity proposition of thought and being, the reconciliation of opposites, non-being and being. If the idea of Right makes itself intelligible to us from systematic foundations, as Hegel argues, this demonstrates that right "as" right in history is capable of surviving the battle with the empiricist and intellectualist discourses of seventeenth and eighteenth century legal science, of right to become philosophical. As Hegel emphasizes, "The Idea of right is freedom, and in order to be truly apprehended, it must be recognizable in its concept and in its concept's existence [*Dasein*]."[16] Freedom's existence, its being, is coextensive with the living body of Objective Spirit, its thought.

From the standpoint of method, Hegel takes it that freedom's being "self-external" just means "natural" – each opposite having an equal claim on the activity of the subject. The process of appropriating and claiming the subject by the self-movement of the concept and contradiction, implies negating the impulse's immediacy. This negating is at the same time that of making use of the ego, or I that wills, as object (*Gegenstand*)[17] internalizing this externality, in settling upon one of these impulses and "resolving" to act.

Furthermore, this third moment, "resolving upon" some action is the birth of the dialectical will for Hegel: it is a sublation of impulse, through undergoing a transformation itself, which is an outgrowth of impulse. From this we conclude that the primary criterion of free action in Hegel is freedom, yet not as alienable property of the will and something itself alien at heart of the subject. Instead, individuating the particular is grasped as freedom's self-externalizing and immanent self-beginning, and therefore as a "self-determination criterion."

We can restate this point about agency, linking it to the method. Hegel counters an one-sided, epistemic normativity by demonstrating that what appears from one aspect as the internalization of the idea from out of its other, appears from another aspect as the externalization of the subject through action: the finite will's (the object's) ends are realized, made objective in the sense of negating subjective immediacy. Free action externalizes itself (*Entäußerung*),[18] its being thrust into the world makes it the *objectivity* condition. Through action, again, the objective conditions that undergird free action in the first place are themselves the test. This freedom as normative condition of possibility of the system of Right, as "retrogressive grounding" (in Thompson's words) taken together with the conditions that enable free action, just is what Hegel calls "right."

To put the same claim more strongly, the *Philosophy of Right* logically brings Hegel to engaging the legacy of the French Revolution on systematic foundational grounds, he urges the reader to practice "freedom toward the object."[19] On a first approximation, the systematic interpretation changes normativity into a question about lacking foundations in a first origin, and this demands demonstration of how the social "whole" as subject gives rise to public institutions, values and practices through which the living concreteness of logic forms a nexus with history.

The second most important contribution more properly concerns the method in the Logic. The systematicity account of method in the *Science of Logic* motivates a dialectic of thinking and process not merely as substance-ontological but as well, as epistemological normativity. The *Logic* establishes the "true way of knowing, the way of knowing things in their truth," and this is nothing other than the "process of development that is proper to being itself, and this is to grasp the rationality, the dialectic of the concept, within all that is."[20] The philosophies of Nature, and of Spirit, the latter of which the *Philosophy of Right* is a part, are "exhibiting normativity," so far as each is to "discern the movement of the concept, the movement set out and established by the Logic."[21]

The corollary is that since the method of the logic undergirds historically specific and always ontologically concrete forms of rationality, a necessity of contingency, then, for reasons of the immanence of ground, the criterion for objectivity is internal to all these forms. For example, as Kevin Thompson argues immanence understood as ground's necessary entailment, *PR*, §142 demonstrates that "the potential conflicts between the principles of Abstract Right and Morality are resolved and the ethical objectivity of *Sittlichkeit* is able to be the rightful criterion to which ethical subjectivity … is obligated to measure up."[22] The ontological claim is that the identity of Ethicality is a systematic concept (rather than a representationalist or 'culturalist') deriving its self-justification from the logic of ground as being determinate being without a "first" origin in a pre-determined foundation. The concreteness of *Sittlichkeit*, for Hegel, is therefore not, and cannot be, about being simply a historically specific set of expectations embodied in the customs. Hegel's logic of the non-founded ground does not allow that duties are simply prescribed by one's "historically contingent situation." Importantly, the concreteness of the "identity of conscience and the good, the particularity and the universality of right" already denotes the institutional order as determinate being but as demanded by the "complete actualization" of freedom as self-determination and as self-movement, imminent cancellation of itself as return from being for another.

Hegel's account of the self-justification of the existence of freedom "as" right in history in turn, deepens, and radicalizes the method of the *Logic*. The logic provides grounding in the speculative idea of rationality traced out of the objective development of the "whole" subject, together with its self-actualizing concept "as" rationality in history, deployed in its public life and institutions. That is, the logical totality of the idea provides a horizon of meaning, on which the subject is not opposed to the object but becomes unfolded to the point of harmonious unity of the self and its other, as ideal embodiment. As Hegel puts it, in the activity of free will we find the *essential development* of the substantial content of the Idea" – the will essentially develops the *substantial* content of the Idea. In this essential development, the activity of the will cancels the abstract contradiction of objectivity and subjectivity. The will must translate its subjective ends into objective determinations while at the same time "remaining *with itself* in objectivity."[23] This means that the cancelling here cannot be merely theoretical or abstract – it cannot be purely subjective, it must eventually take on objective form. This is why the subjective free will must already be working towards its mediation in sustainable or durable institutions.

Third, the thesis about method as presuppositionless thinking of the early 2000s, in Houlgate, opens the philosophy of right to systematic foundations by arguing more specifically for an ontological normative interpretation of freedom in the *Philosophy of Right*. This is precisely because the activity of the will and of freedom must grasp and exhibit its systematic foundations, which means this activity must track some of the ontological issues crucial to the *Logic*. The pivotal point is that the dialectic of the will and its activity, in the transition from Subjective to Objective spirit, tracks the transition as deriving from the logic of Being as ground, as being without a pre-determined foundation, and into the logic of Essence.

Indeed, what is at stake, as Houlgate influentially argues, is a transition from particular actions of an individual, to those actions as reflecting universal principles, which must find stability in existence. "Being transforms itself logically into a multiplicity of ways of being, therefore, because of the moment of *negation* that it necessarily bears within itself."[24] The logical thus involves a peculiar ontological necessity: the category of necessity, its reason for being, is not predetermined or given but becomes *what is*. Pure "being proves to be not just sheer being after all but the unity of being and the *not*" – being exists as bearing residues of articulating this inborn not.

In proper terms, the first major role from Houlgate lies in evaluating freedom's necessity as ontological contribution, and with it reopening the question of the subject, in Hegel, as a question of method of transformation and as permanent self-critique, and this implies as internal social critique. The key difference is regarding the method in relation, in particular, to the categories of the *Logic*. The categories, for Houlgate, are "both forms of thought *and* structures of being as such." Consider that this considerably lowers the threshold of signification of the self established by the normativity view of the 1990s through the advances in scholarship made by Pippin. For Pippin, Hegel's method is transcendental, "insofar as [for Pippin] it starts with the bare thought of being and then *regresses* to ever more fundamental conditions of the successful thought of determinate being."[25] A second major transformation through Houlgate is that it allows for Hegel's philosophy of history to take on new interpretation through the Logic as method.

Let me now move, finally, to issues that prove transformative for receiving Hegel's *Phenomenology of Spirit* in this turn between Logic and History. The *Philosophy of Right* approached this way, I argued above, functions as providing the standpoint of the rational unfolding of the theory of right *as* "right" in history. Hegel impels the reading audience to cultivate rigour and be able to identify the thread of necessity prevailing through this seeming contingency. The challenge lies in how to turn to the systematic rational structure of thought itself, through which rationality finds itself as pure unfolding. The point about method, as I recount below, is as well advantageous to reconceiving a theory of origin, and this implicates a fractured origins theory, including theorizing like Hyppolite did argue, omitting the doctrine of Statism out of the corpus in 1948 (on occasion of the 1920s appearance of works from the 1803 and onwards of Hegel's early systems drafts).[26]

Again, Houlgate defends the view that presuppositionless thinking must lie at the foundations of rationality as practice of the idea of philosophy, the beginning of the science of logic. To arrive at this, Houlgate summarises some of the history of discussion of presuppositionless thinking (Schelling was the first to conceptualize this idea which crystalizes in Hegel). For Hegel, the pure being of thought as scientific (*wissenschaftlich*) Logic and based on it his account of method, derives from not a phenomenological bracketing (e.g., instrumental rationality in Husserl), not a noumenal, suprasensible "beyond" of the idea (e.g., world of forms in Plato). Houlgate writes about "thought that sets aside all its assumptions about *what* it is," and "is left with nothing but the simple thought *that* it is."[27] "Hegel's presuppositionless science of logic begins, therefore, with the thought itself as simply being – not being anything in particular but simply *be-ing* as such." The first prong of this is that for Hegel, "the necessary categories of thought have to be derived" "from this pure being of thought."[28] The second prong is that none of Hegel's arguments are invulnerable to rational critique – rather, we are "not permitted to take any such criteria for granted in a fully self-critical philosophy."[29]

How has the last decade transformed approaches to the *Phenomenology of Spirit*? The early Frankfurt School of Benjamin and Adorno and the legacy of Hyppolite in the French reception in the last half of the twentieth century significantly transformed the approaches to Hegel of the 1806 Jena *Phenomenology of Spirit*. Through the themes that came to prominence in the legacy of 1960s post-war heightened attention to instrumental reason, self-destruction, and overall a dialectic of the Enlightenment that understood itself as not being enlightened about itself, Hegel became mobilized for the needs of leftist social critique, and a new paradigm for freedom and history.

Recent scholarship approaches the early work as valuable, intrinsic component from which to reflect on the system's own relations of internal reflection, deploying Hegel's method of intelligibility understood as method of self-critique from within. So for example, in the memorable chapter 6, "Self-Alienated Spirit. Culture," Hegel traces the re-commemoration process of the Spirit, part of the progressions of Self-consciousness. Culture is Hegel's critique of the contemporary ideology and body politic of world-historical Modernity, particularly, through the aporia that the centrality of the French Revolution presents for the actors. Alienation and self-alienation are the experiences of Self-consciousness characterizing its normative commitment in structuring modernity, and the role that tragic action plays in this commitment. The construct of tragic action and transmission of trauma, on which we find foregrounded the worth of remembrance as being in need of re-conceptualizing the past as opposed to mechanically repeating, leads Hegel to develop a notion of history, as Comay has argued in 2011, on the model of a logic of forgiveness. Hegel's account is centred on the traumatic chain of empty transmission of History, as representing a finite history of the Spirit in Time.

More broadly, in the objective movement of Hegel's oblique negation, a "genuine negativity" finds the *free* subject as emerging in the continuous movement – from "comedy inherent in the Greek democracy," and through the advent of revealed religion, and into the logical totality traced out of the French Revolution. Yet in Hegel, the subject rightly, does not strive towards an other in order to reduce it to the same. Precisely the opposite. Hegel writes early in the *Phenomenology*: "But that an accident and such, detached from what circumscribes it, what is bound and is actually only in this context with others, should attain an existence of its own and the separate freedom – this is the tremendous power of the negative; it is the energy (*Energie*) of thought, of the pure 'I'."[30] The boldness of phenomenological articulation here stems from a negativity that is not posited in a subject anguished by an inaccessible sociality or transcendence.

The *Phenomenology of Spirit* construed in recent reception, taken together with the *Science of Logic* and the *Philosophy of Right* teaches us that Hegel posits a normativity of "freedom," its "necessity" – as a socio-political and as well an ontological question. Over and above the intersubjective, or the imaginary domain of master and slave, Hegel is to account not only for society, but for history itself. There is no relation of simple succession between the imaginary (the social or intersubjective master and slave bond) and the symbolic plane, which actually binds. What binds is a semiotic collapse at the limit of our experience – no longer biologically defined, death is never experienced as such. That which actually binds, then, is the symbolic game, the subject/other structure: desire for the recognition of the desire of the other's desire. Fear of death, not defined on the biological/ imaginary register depends on taking a leap of faith, into an impasse, rejection/ negation taking it back to the "original myth" and another plane, the symbolic. Arguably, Hegel approaches on structuralist premises what meaning is. Meaning is generated by the bifurcation of the subjective and the objective, concept and object, being and essence, through the friction of one binary element against another, as these form the fundamental oppositions implicit within any speech act. Hegel thus situates the subjective spirit and objective spirit in relation to the priority of ground – both these are at origin thrown into language, the plane of signs and symbols. In Hegel, then, the symbolic is always already prior to the subject. Language and culture precede the coming into being of the subject. In this sense, the symbolic in being prior, cuts the subject and casts it as "whole" in the system of signifiers. The Terror, then, as the culmination in chapter 6 B, Culture, hints at, is interminable battle, susceptible to reverting to myth at any given moment – between Enlightenment and Faith.

The Chapters and the Organization of the Collection

This collection is organized in three parts that link chapters together in relation to the conceptual lines of inquiry discussed above. The first part shows how issues of freedom and history, arising in terms of normativity and trust, help situate the *Philosophy of Right* in Hegel's system, and how the method of the *Science of Logic* informs and structures the science of right. The second part shows how attention to historical experience sheds light on the role of the concept in the *Phenomenology*, *Lectures on History*, and how this in turn informs Hegel's concept of history, in particular, as essence and ground of the necessity of freedom. As well, in this part study of the *Logic* and *Aesthetics* shows that for

Hegel modal categories need to be understood not in abstract terms (as in Kant) but as arising in the temporality of history, in ways that bring freedom into play. The third part contains a discussion of Comay's recent monograph about Hegel and the French Revolution. This discussion sharply focuses attention on key issues in Hegel, such as the absolute, necessity, contingency, and experience, and the ways these cross-cut his discussion of historical revolutions, and his view of philosophy revolutionizing the concept.

The first part concerns "The Logic of Freedom and Its Necessity." Its chapters defend and elaborate the central point of the "systematicity interpretation," namely that freedom needs to be understood as a sort of necessary contingency that articulates itself from a systematic ground that it itself establishes.

In chapter 1, "Right and Trust in Hegel's *Philosophy of Right*," Stephen Houlgate expands his earlier results regarding Hegel's pursuit of philosophy as the science of presuppositionless thinking. He shows the implications of this project with respect to the *Philosophy of Right* and its role in the system. Specifically, Hegel's project leads to a view in which truth can only be understood as folding or doubling back on itself (*Einfaltung*, or enfolding via a kind of repetition) in spirit's achievement of itself, and that this means that the "System" necessarily has to be a self-contradictory unity – which means that issues of freedom and history are coimplicated even at this logical level of the system. Because of this, fully grasping the speculative dimension in Hegel (that is, his discussion of logic and the initially abstract categories as behind the system's concept), requires taking both experience and phenomenology into account. On the other hand, to understand how experience contributes to this speculative dimension, we cannot stay within immediate experience, we need to understand how that experience is driven by conceptual and logical issues. As Houlgate argues, in our experience of contradictions (at a phenomenological level) our ontological commitments are at stake (at a logical, conceptual level, what he calls the metaphysical idealist level). With regard to the *Philosophy of Right*, this approach lets him show (in ways that resonate with the sort of results we find in Quante and Nuzzo) that the reasoning about right that grounds this work needs to be understood as involving both concepts and experience. Houlgate brings this out by especially attending to issues of trust, as not a merely anthropological or psychological category, but not as a purely logical or epistemic category either. Conversely, this analysis lets him show that this has implications for Hegel's logic and as well, for example, how experiential issues, are not external to this logic.

In chapter 2, "Hegel's Cognitivist Ascriptivism," Michael Quante begins by noting that for Hegel in the *Philosophy of Right*, the only adequate basis for judging actions right are reasons manifest at the level of historical stages (e.g., Greek tragedy, the Ethical order). But, Quante observes, Hegel needs to show why this is the case, and to give some basis for this claim about right via his concept of history. Pursuing this line of investigation lets Quante show that Hegel's claims about right are not based, for example, in meta-ethical claims: Hegel insists that we have to grant history its weight, we have to see that for each epoch, there is a corresponding thought (e.g., in the stages of Objective Spirit, its Art, Philosophy and Religion) that shapes concepts of right. Quante shows, however, that the sort of history in question is not the sort of grand or totalizing narrative often attributed to Hegel, rather Quante argues for a deflationary view of history and the absolute, a "discursive dialectic," in which reason always relates to the manifestations of the special practices and institutions. Conversely, as we ourselves are this historically realized agency, we as agents share in these institutional representations and share in the interpretations of rationality that govern individual action, individuals' wills, and souls. Quante thus provides an "ascriptivist cognitivist" account for the rationality of agency (vs. a normatively prescriptive one), in which reason is worked out through its dialectical, dialogical history. He shows how the speculative, logical development must in fact be understood as a discursive dialectic. In terms of the system, Quante shows that this dialectic, which shapes reason, and is tracked in the *Science of Logic* (and *Encyclopedia Logic*), in fact takes place via an "ascriptive" practice, through the history of reason. On the one hand, the rational basis of right needs to be understood in terms of issues of the concept discussed in the *Logic*. But, on the other hand, these issues in the logic need to be understood through the historical shapes of spirit, a point that has been made in prior scholarship, but to which Quante adds innovative claims via what he calls a "hermeneutical therapeutics" that focuses on the temporality of speaker positions in language as crucial to this history (in ways that challenge the Habermasian deliberative consensus).

Chapter 3, Angelica Nuzzo's "The Justice of Contradiction: History and the Realization of Freedom in Hegel," draws out the implications of the systematic foundation of Hegel's philosophy of Objective Spirit in the *Science of Logic*. What is at stake in Hegel's concept of "history" is the process of generating the norms of the "social," where the rationality of norms arises as a reflection about, yet from within, a presuppositionless thought working itself out.[31] But this also means that in working itself out, this thinking is not driven by abstract, arbitrary or rigid concepts or reasoning, it is rather driven by a historical dimension internal to "the very idea of philosophy that one systematically practices." Nuzzo defends the claim that in Hegel, logical method is crucial to the philosophy of history, and that this nexus of logical method and philosophy of history, is in fact central, such that the logic itself is the unity of subjective and objective concept. That is, for Hegel, the idea of history is the culmination of the movement of freedom's realization in the sphere of ethical life, but we must understand this movement in terms of the normativity of logic as method. In particular, Nuzzo analyses the role that contradiction and negativity play in structuring logical, practical, and historical processes. On the basis of an analysis of this issue, and in contrast with a long-standing interpretation of Hegel's idea of history, she claims that the most innovative and most useful feature of such an idea is the way it must be brought back to history's *logical* foundation. This overall claim emphasizes the fundamental solidarity between Hegel's logical thought of contradiction and his awareness of its practical and historical relevance.

Chapter 4, Iain Macdonald's "Adorno's Modal Utopianism: Possibility and Actuality in Adorno and Hegel," shows how, on Adorno's reading, Hegel falls into a longstanding metaphysical tradition in which actuality is prior – and in some ways superior – to possibility. That is, Adorno criticizes Hegel for being limited to an anthropogenic subject that is neatly defined by the *Phenomenology* and caught within the limits of its own experience, that is, within historical epochs that inscribe thought in pre-existing categories via a negative and rigid dialectic that instrumentalizes reason. Macdonald does not take sides in Adorno's polemic against Hegel, but makes an important contribution to the collection and this part, by meticulously tracing the points of argument, as well as linkages between these and issues of critical social theory. Showing how Adorno's way of reading the *Logic* through the *Phenomenology*, and his modal utopianism, which uproots modality from the system, can lead Adorno to this conclusion, Macdonald's result implicitly highlights the importance of attending to the *Logic* as well as the roots of modality in the normativity of freedom, and not necessarily committing Hegel to utopia.

Chapter 5, Nahum Brown's "Possibility Necessarily Entails Itself in Actuality: Hegel's Theory of Conditions," focuses on immanent conditions as having a crucial role in the *Science of Logic*. Brown concentrates on Hegel's Argument from Modality, because it leads to the unusual consequence that possibility necessarily "entails itself in actuality." Traditionally, classical modal theories assume that although actuality entails possibility, possibility does not necessarily entail actuality. But

Hegel claims that if each actuality is a condition for the possibility of others, then immediate actuality is really possibility resulting in further actualization. This consequence leads Hegel to reject metaphysical theories that divide reality into a two-world system. In a two-world system, essence and appearance are divided, and the question whether an essence must necessarily appear is a non-question, because essence is disjoint from questions of necessity and contingency, which attach only to appearances. Hegel rejects this disjunction as artificial and abstract, and this leads him to a very different view of possibility and actuality as concretely related, such that their relation is necessitated by, yet contingent on the way things work out. Put another way, if conditions of things involve *both* actuality and possibility, one must rethink whether "unactualized" possibility is a viable category at all. Altogether Brown shows how these modal categories therefore do not turn on a relation between essence and appearance, but rather they transform into one another in a historical process that involves a kind of freedom, since it is not limited in advance by such abstractions as unactualized possibilities, essences, etc., or even historical epochs as pre-existing categories of thought.

The second part concerns "Phenomenological and Aesthetic Approaches to the Necessity of Freedom and its History." Whereas chapters in the first part focus more on formal aspects of the 'systematicity interpretation' (on the conceptual logic at work in the necessity of freedom), chapters in this part focus on the experiential and aesthetic content through which freedom unfolds. As well, chapters in this division discuss implications regarding Hegel's understanding of the meaning of the progress of history. This turns out to have a more radicalized sense than is usually thought. It is well known that for Hegel, history is not a matter reducing to or being founded upon existing historical records, history is rather the self-articulation of the sorts of meaning of historical consciousness. This includes memorialization and representations of memory through which history makes sense as a process. Often it has been claimed that for Hegel this self-articulation of history is closed up, that, for example, it does not give a voice to suffering as condition of all truth, and is predestined to an end. The chapters in this section work against this claim. This is because the self-articulation of history proceeds through a theory of freedom as a nexus of logical method and philosophy of history that does not commence from a first beginning that is a historical given. History contingently develops its own systematic grounds. So it cannot operate as some sort of closed system. The connection to Hegel's logic shows us that, given the necessity of freedom, history as experienced is an openness to beginnings in a "more radicalized sense."[32]

Chapter 6, Alberto Siani's "Hegel on the Self-Fulfilment of Philosophy as the Opening of Human History," offers exegesis and interpretation of several programmatic statements from the Preface to the *Phenomenology of Spirit*, to show that Hegel's project of the self-fulfilment of philosophy into its scientific form does indeed open, and not close, the time and space of actual human history. Siani advances this argument by discussing the implications of Hegel's statements, showing how the self-fulfilment of philosophy implies its liberation from positive given principles or assumptions based on a presumed fixed and static human nature. Assessing Hegel's relevance for a philosophical understanding of our time depends largely on the meaning to be assigned to his conception of the relationship between philosophy and history. Siani thereby places Hegel in contrast to and against widespread interpretations, such as the one given by Francis Fukuyama. Furthermore, Siani distinguishes different philosophical patterns of the separation between subject and object and the possibility of its overcoming, outlining the main characteristics and possible appeal of a Hegel-based philosophy of history.

Chapter 7, Jennifer Ann Bates's "Organic Freedom: Hegel's Four-Way Dialectic," pursues the thorny question of how we are to understand Hegel's frequent use of the word "organic" in his writings – and how is it related to Hegel's conception of freedom. Bates begins with the *Philosophy of Right* where extant wholes (e.g., the State) and the speculative method are understood as analogically organic (vs. literally organic). Bates contrasts this with the organic as dialectical, Hegel's "dialectical organic." This is a four-way dialectic consisting of the relation of the concept and reality *in dialectical relation to* the relation of subject and substance, dating back to the *Science of Logic*, and before that to the four-way dialectic of "organic" and "inorganic" in the *Phenomenology of Spirit*. Against some commentators' erroneous back-dating of a *determinate*, organic "life of the concept" to Pure Being, Bates defends Hegel's four-way dialectic, i.e., the simultaneous emergence of life and self-consciousness, as more fruitful and exegetically justified method of approaching issues of the organic in Hegel. The organic-inorganic dialectic of Freedom in the *Logic*, and the maturation of the "person," Self-consciousness's and spirit's encounters with the inorganic in the *Phenomenology*, show how the dialectic of organic and inorganic becomes, through the work of burial and recollection, the way in which spirit sustains itself. This "sustaining" work is accomplished at first through the burying of the dead, and it is then socially developed in elaborated forms in subsequent chapters, and it finally culminates in the "Calvary of Absolute Spirit," in Absolute Knowing. On Bates's view, the four-part dialectic of Hegel's "organic" philosophy shows us how to think and be in a free and sustaining way, in our ethical and natural environments. In terms of the collection, this result shows that logical dialectic needs to be understood in terms of such environments and their history as involving freedom, but also that these environments and history articulate themselves via a logic worked out in the dialectical organic.

Chapter 8, Jim Vernon's "Hegel on Language and Freedom" offers exegeses of both the resolution to the Unhappy Consciousness in the *Phenomenology* and the transition from affection to thought in the *Encyclopedia*. This yields the result that for Hegel, freedom is a species-specific property that implicitly demonstrates that all humans are essentially free. Hegel, however, more deeply understands that the very essence of humanity is freedom. For Hegel, though, we can remain, and for the most part have remained, in ignorance of our essence, and, by the same token, even as we are making possible our freedom, we can fail to actualize or become aware of being free more essentially. While Hegel's arguments are unique, his overall account places him within a well-established lineage of philosophers who identify our unique capacity for language with our essential freedom. This is a humanist idea of language, in which Hegel grounds our freedom in the universal, finite grammar through which an infinity of particular expressions can be constructed. Vernon argues that Hegel needs to be understood in this context, and this explains the importance of Hegel's defence of the free will, and that bringing this view of language to the *Philosophy of Right* helps us more fully understand his political philosophy. Vernon's connection between freedom and language, which also shows how this connection arises through history and issues of right, advances the connections between logic and history discussed in the collection.

Chapter 9, Jeffrey Reid's "Re-presenting the Past: The Reason in Hegel's History," argues that Hegel assigns a role to Reason in history that is not fully grasped if interpreted only from the perspective of Hegel's *Philosophy of History*. Reason's role in history must instead be understood in terms of the analysis and concept of reason in the *Phenomenology of Spirit*. The *Phenomenology* overcomes the Kantian view of abstract reason, and dualisms of noumena and phenomena, subjective and objective, essence and appearance, etc., by arguing that "Reason is the certainty that self-consciousness has of being all reality." This leads Hegel to think of "reason in history," of reason taking place in, and only in, our coming to recognize ourselves in our past. This process of self-knowledge in history is only carried out through historiography, which, for Hegel, involves writing history in original (document gathering), reflective (analytical/ critical), but also and ultimately philosophical form. That is, for Hegel, writing history and grasping reason in history requires the philosophical and hermeneutic work of grasping the rational concepts and meanings by which history has operated, in its own terms. Doing history and the history of reason in history cannot just be document gathering or critical analysis of what is recorded in documents, it requires re-presenting the conceptual worlds articulated and developed in this history. Reid's argument underscores the point that the relation between these forms of historiography (famously presented in Hegel's Introduction to the *Lectures on History*) should be seen as a dialectical epistemology whereby history is represented "for us." The final articulation of this writing on Reason as normative in history is found in the pedagogical discourse of Science itself, i.e., in the *Encyclopedia of Philosophical Sciences*. That is, Reid's highly original proposal is that we read the *Encyclopedia* not as an abstract logical deduction of the concept and as merely propaedeutic to the system, but as representing the transformative historical process of reason, in such a way as to understand it in terms of its own dialectical process.

Chapter 10, Timothy Brownlee's "Hegel on the Need for a Philosophy of Art: An Ethical Account," speaks to a longstanding discussion of Hegel's claim that "Art is something past for us," which interpreters have rightly understood to constitute a declaration that the conditions for the production, experience, and meaning of art have profoundly changed in modernity. Some even attribute to Hegel the view that art is at an end. Brownlee's point of departure lies in an examination of a question to which, he argues, interpreters have devoted insufficient attention, namely who the "we" is, for whom art is now "something past." He argues that Hegel identifies "our standpoint" with what he calls "morality," a view founded on a radical disjunction between the domains of reason and sense. At the same time, Hegel's portrayal of the aesthetic culture of his day is ambiguous, insofar as he also presents a powerful criticism of predominant attitudes towards art that are anchored in the "moral standpoint." Brownlee shows that the aim of Hegel's philosophy of art is analogous to that of his practical philosophy, namely, to reconcile the radical oppositions found within the culture of Hegel's day, thereby offering a critique and ultimately overcoming of the "moral standpoint." To do this, Brownlee examines Hegel's arguments for the need for a philosophy of art, pointing out important links between that philosophy and Hegel's theory of "ethical life" (*Sittlichkeit*), concluding that in Hegel's philosophy of art, the idea of freedom plays a role analogous to *Sittlichkeit*, since freedom, in both "ethical life" and art, demands a reflective engagement with the shared social world. For this reason, art can remain vital and lively only to the extent that it contributes to the realization of human freedom. This implies, though, that the "we" for whom "art is now past," is not a 'we' already defined in the present or past, but a 'we' who works itself through and in practices like art making. Brownlee's chapter, like Vernon's on language, gives us an insight to the way that freedom, situation, and history interweave in spirit working itself out, and Brownlee makes an important contribution to the collection, since his focus on this issue of the way spirit works out its identity, exposes a logic of art that structures the process of this identity, and gives insight into this as knotting together concept and history.

Part III, "Hegel on the History of Freedom and the French Revolution – On Rebecca Comay's *Mourning Sickness: Hegel and the French Revolution*,"[33] comprises a synopsis of Comay's monograph, two commentaries on it, and the author's response. Comay's book and the commentaries on it fit within the overarching themes of the books, as ancillary to key points in parts one and two above, midway between Part I's emphasis on formal connections between history and logic, and Part II's consideration of the experiential and aesthetic content that shapes this connection. This is because Comay, in connecting the *Phenomenology of Spirit* to the French Revolution specifically, is contributing to longstanding debates about the role of the *Phenomenology* in Hegel's system. Her book shows that the *Phenomenology* is not so much an abstract deduction of the experiential forms that spirit must take, but a study of spirit's passage as a concrete, actual historical matter, driven by the unity of the subjective and objective concept, and thus by the issues of logic and history discussed above. That is, by putting the French Revolution at the centre of Hegel's *Phenomenology*, she opens up the *Phenomenology* as a case study for the connections between logic and history that are at the heart of Houlgate's systematicity interpretation, which is why it belongs here.

In terms of Hegel scholarship, Comay's return to the Revolution is quite significant. The only prior study of note is Joachim Ritter's[34] influential work on the topic, from five decades ago, and Comay's contribution is clearly generating great interest, with many translations of her book and symposia on it.[35] For our purposes, what is important is that Comay puts the Revolution at the centre of the *Phenomenology*, by underscoring its role in Hegel's analysis of the transition to Morality, and the significance of this for his system. In terms of the systematicity interpretation, the point is that the transition to Morality is not achieved by way of liberal means of progress, such as money, economic supersession, industrial revolution, and so on. Instead, the pre-history of Culture (Hegel's word for the project of Modernity) finds itself necessarily exposed to violence, a continuation of the battle of Faith and Enlightenment. In other words, Comay offers us, within the *Phenomenology*, a version of the system elaborating itself from within from its own grounds, in and through an actual concrete history. Three points are worth briefly mentioning here.

First, with regard to Culture, Comay recasts Kant as Hegel's true opponent and rival. On Comay's view, Hegel develops a new model of doing philosophy, namely, as phenomenology that proposes a novel method, one to do with self-description and inquiry into the temporality of experience. For Hegel, the object-cause that stirs the mind to critical critique and reflection, is that of the splitting, doubling and "despair of Consciousness"[36] in the mutual encounter with another consciousness. Fear of loss of love, and connectedness with the sociality of the essence of the other takes priority over a simple being of awareness or reflection. That is, what drives the system is not some pure, abstractly theoretical demand for unity, as exemplified, say, by the transcendental unity of apperception, but a genuinely and concretely conflicted consciousness that can only sort itself out through the work of Culture, by the sort of work we find self-consciousness undergoing as Unhappy Consciousness in actual histories, such as the French Revolution. In this regard, her book gives us an insight into the *Phenomenology* as a study of the logic of the system working itself out from within its own grounds (as opposed to other readings of the *Phenomenology* as a much more tidy progression of shapes of experience).

Second, Comay's book thereby reveals important points about freedom. In its logic and ontology, freedom is no longer an empty formalism of right, an empty essence. Freedom exists as the result and the cause of its own deed: it is in bursting out in existence that any essence of freedom is experientially and experimentally tested. In particular, Comay shows how this freedom involves the development of the Spirit in Time, and how history's occurrence in time, is based on repeating. In this way Hegel anticipates Lacan. Indeed, Comay shows us how Hegel is moving very far away from Kant, precisely because this development of freedom involves a sort of working through symbols, language and culture that echo psychoanalytic labour.

Third, Hegel's radicalisation of the philosophical concept of freedom nevertheless productively moves beyond Kant, to the point where, as Comay rightly argues, key Kantian particulars are no longer intact.[37] As Comay puts it, in the French Revolution "the king's trial" makes "painfully visible," "the originality of a law that had to invent itself in the absence of any precursor."[38] This is precisely the point at the centre of the systematicity interpretation: the system cannot begin from an already given faculty of will that operates as the law of a system, the system instead has to elaborate its ground of existence from within, and as a contingent, free matter. Houlgate's 'systematicity interpretation' is thus reinforced by Comay, who rightly singles out Hegel's deeply disturbing work on action, conscience, and forgiveness, as the culminating matter of the *Phenomenology of Spirit*. Hegel thus reflects deeply on the conditionality and unconditionality of law, and anticipates contemporary problematics as to the moral foundations of judgment including in international justice cases and court tribunals, war, and genocide, in the second half of the twentieth century. Comay thereby reveals Hegel as a sobering and materialist thinker and a revolutionary, one who recognizes a practical need for regulations of life in the rational state – encompassing political practices, institutions, procedures, and sciences as prerequisites of modern life.

Chapter 11, written by the editor, gives a more detailed introduction to Comay's book. This leads the way into chapter 12, John McCumber's "Against a Literalist Account of Time in the *Phenomenology*." McCumber contributes to the discussion of Comay's book by first of all giving a concise summary of its argument that highlights connections to accounts of absolute knowing. But McCumber also finds and draws out some important insights brought to light by Comay's study of linkages between revolution as a matter internal to philosophy (in dialectically overturning old ideas) and as a historical matter seemingly external to philosophy. He draws attention to Comay's point that for Hegel, philosophical reflection on the French Revolution is reflection on the most "reflectable" or 'philosophical' historical event (since it proclaims a radical freedom to reflect on things in history, a new sort of historical subject), in such a way that philosophical reflection is "thus driven by the nothingness at the core of that historical given itself." The French Revolution is thus "not so much the object of the philosophical reflection as it is what generates it." McCumber thereby finds that he and Comay are on the same side (contra Kantianism) in opposing a "literalist" account of time, which claims that the sort of time that matters to history or philosophy is time that is over and done with, that is recorded on paper in the historical documents. Instead, the time that is the transformative matter of history and philosophy itself, including the time that internally structures the *Phenomenology* itself (as a book, as a document of a philosophical system and thinking, and a study of experience), is defined by a complex relationship, involving its internal self-structuring dynamic and the external world on which and in which it conducts its reflections. McCumber thus contributes important insights to the collection about the relation between freedom, history, and the absolute, and in relation to Comay's complex reading of the *Phenomenology* and revolution, contributes the important point that we need to understand the revolutionary act of philosophical reflection not as utterly destroying past ideas in the name of an already fixed future, but as a *"distortion"* of givens from within their complex temporality of historical experience.

Chapter 13, Ian Balfour's "Hegel before Comay: *Mourning Sickness* and the Absoluteness of Freedom," situates and contextualizes Comay's work in relation to other scholars who have taken up Hegel on the French Revolution (e.g., Marcuse, Hyppolite, and Bloch), focusing on the question of the sort of freedom at work in the French Revolution, and how it can, for Hegel, be "qualifiedly unqualified," that is, *"absolute* freedom." Balfour shows how Comay's approach enables a novel contribution to this question, because of her attention to the intersection of philosophy, reflection, and historical experience that brings out the sort of temporal complexities identified by McCumber. Specifically, absolute freedom could not arise, as Balfour emphasizes, as a series of "existential decisions made by agents" who, as individual, are trying to make their way through the winds of history, responding to the past through a capacity for freedom they already have; rather it involves a much more complex and paradoxical movement that is "oriented to both past and future," and beyond a so-called immediate future that would, e.g., already be determined as an immediate consequence of present actions. The absoluteness of freedom is thus not above historical experience or time, it arises from within (in something like the manner of the distortion that McCumber describes), via a paradoxical temporality that unfolds into both a (past) memory and a (future) promise. Balfour also shows that Zizek's analysis of dialectic fails to grasp this radical and complex temporality, and Balfour thus shows how these points from Comay, which resonate across the collection and McCumber's earlier work, lead to a new appreciation of the way Hegel's system and its dialectic are open to historical experience. Balfour and McCumber together draw out some key points and questions about the relation between system, dialectic and history.

In chapter 14, "The Actuality of Anachronism, or, Absolute-Freedom-and-Terror Today (Response to Balfour and McCumber)," which also serves as a postscript to her book and its reception, Comay responds to Balfour and McCumber by taking up the psychoanalytic term "exaggeration," asking why Hegel's reflections insist on the "unprecedented strangeness of the French Revolution," its "shocking incongruity," which would perhaps seem to rupture time. Comay's approach lets her show that it would in fact be wrong to take this exaggeration and rupture as situated within a time that is either literal (the time recorded in documents), anachronistic (as involving breakages via projecting a monumental time back into the past), or an-achronistic (as series of events constructed and held together by agents according to already given principles of cohesion), or anarchic (without principle). Rather, this time involves precisely the sorts of complexities that Balfour and McCumber articulate. Comay thus radicalizes and amplifies the issues of the temporality of experience, and the relation to the absolute, that Balfour and McCumber contribute to the collection – and that are central to the sort of logic and history that is at the centre of the systematicity interpretation.

NOTES

1 G.W.F. Hegel, *Elements of the Philosophy of Right*, trans. H.B. Nisbet, ed. Allen W. Wood (Cambridge: Cambridge University Press, 1991). Henceforth cited as *PR* followed by paragraph number.

2 G.W.F. Hegel, *Wissenschaft der Logik* (2 *Bände*) (1812–16, second edition 1832), ed. E. Moldenhauer and K.M. Michel, 2 vols., *Werke in zwanzig Bänden*, vols. 5 and 6 (Frankfurt am Main: Suhrkamp Verlag, 1969)/ *Hegel's Science of Logic*, trans. A.V. Miller (Amherst, NY: Prometheus Books, 1997).

3 *Phänomenologie des Geistes* (1806), H.-F. Wessels und H. Clairmont (eds.) (Hamburg: Felix Meiner Verlag, 1988)/ G.W.F. Hegel, *The Phenomenology of Spirit*, trans. A.V. Miller (Oxford: Oxford University Press, 1977). Henceforth cited as *PS* and indicating a paragraph number.

4 See Bowman, Brady (2013). *Hegel and the Metaphysics of Absolute Negativity*. (Cambridge: Cambridge University Press); and Sedgwick, Sally (2012). *Hegel's Critique of Kant: From Dichotomy to Identity*. (Oxford: Oxford University Press).

5 Ng, Karen (2020). *Hegel's Concept of Life: Self-Consciousness, Freedom, Logic*. (Oxford: Oxford University Press); and Kreines, James (2015). *Reason in the World: Hegel's Metaphysics and Its Philosophical Appeal*. (Oxford: Oxford University Press). Also see Wretzel, Joshua, "Constraint and the Ethical Agent: Hegel Between Constructivism and Realism" in Stein and Gledhill (eds.) *Hegel and Contemporary Practical Philosophy: Beyond Kantian Constructivism*. (New York: Routledge, 2019).

6 Stephen Houlgate, *The Opening of Hegel's Logic: From Being to Infinity* (West Lafayette, Indiana: Purdue University Press, 2006), 29–53.

7 Kevin Thompson, *Hegel's Theory of Normativity: The Systematic Foundations of the Philosophical Science of Right* (Evanston, Illinois: Northwestern University Press, 2019), 77. Cf. *PR*, §§ 91, 92.

8 For a strong claim and defence of Hegel's account of the method in a similar vein, see Rocio Zambrana, *Hegel's Theory of Intelligibility* (Chicago and London: University of Chicago Press, 2015), esp. 115–34. Similarly important is an earlier account of the method and system by Angelica Nuzzo, "The Idea of 'Method' in Hegel's Science of Logic – a Method for Finite Thinking and Absolute Reason," *Bulletin of the Hegel Society of Great Britain* 39–40 [1999]. Also see Stephen Houlgate, who argues that the Logic establishes that being is nothing less than nature, esp. in *Freedom, Truth, and History: An Introduction to Hegel*, 2nd ed. (Oxford: Blackwell, 2005).

9 See e.g., *The Freedom of Life: Hegelian Perspectives* (2013). Eds. Thomas Khurana, James Kreines, Catherine Malabou, Karen Ng, Matthias Haase, and Sally Sedgwick. (Berlin: August Verlag). The initial influences on Houlgate's systematic foundations approach include interpreters specifically concerned with recasting the reception of Hegel's Logic. See e.g., Winfield, Richard (1994). *Overcoming Foundations: Studies in Systematic Philosophy* (New York: Columbia University Press); and Maker, William (1994). *Philosophy without Foundations: Rethinking Hegel* (Albany: SUNY Press). Further influences derive from a novel reception of Hegel's notion of the syllogism (*Schluß*) initiated through e.g., John Burbidge, "Hegel's Logic," in *The Rise of Modern Logic: from Leibniz to Frege*, vol. 3 of the Handbook of the History of Logic, ed. Dov Gabbay and John Woods (Amsterdam: Elsevier North Holland, 2004). Finally, more generally, of influence is the return of Hegelian thought in analytic philosophy, see e.g., the account of the relation between *Schluß* and *Anerkennung* by Paul Redding in *Hegel's Hermeneutics* (1996). (Ithaca: Cornell University Press). Also see Nuzzo, Angelica (2010). *Hegel and the Analytic Tradition* (London: Continuum).

10 Wood, Allen W. (1990). *Hegel's Ethical Thought*. (Cambridge: Cambridge University Press).

11 Longuenesse, Béatrice (2007). *Hegel's Critique of Metaphysics*. (Cambridge: Cambridge University Press).

12 Yeomans, Christopher (2011). *Freedom and Reflection: Hegel and the Logic of Agency*. (Oxford: Oxford University Press).

13 Pinkard, Terry (1994). *Hegel's Phenomenology: The Sociality of Reason*. (Cambridge: Cambridge University Press).

14 See e.g., Axel Honneth, "*Von der Begierde zur Anerkennung: Hegels Begründung von Selbstbewußtsein*," in *Hegel's Phänomenologie des Geistes: Ein kooperativer Kommentar zu einem Schlüsselwerk der Moderne*, ed. K. Vieweg and W. Welsch (Frankfurt a. M.: Suhrkamp, 2008).

15 R. Pippin, *Hegel's Idealism*: The Satisfactions of Self-Consciousness (Cambridge: Cambridge University Press, 1989), 246; 219, 233. Pippin's argument is that Hegel's account of method is transcendental, in a

manner similar to Fichte, thought begins with an "immediate object of consciousness" and then goes on to "display the conditions of the same." For a more recent iteration, see his *Hegel on Self-Consciousness: Desire and Death in the Phenomenology of Spirit* (Princeton University Press, 2011).

16 *PR*, §1.

17 *PR*, §§ 59–64, 65–71.

18 *PR*, §§ 65–71.

19 *PR*, §10.

20 Thompson, *Hegel's Theory of Normativity*, 32.

21 Thompson, *Hegel's Theory of Normativity*, 32.

22 Thompson, *Hegel's Theory of Normativity*, 81.

23 *PR*, §28.

24 Houlgate, *The Opening of Hegel's Logic*, 436.

25 Cf. Pippin, *Hegel's Idealism*, 246, 219, 233.

26 Hyppolite, Jean (1996). *Introduction to Hegel's Philosophy of History* (Florida: University Press of Florida).

27 Houlgate, *The Opening of Hegel's Logic*, 31.

28 Houlgate, *The Opening of Hegel's Logic*, 32.

29 Houlgate, *The Opening of Hegel's Logic*, 35.

30 *PS* M19.

31 See Nuzzo, *Philosophy and Social Criticism*, issue 33 (1) 2007: 41–4.

32 Theodor W. Adorno, *History and Freedom*. Lectures 1964–5, ed. Rolf Tiedemann, trans. Rodney Livingston (Cambridge: Polity, 2006), xv.

33 Rebecca Comay, *Mourning Sickness: Hegel and the French Revolution* (Stanford: Stanford University Press, 2011)

34 Joachim Ritter, *Hegel and the French Revolution: Essays on the Philosophy of Right* (MIT Press, 1982).

35 Comay's monograph was at the centre of nine academic symposia worldwide, six in the US, two in Australia, one in Canada (at Trent University in 2012, where early versions of most of the chapters in this collection were presented as papers). It has been translated in Spanish, German and Farsi languages. It was widely reviewed, including in "Missed Revolutions, non- revolutions, and revolutions to come: A Conversation on Rebecca Comay's *Mourning Sickness*," extended interview with Josh Nichols, in *PhaenEx*, Spring Issue, 2012; "The Uses of Disenchantment: Remarks on Rebecca Comay's Mourning Sickness: Hegel and the French Revolution," in *Parrhesia* (2013) 17: 41–9.

36 In *PS* M18.

37 Cf. *Mourning Sickness*. Comay cites Kant: "But this disguising of the deed miscarries ... such a presumption on the people's part is *still worse than murder*" (45). It is at the heart of this Kantian theater of sensibility that Comay will place the "whole" that for Hegel represents a broken middle

ground, the mediating concept of the vanishing third. Hegel is only too attentive to a discerning thought in Kant's own late writings, *Metaphysics of Morals*, about a pathology. Namely, for Comay, "it turns out to be a case of legality hiding behind the appearance (Kant himself has discerned it, after all) of pathology" (45). The pathology of the drives of moral reason in humans is concern with the type and typology of a "disguising of the deed [that] miscarries."

38 Comay, *Mourning Sickness*, 44.

REFERENCES

G.W.F. Hegel, *The Phenomenology of Spirit*, trans. A.V. Miller (Oxford: Oxford University Press, 1977).

G.W.F. Hegel, *Elements of the Philosophy of Right*, trans. H.B. Nisbet, ed. Allen W. Wood (Cambridge: Cambridge University Press, 1991).

G.W.F. Hegel, *Science of Logic*, trans. A.V. Miller (Amherst, NY: Prometheus Books, 1997).

Kevin Thompson, *Hegel's Theory of Normativity: The Systematic Foundations of the Philosophical Science of Right* (Evanston, Illinois: Northwestern University Press, 2019).

Stephen Houlgate, *The Opening of Hegel's* Logic: *From Being to Infinity* (West Lafayette, Indiana: Purdue University Press, 2006).

PART I

The Logic of Freedom and Its Necessity

1 Right and Trust in Hegel's *Philosophy of Right*

STEPHEN HOULGATE, UNIVERSITY OF WARWICK

What is the principal aim of Hegel's philosophy of right? It is, in my view, to set out the true concept of *freedom*. Hegel was long accused of being a supporter of the Prussian Restoration, but, like Kant and Fichte before him, he is above all a philosopher of freedom.

The Arbitrary Will

In his *Elements of the Philosophy of Right* (1820) Hegel maintains that "the commonest idea we have of freedom is that of *arbitrariness* [*Willkür*]" (§15 Remark).[1] The arbitrary will, we are told, encompasses three different moments. The first is the "*absolute possibility* of *abstracting* from every determination in which I find myself" (§5 Remark). This capacity for abstraction rests on the "pure reflection of the I into itself" or the "pure *thinking* of oneself" (§5). As creatures of nature we are determined in manifold ways by natural drives. In understanding myself to be a pure *indeterminate* I, however, I am conscious that my identity is not bound to these drives and that I can always separate myself from them.

Second, the arbitrary will includes the capacity, not just to distance oneself *from* one's natural drives, but to return *to* them and to identify oneself positively with one or other of them. In this case, the I is no longer passively determined by the drive concerned, but *lets itself* be determined by it.

Third, in giving itself a determinate character in this way, the arbitrary will retains the capacity to separate itself from the drive once again and to let itself be determined by a different drive. The I thus remains "indifferent" to the drive with which it has provisionally identified itself. It considers that drive to be "a mere *possibility* by which it is not restricted but in which it finds itself merely because it posits itself in it" (§7).

Understood in this way, the freedom of the arbitrary will consists in the capacity to *choose* in an unconstrained manner between one's drives (and their objects). Hegel does not deny at all that we enjoy this freedom. He believes, however, that it is inherently contradictory.

The freedom of the arbitrary will consists in determining oneself and not simply being determined by one's given nature. In order not to be determined by nature, the I abstracts itself from its natural drives and thinks of itself as purely indeterminate. This I, however, also gives itself a determinate character, so that it is free not just in a negative, but also in a positive way. Yet since it is indeterminate in itself, it turns back to its natural drives to find the determinacy it seeks. That is to say, the *indeterminate* I freely lets itself be determined by its *given* nature. In so doing, however, the I, in its unrestricted freedom, makes itself *dependent* on that given nature; but this dependence is at odds with the self-determination that it claims for itself.

How then is this contradiction to be avoided? This is possible, Hegel claims, only when the content affirmed by the free will is no longer simply *given* to it, and this happens when the free will has itself and its own freedom as its content and object. In this case, the indeterminate I lets itself be determined not by something else – by a drive that we are simply found to have – but by itself. The choosing will imagines that it is a truly self-determining will. Unfortunately, it can only choose from among the drives and objects that are available to it, and this is initially determined by nature, not by the will itself. The will casts off this moment of dependence, however, when it takes as its content its very own freedom. In this way, it achieves unambiguous self-determination, because it lets itself be determined purely by itself and its own freedom. "The absolute determination, or if one prefers, the absolute drive, of the free spirit" is thus, in Hegel's view, "to make its freedom into its object" (§27). We do not yet know what this will mean; we know, however, that the truly free will *must* take this form, for only in this way can it avoid the contradiction in arbitrary freedom.

Right As Such

When freedom is understood as the object of the will in the strongest sense – that is, as an "immediate actuality" (§27), rather than something merely imaginary – it is understood as *right*. For Hegel, therefore, the essence of right is *freedom*; indeed, right is simply "the *existence* [*Dasein*] of the *free will*" (§29). The free will as such is something subjective. When this will is regarded as its own object, however, as something that exists *for* the will itself, it gives itself the form of right. Right is thus nothing but freedom, understood as an object, an actuality, for the will.

It should be emphasised that the free will *must* have its freedom as its content and object, if it is to free itself from dependence on what is given and relate only to itself. The will has no choice in the matter: if it wants to be truly free, it must make itself the object of its own willing. Right is thus freedom, understood not only as something actual and objective, but also as that which the will *must* will and affirm, if it is to be truly *free*. This moment of necessity belongs essentially to the concept of right. A right does not have the compelling force of a natural event or law; nonetheless, it demands recognition from the will. It confronts the will, therefore, with normative, not natural necessity. In the *Philosophy of Right*, Hegel points to this necessity in the concept of right by maintaining that "right is something *utterly sacred*" (§30). In the lectures of 1821–2 the moment of necessity is made more explicit: "People say that the will is free, because it can *choose*. Rational freedom, the will in and for itself, does not choose, but also has necessity … Right is *necessary* [*Das Recht ist* notwendig]."[2]

The modality of freedom in the usual sense is that of being able, of possibility: I am free, insofar as I *can* … but do not *have to* … In order to avoid the contradiction in this conception of freedom, however, the will *must* have itself and its own freedom as its object. This "must" is immanent in the free will: the truly free will is necessarily *"the free will which wills the free will"* (§27). Freedom understood *as* that which the will must affirm and respect is called "right." The truly free will must, therefore, will and affirm right. One *can* always violate right, because the abstract freedom of choice is not a fiction. Yet the concept of right itself *demands* that right be respected. Not to see this is not to understand what the word "right" means. It is to lack the proper concept of right and of true freedom.

The notion of right is, of course, not unknown to ordinary consciousness. Yet right is often understood as merely a *"limitation* of my freedom or *arbitrary will"* (§29 Remark). According to Hegel, by contrast, true freedom does not consist merely in arbitrariness that is then limited by right, but in the free willing *of* right itself, a willing that freely submits itself to its own immanent necessity.

Abstract Right

Hegel endeavours, when he discusses a specific topic, to set aside unjustified presuppositions. In his view, this means that, to begin with, he may take up nothing but the bare matter itself in its simple immediacy.

The truly free will in *its* immediacy relates immediately to itself in two ways.

On the one hand, it is conscious of being a finite subject with various determinate drives: "the *inherently individual* will of a subject" (§34). On the other hand, it is conscious of its freedom as an indeterminate, abstract I (§35 Remark). Furthermore, it conceives of its freedom as *right* and so understands itself to be a *person*. A person, for Hegel, is thus a self-conscious individual, who understands his freedom to lie not just in the ability to choose, but also in the capacity for right (*Rechtsfähigkeit*) (§36).

Personality as such is indeterminate in itself, since I know myself to be a person only insofar as I understand myself to be a pure, universal I. My personality – that is, my freedom, my right – is thus not bound to any specific drives or external objects. Like the arbitrary will, therefore, the person still enjoys the abstract freedom to *choose* this or that – the freedom that consists in being *able* to …, in unconstrained possibility. Yet the freedom of the person is not reducible to that of the arbitrary will.

The arbitrary will identifies its freedom completely with the *ability* to choose. The person retains this freedom, but he also knows that this ability to choose is a *right* that must be respected. The modality underlying the freedom of the person is thus not mere possibility, but the necessity of possibility. The person *can* appropriate whatever he likes (as long as the limits set by the rights of others are respected). Yet he knows not only that he enjoys this freedom as a matter of fact, but also that he has the *right* to appropriate things (or not), as he sees fit. As a person, therefore, my freedom consists in the *rightful* possibility of choosing as I please – a possibility that must be respected by all. Consequently, the right of the person takes the form, for himself and for others, of an inviolable "*permission* or *warrant*" (*Erlaubnis oder Befugnis*) (§38) to appropriate things that are not already owned by someone else.

In the sphere of abstract right, for Hegel, arbitrary freedom is not just limited but also *secured* by right. The consciousness of right necessarily coexists, therefore, with the freedom of the arbitrary will. This means, as we have just seen, that persons have the right to appropriate things as they please, as long as they are not the property of another. Yet it also means that their very *willing and maintaining of right* is itself exposed to the contingency of the arbitrary will. A person is conscious that his or her freedom must be respected. But what guarantees that this freedom will be respected in fact? Nothing other than another person's arbitrary will. The necessity and actuality of right are thus dependent on the *contingency* of arbitrariness. The fact that in a contract two persons come together to exchange property rightfully does not alter the situation:

rightful property simply becomes dependent on two contingent wills, rather than one (§81). Due to this moment of contingency, therefore, there is always the danger that persons will choose *not* to respect the rights they know they must respect, if such respect conflicts with their arbitrary will. This is the danger of wrong (*Unrecht*).

In merely abstract right, therefore, right is not yet present in its fully realized form. Right is freedom, understood as something actual and necessary; in abstract right, however, contingency undermines the necessity belonging to right, because the respect that is owed to the right of persons depends upon the arbitrary wills of those persons. Abstract right *must* be respected; yet it *can* happen that such right is not respected, and this possibility is logically necessary. Abstract right thus lacks true necessity, the necessity that holds sway in spite of contingency. In this sense, right is not yet fully realised in the sphere of abstract right.

Morality

The person sees his freedom embodied in the external *thing* that he appropriates and owns. In what Hegel calls the sphere of "morality," by contrast, freedom is actualised and acquires "existence" in and through the free will itself, that is, in *subjectivity* (§§106–7). The moral will does not just appropriate external things, therefore, but externalises itself and its freedom in its own *action* (§113). This will gives itself a particular, subjective content – an aim or purpose – and then carries it out in the external world (§§109–10).

Both the choosing will and the rights-bearing will are dependent in their freedom on what is given to them (their natural drives and the things around them). The purposes and intentions of the acting will are also determined in part by naturally given drives. Yet they are not merely found, but are formulated by the acting will itself. To this extent this acting, moral will demonstrates a more developed form of self-determination than the two wills that precede it.

Yet the moral will not only actualizes freedom and right in its action. Insofar as it is a subjective, individual will, it also *differs* from and stands in *relation* to right, which is something objective and universal (§108). In the sphere of morality, such right unites the abstract right of the person to property and personal security with the right of the moral subject to achieve satisfaction and well-being through its actions. This unity of abstract right and well-being, Hegel tells us, is the *good* (§129). Insofar as the moral will understands this good as something distinct from itself that nonetheless must be respected, it considers the good to be its *duty* (*Pflicht*) (§133). The moral will is thus necessarily subject to duty, because, on the one hand, it knows that it must affirm right in the form of the good, but, on the other hand, it considers the good to be something that stands over against, and binds, the subjective will.

The modality of moral freedom differs from that of abstract, rightful freedom, because moral freedom is subject to a "should" or "ought" (*Sollen*), rather than a simple "must" (§131). The must contained in abstract right is a normative, not a natural necessity: it does not have the power to force us to do something, but directs itself at our freedom. Specifically, it requires us to obey its command immediately without further reflection; and, as we have seen, the person obeys this command, and respects right, as long as doing so is in agreement with his arbitrary will. The should, by contrast, does not just demand immediate obedience, but directs itself at our subjective, *inwardly reflective* freedom. When I am conscious that I should do something, that it is my duty, I am conscious, not just of an immediate requirement that must be fulfilled, but rather of a demand that *I* have to fulfil through my *own* subjective freedom. To put it another way, a moral duty is not just something that must *be done*, but something that *I myself* am responsible for doing.[3] Indeed, the moral will considers it to be its right to take upon itself the responsibility for doing what duty commands and upholding right. In this sense, the moral will is characterised by a certain heroism: it always thinks that in the absence of its *own* activity right would not be actualised.

The moral will also presumes that it can determine by itself the content of the good. As is well known, Hegel believes that the concept of moral duty in itself is empty of content. Whether this is true of Kant's conception of duty, we shall leave to one side; Hegel shows, however, that duty, as it is conceived by the moral will that has emerged in the course of the *Philosophy of Right*, must be empty and without content. Since this concept of duty prescribes no specific duties, it falls, in Hegel's view, to subjective conscience to decide what the duty-bound will should do. Subjective conscience thus becomes the "power of *judgement* which determines solely from within itself what is good" (§138). Indeed, conscience claims for itself the *right* to exercise this power of judgment, for it sees itself as a "sanctuary [*Heiligtum*] which it would be *sacrilege* to violate" (§137 Remark).

The moral subject who abides by his conscience is convinced that his actions are justified. Conscience, however, is something subjective; the moral subject thus always runs the risk that, even though he is convinced he is doing his duty, he actually gives free rein to his own subjective arbitrariness. In this case, the moral subject does not regress to the standpoint of the person, who consciously violates right when it conflicts with his arbitrary will; rather, he becomes an *evil* will that indulges its own, arbitrary inclinations while considering itself to be perfectly good and dutiful.

Hegel does not maintain that evil is unavoidable in human life, but he argues that the moral will runs the risk of becoming evil by claiming the right to determine purely by itself, through its conscience, what counts as the good. In the sphere of morality, therefore, the actualisation of right and the good is made dependent upon the subjectivity of the particular individual. This means that the good lacks true actuality and necessity, because its actualisation is exposed to *contingency*.

Ethical Life

Let us briefly recapitulate. Arbitrariness is freedom understood as possibility: it consists in being *able* to choose, as one sees fit. Since the I that enjoys this freedom is utterly indeterminate, it finds determinacy only in what is *given* to it, namely natural drives and their corresponding objects. The freedom to choose is thus *dependent* on this given: however unconstrained such freedom may be, we can choose only what is available to us.

To free itself from such dependence, the free will must have itself as its object: it must be the *"free will which wills the free will"* (§27). Insofar as the free will has its own freedom as its object, it understands that freedom to be something actual and existent, not merely to consist in the possibility of selecting this or that. At the same time, the will understands its freedom to be that which it *must* will, to be something necessary for the will. When freedom itself is understood as the actual, necessary object of the will, it is conceived as *right*. The concept of right then determines the further logical development of Hegel's philosophy of freedom.

First, right is understood as something *immediately* actual and necessary, something that simply *must* be respected by the individual will. Understood in this way, however, right remains dependent on the arbitrariness of the individual, who can, if he chooses, violate right. Second, right is understood as something whose actuality and necessity is *mediated*. It is seen as something that is necessary, but that is actualised only in and through our own inner, subjective freedom. Right is here once again made dependent on subjective arbitrariness, though in this case such arbitrariness is convinced that it is in conformity with right, duty and the dictates of conscience. In both these cases, therefore, right is present in a form that lacks true actuality and necessity.

Only in *ethical life* (*Sittlichkeit*) is right something *truly* actual and necessary, and so present in its fully developed form. Ethical life, Hegel writes, is freedom as "the living good," as an "existing world" of objective laws and institutions (§§142, 144). These laws and institutions have "a fixed *content* which is necessary for itself, and whose existence [*Bestehen*] is exalted above subjective opinions and preferences" (§144). They thus constitute a "circle of necessity" (§145) that is no longer dependent on subjective arbitrariness, but that precedes and grounds it – a world within which subjective arbitrariness first arises and comes to expression. The concept of ethical life is introduced by Hegel, therefore, not just because it gives content to empty, contentless moral duty, *but because ethical life is the true actualization of right*. Indeed, ethical life is made necessary by the concept of right itself.

Ethical life has its actuality in the practical action of self-conscious subjects and does not lie, like external nature, outside of subjectivity: the institutions of ethical life are organisations of active *human beings*. Yet for the ethical individual, who grows up and is educated in these institutions, "the ethical substance and its laws and powers ... *are* [*sind*], in the supreme sense of self-sufficiency" (§146). Ethical laws and institutions have the normative authority of right, so the individual knows that he must respect them; but they also constitute an *existing actuality*, in which the individual can participate, but which ultimately do not depend on *his* action or will. This point is important: the moral subject always thinks that the good is first realised through his own action. The ethical individual, by contrast, understands the good to be a reality that precedes him – one that he must sustain and can reform through his action, but whose independence he must also acknowledge and allow to hold sway.[4]

In the ethical world around him the individual sees other human beings who actualise right and the good in their actions. In such ethical human beings, acting in accordance with right and the good has become a habit or "*second nature*" (§151). They do what is good without further ado, without having at the forefront of their minds that it is their responsibility and duty to do so. Or, to put it another way, they actually *do* what is good, rather than just thinking that they *should* do so. Yet the ethical individual not only encounters a world of ethical human beings around him; he also actualises the good in his *own* habitual action. He knows, therefore, that freedom is a reality both in the world and in his own action.

The ethical individual, for Hegel, is thus a practical subject: ethical life is actualised in the *actions* of self-conscious individuals (§142). The relation of the ethical individual to the laws and institutions of ethical life cannot, however, be a purely practical one, for the individual relates to a world of freedom, right and reason, whose existence is objective and independent of his own particular action. The appropriate relation for the individual to have to this objective, independent realm of freedom is a *theoretical* one, in which the individual *recognises* that the world around him is the embodiment of freedom.

According to the *Encyclopaedia*, the truly free will is "the unity of theoretical and practical spirit."[5] Crudely stated, theoretical spirit is the knowing of what *is*. In the practical sphere, by contrast, something is brought *into* being by me. The will is obviously practical, insofar it brings about changes in the world through its actions. Yet insofar as the ethical will understands freedom to be something already existent and actual in the world, it is practical spirit that is mediated by a *theoretical*, cognitive relation to actualized freedom.

Recall that right is freedom, understood not just as possibility, but as something actual and necessary: that which the free will *must* will. Recall, too, that right must take the form of ethical life, if it is to be freed from dependence on the arbitrary will and to be something truly actual and necessary: the modality of right itself leads it from abstract right, via morality, to ethical life. As we have just seen, the appropriate relation for the individual to have to the actual, existing world of ethical life is a theoretical one: that of cognition. It follows from this that *right* itself in its fully developed form requires the individual to stand in a *theoretical* relation to it. The free will is always practical: it chooses, acts and produces. In the ethical sphere, however, such practical activity is subordinated to, and informed by, theoretical cognition of the actuality of freedom and right.

Note that in ethical laws and institutions the individual does not see an alien authority, but objective structures that guarantee and actualize his *own* freedom. "The subject bears *spiritual witness* to them as to *its own essence* in which it has its *self-awareness* [*Selbstgefühl*]" (§147). Such "spiritual witness," Hegel tells us, takes the form of *trust* (*Zutrauen*). The properly ethical individual thus *trusts* the laws and institutions of ethical life; indeed, his relation to them is "immediate and closer to identity than even *faith* or *trust*."

Trust, for Hegel, is "the consciousness that my substantial and particular interest is preserved and contained in the interest and end of an other" (§268). It is the feeling that my well-being and freedom are secured by that other, and that in relating to the other I am in fact relating to myself and my own essence. Such trust can remain naive and immediate, or it can "pass over into more or less educated insight" (§§268, 147 Remark). The main point is that trust is an essentially *theoretical* relation to ethical life – a *knowing* of oneself in the other – that underlies the ethical actions of people. Ethical action is action grounded in the consciousness and recognition that right and freedom are indeed actualised in the world; this consciousness is our trust in the institutions of ethical life; action must, therefore, be rooted in trust, if it is to be truly ethical.[6]

Note that, for Hegel, true trust is not blind, but it is the immediate or educated *recognition* that right is actualised in the world. It is the understanding, in the form of *feeling*, that right and the good – which include my right and my well-being – are embodied in the laws and institutions around me. This point is crucial: trust and understanding are not at odds with one another, but true trust is itself a form of felt understanding and insight. Such trust is not merely peripheral to ethical life, for Hegel, but belongs to the very essence of ethical life, because it is the appropriate subjective relation to objectively existing right. In the spheres of abstract right and morality there can be no trust that right is actualised, because right has no properly independent existence, but depends utterly for its maintenance on the arbitrary will of the individual or the actions of particular subjects. In ethical life, by contrast, where right is something actual that precedes and grounds my subjective activity, the appropriate relation to right is above all that of felt recognition or trust.

This trust is itself a distinctive form of freedom that can be found only in ethical life.[7] For both the abstractly rightful person and the moral subject the actualisation of right depends on their will and their activity. The ethical individual, however, enjoys the freedom of seeing right already actualised in a world that is in an important respect independent of him. The ethical individual can thus, so to speak, relax and does not need constantly to take responsibility for actualising right, because his life is informed by trust in the existing institutions of ethical life. This freedom that consists in trusting the world around us and not always wanting to put the world right through my own efforts is to be found only in ethical life and is unknown to the bearer of abstract rights and the moral subject.

If, however, trust is to be the *consciousness* and *recognition* that right is actualised in the world, then the laws and institutions to which I relate must, indeed, actualize right: they must actually correspond to the trust I have in them. This means, among other things, that such laws and institutions must protect the abstract right to property and the moral right to freedom of action and particular well-being (§154). As I have stressed, ethical trust is not blind, but the immediate or educated *recognition* of the actuality of freedom. Trust can be such recognition and insight only if there is a reality there to recognise, that is, only if freedom in all its forms *is* actualised in the world about us. Those who are afraid of trust and always urge us to be vigilant in face of the state because they fear that trust will enable corruption among officials to flourish, misunderstand Hegel's concept of trust. True trust, as the felt *awareness* that freedom is realised in society, is possible only when freedom is indeed realised in society.

The actuality of freedom and right must, therefore, precede the trust we place in it, and, according to Hegel, the most important objective guarantee of public freedom is the *division of powers* (provided that this is taken in its true sense as a moment in an organically unified state) (§272 Remark). This not only means that the executive and legislative powers must be distinguished from one another – something that Hegel thinks did not happen in the French Revolution, with devastating consequences.[8] It also means that local communities and corporations must be accorded legal recognition and rights in order to protect the state and those who are governed by it "against the misuse of power on the part of the official bodies and their members" (§295). The objective actualization of freedom also requires that the deliberations in the Estates' assemblies be public and that there be "freedom of public communication," including the press (albeit within limits set by right and law) (§319). All of this constitutes the objective condition of public trust. Such trust is, however, itself essential to ethical life and constitutes a distinctive form of freedom: the freedom of being and feeling at home in the world that is denied to the mere rights-bearing person and the merely moral subject.

I come now to my concluding remarks. What I wish to highlight here is the close connection, to which Hegel directs our attention, between right and trust. For Hegel, freedom consists in part in the ability to choose; true freedom, however, consists in the willing and maintaining of right. Right always has priority, in Hegel's view, over the unconstrained choices exercised by individuals. This right must encompass the rights of the person and of the moral subject, but its true actualization is to be found in the laws and institutions of ethical life together with the people in whom acting in accordance with the demands of right has become habitual and "second nature." If such people are to enjoy the full freedom of ethical life, they must be able to trust that their freedom and rights are secured by the laws and institutions under which and in which they live. They must also enjoy the freedom that lies in this trust itself and the feeling of being at home in the world that it involves. Hegel does *not* maintain that the citizens of every state in the modern world live in this trust: he is well aware that there are bad states in which such trust is lacking (for example, the French Republic after 1792).[9] According to Hegel, however, a life without this trust cannot be a truly *free* life.

On the basis of Hegel's insight into the close connection between right and trust, we can identify two very clear dangers that people face in the modern world. The first is that our trust might be blind after all and not involve any recognition of what there actually is. In this case, we may well place our trust in institutions that do not merit it. Genuine trust, however, is an essential element of modern freedom, for Hegel. It is important, therefore, that modern states maintain the division of powers and protect themselves from public corruption by (among other things) publicising proceedings in the assemblies and according appropriate rights to local communities and corporations. It is also important that the press and education system make it possible for citizens to gain a proper understanding of the real political and social situation in which they live. Only under these conditions can the trust that citizens place in their laws and institutions become genuine trust, as Hegel conceives it, namely, the felt *recognition* that freedom is, indeed, realised in those laws and institutions.

The second danger is that we might refuse ever to place our trust in the institutions of ethical life, even when they do in fact merit it, and instead cultivate an attitude of perpetual vigilance and suspicion. Vigilance is certainly warranted when signs of corruption are evident. Such vigilance and suspicion are, however, not always well grounded and can degenerate into a self-sustaining "culture of suspicion," to use Onora O'Neill's term, that undermines the possibility of trust.[10] In this way, our zealous efforts to be alert and to avoid naivety threaten the very ethical life we claim to be protecting.

A life in which we trust our fellow human beings is not altogether without risk; but a life without genuine trust lacks an essential element of ethical freedom. Some see trust, especially that placed in the laws and institutions of the state, as nothing more than naivety. Hegel's insight, however, is that a life lived in a *trusting* relation to laws and institutions, that are themselves free of corruption, is one to which we all have an inalienable *right*.

NOTES

1   G.W.F. Hegel, *Elements of the Philosophy of Right*, ed. A.W. Wood, trans. H.B. Nisbet (Cambridge: Cambridge University Press, 1991); G.W.F. Hegel, *Grundlinien der Philosophie des Rechts oder Naturrecht und Staatswissenschaft*

im Grundrisse, ed. E. Moldenhauer and K.M. Michel, vol. 7 of *Werke in zwanzig Bänden* (Frankfurt am Main: Suhrkamp Verlag, 1970). Note that I have occasionally amended Nisbet's translation.

2　G.W.F. Hegel, *Die Philosophie des Rechts: Vorlesung von 1821/22*, ed. H. Hoppe (Frankfurt am Main: Suhrkamp Verlag, 2005), 50, 56.

3　This difference is obscured by Robert Brandom when he writes that "treating others as *selves*" at all means treating them as "ones who are *responsible* for their doings and attitudes" – which is not to say that Brandom would not draw the distinction. See Robert B. Brandom, *Reason in Philosophy: Animating Ideas* (Cambridge, MA: Harvard University Press, 2009), 3.

4　Frederick Neuhouser writes that free individuals understand themselves to be "*re*-producers" of their institutions. See Frederick Neuhouser, *Foundations of Hegel's Social Theory: Actualizing Freedom* (Cambridge, MA: Harvard University Press, 2000), 87.

5　G.W.F. Hegel, *Philosophy of Mind*, trans. W. Wallace and A.V. Miller, revised by M. Inwood (Oxford: Clarendon Press, 2007), 214, §481.

6　Neuhouser understands the relation between the theoretical and practical attitude in Hegel's concept of ethical life to be the other way around. The trust of individuals in the institutions of ethical life can, indeed, be conceived as "a theoretical stance," but "this attitude itself is derivative of their 'being-with-themselves' in their social institutions in a way that is more clearly practical in nature." See Neuhouser, 105–6.

7　See Neuhouser, 105, 111.

8　G.W.F. Hegel, *Vorlesungen über die Philosophie der Weltgeschichte. Zweite Hälfte*, 2nd ed, ed. Georg Lasson (Hamburg: Felix Meiner Verlag, 1923), 929: "for the whole power of the administration was placed in the legislature."

9　Hegel, *Vorlesungen über die Philosophie der Weltgeschichte*, 930: "thus suspicion [*Verdacht*] reigns."

10　See Onora O'Neill, *A Question of Trust* (Cambridge: Cambridge University Press, 2002), 57. See also Hegel, *Elements of the Philosophy of Right*, §272 Remark: "to make malevolence and distrust of malevolence the primary factor … is, as far as thought is concerned, characteristic of the *negative understanding* and, as far as the disposition is concerned, characteristic of the outlook of the rabble."

REFERENCES

Brandom, Robert B. *Reason in Philosophy: Animating Ideas*. Cambridge, MA: Harvard University Press, 2009.

Hegel, G.W.F. *Vorlesungen über die Philosophie der Weltgeschichte: Zweite Hälfte*. 2nd ed. Edited by Georg Lasson. Hamburg: Felix Meiner Verlag, 1923.

—— *Grundlinien der Philosophie des Rechts oder Naturrecht und Staatswissenschaft im Grundrisse*. Edited by E. Moldenhauer and K.M. Michel, Vol. 7 of *Werke in zwanzig Bänden*. Frankfurt am Main: Suhrkamp Verlag, 1970.

—— *Elements of the Philosophy of Right*. Edited by A.W. Wood and translated by H.B. Nisbet. Cambridge: Cambridge University Press, 1991.

—— *Die Philosophie des Rechts: Vorlesung von 1821/22*. Edited by H. Hoppe. Frankfurt am Main: Suhrkamp Verlag, 2005.

—— *Philosophy of Mind*. Translated by W. Wallace and A.V. Miller. Revised by M. Inwood. Oxford: Clarendon Press, 2007.

Neuhouser, Frederick. *Foundations of Hegel's Social Theory: Actualizing Thought*. Cambridge, MA: Harvard University Press, 2000.

O'Neill, Onora. *A Question of Trust*. Cambridge: Cambridge University Press, 2002.

2 Hegel's Cognitivist Ascriptivism

MICHAEL QUANTE, UNIVERSITY OF MÜNSTER

TRANSLATION FROM GERMAN BY: NIELS FEUERHAHN

To comprehend *what is* is the task of philosophy, for *what is* is reason.

G.W.F. Hegel

Introduction

It is an ambitious undertaking to add a new interpretation or a new systematic reconstruction to the almost unmanageable literature on Hegel's philosophy in general, and on his *Elements of the Philosophy of Right* in particular.[1][*] Nevertheless, the following reflections aim at presenting the framework of an innovative proposal. Its core idea is that Hegel's philosophy of right should be understood as a descriptive analysis and systematization of the central evaluative and normative practices of attributing, asserting, and recognizing justified claims that agents express. On this account, the theoretical structure of *Elements* can be conceived of as a descriptive metaphysics understood in the Strawsonian sense. On this interpretation, Hegel's philosophy of right does not occur on the ethical level where we assert, justify, and criticize claims, norms, and institutions. It rather brings the various social practices of these evaluative and normative attributions into a philosophical order, mediated by the "concept of the will" (§4A).[2] For this reason, Hegel explains, the analysis has a "determinate *starting point*" (§2) and

---

[*] Translator's note: Throughout this text I have used H.B. Nisbet's translation of *Grundlinien*, edited by Allen W. Wood and published by Cambridge University Press as *Elements of the Philosophy of Right*. Since Hegel's handwritten notes are not included in this edition, I have provided my own translations of the respective passages. All other translated passages of Hegel's *Grundlinien* stem from Nisbet's translation and are included here without alteration.

the structure of a philosophical explication and justification, which are not derived from the practices themselves. Whether such an interpretation is sensible, and whether the position that we are sketching here is systematically fruitful, only the complete execution can show. It goes without saying that the latter cannot be performed in a single contribution. In the following elaborations, the only claim that I can, and want to make, is to sketch the outline of this project and to provide reasons that motivate its implementation.

To reach this goal, I will first elaborate the two concepts that I use in the title of this contribution: cognitivism and ascriptivism. Subsequently, I will present and briefly explain my thesis; I will expound the advantages of my interpretation of Hegel's philosophy of right, and I will determine the relationship between my interpretation and Hegel's "strong" metaphysical premises and aims. Finally, I will pursue the questions of the scope and limits of my systematic interpretive proposal; I will also discuss some obvious objections.

Conceptual Clarifications

Since the terms "cognitivism" and "ascriptivism" are anachronistic in relation to Hegel's philosophy and lack a uniform use in the secondary literature, a few preliminary clarifications and stipulations, some of which pertain to definitions, are necessary. In addition, some short remarks will provide reasons for my proposal that we need to assign the systematic conception that is indicated by these terms to Hegel's philosophy of right. I begin with a brief explanation of what "cognitivism" means in the domain of practical philosophy.[3]

COGNITIVISM

In the domain of practical philosophy, I take *cognitivism* to be the view that ethical statements, among which I count attributions of justified claims and of responsibility, are capable of justification and truth. Within the framework of moral objectivism, it is assumed that we possess intersubjective standards of judgment and justification for such statements; within the framework of a moral realism, it is assumed that these statements denote moral facts and can thus be true or false.

Conversely, in the domain of practical philosophy, non-cognitivism is the view that ethical statements are capable neither of being justified nor of being true or false. Whether non-cognitivism takes these statements to be mere expressions of feeling or imperatives or decisions, plays no role for us here.[4]

It is evident that Hegel commits himself to a kind of cognitivism in his philosophy of right. This can be proven conclusively through two points: in his handwritten notes to §4 of *Elements*, Hegel elaborates that as far as the relation between thinking and the will is concerned, we find "not two separate faculties at all" (§4R)*, but that the subjective end (*Zweck*) of the free will becomes epistemically accessible to the latter in the form of first-person propositions. Furthermore, Hegel adds that the self-reference by means of the "I" also contains a dimension that can be reconstructed cognitivistically, because the "I [is] the object of thinking" and the will always wills itself "as something general" (ibid.).**

Secondly, Hegel elaborates in the Remark to §132 of the section titled "Good and Conscience" as follows: "The *good* is in general the essence of the will in its *substantiality* and *universality* – the will in its truth; the good therefore exists without exception only *in thought* and *through thought*" (§132A). Even though it must be left open whether Hegel's remark assumes the position of moral objectivism or that of moral realism, it is nevertheless clear that he held a version of cognitivism in his philosophy of right.[5] This can be plausibly assumed in so far as in *Elements* Hegel himself vehemently engages with the different moral irrationalisms of his contemporaries (for instance in his critique of inadequate concepts of conscience).[6]

ASCRIPTIVISM

The core idea of the ascriptivism that goes back to H.L.A. Hart is the thesis that the statements that we use to speak about actions not only serve to describe the events in question, but also to attribute responsibility in an ethical or judicial sense: "My main purpose in this article is to suggest that the philosophical analysis of the concept of human action has been inadequate and confusing, at least in part because sentences of the form 'He did it,' have been traditionally regarded as primarily descriptive whereas their principal function is what I venture to call *ascriptive*, being quite literally to ascribe responsibility for actions much as the principle function of sentences of the for 'This is his' is to ascribe rights in property" (Hart, "The Ascription of Responsibility and Rights," 145).

Hart's conception of ascriptivism suffers from an ambiguity in the exact determination of the meaning of his thesis that statements about actions are "fundamentally ascriptive" (ibid., 146). Hart vacillates in

---

* Translation mine. [NF]
** Translation mine. [NF]

his contribution between: the *weak* thesis that many ascriptions of action are not only descriptions or explanations but also attributions of responsibility; the stronger strong thesis that the primary function of these attributions of action consists in the attribution of responsibility; and the strong even stronger thesis that the exclusive function of these attributions of action is to attribute responsibility.[7]

A strong version of the ascriptivist position could be consistently formulated in a cognitivist version, namely if one held the view that ascriptions of responsibility rest also on criticisable conditions of application. However, a look at the use of statements about action shows very quickly that the strong version of ascriptivism one-sidedly over-emphasizes, without need but also without any gain, an aspect that is admittedly central, but one that is presumably not even primary in all contexts. If a detective tries to reconstruct the course of events of a crime, during an interrogation, many of her statements about the action will primarily have a descriptive function. The early criticism of Hart's conception was thus able to show very quickly that this conception suffers from ambiguities and a persistent under-complexity regarding the manifold uses of statements about actions.[8] Hart himself subsequently dropped his proposal and did not pursue it further.

In his monograph *Action and Responsibility*, Andrew Sneddon takes the fundamental idea of ascriptivism anew, because he is convinced that: "ascriptivists were on to a good idea, but that they failed to see clearly just what that idea was" (Sneddon, *Action and Responsibility*, 5).

His new ascriptivism is based on the central thesis that "the possibility of attributing responsibility for an event is a type necessary condition of that event counting as an action" (ibid.). A "type necessary condition" is a condition which is necessary "for the exemplification of a kind, or type" (ibid., 5, fn 13). While Hart had put forth an analysis of linguistic statements, the claim of Sneddon's conception is to develop a "project in metaphysics" (ibid., 10). He regards this as a central difference between his own claim and that of the original ascriptivists. However, with regard to a systematic reconstruction of Hegel's philosophy of right this difference is not essential, because Hegel does not accept the strict separation of concept and object that this difference implies. In contrast, it is important that Sneddon rejects the strong interpretation of Hart's proposal and thus concedes that statements about actions also have a descriptive function. Sneddon's most central insight, however, is that the criteria that Hart had singled out as the basis of the attribution of responsibility must not only be understood as characteristics of our concept of actions, but also as constitutive conditions for actions themselves. Furthermore, in view of Hegel's cognitivist ascriptivism, it is pertinent that both Hart and Sneddon draw these criteria from the social practice of the use of these attributions, hence, as it were, from pragmatics (ibid., 25). In other words, it is the rules of a social practice which, in the form of *type necessary conditions*,* provide the role of constitutive criteria that make an event into an action of a particular type. Sneddon makes this "socio-pragmatic aspect" (ibid., 41), which Hart had still limited to the concept of an action, into a criterion that constitutes actions themselves.[9] Thus, he rejects naturalistic reductions and methodologically individualistic conceptions of human action as fundamentally inadequate approaches.[10]

For the purposes of my contribution, a brief sketch of Hart's basic idea and its advancement through Sneddon will suffice. The characteristics that are central for a reconstruction of Hegel's cognitivist ascriptivism are these:

> the essential and irreducible function of statements about actions as attributions of responsibility;
> the recognition of descriptive aspects of such attributions;
> the recognition of descriptive presuppositions and conditions of adequacy for such attributions;
> the function of social practices of attribution as constitutive criteria for actions;
> the social constitutedness (*Konstituiertheit*) of actions.

Hegel extends the basic features of the attribution of responsibility, which also forms an essential component in his philosophy of right, to the attribution of justified claims in general, and he understands the (institutional or individual) recognition and the (institutional or individual) demand (*Einforderung*) of these justified claims as the main forms of these attributions.

Hegel's Philosophy of Right as a Cognitivist Ascriptivism

The interpretation of Hegel's practical philosophy as a cognitivist ascriptivism has two main points. *On the one hand*, it means that the philosophy of right assumes a descriptive-metaphysical attitude towards the phenomenal domain of practical philosophy, and it does this in a double sense. First, philosophy describes and reconstructs its subject area, which means that it does not formulate any claims on the

---

* English in the original. [NF]

level of the practices themselves. Hegel discerns the function and the achievement of the philosophy of right in its ability to identify and to systematize the claims that subjects make against each other in their social practices and institutions. Second, it describes and reconstructs the grammar of social practices, as that which is actual (*wirklich*) in the domain of phenomena, by making it explicit and by rendering it systematic by means of philosophical categories and patterns of justification; this is the metaphysical aspect.[11] Based on the metaphilosophical and philosophical presuppositions, which Hegel only briefly alludes to at the beginning of *Elements*, such a reconstruction also assumes a critical and normative function towards the given domain of objects, because an external standard – "the Idea of right – the concept of right and its actualization" (§1) – is applied to it in general, to individual subdomains or to concrete enactments. Hegel's premise is that "[t]he science of right is *a part of philosophy*" (§2), and that the domain of phenomena can and must therefore be measured by a standard that, as far as "its *coming into being* is concerned, falls outside the science of right" (§2), and yet it gives itself actuality (*Wirklichkeit*) and shape (*Gestalt*) in the domain of phenomena, so that the unfolding of this concept of right can be understood at the same time as "the proper immanent development of the thing [*Sache*] itself" (§2) of this domain of phenomena itself.[12]

On the other hand, and this is the second crucial point, my interpretation implies the thesis that Hegel understands cognitivistically the practices that are present in our social institutions in which subjects make and recognize (or reject) claims. These claims, and the interactions through which they are negotiated, have a cognitive core which Hegel derives, on the one hand, from the relation between thinking and willing, and on the other, from his rationalistic conception of the first-person self-reference by means of "I." Willing has a propositional constitution and points to intersubjective standards of rationality by means of which we can justify, but also criticize, claims. In order to function as the constitutive principle of rights (in the general sense of justified and justifiable claims that subjects direct at each other), the free will must always have the form of first-person-propositional attitudes; this is one of Hegel's overarching philosophical aims, which he already attempts to deliver in the part of the system titled "Subjective Spirit."[13] Therefore, all of our social practices and institutions in which subjects assert claims against each other, are based on the principle of the free will, and thus on a common structure which philosophy can make explicit and show to be the organizing principle of the entire domain of phenomena.

THE CENTRAL INTERPRETIVE HYPOTHESIS: SOME INDICATORS
The interpretive hypothesis at the basis of my reflections can be formulated as follows:

(Thesis)   Hegel's philosophy of right is a philosophical explication and systematization of our practices of asserting and redeeming evaluative and normative validity claims.

Before I discuss three advantages of my interpretation, I want to present two pieces of evidence that suggest that Hegel approaches the subject area of practical philosophy from a primarily descriptive-metaphysical perspective. In general, such an approach does not aim at intervening on the level of the evaluative and normative practice itself, for instance, by presenting justifications for particular norms or ethical judgments. Rather, the goal is to explicate these practices along with the rules and principles (i.e., the grammar) that organize them. If norms and ethical judgments make their occurrence in the course of such a depiction (*Darstellung*), the philosopher should, if he remains true to his program, make mention but not use of these.

If we look at Hegel's remarks in light of these presuppositions, we find numerous traces of precisely this structure. A *direct* proof of this is, for example, Hegel's introduction of the commandment of right which lies at the basis of the concept of abstract right: "(1) Personality contains in general the capacity for right and constitutes the concept and the (itself abstract) basis of abstract and hence *formal* right. The commandment of right is therefore: *be a person and respect others as persons*" (§36). The first point on which I want to draw is one that can be found at the end of this paragraph in Hegel's text. The commandment is obviously an imperative, so we should have expected an exclamation mark at the end if Hegel had issued this imperative himself. The ductus of the paragraph, however, unambiguously shows that Hegel merely mentions this commandment of right and does not assert the validity claim of an imperative itself.

The second point, which also speaks for my interpretive hypothesis, consists in the fact in this paragraph Hegel derives the commandment of right as an interference (by means of "therefore") from the preceding sentence. This is only admissible if the preceding sentence contains an element from which an imperative or other forms of commandments can actually be derived. Let us assume that Hegel does not simply depict a logically defective inference which we make in our practices, but rather assumes the correctness of this derivation.[14] In that case, "personality" has to be a characterization or an attribution of a status whose enactment involves the attribution of rights and duties.[15] This, however, is the core of the ascriptive analysis of such statements, as we have explained above: only if the characterization of an X as a person represents at the same time the ascription of an evaluative or normative status, can an imperative be inferred from it.

An *indirect* proof of my interpretative hypothesis can be gained from the following observation. In §§110–112, where Hegel explicates the first-person structure of intentions, his depiction changes from the reporting perspective of the third person to that of the first person:

> But this identity of content receives its more precise and distinctive determination within the moral point of view, in which freedom, this identity of the will with itself, is present *for* the will. (§105)
>
> (a) The content is determined for me as *mine* in such a way that, in its identity, it *contains* my subjectivity *for me* not only as my *inner* end, but also in so far as this end has achieved *external objectivity*. (§110)

While the first sentence of this paragraph is written from a perspective that reports (*berichtend*) and applies from an external point of view (*herantragen*) its philosophical instruments to our self-understanding as moral subjects ("for the will") from an external point of view (*herantragen*), in the second paragraph Hegel switches into the first-person mode. The subsequent paragraph assumes the perspective of the first sentence of §110 again, yet the first sentence of §112 is then again written in the first-person mode, while the second sentence switches the mode yet again.[16] Similar switches can be observed in other places of the text of *Elements*, for instance in the Remark to §132, and it systematically occurs wherever Hegel is confronted with the following problem: he wants to mention a first-person-propositional attitude in order to be able to make the grammar of this attitude recognizable (*kenntlich*), in this case the grammar of an intention.[17] If the particularity of the first-person self-reference by means of the "I" is constitutive of the phenomenon in question, then this particularity must not be absent when the attitude is mentioned. According to Hegel, the particularities of this self-relation expressed through the "I" are of crucial importance for the philosophy of right, and must be explicated in all their detail, especially in the analysis of the intentionality of actions, so that the different aspects of our practice of evaluating actions can be grasped. To respect this, one either has to quote the first-person self-reference of another subject, which, however, would refer only to the concrete occurrence and could not make the general structure visible, since the latter would presumably not be explicitly contained in the quoted self-reference. Or, one has to choose a depiction of the self-reference by means of the "I" in a third-person formulation that further conveys the information that the speaker who is referring to himself also knows that he is referring to himself.[18] In Hegel's time, the logical and semantic tools that could also preserve the special epistemic relationships of the "I" in descriptive sentences are not yet developed. Therefore, Hegel resorts to the solution of preserving these particularities by means of a switch to the first-person mode of depiction. Since here Hegel evidently leaves the level of a descriptive mention, these passages are not to be taken as a refutation of my interpretive hypothesis. On the contrary, the fact that Hegel controls this switch of depiction, which he performs for reasons that have to do with the subject matter itself and that can be reconstructed, shows that he was conscious of the descriptive-metaphysical approach of his philosophy of right.

ADVANTAGES OF THE PROPOSED INTERPRETATION

The proposal to interpret Hegel's practical philosophy as a cognitivist ascriptivism, and as a systematizing reconstruction of the social practices in which we either make claims against each other, recognize these claims, or legitimately reject them, has three advantages that I would like to present briefly in this section.

The *first* advantage lies in its ability to make visible and understandable the structure of Hegel's practical philosophy. Hegel builds his philosophy of right into his encyclopaedic System (*Gesamtsystem*)* as "Objective Spirit," and he sketches an outline of this part of the system in *Elements*. The upshot of this is that in the philosophy of right Hegel pursues two philosophical goals at once; these goals, in turn, stand in a systematic context of justification: on the one hand, the fundamental principle of Hegel's philosophy – subjectivity as concept and as idea – evolves and unfolds in the part of the system "Objective Spirit" in the form of the will, by way of manifesting itself in the form of a system of social practices and institutions. On the other hand, Hegel's depiction of the development of the will also captures the grammar that underlies these practices and institutions as their organizing principle, which

---

* Translator's note: I have translated the word "*Gesamtsystem*" as "System" (with a capital "S"). The words "*System*" and "*Systemteil*" have been translated as "system" and "part of the system," despite the fact that in the English literature it is not uncommon to refer to Hegel's "System" with a capital "S." Nevertheless, I have maintained this distinction between lower-case "s" "system" and capital "S" "System" throughout the text to preserve Quante's distinctive use of the words "*System*" and "*Gesamtsystem*."

thereby can be comprehended philosophically in its rational context (*Zusammenhang*). These two aspects of the conceptual development which Hegel unfolds in *Elements* serve two justificatory functions: on the one hand, the rational fundamental structure of our social practices and institutions becomes visible both in its ideal rational structure and in its concrete social manifestation.[19] Through this, these practices and institutions themselves receive a philosophical justification.[20] On the other hand, in the course of the execution of the task of showing the rational character of our social practices and institutions Hegel's System also proves itself. Hegel's central metaphysical premise, the development of subjectivity as a concept and as an idea, cannot be justified externally. It can only prove itself in the course of the justification of the different subject areas and phenomena.[21] Hegel's speculative premise (*Vorgabe*) proves itself to the extent that he succeeds at developing a philosophical systematization and reconstruction of the grammar of our social practices and institutions.

This double perspectivity of the conceptual process of development, which Hegel unfolds throughout his encyclopaedic System, takes on different forms in the different parts of the System; only the double and interdependent context of justification remains constant. Hegel, then, uses the latter to integrate the local grammars and the principles that are constitutive of the individual domains into a philosophical context of development, which, in turn, follows the conceptual process of development of his speculative logic.

On the one hand, the interpretation that we are presenting here is able to capture the general double perspectivity of the encyclopaedic System. On the other hand, the concrete form, which we determine here as a cognitivist ascriptivism, is the shape that the systematic context takes on specifically in practical philosophy. It goes without saying that this interpretation is not suitable for the reconstruction of this total constellation in the domain of natural philosophy.[22] However, this is not a weakness of my proposal, but rather an indication for one of its strengths: its context sensitivity.

The *second* advantage of this proposed interpretation is that it allows us to distinguish the different levels on which in *Elements* we find Hegel's depiction, and to explain why, and in what way, this is connected with the general orientation of his philosophy of right.

On one level, Hegel is able to reject concrete patterns of justification as these occur in the social practices and institutions, as it were, as the reasons of interacting subjects themselves. He can reject these if it happens that they are incompatible with the grammar of underlying social practices and institutions, either directly or on the basis of their presuppositions. To illustrate this type of criticism, let us look at two examples: (i) in his analysis of the making and acceptance (or also rejection) of excuses, Hegel shows that the excuse of an agent, which focuses on the absence of criminal responsibility or on reduced responsibility, for one, disregards the difference between the general exemption of an agent from the practice of attributing responsibility, and the presentation of exculpatory considerations in a concrete, singular case. Furthermore, he points out that the former in fact does not constitute an exoneration of the subject but rather comes at a high price, namely, because the agent in question would thus lose the normative status of a person (or of a moral subject). However, for Hegel, this constitutes a greater harm and a more massive violation than the pronouncement of a sanction.[23] (ii) The second example is found on the level of the functionality of a social institution: in his explication of legal sanction through punishment, Hegel elaborates the motive of the avenging reason as a possible intention for the justification of this institution (§102). He then rejects this justification as deficient because it leads to an infinite regress, i.e., the provocation of an avenging reason on the part of the sanctioned. This regress does not lead to the pacification of the situation and to the compensation of the injustice that occurred, but rather to further violations of the law and to a destabilization of the situation in general. We can take Hegel's remarks to mean that it is therefore a philosophical task to justify the legal institution of punishment without reference to revenge as a motivating and legitimizing element.[24]

On another level, Hegel is able to reject proposals for a philosophical interpretation and reconstruction of the grammar of our social practices and institutions, in case that they are directly or on the basis of presuppositions incompatible with the grammar of these social practices and institutions, which at this point also means, with the self-understanding of the subjects that act within these. One example of Hegel's engagement with such philosophical errors is his criticism of the conception of the erring conscience (§140A), which, in his opinion, amounts to an inconsistent position that thus undermines the cognitivist core of social practice. Further examples are all subjectivist conceptions of the good, which either reduce the good to a feeling and thus represent emotivist versions of the non-cognitivist thesis (§126A), or tie the standard of the assessment of the good to the judgments and values of the individual subject (§140A and §132A).[25]

Had the philosophical positions that Hegel criticizes been adequate, it would inevitably follow that our practice of putting forth, accepting, and criticizing reasons for or against the recognition of mutual claims have been based on an error. This, however, is neither compatible with the self-understanding of the individuals, nor with the grammar of these social practices and institutions whose rationality is shown in Hegel's System. Therefore, Hegel criticizes his opponents, on the one hand, on the level of philosophy, by giving proof of their philosophical errors. On the other hand, he points to the consequences of the erroneous philosophies that will corrode our practices and institutions if the subjects who act in the social practices and institutions adopt (or were to adopt) these philosophical interpretations as their self-understanding.

A *third* advantage that I see in the interpretation that I am proposing here consists in that the overall orientation of Hegel's practical philosophy underscores a self-restraint of philosophical ethics with regard to the formulation and justification of concrete moral statements. Such self-restraint, which Hegel emphasizes time and again in his critique of philosophical utopias, is not only expressed in the overall orientation of the entire undertaking as a critical-reconstructive hermeneutic(s) of the social reality (*Wirklichkeit*) of the spirit that has historically become (*gewordenen*) what it is. The level of abstraction on which his justification, and his critique of our social practices and of individual moves within them occurs, also represents, in my opinion, a plausible self-restraint of philosophical ethics: on the level of concrete normative judgments philosophical ethics plays no expert role (with the exception of the rejection of strategies of justification and critique on a general level). Which penalty is appropriate (§101A), which excuse is acceptable in a given case (§132A), or who is to be pardoned under what circumstances, as Hegel discusses in relation to the monarch (§282A): all of this has to be left to the members of the social practice in the given institutions, or even to the individual subjectivity of a particular agent. Those who deduce their application to individual cases from the level of general norms and principles, which is the only level that is accessible to practical philosophy, commit the mistake of the "misplaced exactitude," for this eliminates the constitutive role of the power of judgment of the individual and thus leaves us unable to adequately accommodate the situatedness of practical reason or the autonomy of the individual decision-maker.[26]

HEGEL'S "STRONG" PREMISES AND AIMS

Hegel's philosophy of right is based on the thesis that all of our social practices and institutions can be explicated as *shapes* (§32) and as increasingly more complex differentiations of the concept of the free will, and that they can be brought together in a context that can philosophically be shown to be rational. In the context of the domain of phenomena of practical philosophy this is certainly a strong systematic assumption. It stems from Hegel's demanding metaphysical premises and aims, owing to the systematic character of Hegel's philosophy, for these go far beyond the claim of a philosophical reconstruction and systematization of our social practices and institutions. The conceptual differentiation of the concept of the will itself follows a general structure that Hegel develops in his *Science of Logic*, and he justifies the latter by showing that it is the necessary and complete totality, without alternative, of the categories in which subjectivity constitutes itself. This also impacts the validity claim of his philosophy of right: that is, Hegel does not need to claim that the logical categories capture the logic of the domain of phenomena in all its details. Depending on the exact structure of the development of the categories, he can also conceivably allow for the fundamental principles of the philosophy of right to remain underdetermined and capable of further specification through the contexts at hand. And yet, he must claim that his philosophical explication and systematization is without alternative and that it is complete on the philosophically fundamental level, so that our social practices and institutions become understandable in their functional necessity, and thus become justified in the Hegelian sense.[27]

To be sure, every interpretation of *Elements* has to heed these general metaphysical conditions and aims of Hegel's philosophy, yet if one forgoes with good reason the strong justificatory claims of the philosophy, it is possible to take seriously Hegel's philosophy of right from a systematic point and to consider it viable without taking on the high burdens of proof.[28] Under these circumstances, two systematically valuable aspects can be gained from the fact that Hegel's philosophy of right is part of an encyclopaedic System. For one, the beginning and the end of the philosophy of right point to the other parts of the System and thus to "adjacent" phenomenal domains. With regard to "Subjective Spirit," the part of the system that precedes the philosophy of right, it opens up the possibility of relating the practical philosophy to the philosophical anthropology and the general philosophy of mind (in the sense of the contemporary *philosophy of mind**).[29] As for "Absolute Spirit," the subsequent part of the system, there becomes possible a reflection on the question of the philosophically explicable connections between our social practices and institutions, and the central cultural media of self-interpretation becomes possible. As is well known, here Hegel mentions art, religion, and philosophy.[30]

---

* English in the original. [NF]

Furthermore, the speculative-logical general orientation of the development of the concept allows for an attractive interpretation of Hegel's thesis of the sublation of morality in "ethical life" (*Sittlichkeit*), which Hegel himself characterizes, with an explicit reference to his "Logic" (§135A), as a movement of integration.[31] If we take this description, it becomes possible that we do not need to interpret Hegel's determination of the relationship between morality and the ethical life as a lexical priority of the validity of the latter over the claims of the former. A more plausible interpretation (one that can be reconciled better with Hegel's own remarks) would assume that here Hegel puts to use the pragmatic argumentative pattern of the *default-and-challenge*, a variation of the logical figure of positing and presupposing the logic of reflection: according to this interpretation, the assertion of specifically moral claims presupposes the validity of moral convictions, that is to say, of norms that are actually shared, because otherwise moral claims could not be formulated or made comprehensible at all. Moral conflicts require a lived ethical order as the shared normative and evaluative background, or else there would be no possibility of dissent. This general relationship of dependence, therefore, excludes the possibility of founding or justifying the *totality* of validity claims of the ethical life through those of morality. But of course it allows for the possibility that in individual cases moral claims not only demand priority over ethical claims, but that this priority can indeed be acknowledged.[32] Nowhere in his philosophy of right does Hegel develop answers for questions that arise from concrete moral conflicts or conflicts between moral and ethical claims. His discussion of Greek tragedy or his remarks on moral revolutionaries, for instance, show that his answers always remain on a general level that pertains to the principles and the grammar of our social practices. The reservation expressed by Hegel's thesis of the limited power of practical philosophy is certainly regrettable, and perhaps it can be corrected through a philosophical ethic with a different focus. This self-limitation notwithstanding, Hegel's approach at least has the potential to make understandable the structure of conflicts that arise in a given case from tensions between the different social practices and between conflicting institutions.

Scope and Limits of this Interpretation

I would like to conclude this contribution by identifying the scope and the limits of my interpretation, and to do so I discuss three, in my opinion, central objections that can be raised against my proposal.

First: it is by no means apparent that the free will should be the philosophical principle that constitutes and organizes our social practices and institutions. This objection allows for a number of different readings, which, in my opinion, require different replies. This could mean (i) that Hegel is unable to show that our social practices and institutions are necessarily explicated and systematically reconstructed in only one way, namely, through his conception of the will. Why should it not be the case, this reading might object, that practical philosophy is able to analyse our social practices and institutions in various ways, thereby relying on alternative principles and conceptions? Since in this contribution I have argued in favour of relinquishing the claim that Hegel presents an ultimate justification without alternatives, this objection poses no challenge to me. Nevertheless, one can reply to this objection that its plausibility depends on its own ability to present such alternatives and to show that they are at least as powerful as Hegel's philosophy of right. The first objection can also mean (ii) that Hegel's conception of the will alone is not sufficient to explicate and systematize all of our social practices and institutions adequately. According to the counterproposal required by this reading of the objection, in order to develop an adequate practical philosophy we need additional ethical principles that are independent of Hegel's conception of the will. If this objection were justified, which would have to be shown by means of its own suitable outline of a theory, I could hold on to my interpretative hypothesis that Hegel indeed pursues such a monistic conception, yet I would have to concede that Hegel's conception of the will is not rich and complex enough to integrate these other principles that are brought into play by competing philosophical ethics and that are *prima facie* plausible. Since a systematically oriented interpretation of Hegel's philosophy is not committed to the thesis that the theory that Hegel develops is adequate from a systematic perspective, this would, in principle, not cause any harm, even though the appeal of conducting the interpretative project outlined here would noticeably decrease. Again, the strength of this reading of the objection depends on the plausibility of the prospective alternatives and on how powerful Hegel's conception of the will ultimately proves to be.[33] Finally, the first objection can also be understood to mean (iii) that by assigning this role to the free will, one would need to posit an individualistic (or monological) and psychological criterion as the foundation of ethics, which would be inappropriate in substance (*sachlich*). On this reading, the first objection can be rejected convincingly. For one, Hegel's conception of the will is not

a psychological criterion but rather pertains to the grammar of the
propositionally constituted content of claims that we assert, recognize but also criticize in social practices and institutions.[34] On the
other hand, it is evident that freedom means neither the mere freedom of action nor the freedom of the will, but rather the proof of the
success (*Bewährung*) of claims that are made through actions in the
social space. This is, as an analysis of Hegel's conception of action
shows, a socially constituted and cognitive freedom, so that on this
reading the first objection comes to nothing.

Second: according to the second objection, by embedding practical philosophy in Hegel's metaphysically highly charged System, one will
distort the explication and reconstruction of our social practices and
institutions in a way that is ethically not defensible and that yields
a systematically inadequate reconstruction.[35] Prominent versions of
this objection are the talk of a repressed intersubjectivity in Hegel's
philosophy of right or the underdevelopment of individual protec-
tive rights against an idolized state, which is due to the totalizing
movement of identity and the conservative preservation of the existing order *qua* reason.[36] To this objection we can say that its claims
need to be shown in their specific varieties in Hegel's *Elements*. If
such a proof should succeed, one must ask if these distortions are
truly unacceptable in substance and, if this is the case, if they follow
as an inevitable consequence from the general structure of Hegel's
practical philosophy. It is possible that the relationship between
the metaphysically organizing level of Hegel's philosophy and the
grammars of the individual phenomenal domains is more indirect,
and leaves more room for interpretation than Hegel assumes (or it
leaves room for different emphases than those that Hegel himself
considers appropriate in substance). If such a close necessary connection (*Zusammenhang*) could be proven, as the second objection
alleges, the following strategy would be left as a possible reaction: in
a first step, one would have to decouple the interpretative hypothesis from the thesis that Hegel presents a practical philosophy that
is appropriate in substance. In a second step, one would have to
determine which modifications of his systematic development
would have to be carried out in order to avoid the unwanted consequences which, for good reasons, are considered to be implausible.
If one does not adopt the strong metaphysical justificatory claims
of Hegel's System, there is some conceptual latitude in which one
could further develop, or also correct, Hegel's practical philosophy.[37]

Third: the interpretative proposal that I have sketched here is unable to
adequately reconstruct the function of the section "World History,"

which concludes Hegel's philosophy of right. This objection, as well, allows for (at least) two different readings. *On the one hand*, this can mean that it makes no sense to conceive of world history itself as a social practice, one that could be captured in the sense of the interpretative strategy that we are proposing here. To my mind, this is necessarily true for two reasons: the first reason is that Hegel conceives of states as institutions that stand in relations of recognition, thus forming a self-consciousness of their specific identity.[38] Second, the function of history can also be determined, admittedly in a depotentiated form, in such a way that the reference of a system of social practices and institutions to another system of social practices and institutions, which is historically distinct from the former, is constitutive of the becoming-conscious of the states' own specific evaluative and normative orientation. If, for example, historical (*historisch*) experiences belong to the self-understanding of the subjects who act in these practices and institutions, then the historical (*geschichtlich*) dimension of the normative self-understanding constitutes a systematic reason why Hegel ends his practical philosophy with world history.[39] *On the other hand*, the third objection can also express the assertion that Hegel needs to make use of his metaphysically demanding philosophy of history in order to deliver on his program, i.e., he needs it for the explication and justification of the totality of social practices and institutions.[40] If this is how the objection is understood, then my answer is simply the same as it was in the other two cases; namely, that as long as one distinguishes the burdens of proof and the claims of Hegel's philosophy of right from those that arise from the orientation of his logic and of his System, the objection comes to nothing. However, if the third objection is understood in this manner, then a follow-up problem arises that needs to be taken into account by assessing if, and where, Hegel's reconstruction of our social practices and institutions does not do justice to the subject area for reasons owing to the general metaphysical orientation of his philosophy. And yet again: it is necessary first to justify that we are dealing with an inadequacy in substance, and then show further that the latter follows from the systematics of Hegel's logic.

But perhaps there is another obvious objection that forces itself on my reader, who, to this point, has followed my interpretation patiently: does the interpretative strategy that I have presented here fit the whole of Hegel's philosophy of right, and can it be sustained throughout the entire text of *Elements*? While this is a justified objection, it can only be answered by means of the attempt to execute the interpretive strategy sketched out in this contribution. The viability of the proposed interpretation of Hegel's philosophy of right as a cognitivist ascriptivism will become apparent only then, and with this it will become apparent also whether it can be positioned as a systematically productive conception in the contemporary philosophical discussion.

NOTES

1 In this contribution, when I speak of "Hegel's philosophy of right" I refer solely to Hegel's practical philosophy as he developed it in *Elements of the Philosophy of Right*. I quote *Elements* directly in the text with the appropriate citations of the respective paragraphs. I use the text of the critical edition, volume 14.1 of Hegel's *Gesammelte Werke* (I use "A" to refer to the Remarks to the paragraphs and "R" to refer to Hegel's handwritten notes which can be found in his personal copy and which are contained in volume 14.2 of the critical edition): G.W.F. Hegel, *Grundlinien der Philosophie des Rechts*, vol. 14.1, eds. K. Grotsch and E. Weisser-Lohmann (Hamburg: Meiner, 2009); and Hegel, *Grundlinien der Philosophie des Rechts*, vol. 14.2, eds. K. Grotsch and E. Weisser-Lohmann (Hamburg: Meiner, 2010). Such an undertaking is not only ambitious, but in light of the plethora of existing interpretations it is also not without risk. My only claim is that I am not aware of an interpretation that points in the same direction as the one that I will outline and justify in this contribution. A basic idea that is related in substance can be found in A. Honneth, *Leiden an Unbestimmtheit* (Stuttgart; Reclam, 2001), 53ff and in D. Moyar's concept of a "performative view of practical reason" (*Hegel's Conscience* (New York: Oxford University Press, 2011), 38ff).

2 This constellation is comparable to the one between the phenomenal domain of reactive attitudes and the analysis of the social practices in which we articulate these attitudes, as put forth by P. F. Strawson, "Freedom and Resentment," in *Free Will and Reactive Attitudes: Perspectives on P.F. Strawson's 'Freedom and* Resentment,' eds. M. McKenna and P. Russell (Surrey: Ashgate Publishing Limited, 2008), 19–36. This parallel must of course not obscure the crucial difference between Hegel and Strawson, which consists in the fact that Hegel integrates these practices themselves further into a philosophical System, thereby supplying their philosophical justification – understood in the Hegelian sense! For a similar discussion see H. Schnädelbach, *Hegels praktische Philosophie* (Frankfurt am Main: Suhrkamp, 2000), 37. Schnädelbach reaches the conclusion that Hegel advocates a "normativism of its own kind" (ibid., 351 [translation mine, NF]), yet he fails to clarify what this normativism looks like.

3 In this contribution, I am solely concerned with cognitivism in the domain of practical philosophy, which is why additional qualifications (e.g., as "ethical cognitivism") can be omitted.

4 For further explanations of these metaethical distinctions and the ethical positions that are captured by them, see M. Quante, *Einführung in die Allgemeine Ethik*, 4th ed. (Darmstadt: Wissenschaftliche Buchgesellschaf, 2011), chaps. 3–6.

5 In his overall favourable discussion of the above reflections, S. Ostritsch criticizes that, by setting this course, I have neglected one possibility: "[w]hat is thus not pursued is the possibility that Hegel's philosophy could not only circumvent the non-cognitivist position but the distinction between cognitivism and non-cognitivism as such" ("'Freiheit – Liberté – Freedom.' Der Internationale Hegelkongress 2011 in Stuttgart,'" *Zeitschrift für philosophische Forschung* 65 (2011): 594). Aside from the fact that Ostritsch gives no indication as to how Hegel could do this, which, to be sure, is difficult to do in a congress-report, it is not clear what such a manoeuvre would look like. If one keeps in mind that the cognitivist thesis is compatible with the notion that moral statements can satisfy other functions as well, then no material (*sachlich*) reason can be found as to why Hegel, who was familiar with the rejection of the moral non-cognitivism of his time and thus also with the essence of this distinction, should have dismissed it.

6 A comprehensive systematic investigation of Hegel's conception of conscience can be found in Moyar, *Hegel's Conscience*.

7 Cf. H.L.A. Hart, "The Ascription of Responsibility and Rights," in *Logic and Language*, ed. A.G.N. Flew (Oxford: Blackwell Publishing, 1951), 160ff.

8 Cf. P.T. Geach, "Der Askriptivismus" in *Analytische Handlungstheorie Band 1: Handlungsbeschreibungen*, ed. G. Meggle (Frankfurt am Main: 1977); J. Feinberg, "Handlung und Verantwortung," in *Analytische Handlungstheorie Band 1: Handlungsbeschreibungen*, ed. G. Meggle (Frankfurt am Main: Suhrkamp, 1977); or G. Pitcher "Handlung und Verantwortung bei Hart," in *Analytische Handlungstheorie Band 1: Handlungsbeschreibungen*, ed. G. Meggle (Stuttgart: Bad Cannstatt, 1933).

9 Elsewhere I have shown in detail that Hegel also committed himself to the thesis of the intersubjective constitution of human action, so that in this regard as well a parallel between Sneddon's ascriptivist conception and Hegel's concept of action arises in this regard. Cf. R.B. Pippin, *Hegel's Practical Philosophy: Rational Agency as Ethical Life* (Cambridge: Cambridge University Press, 2008), chap. 6; as well as Quante, *Hegels Begriff der Handlung* (Stuttgart: Bad Cannstatt, 1993) 111–24; and Quante, "Hegel," in *Companion to the Philosophy of Action*, ed. T. O'Connor and C. Sandis (London: Blackwell Publishing, 2010). Moreover, it is evident

that Hegel considered any kind of scientistic naturalism about the mental
to be fundamentally inadequate; cf. Quante, *Die Wirklichkeit des Geistes*
(Frankfurt am Main: Suhrkamp, 2011), chaps. 4–6.

10 Cf. also R.B. Pippin, *Hegel's Practical Philosophy: Rational Agency as Ethical
Life*, chap. 2; and F. Neuhauser, *Foundations of Hegel's Social Theory*.
Cambridge, MA: Harvard University Press, chap. 6.

11 It is apparent that Hegel's interpretation and reconstruction of the
social practices and of the subjects' self-understanding inherent in
them makes revisions (grounded in his philosophical premises) that are
considerably more far-reaching than the ones that arise from Strawson's
original conception; compare on this point the introduction in Strawson,
Individuals. An Essay in Descriptive Metaphysics. London: Methuen. See also
Quante (2011, chaps. 2 and 3) for a determination of Hegel's philosophy
between the poles of therapeutic philosophy and revisionist metaphysics.

12 For an informative exposition of the specific characteristics of Hegel's
understanding of metaphysics, cf. S. Houlgate, *Hegel, Nietzsche, and the
Criticism of Metaphysics* (Cambridge: Cambridge University Press, 2004),
chap. 5.

13 In the morality chapter of *Elements* (§§110–12), Hegel further determines
the structure of first-person propositional attitudes, through an explication
of our concept of action and of our self-understanding as free agents,
as a conception of the intentionality of actions. Cf. in detail Quante,
Hegels Begriff der Handlung, chap. 2; as well as H.C. Schmidt am Busch,
Anerkennung' als Prinzip der Kritischen Theorie. Berlin: de Gruyter, 2011),
157–70.

14 In view of the significance that the concept of a person has for Hegel's
entire philosophy of right in general and for his systematic reconstruction
of abstract right in particular, this assumption is, in my opinion, without
alternative.

15 For a closer analysis of Hegel's concept of personhood, cf. Quante
(2011, ch.8). A systematic account of the different manners of use of the
concept of a person can be found in Quante, *Person*, 2nd ed. (Berlin: de
Gruyter, 2012), 1ff. I discuss the problem of justificatory connections
(*Begründungszusammenhänge*) between the descriptive and the prescriptive
use of the concept of a person – a problem that is central to both practical
philosophy and the philosophy of right – in Quante, "Die Bedeutung des
Personenbegriffs für den moralischen Status der Person," in *Der Mensch als
Person und Rechtsperson*, eds. E. Klein and C. Menke (Berlin: 2011).

16 The following sentences, which are contrasted from the first sentences of
§112 by means of dashes, bring along further changes of perspective.

17 To be sure, this type of statement needs to be distinguished from those
first-person sentences, in which Hegel uses them simply in order to

announce his further proceedings to the reader (as for instance in the Remark to §140 where Hegel writes, "In these present Remarks, I shall briefly indicate the principle shapes which this subjectivity commonly assumes.").

18 The sentence, "He is currently speaking about himself [*über sich*]," can be true even when the speaker denoted by "he" does not know that he is currently speaking of himself (for instance, when he uses a designation that is factually accurate yet escapes his knowledge). In order to close this epistemic gap, which cannot occur where "I" is used correctly, the sentence has to say "He is currently speaking about himself'" [*über sich selbst*]" where "himself' [*selbst*]" indicates the knowledge of the self-reference. The quasi-indicators introduced by Castañeda satisfy in essence precisely this function.

19 As E. Rózsa shows in *Versöhnung und System* (München: Wilhelm Fink, 2005), this constitutes a practical goal that Hegel pursues in his reconstructive-hermeneutical project: to make possible the individual's reconciliation with the prosaic relations of modern society.

20 This justification is not to be understood as an internal one, put forward in the practices themselves as a justification for a move within a given practice. Put very briefly, what is thus shown is the rationality of the acknowledgment of excuses or of the conclusion of contracts, yet the appropriateness of a concrete excuse in a specific situation or the individual conclusion of a particular contract is not established.

21 This is the – admittedly deflationary – sense which Hegel's talk of the "absolute" acquires in the interpretation that I propose here. The consequences that follow from this, for instance for Hegel's philosophy of religion, cannot be looked into in this contribution.

22 In my view, the numerous misinterpretations of Hegel's philosophy of nature, which in part want to pin him down to an interpretative perspective towards nature (in opposition to the explanatory perspective of the natural sciences), have their material reason here. On the level of the encyclopaedic overall context there exists indeed a speculative-logical development which must be understood in the sense of a discursive dialectic. From this it does not follow, however, that the development within the grammar of the phenomenal domain itself should follow the same ordering pattern. What follows indeed is that Hegel has to effect a meta-reflection on how to make the different constellations between the two levels philosophically comprehensible, and on how to integrate them, at the same time, into the development of the concept on the level of the System. In my opinion, Hegel attempted to meet the burden of proof already in *Phenomenology of Spirit*. For the reconstruction of this context in relation to observing reason and the

natural sciences' treatment of the mental, cf. Quante, *Die Wirklichkeit des Geistes*, chap. 4.

23 To be sure, Hegel does not want to deny in principle the possibility that such exemptions may be permissible. His argument rather aims at correcting the error that *can* underlie the inflationary use of this strategy intended to exonerate and spare the involved agents; on this point, cf. my extensive analysis of Hegel's argument in Quante, *Die Wirklichkeit des Geistes*, chap. 10. The therapeutic and hermeneutic-reconstructive orientation of Hegel's philosophy of right, the traditional reproach notwithstanding, does not necessarily lead to quietism. However, this orientation of Hegel's philosophy in general bears the danger of judging the prevailing conditions too quickly as adequate manifestations of reason, and of making too little use of the critical potentials of philosophy, which is a danger that Karl Marx identified as the positivism of Hegel's philosophy.

24 For the argumentative structure of Hegel's theory of the will, cf. Quante, *Hegels Begriff der Handlung*, 59ff.

25 In his discussion of the question how the right of the individual will can be integrated into a cognitivist conception of justification that maintains intersubjective standards, Hegel shows both where the material motivation for this philosophical error lies, and why those who make this error are led to untenable consequences. For a detailed discussion, cf. Quante, *Hegels Begriff der Handlung*, chap. 10.

26 It is of course a controversial point, which hinges on my very own metaethical premises, whether one views this aspect of Hegel's practical philosophy as an advantage. Cf. on this point A. Vieth and Quante, "The structure of perception in particularist ethics," *Ethical Perspectives* 17 (2010): 5–39.

27 Ostritsch has criticized my conviction (which I voiced in a paper at the Stuttgart Hegel Congress) that we have good reasons not to accept Hegel's strong metaphysical assumptions and aims. In his criticism, Ostritsch assumes that it is my view that "in the case of the philosophy of right, the supposedly highly metaphysical premise amounts to nothing more than the claim to carry out an immanent conceptual investigation of the free will" (Ostritsch, "'Freiheit – Liberté – Freedom.' Der Internationale Hegelkongress 2011 in Stuttgart,'" 594; [translation mine; NF]). This is, however, not my position: the distinction that I make above, between the strong systematic thesis regarding the practical philosophy, and the demanding metaphysical premise of the System, is meant to make this explicit. Consequently, Ostritsch's criticism comes to nothing, yet I thank him for it because it has helped me to formulate this point of my interpretation in clearer terms.

28 Elsewhere I have presented the reasons for my view that Hegel cannot claim necessity for his metaphilosophical assumptions (Quante, *Die Wirklichkeit des Geistes*, chap. 3).

29 On the topic of the link [*Zusammenhang*] between Hegel's practical philosophy and the philosophical anthropology, cf. L. Siep, *Praktische Philosophie im Deutschen Idealismus* (Frankfurt am Main: Suhrkamp, 1992), chap. 11; on its link with *the philosophy of mind*, cf. C. Halbig, *Objektives Denken* (Stuttgart: Bad Cannstatt, 2002), chaps. 1–3.

30 On this point, cf. W. Dudley, *Hegel, Nietzsche, and Philosophy* (Cambridge: Cambridge University Press, 2002), chap. 4.

31 On this point, cf. Siep, *Praktische Philosophie im Deutschen Idealismus*, chap. 12; and Neuhouser, *Foundations of Hegel's Social Theory*, chap. 7.

32 On this point, cf. my more detailed analysis in Quante, *Die Wirklichkeit des Geistes*, chap. 13.

33 The reasons for my optimism about this point can be found in Quante, *Die Wirklichkeit des Geistes*, esp. chaps. 12–14.

34 On this point, compare the more extensive account of Pippin, *Hegel's Practical Philosophy: Rational Agency as Ethical Life*, chaps. 4–6.

35 On this point, cf. the discussions in M. Theunissen, *Sein und Schein* (Frankfurt am Main: Suhrkamp, 1980), 472ff; and A. Honneth, *Leiden an Unbestimmtheit*, 28ff.

36 On this point, cf. Siep, *Praktische Philosophie im Deutschen Idealismus*, chap. 15; and Siep, *Aktualität und Grenzen der praktischen Philosophie Hegels* (München: Fink, 2010), 93–114 and 117–30.

37 I do not wish to deny the possibility that a gap may open up here between, on the one hand, the claim to present as faithful an interpretation as possible, and, on the other, the wish to reveal a conception that is systematically sound and attractive. If the second objection is plausible, how far one is ready to open this gap will ultimately depend on the epistemic interests of the interpreter.

38 I give an overview of the different constellations of recognition that Hegel integrated into his concept of the will, including the constellation that holds between states, in Quante, *Die Wirklichkeit des Geistes*, chap. 12.

39 This historical dimension is, however, not necessary for the formation of such an identity constituted by the experience of difference, for it could also be rooted in a plurality of coexisting systems of social practices and institutions. Alternatively, one could presumably show the limit case of a universal, internally differentiated totality of such social practices and institutions which would constitute a sufficient framework for the formation of such an identity; namely, if one assumes that the specific internal grammars of the individual subsystems could be prompted to

become reflexive through the delimitation of a given subsystem from other subsystems.

40 On the topic of this problem, cf. E. Weisser-Lohmann, *Rechtsphilosophie als praktische Philosophie* (München: Fink, 2011), chap. 9; and E. Angehrn, "Geschichte und System," in *Logik und Realität: Wie systematisch ist Hegels System?* eds. Christoph Jamme and Yohichi Kubu (München: Fink, 2012).

REFERENCES

Angehrn, E. "Geschichte und System." In *Logik und Realität: Wie systematisch ist Hegels System?*, edited by Christoph Jamme and Yohichi Kubu, 247–58. München: Fink, 2012.

Dudley, W. *Hegel, Nietzsche, and Philosophy*. Cambridge: Cambridge University Press, 2002.

Feinberg, J. "Handlung und Verantwortung." In *Analytische Handlungstheorie Band 1: Handlungsbeschreibungen*, edited by G. Meggle, 186–224. Frankfurt am Main: Suhrkamp, 1977.

Geach, P.T. "Der Askriptivismus." In *Analytische Handlungstheorie Band 1: Handlungsbeschreibungen*, edited by G. Meggle, 239–45. Frankfurt am Main, 1977.

Halbig, C. *Objektives Denken*. Stuttgart: Bad Cannstatt, 2002.

Hart, H.L.A. "The Ascription of Responsibility and Rights." In *Logic and Language*, edited by A.G.N. Flew, 145–66. Oxford: Blackwell, 1951.

Hegel, G.W.F. *Grundlinien der Philosophie des Rechts*, Vol. 14.1. Edited by K. Grotsch and E. Weisser-Lohmann. Hamburg: Meiner, 2009.

—— *Grundlinien der Philosophie des Rechts*, Vol. 14.2. Edited by K. Grotsch and E. Weisser-Lohmann. Hamburg: Meiner, 2010.

Honneth, A. *Leiden an Unbestimmtheit*. Stuttgart: Reclam, 2001.

Houlgate, S. *Hegel, Nietzsche, and the Criticism of Metaphysics*. Cambridge: Cambridge University Press, 2004.

Moyar, D. *Hegel's Conscience*. Oxford: Oxford University Press, 2011.

Neuhouser, F. *Foundations of Hegel's Social Theory*. Cambridge, MA: Harvard University Press, 2000.

Ostritsch, S. "'Freiheit – Liberté – Freedom.' Der Internationale Hegelkongress 2011 in Stuttgart'." *Zeitschrift für philosophische Forschung* 65 (2011): 586–95.

Pippin, R.B. *Hegel's Practical Philosophy: Rational Agency as Ethical Life*. Cambridge: Cambridge University Press, 2008.

Pitcher, G. "Handlung und Verantwortung bei Hart." In *Analytische Handlungstheorie Band 1: Handlungsbeschreibungen*, edited by G. Meggle, 225–38. Stuttgart: Bad Cannstatt, 1933.

Quante, M. *Hegels Begriff der Handlung*. Stuttgart: Bad Cannstatt, 1993.

——— "Hegel." In *Companion to the Philosophy of Action*, edited by T. O'Connor and C. Sandis, 537–45. London: Blackwell, 2010.

——— *Die Wirklichkeit des Geistes*. Frankfurt am Main: Suhrkamp, 2011a.

——— "Die Bedeutung des Personenbegriffs für den moralischen Status der Person." In *Der Mensch als Person und Rechtsperson*, edited by E. Klein and C. Menke, 69–87. Berlin, 2011b.

——— *Einführung in die Allgemeine Ethik*. 4th ed. Darmstadt: Wissenschaftliche Buchgesellschaft, 2011c.

——— *Person*. 2nd ed. Berlin: de Gruyter, 2012.

Rózsa, E. *Versöhnung und System*. München: Wilhelm Fink, 2005.

Schmidt am Busch, H.C. *Anerkennung' als Prinzip der Kritischen Theorie*. Berlin: de Gruyter, 2011.

Schnädelbach, H. *Hegels praktische Philosophie*. Frankfurt am Main: Suhrkamp, 2000.

Siep, L. *Praktische Philosophie im Deutschen Idealismus*. Frankfurt am Main: Suhrkamp, 1992.

——— *Aktualität und Grenzen der praktischen Philosophie Hegels*. München: Fink, 2010.

Sneddon, A. *Action and Responsibility*. Dordrecht: Springer, 2006.

Strawson, P.F. *Individuals: An Essay in Descriptive Metaphysics*. London: Methuen, 1959.

——— "Freedom and Resentment." In *Free Will and Reactive Attitudes: Perspectives on P.F. Strawson's 'Freedom and Resentment,'* edited by M. McKenna and P. Russell, 19–36. Surrey: Ashgate Publishing Limited, 2008.

Theunissen, M. *Sein und Schein*. Frankfurt am Main: Suhrkamp, 1980.

Vieth, A., and M. Quante. "The Structure of Perception in Particularist Ethics." *Ethical Perspectives* 17 (2010): 5–39.

Weisser-Lohmann, E. *Rechtsphilosophie als praktische Philosophie*. München: Fink, 2011.

3 The Justice of Contradiction: History and the Realization of Freedom in Hegel

ANGELICA NUZZO, CITY UNIVERSITY OF NEW YORK

In this essay I look at the implications that the systematic foundation of Hegel's philosophy of objective spirit in the Logic and the logical method has for his idea of freedom and for his conception of history as the culmination of the movement of freedom's realization within the sphere of ethical life. In particular, I am interested in the role that contradiction plays in structuring logical, practical, and historical processes *as processes*. I suggest that the most innovative and, for us today, useful features of Hegel's idea of history must be brought back precisely to history's *logical foundation*. My overall claim regards the fundamental solidarity between Hegel's logical thought of contradiction and his awareness of its practical and historical relevance.

The structure of my argument is informed by the questions that the end of the *Phenomenology of Spirit* poses with regard to the issue of history's position within the system. The phenomenological movement yields two general results: first, it establishes the concept of *Geist*, which is now the historical, developmental reality assumed by the "subject" into which "substance" has been transformed;[1] second, it systematically introduces to the dimension of the speculative *Begriff*, the point in which the spirit's phenomenology ends and the "science of logic" can begin.[2] And yet, for the logic to begin history and its temporality must be overcome, the movement of spirit left behind, and its memory forgotten so as to allow for a pure and absolutely 'presuppositionless' logical beginning. Once "absolute knowing" has been reached and the dimension of Hegel's post-revolutionary present (or the standpoint of the Preface) is gained, phenomenological *Erinnerung* yields a "logical" or "virtual" memory that brings phenomenological history to an end thereby producing the transition (or alienation) to the a-temporal and a-historical element of the concept, free once and for all of the "opposition of consciousness."[3] At this point, memory and history part ways.

Disclosing its one-sidedness, memory turns against history. Both memory and history are transformed by such a separation. Memory becomes a purely logical movement but also gains a psychological, subjective depth from which its collective, ethical, and social significance must be recuperated. History proper or world-history becomes highly political; its subject is neither the individual consciousness nor the free agent nor the (ancient) individual in immediate unity with the ethical whole but the modern institution of the nation state. Concluding the development of objective spirit, *Weltgeschichte* discloses the reality of logical contradiction.[4]

Now, coming from the conclusion of the *Phenomenology*, this is the question I shall presently address: how do we (re)gain history in the system after phenomenological memory has been left behind, forgotten, as it were, once and for all; after the a-temporal and a-spatial movement of the Logic has run its course, and the development of the philosophy of subjective spirit has first recuperated the concept of spirit in its subjective, individual, and psychological dimension? What does the dialectic-speculative movement of the Logic bring to the new, post-phenomenological (and post-revolutionary) idea of history? What are the systematic conditions that make spirit's actuality and the reality of freedom properly *historical*?

I first consider the Logic and then turn to objective spirit.

The Logic as Condition for Thinking History

My claim is that Hegel's idea of a dialectic-speculative logic (in contrast to Kant's transcendental logic and more generally to the entire tradition of what Hegel calls *Verstandeslogik*) constitutes the most adequate basis for the introduction of history in the systematic of spirit but also for the understanding of the specific developmental structures of history itself. On my view, to claim that history has its systematic foundation in the Logic means that it is the Logic and not some metaphysical or theological or even moral assumption or goal that guides its development. I will argue in favour of the following three points that make of the Logic the condition for thinking history and for articulating history dialectically. Hegel's Logic is the best-suited tool for articulating the structures of history, first, because it is the logic of the transformative process that pure thinking itself undergoes when considered in its immanent activity; second, because such logic replaces the metaphysical problem of *origin* with the methodological problem of the *beginning* of thinking's most proper activity; and finally, because the logical movement is a movement of advancement fueled by the dynamic of contradiction and the practice of judgment. Hegel's specific conception of history as freedom's realization and, more precisely, as freedom's *advancement* directly follows from and is shaped by these three programmatic, logical objectives. History is the immanent development of real transformative processes, which display human, worldly beginnings, advancements and epochal transitions but is not the search for metaphysical first 'origins' or ultimate, merely 'ideal' (hence unreachable) goals or transcendent final ends. Moreover the motor of history and the authority to which history is subject is the justice done by the power of contradiction, by the same immanent contradiction that determines historical advancements.

The Logic of Transformative Processes

One of the distinctive characters of Hegel's dialectic-speculative logic is its being a "logic of transformative processes,"[5] namely, a logic that has the immanent movement of "objective thinking"[6] as its topic and is itself the dynamic, transformative movement of such thinking. The historian Arnaldo Momigliano once said, "we study transformation because we are subject to transformation. This gives us a direct experience of change – this is what we call memory."[7] History, in the sense of the historical science, is directly linked to our historical nature. Herein 'historical' means, minimally, to be capable of transformation both in the active and in the passive sense: capable of *producing* transformation and capable of *undergoing* it. Memory is the *direct experience* of change. Hegel claims that history concerns only that which can be recollected; but recollection is possible only of that which changes.[8] But what is the logic of change and what are its structures – or simply: what is change? This is the question that Hegel raises after he has explored, with the *Phenomenology*, the issue of consciousness's experience and of spirit's historical memory. What is the internal logic of such experience and what are its structures once consciousness and spirit are taken out of the picture, i.e., once the movement of transformation is no longer considered as dependent on the subject who undergoes it or meaningful only for it?[9] If we study historical transformations because we ourselves are beings immersed in, subject to, and producers of transformation – agents in and of change – then, philosophically, we must undertake the step that leads us to grasp the formal structures of transformation itself, independently of the specific empirical, spatial, and temporal conditions in which it is manifested. This study of transformation "in and for itself" (in contrast both to the phenomenological 'for consciousness' and to the *realphilosophisch* specification of change as occurring in determinate empirical objects and subjects) is Hegel's dialectic-speculative logic. After the *Phenomenology*, it is the task of the Logic – of the "dialectical memory" that is, I submit, the "method" – to present the dynamic of transformation independently of its object and subject. At stake now is the movement of transformation taken purely and formally, i.e., "in and for itself."[10] For, it is such on-going, overarching, purely logical movement that shapes the subject as spirit, not the reverse. To understand what the process of change and transformation is, logically, i.e., in its pure form, all that pure thinking needs to do is to perform change. Accordingly, Hegel's Logic stages the action in which the dynamic process of objective thinking unfolds. It is not the logic of fixed, abstract, a priori concepts disposed in a neat but unmoved "table of categories." It is rather the movement that thinking itself *is* when all that thinking *does* is simply and purely think. Now, it is precisely in this respect that the Logic becomes the systematic basis of Hegel's philosophy of history.

If contrasted to the aims and the accomplishments of both Kant's transcendental logic and formal logic in the classical and modern traditions, Hegel's dialectic-speculative logic is the only one that sets itself the task of accounting for the dynamic of real *processes*. It is a logic that attempts to think of change and transformation in their dynamic flux, not by fixating movement in abstract static descriptions, but by *performing movement itself* before its differentiation and specification in real occurrences as natural, psychological but also social, political, and historical processes. By bringing change to bear directly on pure thinking, by making thinking one with the movement that it aims at explaining, Hegel's logic *does* the very thing that it purports to understand. Thereby the question of the intelligibility of actuality taken in its purely logical form becomes a practical issue or an issue of praxis as much as one of theory.[11] The descriptive function that the Logic advocates to itself with regard to actuality goes hand in hand with a fundamentally normative function that concerns the ways in which transformations are actually (and rationally) produced. Unlike the philosophy of nature and spirit, the Logic offers an account of the structures of change independently of the question of what is it that changes and what is it that produces change, that is, it takes transformation in the constellation of its pure forms, independently of the particular contingent and empirical conditions under which it may occur and manifest itself – and, first and foremost, independently of the conditions of time and space. Herein lies one of the differences between logical and historical processes of transformation.

Logical Method: Metaphysical Origins, Logical and Historical Beginnings

Hegel's Logic stages the dynamic process of thinking's pure activity. At stake in this movement is neither an activity dependent on a presupposed subject (a metaphysical substrate or substance, Kant's transcendental "I think," a phenomenological consciousness) nor an activity dependent on a content (the object as that which is being thought in its specific constitution). The Logic is instead the immanent presentation of the process that eventually constitutes thinking into a subject which intentionally – theoretically and practically – refers to particular, empirically determined objects. A crucial role in shaping the structure of the logical movement is played by what Hegel calls the "method." On Hegel's account, the method is one with the developing logical activity of thinking. As "method," it emerges at the end of the entire movement in the chapter dedicated to the Absolute Idea. At this juncture, Hegel reveals that the process staged by the Logic is not only the action *successively performed* by pure thinking but also the action conclusively and *retrospectively re-collected* in the unitary presentation that is the method. As method, the concluded logical process is both that which logical thinking has successively produced or achieved, and the modality in and by which all processes are internally structured or produced. We are here at the intersection of theory and praxis (the "absolute idea" is the unity of the theoretical and the practical idea).[12] These two modalities are crucial for the understanding of history on the basis of Hegel's logic. Significantly, there is a re-collective, memorializing dimension to the logical method insofar as this is the result of the logical process *taken in its entirety*. Thus, I maintain that the "absolute method" is the logical or "dialectical memory" on which the entire logical process is built.[13] Furthermore, my suggestion is that this memory is, in turn, the logical basis on which philosophy articulates its dialectic-speculative understanding of history (*historia rerum gestarum*) as well as the basis on which spirit itself proceeds in the actual realization that is world-history (*res gestae*).

Three are the moments of the "absolute method": beginning, advancement, and end. They constitute the fundamental structures of all transformative processes. In its conclusive stage, the retrospective, "methodological memory" of the logic re-collects the entire movement thereby discerning, retrospectively, such moments at work in it. These, I suggest, are also fundamental structures of all historical transformations. The moments that account for the development of logical truth are, at the same time, the crucial structures of the historical actualization of freedom. And this is because, in the first case, the method discloses the generative forms of thinking's pure activity, while in the second case, history brings to light, in their actual realization, the structures of spirit's own free activity.

Hegel's presentation of the "absolute method" begins with the beginning.[14] What does it mean to raise the question of the beginning as a *methodological* question? Unlike the beginning of the Logic, where at stake is the very first logical form (and the first logical content); and unlike the introductory considerations on the topic, i.e., "with what must the science begin?,"[15] which occupies the logic before the beginning (and is still a question of content), we are now dealing with the problem of beginning once the logic as a whole *has already begun*. Now, the beginning becomes a question of method or of dialectical memory: it is the recollection of all those partial beginnings once the entire logical development has reached its conclusion (that is, once those beginnings belong to the logical past). It is the same logic, whereby the dimension of the historical present (the *Gegenwart* as the conclusion of a particular movement of spirit) discloses the possibility for philosophical thinking to grasp the deeper, necessary features of the historical world (its "rationality" as it were). It is the logic that supports the famous claim of the preface to the *Philosophy of Right*, according to which, if "philosophy is its own time apprehended *in thoughts*," then, "as thought of the world it appears in time only after actuality has concluded the process of its formation."[16] Philosophical comprehension and historical transformation are never synchronic. The delay that separates the former from the latter is measured by the movement of dialectical memory. At stake, more specifically, is the issue of the logical structure that allows the philosopher to recognize in the development of spirit's activity the *beginning* of a new epoch and the *end* of an old one. This is the problem that Hegel addresses in 1807 in the preface to the *Phenomenology* and yet again in 1820–1 in the preface to the *Philosophy of Right*, which ends, significantly, with the moment of "*Weltgeschichte*." This is indeed crucial for the understanding of history. History is not just process; it is the structured process that unfolds discerning in spirit's activity and realization the beginning, the advancement, and the end of successive epochs. Such is the identical rhythm of logical and historical dialectic.

But first comes the logical question: what does it mean for action to begin? What is the beginning "in and for itself," as "mode"[17] of movement? Methodologically, *to begin* is the action characterized by being "immediate" and by displaying the form of "abstract universality."[18] As moment of the method, "the beginning has no other determinateness than this: being simple and abstract,"[19] immediate and universal. Here, however, immediacy and abstractness are not characters that define the content of a certain beginning. They are rather the very *modality* or form with which logical thinking *begins to act as logical thinking* and *begins to know* what logical thinking, as such, is. Dynamically viewed, the act of beginning entails "the instance of the realization of the concept," the *Trieb* for a further advancement.[20] This is the structure that becomes relevant in history – in the understanding and making of history.

There is one crucial implication that we can draw from the first moment of the method with regard to the issue of the nature of a philosophy of history developed on the basis of the dialectic-speculative logic. Hegel *transforms the metaphysical problem of origin* – which has vexed, last but not least, speculative reason in Kant's Transcendental Dialectic – *into the methodological issue of the beginning action* (or the action that begins). It is only on the basis of this transformation that the problem of historical beginnings becomes the meaningful topic of a philosophy of history that freed from the metaphysical and mythological assumptions implied by the search for "origins," can have the worldly realization of spirit's freedom as its topic. In other words, it is this crucial tenet of his dialectic-speculative logic that allows Hegel to frame history in terms of the worldly realization of spirit's activity, in terms of the realization of freedom – and not as the search of a-historical or pre-historical origins.

It is clear that the transformation of the problem of origin into the problem of beginning carried out in the Logic has far-reaching consequences for Hegel's conception of history. The point is that, while origins are not historical (they are beyond history, preceding it), beginnings are immanent in history's development. The origin is fixed and a-historical, even divine or sacred or mythological, while beginnings are dynamic and historical; the origin does not immanently 'originate' processes, only beginnings do. The origin is a detached, self-contained, isolated point or entity, while beginnings actively lead to and enable developments and are immanently tied up to the development by complex relations; origin implies isolation, beginnings programmatically defy it; the origin is unique, beginnings are plural, capable of multiple figurations, and possibly eccentric.

Indeed, a logic that searches for first origins can by no means consequentially lay the foundation of a philosophy of history rooted in the present time and fundamentally secular, political, and immanent in its presuppositions.[21] If, however, the logic of origin is considered as the only epistemological possibility for the understanding of history, then an alternative still lays open. This is the alternative that seems to guide many philosophies of history during Hegel's time. Either the logic of origin is accepted, as in Schelling's late philosophy where history is viewed as the progressive realization of the Absolute or as the development out of a mythological origin placed in an absolute pre-historical past – and, in this case, it is not so much the structure of history as that of the Absolute that comes to light.[22] Or the logic of origin – and with it logic *tout court* – is rejected as a possible foundation of history, as in Kant, who looks for a different, alternatively moral, juridical or ethico-theological basis for history. For Kant, the search for conjectural origins, while constituting one legitimate type of history, is not a properly philosophical enterprise.[23]

Hegel overcomes this alternative. As he turns the metaphysical problem of origin into the methodological problem of beginning, the way of thinking history fundamentally changes. History no longer requires a metaphysical basis, no longer searches for mythological origins or for an absolute first, and no longer claims a moral justification, but gains, instead, a logical, that is, dialectic-speculative foundation. This, in turn, allows Hegel to re-claim history as the intra-worldly activity of spirit and as the "objective" realization of freedom; but allows him also to reject all search for obscure, archaic origins, all theogony and mythology; and, correspondingly, as the problem of the beginning connects with that of the end, to reject all ideas of a transcendent end of history. As Hegel polemically claims against the "fanaticisms of the church" in the conclusion of the Jena *Realphilosophie*, the end of history – the *Himmelreich* – does not belong to history because history is the history of political states.[24] Hegel's early dispute with Schelling on the beginning of the philosophical science with the Absolute, which occupies Hegel in the preface to the *Phenomenology*, shows its far-reaching consequences in disclosing the possibility of a philosophy of history on a logical basis. To begin with the Absolute – that is, to posit a first (metaphysical, theological) origin – renders not only a developmental, discursive logic impossible (which was Hegel's point in 1807) but ultimately undermines the very possibility of thinking history in immanent, secular terms; it undermines the possibility of understanding historical transformations in their own right without appealing either to an original Absolute or to a final, transcendent end or, in any case, to an unreachable goal posited outside of history, be it the *Himmelreich* or the ideal of perpetual peace. What the method recollects at the end of the Logic is not the first origin but the mode in which the beginning is made in the pure process of thinking so that an immanent development ensues, i.e., so that the beginning is truly proved as the beginning of a dynamic process. Significantly, it is the very structure of the methodological beginning (its incompleteness, indeterminateness, one-sidedness, and deficiency), not an alleged presupposed goal of the process that drives the movement on.[25]

In sum, my claim is that the methodological beginning of Hegel's Logic liberates the understanding of history from the search of a-historical origins (which remains in the frequent appeal to the *Genesis* of eighteenth- and early nineteenth-century philosophies of history)[26] as well as from alleged final goals, and yields instead an essential structure of the historical process, namely, the intra-historical, autonomous beginning of spirit's own activity, itself endowed with the immanent *Trieb* to its further actualization.[27] Now, a crucial role in the realization of the beginning or in the further step out of the immediacy and simplicity of all beginnings is played by contradiction, the moment of the concept's split or *Ur-teil*.

Logical Judgment, Contradiction, and Justice

The second moment of the logical method considered in its formality is the advancement – *Fortgehen*. This is immanently developed from the first moment because the *Anfang* is the beginning *of a process and a development*.[28] And yet advancing is not a mere "excess" (*Überfluß*) over and above the beginning, is not a mere implication of it.[29] The advancement is both synthetic and analytic in relation to the beginning.[30] The methodological question of the advancement is: what does it mean for action to proceed, to move on once it has begun? At stake, again, is the advancement not with regard to a particular action (or content) or to a particular agent (most generally, nature or spirit) but with regard to the overall structure of the logical development that is finally re-collected in the method. Advancing is the activity of dialectical contradiction. What characterizes the advancement is the intervention of "difference" (*Unterschied*, *Differenz*) and negativity, the transition to otherness, and the "judgment" that draws differences and acknowledges, reflectively, that the simplicity of the beginning is re-visited in the advancement as the unity of that which carries difference within itself.[31] Although the advancement in its split negativity seems to do violence to the beginning and to betray its simplicity, it is truly the act that does justice to it, bringing the beginning to completion, making it real, and thereby manifesting what the beginning *truly* is. Methodologically, dialectic is the "standpoint in which a universal first, considered in and for itself reveals itself as the other of itself."[32] This standpoint is crucial to Hegel's notion of freedom as self-actualization in otherness. In the final perspective offered by the method, dialectic makes clear that the process in its entirety is both continuous (the method is analytic, difference is immanent) and fundamentally discontinuous (the method is synthetic, difference is in the gap that produces the transition to the other).[33] This, again, is the fundamental logical structure that underlies all historical transition and epochal transformation – the ground of historical continuities and discontinuities, the basis of the negativity and destructiveness but also of the recovery from such destructiveness that characterizes historical development.

The account of the second moment of the method offers a first insight into the connection between contradiction, judgment, and justice – the connection that appears in Schiller's verse *Weltgeschichte* is *Weltgericht*. Being the result of the logical activity of judgment, justice discloses the "truth" of the beginning but also subverts it by mediating its simplicity and immediacy. As such, justice is neither the starting point nor the conclusion of the process, and is not the absolute value positioned in an original moment before the beginning. Justice is, instead, the intermediary 'critical' moment of the advancement – a moment of fragmentation and split in which it is contradiction (not a unified ideal) that is responsible for orienting the overall movement. This, I suggest, is the crucial dynamic structure of the dialectical process of history. Justice is the loss of the innocence of immediacy that advances historical processes. Justice is neither a first nor a last but lies in the middle. Viewed on this logical basis, the historical movement is carried on neither by an absolute origin nor by a final goal (both placed beyond history – before or after it) but by the capacity that the middle, mediating force of contradiction has to produce difference and thereby to discriminate or judge – to be both the *crisis* in the process and the *critic* thereof. Justice is precisely this intermediary 'critical' moment that immanently moves on the logical and the historical process.

The idea of dialectical contradiction is directly connected to the task of thinking transformation in its pure logical forms. In this regard, Hegel's Logic is framed as the last chapter in the history of the dialectic, which begins with ancient Greek philosophy. "One must realize that war is common and Conflict is Justice, and all things come about by way of conflict and necessity," reads a famous fragment by Heraclitus.[34] On his view, constant transformation constitutes the essence of reality, the principle to which nothing escapes. Change, however, is generated by conflict, i.e., by the clash of opposites and their coexistence. Opposing Pythagoras, who proposed the ideal of a peaceful and harmonious universe, and Anaximander, who saw the warfare of opposites as outright injustice, Heraclitus identifies conflict and its necessity with justice (*dikē*).[35] Justice is not harmonious and changeless balance but the restless tension of strife. Contradiction does not lead to chaos but to a just order that is the dynamic order of universal transformation. Herein Heraclitus runs counter to the tradition of Hesiod (with his distinction between good and evil strife) and Solon (for whom conflict and violence are the outright opposite of justice and law). The Pythagorean tradition is continued in Plato and Aristotle. In their view, conflict – political, social, but also psychological as imbalance and disharmony of the different parts of the soul – is considered the great evil to be corrected by the harmonious force of reason which is itself justice. On this crucial point, Hegel follows Heraclitus. Reason is justice because reason is fundamentally dialectical, i.e., because it bears in itself conflict in its utmost necessity. But reason is also, at the same time, the power that is able to overcome contradiction. Unlike Kantian reason, Hegelian reason does not remain stuck in the still-stand of its antinomies. As the dynamic unity of conflict and its resolution, Hegel's *Vernunft* is justice. The verse from Schiller's poem *Resignation* that Hegel takes up in framing his idea of world-history has, after all, a pre-Socratic root in this form of Heraclitean dialectic. Conflict is Justice: *Weltgeschichte* is *Weltgericht*[36] because historical change is produced by strife and strife is justice. Ultimately, Hegel's rejection of Kant's ideal of perpetual peace has the same metaphysical motivation as Heraclitus' polemic stance towards Pythagoras' harmonious universe.[37] Contradiction determines the ongoing movement of the historical process the justice of which lies in the self-regulating development of contradiction. The order of justice is the very order of (historical) change; not a changeless state beyond transformation and conflict. Contradiction is 'critical' in the sense of discriminative and ordering; it leads neither to chaos nor to nothingness.

History and Justice

By bringing to the fore the central role that the method plays in the program of Hegel's dialectic-speculative logic, I have established that the Logic offers the systematic basis for thinking the development of history as a movement that: (i) does not depend on a metaphysical or mythical, a-historical absolute origin placed beyond history but looks at the intra-historical beginnings, advancements, and ends of spirit's own activity; (ii) is not teleologically oriented towards or moved by a unified final goal placed at the end of history (an ethico-theological providential goal, the *Himmelreich* or the ideal of perpetual peace) but is fuelled instead by the immanent dynamic force of contradiction; (iii) finally, I suggested that contradiction, that is, the mediating moment of negativity and difference, the *Urteil* of the concept, is the immanent 'authority' that decides of the 'justice' of the process, i.e., of its necessity for the advancement of freedom. We need now see how the Logic informs the systematic of spirit in its historical development. I argue that in the late systematic of spirit, history is introduced and structured by the idea of justice, which, as I have suggested above, is closely linked to the idea of logical contradiction as that which produces the advancement of all transformative processes. Justice is the objective and pragmatic realization of the power of contradiction.

The difficulties met by the conclusion of objective spirit with *Weltgeschichte* are well known.[38] The field of world-history seems to represent an abrupt interruption – even a reversal – in the ascending structure of the progress of freedom from "abstract right" through "morality" up to the different moments of "ethical life." Already in the confrontation among autonomous states (*Völkerrecht*) right loses its power of actuality, is undermined by contingency,[39] and sinks back to the level of a mere *Sollen*,[40] while the anarchy of a renewed state of nature seems to propose, yet again, the resurgent condition of abstract right. Given this situation, how can Hegel attribute to world-history the function of establishing the last "judgment" on the highest and absolute level of right, on the most advanced development of freedom?[41] How can the *impasse* of an un-reconciled confrontation between nature and freedom, which characterizes world-history at this point be proposed as closure for freedom's ascending realization and considered the ultimate *Weltgericht*? Hegel's systematic choice has often been discussed (and rejected) on the ground of the political and ideological implications of its content. Leaving this discussion aside, I want to concentrate instead on the architectonic and logical aspects of the problem. I am interested in the conceptual nature of the figure of history introduced by Hegel at this point. What can we infer with regard to Hegel's idea of world-history from its systematic placement and from the logic that such placement suggests history follows?

The general question, which Hegel faced already in the *Phenomenology*, regards the conditions that structure a process as *historical*, making the movement of *Entwicklung*, which in the Logic and all along in the *Philosophy of Right* was a-temporal and non-historical, into the development in time that is world-history. What is it that transforms, alternatively, a discrete number of successive empirical events or a logical moment in the development of the concept of right into an *epoch* of world-history? What is the systematic principle of history? In Hegel's late system, the answer is the idea of historical justice whereby *Weltgeschichte* in all its contradictory tensions is framed as *Weltgericht* [(and placed above international justice)]. As the political state becomes the agent and subject of history, the traditional idea of God's final judgment is secularized in the idea of historical justice,[42] which now becomes the principle responsible for the immanent "partition" of the historical process, that is, for the historical periodization that concludes the *Philosophy of Right*.[43] On the basis of the dialectical method, the immanent partition/periodization of the process generates the process itself as the totality of history. Significantly, partition/periodization does not presuppose history but first establishes a temporal sequence *as world-history*. The tribunal that judges the actions of the states on the world scene is no longer placed beyond history but is history itself. Historical justice is the immanent principle of historical judgment, i.e., is the principle on which the advancement of the process is made. Here again, the structure of history leads us back to the logic of the process. For the *Weltgericht* of history neither reflects a divine providential order nor dictates ideal conditions of ethical or international justice. Its function is instead to indicate the conditions under which alone the historical process can advance as the immanent process of freedom's realization (and is not stalled, for example, or pushed back to preceding stages or forced to sterile repetitions of the same errors). Because of its logical basis, history's justice is neither theological nor moral but is pragmatic worldly justice. Just is that stage of the process, which allows for and actually accomplishes the *historical advancement* of freedom within the totality of *Weltgeschichte*.[44] Justice does not consist in following immutable, a-historical (or a priori) principles; it is rather the result of the process in which contradictory possibilities have been tested in their real capacity to produce change, and, ultimately, to *advance* freedom. Justice is the *"method"* of advancement. Justice does not precede the historical event; just is the historical moment to which the process of advancement has led.

The introductory remarks with which Hegel comments upon his divisions of the different parts of the system are relevant in this connection. Two are the meanings of a philosophical "partition" (*Einteilung*). The first is that of a merely provisional *Historie* of the process that, by way of an external description of temporally successive stages, anticipates the movement of the whole. The second meaning is given by this very movement itself: partition is the immanent law that constitutes the process as a whole (and the whole as a process) by articulating it in its stages – it is, accordingly, "method," the final recollection of the whole. These two meanings of partition parallel the two forms of *Geschichte* – the *historische* and the *philosophische Geschichte* – distinguished by Hegel already in his Nürnberg lectures.[45] On a methodological level, Hegel maintains that it is only the "concept" that can be divided or that *Ein-teilung* can only be partition of the concept. For the partition "lies *in* the concept itself" as that which constitutes it in its most proper activity. Correspondingly, in its partition the concept produces its self-determination. More precisely, in the partition, determination is presented as fully developed and completely and autonomously posited. And since the partition provides the proper determination of the concept as that through which it distinguishes itself from anything else, partition always expresses the moment of difference. *Ein-teilung* is for Hegel *Ur-teilung*. It is the concept's act of (self-) judgment.[46]

This logical and methodological feature of the philosophical partition becomes crucial when enacted on the scene of objective spirit – when that which is divided is now the fully realized concept of *Sittlichkeit*. Herein judgment is pronounced from that "court of justice" that is *Weltgeschichte*. History *is* the final enactment or actual execution or realization of the partition of the concept of right. This judgment provides the methodological "turning point" whereby the *Philosophy of Right* is brought to conclusion.[47] If Hegel's reformulation of Schiller's verse in §340 secularizes an old (biblical) tradition, the possibility of referring world-history to an act of judgment that brings about justice responds, in the first place, to the internal architecture of objective spirit, i.e., ultimately, to its logical foundation.[48] While Hegel explicitly discusses the notion of *Einteilung* only in the introductions of his works,[49] as he presents the provisional division of the matter, this notion belongs to the actual practice of the dialectic method. Now, history is the actual practice of the dialectical method in the element of existence, in the contingency of space and time once at stake is the articulation of the objective reality of spirit and the subject or agent of history, i.e., the authority enacting that judgment is the political state as the culmination of the sphere of *Sittlichkeit*. For history is spirit's most proper "*act*" (*Tat*)[50] in the "element" of ethical actuality, while the political state, whose activity is now projected towards the outside in the confrontation with other states, is its agent.[51] What makes the state (and the succession of the world-historical "realms" (*Reiche*) under the lead of a particular, historically determinate state or *Völkergeist*)[52] the subject of historical judgment/justice is not its moral, cultural or theological authority or alleged superiority, but a logical necessity. It is the conceptual *Einteilung* of the fully developed *concept* of *Sittlichkeit* that structures the historical process labouring on the production of discrete differences and determinations, thereby instituting world-history as the "tribunal"[53] that pronounces the historical judgment. Importantly,

Hegel argues that the court of judgment of world-history is not the "tribunal of spirit's power," namely, the "irrational necessity of blind destiny," but the rationality and necessity that arise "from the *concept*" and is accordingly related to the "development of freedom."[54]

Thus, history as *"begriffene Geschichte"* – or history guided and structured by the concept – is the philosophical comprehension of history reached through the enactment of the dialectical method. In it, the cognitive and the practical-pragmatic meanings of history converge. This act of comprehension is spirit's own *"Auslegung* and *Verwirklichung"*[55] which, in turn, is the act through which world-history itself is made (respectively, as *historia rerum gestarum* in spirit's exposition and self-interpretation or *Auslegung*, and as *res gestae* in spirit's "realization"). Again, the generative principle of history does not lay beyond history but is the very act of its immanent production. I suggest that at the end of the *Philosophy of Right* world-history plays a role analogous to the role played by the "absolute method" at the end of the Logic. In both cases Hegel provides a law of movement by generating the movement itself. This movement is the discrete sequence: beginning-advancement-end. In its pure formality, this sequence is the logical method. In its historical realization, this same sequence yields the periodization or partition of world-history.[56] Far from pleading for a reduction of history to logic, this claim implies that Hegel's dialectical method is not a merely theoretical procedure but is rather, as history shows, a form of practical activity: *Ent-schluß*, the "decision" to be in the externality of space and time, as Hegel suggests at the end of the Logic; the most proper *"Tat"* or action of spirit's judgment within the realm of natural and spiritual existence, of "geographical and anthropological existence," as he maintains in the *Philosophy of Right*.[57] As is the case with the end of the Logic, in the sphere of objective spirit the external conditions of space and time are introduced where a systematic sphere closes its circle and goes back to its beginning. The action whereby spirit grasps and comprehends (the act of *Erfassen*, which is spirit's most proper "being" and its "principle") is, at the same time, the movement of its *"Entäußerung"* and *"Übergang,"*[58] – the movement of externalization and even alienation that always, for Hegel, complements *Erinnerung*. This twofold process is world-history. Accordingly, the level of world-history already discloses the dimension of absolute spirit.[59]

To conclude, I have suggested that once history receives its logical foundation in the dialectic method, the justice that becomes the principle of history is the power and the authority of the "middle," i.e., of contradiction. This principle is responsible both for the advancement of the process, or the realization of freedom, and for the periodization or partition of world-history. The basis of both movements is the logical structure of the concept. Justice is neither in the beginning nor in the end but in the contradictory, fractured moment of the middle. As contradiction is the force that drives the process on by mediating the immediacy of the beginning, the "justice" of a certain stage is measured by the capacity to advance the process in its entirety. Advancement itself, in its contradictory nature, reveals, pragmatically, the character world-history. The dynamic of contradiction involves both the generation of contradictory stances within a certain society or epoch and within collective and individual consciousness, and their resolution. Freedom is the unrestrained capacity to advance through conflict and negativity, to affirm transformation and mediation in reality. There is no moral or providential criterion on which advancement is judged (as being adequate to a presupposed given goal) and justified (in attaining it). Nor does the justice of history imply the elimination of contingency, arbitrariness, unhappiness, and suffering. In fact, considered from a limited human moral perspective, the justice of world-history is indeed, dialectically, highly un-just. Advancement is not always towards (what we think is) the better. The justice of Hegelian history is, in this respect, closer to the *dikē* of Heraclitus' Conflict. Or, to put it differently, in contrast to the ideal of justice as harmony the historical justice of conflict is always pragmatically "imperfect." The dynamic order of justice – Heraclitus' cosmic justice and Hegel's historical justice – is the order of transformation that is higher than the order of morality or (abstract and international) right, higher than the Hesiodean distinction between good and evil conflict. Indeed, what drives history on is not conciliation but the hard, conflictual nature of *"Unglück"*: *"World-history is not the realm of happiness,"* insists Hegel. "The periods of happiness are empty pages in it; for they are periods of concord, of lack of opposition,"[60] and no advancement takes place in them. The "activity" that constitutes history is the activity of the "middle," "which translates that which is universal and internal into objectivity" and exteriority.[61] While this "translation" or "transition"[62] does justice to what is internal and interior and merely immediate, i.e., logically, to the abstractness and simplicity of the beginning, or, at the level of *Sittlichkeit*, to the accomplished sphere of the political state seen and lived from within ethical life, it is also a painful process of exteriorization and alienation, the encounter with negativity, opposition, and war.[63] In sum, *Weltgeschichte* is *Weltgericht precisely because* it is the sphere of on-going, inexhaustible conflicts not in spite of it.

NOTES

1 According to the famous formulation of the program of the *Phenomenology*:
   it all hinges on"presenting and expressing the true not as *substance* but at
   the same time as *subject*": W 3, 23.
2 For this issue, see Hans Friedrich Fulda, *Das Problem einer Einleitung in
   Hegels Wissenschaft der Logik* (Frankfurt am Main: Klostermann,1965), and
   my "Das Problem eines 'Vorbegriffs' in Hegels spekulativer Logik," in
   Der "Vorbegriff" zur Wissenschaft der Logik in der Enzyclopaedie von 1830, ed.
   Alfred Denker and Annette Sell (Freiburg: Alber, 2010), 84–113.
3 See W 5, 43. I have argued extensively for this thesis in *History, Memory,
   Justice in Hegel* (NY/London: McMillan, 2012), chap. 1.
4 See *History, Memory, Justice in Hegel*, chaps. 2 and 4.
5 I have argued fort his thesis in "Dialectic as Logic of Transformative
   Processes," in *Hegel: New Directions*, ed. Katerina Deligiorgi (Chesham:
   Acumen, 2006), 85–104.
6 Enz. §25, Anm. "Objective thinking" for Hegel is rationality as the
   encompassing form of reality and subjective thinking; is rationality in its
   purely dynamic movement: neither as (psychological or transcendental)
   function of a presupposed 'I think' nor as (metaphysical) property of
   reality. It is instead the logical structure that underlies both. See Walter
   Jaeschke, "Objektives Gedanke. Philosophiehistorische Erwägungen zur
   Konzeption und zur Aktualität der spekulativen Logik," *The Independent
   Journal of Philosophy* (1979): 23–37.
7 Arnaldo Momigliano, *Sesto contributo alla storia degli studi classici e del
   mondo antico* (Roma: Storia e Letteratura, 1980), 27. A similar claim for
   the link between history and change in Jaques Le Goff, *Storia e memoria*
   (Torino: Einaudi, 1977) xvii [original publication in Italian].
8 See Georg Wilhelm Friedrich Hegel, *Vorlesungen über die Philosophie der
   Weltgeschichte* (Stuttgart: Reclam, 1961), 114; Jan Assman, "Recht und
   Gerechtigkeit als Generatoren von Geschichte," in *Die Weltgeschichte – das
   Weltgericht?*, ed. Rüdiger Bubner and Walter Mesch (Stuttgart: Cotta, 2001),
   296–311, 297.
9 This is logical thinking free of the opposition of consciousness (W 5, 43).
10 W 6, 557, 560 and 561.
11 Thereby I claim that Hegel's logic cannot be separated (and rejected) from
   his practical philosophy. The contrary view is held by Allen W. Wood,
   Hegel's Ethical Thought (Cambridge: Cambridge University Press, 1990), 3:
   "[t]he Hegel who still lives and speaks to us is not a speculative logician
   and idealist metaphysician but a philosophical historian, a political and
   social theorist, a philosopher of our ethical concerns and cultural identity
   crisis." I completely endorse the last part of this statement. I strongly reject,

however, the dichotomy proposed by Wood. This work will show that the Hegel who speaks to our ethical concerns can do so only because he is a speculative-dialectic logician as well. My position is generally closer to the one articulated by Robert Pippin, *Hegel's Practical Philosophy: Rational Agency as Ethical Life* (Cambridge: Cambridge University Press), 2008.

12 See W 6, 548f.

13 Respectively, in Chapters 2 and 3. See W 6, 570. I argue extensively for this claim in the forthcoming book *Thinking Transformation – Transformations in Thinking*.

14 W 6, 553: "Es ist dabei *erstens* mit dem *Anfange* anzufangen."

15 W 5, 65–79.

16 W 7, 26–8 – my emphasis.

17 W 6, 552.

18 W 6, 553.

19 W 6, 554.

20 W 6, 554f.

21 See for Hegel's critique of this kind of historiography Enz. §549 Anm. (the rejection of the search for an "*Urzustand*" and an "*Urvolk*"); with critical reference against Schelling and Schlegel, Hegel, *Die Vernunft in der Geschichte*, ed. Johannes Hoffmeister (Hamburg: Meiner, 1917), 158ff.

22 See F.W.J Schelling's *Vorlesungen über die Methode des akademischen Studiums*, in *Sämmtliche Werke*, ed. K.F.A., Schelling (Stuttgart u. Augsburg: Cotta, 1856–61), vol. 5, 309 for example, where history is defined, "aesthetically," as the "eternal poem of the divine intellect"; and the *Philosophie der Mythologie*, where Schelling refers to a "pre-history" viewed as "absolut vor-geschichtliche" (see *Sämmtliche Werke* vol. 11, 233, 239). An unsurpassed discussion of Schelling's views is in David F. Krell, *The Tragic Absolute* (Bloomington: Indiana University Press, 2005), 130ff for example. See the comparative considerations in Claudio Cesa, *Le astuzie della ragione* (Torino: Aragno, 2008), 22–30.

23 See Immanuel Kant, *Mutmasslicher Anfang der Menschengeschichte* (1786) and *Ob das menschliche Geschlecht in beständigen Fortschreiten zum Bessern sei* (1797).

24 See Hegel, *Vorlesungen über die Philosophie der Weltgeschichte*, 86; see Cesa, *Le astuzie della ragione*, 39, 42, who quotes Hegel's *Jenaer Realphilosophie* (Hamburg: Meiner, 1967), 270.

25 See W 6, 555.

26 This is the case for Kant and Schiller, for example, see Cesa, *Le astuzie della ragione*, 13.

27 See W 6, 555.

28 It is "Anfang des Fortgehens und der Entwicklung" (W 6, 556).

29 W 6, 555; see the corresponding passage on the relationship between *Anfang* and *Fortgang* in W 5, 71.

30 See W 6, 557.

31 W 6, 556.

32 W 6, 561.

33 See W 6, 557.

34 Heraclitus, D. 80, M 28; see Charles H. Kahn, *The Art and Thought of Heraclitus* (Cambridge: Cambridge University Press, 1981), 66f.

35 Kahn says that such identification "is at first sight utterly perverse" (*The Art and Thought of Heraclitus*, 206; see his further commentary on this fragment at 207).

36 R§340; Enz. §548.

37 Schiller's poem already attests to his detachment from the Kantian ethico-theology he endorsed in his earlier years. *Resignation* entails Schiller's protest "against the very idea of a providential order where virtue is rewarded and vice is punished only in the afterlife" (Frederick Beiser, *Schiller as Philosopher. A Re-Examination* (Oxford: Oxford University Press, 2005), 31).

38 See, for all, Claudio Cesa, "La storia," in *Hegel*, ed. Claudio Cesa (Bari: Laterza, 1997) 281–313, 293–98.

39 R §334 Anm., §335.

40 R §§330, 333.

41 A.T. Peperzak seems indeed to deny that world-history can be the judge (see *Modern Freedom: Hegel's Legal, Moral, and Plotical Philosophy* (Dordrecht: Kluwer Academic Publishing, 2001), 181).

42 Assmann traces the beginning of history in the move taking place from Egypt to Mesopotamia and ancient Israel whereby the idea of a "tribunal of the dead" judging of one individual life (before the life's end) is replaced first by the idea of the worldly responsibility of the kings towards the gods (see "Recht und Gerechtigkeit," cit. 302f), and then by the Jewish idea of a *historia sacra* in which God himself participates. In Hegel's idea of world-history there is a parallel move from the idea of divine justice taking place after the end of history to the idea of an intra-historical judgment that falls within history itself. The tribunal of justice is now history itself.

43 See R§§354–60.

44 The criterion that measures advancement is neither moral nor theological or providential but merely logical.

45 W 4, 410. See Cesa, "La storia," 290.

46 W 5, 56.

47 This "turning point" paralles the *Wendungspunkt* of the absolute method in W 6, 563.

48 Assmann addresses the issue of the "Geburt der Geschichte aus dem Geist des Rechts" in the Mesopotamian and biblical tradition (to which he

sees Hegel referring) in: *Das kulturelle Gedächtnis. Schrift, Erinnerung und politische Identität in frühen Hochkulturen* (München: Beck, 1992), chap. 6.

49 The other place in which Hegel explicitly discusses *Einteilung* is in the "Idea of Cognition" in the logic where the partition is the exterior procedure of finite knowledge. See W 6, 525ff.

50 R §§343; 348; 352; Enz. §549: *Tat*; §551: "Handlung"; *Die Vernunft in der Geschichte*, cit., 67 has "Tat" and "Werk."

51 R §341.

52 See Enz. §549.

53 R §341: *Gericht*.

54 R §342.

55 R §§342–3.

56 This thesis implicitly responds to another *locus communis* of the interpretation. What is at stake in Hegel's philosophy of history is not the fantastic issue of the "end of history," but rather the idea that history is the end (of objective spirit). See for a discussion of this issue and the literature, Perry Anderson, "The Ends of History," in *A Zone of Engagement* (London: Verso, 1992), 279–375, 285–94.

57 R §346.

58 R §343.

59 R §341.

60 *Vorlesungen über die Philosophie der Weltgeschichte*, 70f. – emphasis in original.

61 *Vorlesungen über die Philosophie der Weltgeschichte*, 71.

62 R §343.

63 On the basis of R§345, I suggest to contrast the *"Urteil"* and "imperfect justice" (*Gerechtigkeit*) to which individual and collective events, virtues, and feelings are subject "in the sphere of conscious actuality," i.e., within the state, to the higher judgment and justice taking place "outside of these standpoint" at the level of world-history.

REFERENCES

Anderson, Perry. "The Ends of History." In *A Zone of Engagement*. London: Verso, 1992.

Assmann, Jan. *Das kulturelle Gedächtnis. Schrift, Erinnerung und politische Identität in frühen Hochkulturen*. München: Beck, 1992.

—— "Recht und Gerechtigkeit als Generatoren von Geschichte." In *Die Weltgeschichte – das Weltgericht?*, edited by Rüdiger Bubner and Walter Mesch, 296–311. Stuttgart: Cotta, 2001.

Beiser, Frederick. *Schiller as Philosopher: A Re-Examination*. Oxford: Oxford University Press, 2005.

Cesa, Claudio. "La storia." In *Hegel*, edited by Claudio Cesa. Bari: Laterza, 1997.

—— *Le astuzie della ragione*. Torino: Aragno, 2008.

Fulda, Hans Friedrich. *Vorlesungen über die Philosophie der Weltgeschichte*. Stuttgart: Reclam, 1961.

—— *Das Problem einer Einleitung in Hegels Wissenschaft der Logik*. Frankfurt am Main: Klostermann, 1965.

Hegel, G.W.F. *Die Vernunft in der Geschichte*. Edited by Johannes Hoffmeister. Hamburg: Meiner, 1917.

—— *Jenaer Realphilosophie*. Hamburg: Meiner, 1967.

—— *Phenomenology of Spirit*. Translated by A.V. Miller. Oxford: Oxford Univeristy Press, 1977/*Werke: 3. In Werke in zwanzig Bänden*, edited by E. Moldenhauer and K.M. Michel, 20 volumes and index. Frankfurt: Suhrkamp Verlag, 1969ff.

—— *Vorlesungen über die Rechtsphilosophie, 1818–1831*, edited by K.-H. Ilting, 4 Vols. Stuttgart: Fromann-Holzboog, 1973ff.

—— *Wissenschaft der Logik in der Enzyclopaedie von 1830*. This is a translation of the first volume: *The Encyclopaedia Logic* (with the *Zusätze*). Translated by T.F. Geraets, W.A. Suchting, and H.S. Harris. Indianapolis: Hackett Publishing, 1991.

Jaeschke, Walter. "Objektives Gedanke. Philosophiehistorische Erwägungen zur Konzeption und zur Aktualität der spekulativen Logik." *The Independent Journal of Philosophy* (1979): 23–37.

Kahn, Charles H. *The Art and Thought of Heraclitus*. Cambridge: Cambridge University Press, 1981.

Kant, Immanuel. "Mutmasslicher Anfang der Menschengeschichte." 1786.

—— "Ob das menschliche Geschlecht in beständigen Fortschreiten zum Bessern sei." 1797.

Krell, David F. *The Tragic Absolute*. Bloomington: Indiana University Press, 2005.

Le Goff, Jaques. *Storia e memoria*. Torino: Einaudi, 1977.

Momigliano, Arnaldo. *Sesto contributo alla storia degli studi classici e del mondo antico*. Roma: Storia e Letteratura, 1980.

Nuzzo, Angelica. "Dialectic as Logic of Transformative Processes." In *Hegel: New Directions*, edited by Katerina Deligiorgi, 85–104. Chesham: Acumen, 2006.

—— "Das Problem eines 'Vorbegriffs' in Hegels spekulativer Logik." In *Der "Vorbegriff" zur Wissenschaft der Logik in der Enzyclopaedie von 1830*, edited by Alfred Denker and Annette Sell, 84–113. Freiburg: Alber, 2010.

—— *History, Memory, Justice in Hegel*. London: McMillan, 2012.

Peperzak, A.T. *Modern Freedom: Hegel's Legal, Moral, and Plotical Philosophy*. Dordrecht: Kluwer Academic Publishing, 2001.

Pippin, Robert. *Hegel's Practical Philosophy: Rational Agency as Ethical Life.* Cambridge: Cambridge University Press, 2008.

Schelling, F.W.J. *Vorlesungen über die Methode des akademischen Studiums*, Vol. 5 of the *Sämmtliche Werke*, edited by K.F.A. Schelling. Stuttgart u. Augsburg: Cotta, 1856–1861.

—— *Philosophie der Mythologie, Sämmtliche Werke*, edited by K.F.A. Schelling. Stuttgart u. Augsburg: Cotta, 1856–1861, Vol. 11.

Wood, Allen W. *Hegel's Ethical Thought.* Cambridge: Cambridge University Press, 1990.

4 Adorno's Modal Utopianism: Possibility and Actuality in Adorno and Hegel[1]

IAIN MACDONALD, UNIVERSITÉ DE MONTRÉAL

According to a longstanding metaphysical tradition, actuality is prior – and in some ways superior – to possibility. From Aristotle to Hegel, the exceptions to this fundamental belief are fairly rare. But there is a marked trend in post-Hegelian thought to undermine this traditional priority, with Theodor W. Adorno representing an important line of attack.[2]

In this vein, Jay Bernstein remarks that, for Adorno, "lodged somewhere between logical and actual possibility," there is something that is "neither fully actual nor fully non-actual."[3] This is an extremely important insight into Adorno's thought, but one that neither Bernstein nor Adorno makes fully explicit. What, then, is Adorno's view of possibility and what is the modal status of what he calls "difference with respect to what exists"[4] (*die Differenz vom Bestehenden*)? The answers to these questions will involve showing how Adorno's notion of utopian "difference" relies, crucially, upon a critique of the defective metaphysical thesis concerning the priority of actuality, which finds its highest expression in Hegel's thought. Succinctly put, the trouble is that, "according to Hegel's distinction between abstract [i.e., formal] and real possibility, only something that has become actual is, in fact, possible. This kind of philosophy sides with the big guns. It adopts the verdict of a reality that constantly buries what could be different."[5] Understanding this claim begins with Adorno's critique of Hegel's notion of totality.

The Whole and the "More"

The frequently cited rallying cry of Adorno's critique of Hegel – "The whole is the untrue"[6] – means first of all that the claim to spirit being a whole, a "system of totality,"[7] is untenable. More precisely, as Adorno says elsewhere, any "affirmative and self-assured reference" to such a whole is "fictitious."[8] However, if positive reference to the totality, to the whole, is fictitious, it is not simply because the Hegelian whole is an unattainable metaphysical dream. More concretely, the only totality to which we have direct access takes the form of an antagonistic society that perpetuates itself in denial of its antagonistic character. As Adorno puts it: "The force of the whole ... is not a mere fantasy on the part of spirit; it is the force of the real web of illusion in which all individual existence remains trapped."[9] The whole is thus the web of actuality understood as the sum of repressive forces to which there is no apparent alternative. The task of philosophy is then to criticize and unmask the general and particular structures of the ideological fiction of the "force of the whole" in such a way as to open up the possibility of determinate alternatives. This possibility of determinate negation, says Adorno, is *utopia*, "the utopia of the whole truth [*der ganzen Wahrheit*], which is still to be actualized."[10]

However, this reference to "the utopia of the whole truth" brings with it its own set of problems: are we not replacing one fiction with another, one *telos* with another, and one *whole* with another that would supersede or somehow detach itself from the whole of which Hegel speaks? Adorno assures us that this is not the case. His utopianism "does not mean to suggest a second, secret world which is to be opened up through an analysis of appearances"[11] – *i.e.*, there is no "other" world than this one, other than this untrue whole. On the other hand, if Adorno can invoke the idea of a "utopia of the whole truth" in opposition to the Hegelian whole, then we clearly need to rethink how we conceive of the whole, of actuality itself. Certainly, this desire to reconceive actuality is a pillar of Adorno's thought insofar as it corresponds, for example, to an attempt "to imagine the whole as something that could be utterly different."[12] But this poses a particular problem of interpretation: there is no "other" world than this one, yet we must imagine the "utterly different." What can this mean?

One possibility is that this difference is inscribed in thought itself, in the theories and practices by which we come to grips with actuality. In this respect, one might point out that Adorno's dialectic is not as "closed" as Hegel's: thought's aim is to overcome its own limitations, without positing a moment of completion in totality. In any case, this is how Max Horkheimer handles the question of totality and teleology in Hegel. In an essay whose main theses are taken as read by Adorno, Horkheimer will say that the dialectic is to be understood, *contra* Hegel, as fundamentally *unclosed* (*unabgeschlossen*).[13] He writes: "An isolated and conclusive [*abschlußhafte*] theory of actuality [*Wirklichkeit*] is completely unthinkable."[14] That is, actuality cannot be seen as an internally self-justifying system of beliefs and practices – a world complete unto itself. But how exactly are we to understand this "open" actuality to which Horkheimer seems to refer? Or to put it another way, if the dialectic is unclosed, then what exactly is it open *to*, or what does it open *onto*? Here, Horkheimer's answer is less provocative than Adorno's will be. The dialectic aims at objective truth, says Horkheimer, where this truth is not that to which a proposition *corresponds*, but that which "real events and human activity"[15] *produce:* "to the degree that the knowledge gained from perception and inference, methodical inquiry and historical events, daily work and political struggle, meets the test of the available means of cognition, it is the truth."[16] This claim is the basis of Horkheimer's historicism, whose participative structure ensures its commonness and bindingness for all. Horkheimer's dialectic is thereby "unclosed" in the specific sense of being open to truths different than those we now know, just because truth is not located in static actuality, but in the historically variable requirements and determinations of the nexus of activity that defines it. Not only must thought think thought's own historicality and finitude, but we must understand actuality itself as an active and self-defining network of beliefs and practices that includes both the hypotheses to be tested and the criterion of testing – all of which is encapsulated by what Horkheimer calls human activity.[17] It is through the constant revision of truth on the basis of historically informed theory and practice that actuality's more repressive currents can be overcome. There is no "other world" than this one, but its defects can instruct us on how to transform it for the betterment of all.

Similarly, Adorno's "whole truth" does not correspond to some static ideal to which thinking will one day do justice. In this, his view agrees with Horkheimer's. If the whole is untrue, it is because thinking cannot "close" the circle of the real once and for all. The real must rather instruct thought as to where it should invest its creative powers. However, for Adorno, the whole is false not merely because truth is the result of the historically changing nature of real events and human activity (in Horkheimer's sense); it is also because the *world is not everything that is the case*.[18] As Adorno puts it in one of several similar passages: "Undeniably, being is not simply the epitome of what is, of what is the case. With this anti-positivistic insight we do justice to the concept's surplus over facticity. No concept would be thinkable, indeed none would be possible without the "more" [*das Mehr*] that makes a language of language."[19]

It is this "more" that will help us to determine and clarify the nature of the opposition that Adorno sets up between his own utopianism and the false Hegelian whole. In a word, the Adornian dialectic is open not only because it is somehow more historical or less teleological than Hegel's or because it refuses the claim of totality. It is open because it is marked by an irreducible "more," by a surplus that prevents the whole from closing and the Hegelian circle from returning into itself.

In a word, this "more" is *possibility* – but not just *any* possibility: it is a type of possibility that Hegel's philosophy does not and cannot admit. The question arises, then, as to how Adorno's notions of actuality and possibility differ from Hegel's.

Hegel's Theory of Actuality

For Hegel, actuality and possibility are moments of the absolute and of the whole understood as pure self-manifestation. Or, to put it another way, the absolute's self-manifestation (*i.e.*, in the occurrence of real events in history that correspond to shapes of spirit) is nothing other than the self-movement of actuality as returning to itself through its self-determination as possibility. In fact, according to Hegel, the dialectical identity of possibility and actuality gives rise to a concept of *absolute* actuality that contains (*in sich enthält*) all possibility: "whether this or that is possible or impossible depends on the content," says Hegel, "*i.e.*, on the *totality* of the moments of actuality, an actuality which, in the unfolding of its moments, proves to be necessity."[20]

This unfolding and its necessity are described in greatest detail in the *Science of Logic*, with some interesting and critical points added in the corresponding passages of the *Encyclopædia*. But in every passage and on every level, the traditional priority of actuality over possibility is reaffirmed, though the detail and the terminology are thoroughly modern. The core definition of actuality is succinctly given in the greater *Logic*: "what is actual *can act* [*was wirklich ist, kann wirken*]; something announces its actuality *by what it produces*."[21] What this means, first and foremost, is not that actuality is the mere sum of what is immediately present, but rather that it is *self-producing* because it is always "*full of content*."[22] In other words, *real* actuality is always a *determinate* actuality that contains equally real possibilities that in turn become actual in their own right, just because they are the true content, the in-itself, of this actuality. But this content, which is the condition of possibility of a nascent but not yet existing new actuality, is thereby none other than the *self-same* actuality seen as a totality expressive of a "complete circle of conditions"[23] – a living whole that drives its own development and external, historical transformation. Real possibility is therefore only formally distinct from actuality; or, as Hegel puts it, "it is real insofar as it is itself also actuality."[24] Thus, if actuality contains the moments that make up an emerging shape of spirit, then they will coalesce and that shape will actualize itself – and so on, with each shape taking up its place in the theoretical and practical whole of history as phenomenology. Real possibility resides within the circumstances that precede the transition from one shape of spirit to another.

The dialectical sleight of hand that establishes the identity of actuality and possibility and, more importantly, their self-enclosed, self-reproducing totality, is an admittedly attractive presentation of the internal, logical relation of what *is* and what *can be*. On this view, everything depends upon the definition of existing actuality as a "complete circle of conditions" that implicitly defines an *other* actuality not yet existing. That is, the complete circle of conditions is the middle term in the analysis. Actuality is a complete circle of circumstances; but these are nothing other than conditions for another actuality, which is to be seen as really possible in relation to real actuality. Therefore, in respect of this complete circle of conditions, actuality and possibility are one: "as [actuality's] immediate concrete existence, the circle of conditions, sublates itself, it makes itself into the being-in-itself which it already is, namely the in-itself of an other. And conversely, since its moment of being-in-itself thereby sublates itself at the same time, it becomes actuality, hence the moment which it likewise already is."[25]

In this movement, there is evidently a kind of vanishing (*Verschwinden*), using up (*Verzehren*), or collapsing (*Zusammenfallen*) of possibility, but with neither gain nor loss because real possibility is just latent actuality, *i.e.*, the existing conditions of a nascent actuality that will in turn be the real possibility of yet another expression of actuality.

On a higher level of analysis, this dialectical movement of actuality and possibility, or the counterstroke (*Gegenstoß*) of the one in the other, is also considered utterly *necessary*. Hegel's reasoning on this point is deceptively simple: the circle of conditions is always such that it will give rise to the determinate actuality to which it corresponds: "Hence what is really possible can no longer be otherwise; under the given conditions and circumstances, nothing else can follow. Real possibility and necessity are, therefore, only apparently distinguished."[26] Of course, in terms of *content*, the dialectic is bound to contingency, in the sense that the actuality from which possibility proceeds always has its ground in an other, *i.e.*, in a former actuality that provided the conditions of its emergence. Real necessity therefore appears only as *relative* necessity – *i.e.*, relative to given conditions and open to unforeseen and unforeseeable circumstances. But this openness too is an illusion of history, because the ultimate movement of contingency, in its very becoming in time, obeys the dialectical law of actuality. The stroke and counterstroke of actuality and possibility make up the very form of historical determinateness and contingency. All existence, in spite of its infinite diversity, dependency, and seeming irrationality, unfolds following the same movement. The *"absolute restlessness* of the *becoming* [of actuality and possibility] is *contingency*,"[27] as Hegel says at the beginning of the analysis.[28] At the end, the claim is firmer: "It is necessity itself, therefore, that determines itself as *contingency:* in its being it repels itself from itself [*sich von sich abstößt*], in this very repelling [*Abstoßen*] has only returned to itself, and in this turning back which is its being has repelled itself from itself."[29]

How should we understand this claim? Something possible becomes actual; yet while that specific actualization may not be necessary (it may be contingent, *i.e.*, dependent upon circumstances that are themselves contingent), it is nevertheless determining and shapes what is now possible. For example, that Antigone defies Creon is a contingent fact – *i.e.*, she could have acted otherwise – but her actions' consequences are inevitable and necessary on the level of spirit. In this way, the contingent event participates in the *actual* as the circle of conditions, and in the *possible* as what actuality contains within itself: the being-in-itself that will come to expression sooner or later. The dialectical identity of possibility and actuality is reaffirmed because, as Hegel also puts it, *"essence must appear."*[30]

But what then of possibilities that do not become actual, such as suppressed or blocked possibilities? Or actualities that appear not to conform to their prior circle of conditions ("surprise" actualities)? On Hegel's view, the first are merely formal, impotent possibilities, or the monstrosity of an essence to which no being corresponds.[31] As for "surprise" actualities, they are simply a confirmation of the most basic truth about necessity: that we are often blindly subject to it. The fact that we often mistake what history "ought" to produce is just "the one-sided form of reflection-into-another,"[32] or, in other words, it is the unfortunate result of the narrowness that marks individual consciousness.

Adorno and the "Ought"

It is Adorno's opposition to this definition of actuality as a self-enclosed, self-reproducing totality (of the actual and the really possible) that allows us to grasp the real meaning of his own "unclosed" dialectic. In a word, if the world is not all that is the case in a positivistic sense, nor even self-enclosed, self-manifesting actuality in a Hegelian sense, it is because "what is, is more than it is"[33] in the sense of being marked by a type of possibility that corresponds neither to mere formal possibility, nor to Hegelian real possibility. Or, to phrase it differently, Adorno seems to claim that there is a kind of "middle" possibility that lies between the possibilities that spirit and actuality sanction, and those that are abstract, formal, or absurd.[34]

In Hegel's thought, the category of formal possibility comprises the "unreal" possibilities of the "merely" possible (*e.g.*, the sultan may become the pope or the moon may fall to earth[35]). However, along with absurd possibilities, it is also in this category that Hegel places those possibilities that take the form of mere "oughts" (*e.g.*, war *ought* not to exist) that are too impotent, with regard to the circle of conditions, to become actual: such a possibility is "a *mere* possibility and the *ought-to-be* [*das Sollen*] of the totality of form."[36] As such, an ought cannot rightly be said to be part of the living whole, which *qua* whole is fulfilled in and as actuality. In other words, according to Hegel, what *merely ought to be* but *is not*, is not a true (*i.e.*, real) possibility at all but rather an illusion – not the real in-itself corresponding to something not yet actual, but in truth a straightforward *impossibility*, for otherwise it would either be or become actual. As Hegel puts it: "possibility [in the form of the bare 'ought' or mere formal possibility] is contradiction, or it is *impossibility*."[37] In this way, actuality stands higher than possibility, which it either *contains* and actualizes or *condemns* as an impotent "ought," something only formally possible.

Hegel's critique of the "ought" (*das Sollen*) is well known. Less well known, however, is Adorno's defence of it. The root of the matter is that there are two kinds of "ought" that need to be distinguished: the "ought" of formal possibility – the fantastic wish that Hegel rightly ridicules – and the "ought" that society suppresses in order to maintain itself and the illusion of wholeness, *i.e.*, of its completeness as regards the possible. This distinction appears most clearly when the false reality of a socially necessary illusion *blocks* emancipatory transformation, which is then written off as a vain fantasy, just because actuality does not produce the transformation. On this point, Adorno has the following to say (special attention should be paid to the juxtaposition of the two uses of the modal verb *sollen*): "[the conformist tendency to deny the possibility of what ought to be] stems from the fact that people are only capable of dealing with the contradiction between the obvious possibility of fulfilment and its equally obvious impossibility by identifying with the impossibility, by appropriating it. To use [Anna] Freud's terminology, they 'identify with the aggressor' and say that something cannot be [*nicht sein soll*], when they know full well that it ought to be [*daß es gerade ja sein sollte*], though it is withheld from them through a bewitchment of the world."[38]

For some people, the denial of what merely ought to be and its apparent metaphysical legitimacy may seem readily comprehensible – but this comprehension depends upon an acceptance of the notions of real and formal possibility as Hegel (and much of the metaphysical tradition) understands them. On this view, the denial of what ought to be is just real actuality manifesting itself as an absolute rational norm by which possibilities can be judged. In other words, if real possibility is reduced to what is always already contained within real actuality, then whatever does not fit the norm will inevitably appear to be "impossible." But there is an untenable presupposition at work in the apparent innocence of the simple distinction between formal and real possibility: that the mere reproduction of actuality (if that is what actuality produces) is necessary, just because real actuality is always the expression of what is really possible, understood as an actual and complete circle of conditions that formerly existed. If some other potential or being-in-itself is *really* possible, on the level of spirit, then it will actualize itself sooner or later. The real possibilities of spirit cannot be blocked indefinitely by obsolete forms of ethical life clinging desperately to existence.

It is precisely this presupposition that Adorno implicitly refuses in the passages just cited. For him, the distinction between the "mere" ought and what "really" ought to be, but *nevertheless is not*, is a critical one. It is this "emphatic" ought (a "real" ought that complements "real" possibility) that has no place in traditional theories of possibility, least of all Hegel's. As Adorno puts it: "Negative dialectic penetrates its hardened objects with possibility – the possibility out of which actuality has cheated them, but which nevertheless peers out of each one."[39] For Hegel, such a notion of "negative" possibility – *i.e.*, a possibility of which we are "cheated" or "deprived" – is utterly unthinkable or sheer nonsense. For Adorno, it is just the metaphysical correlate of a humanity that might just destroy itself before actualizing its potential.

Adorno's counter-claim is thus that actuality is currently structured in such a way as to indefinitely *block* and *threaten* possibilities other than those sanctioned by circumstance and that the metaphysical dogma of actuality as a self-enclosed, self-confirming totality further sabotages those blocked possibilities.

A few more examples will bring out the alternative view of modality that Adorno has in mind. First, the well-known and apparently contradictory final lines of the introduction to *Negative Dialectic*, where Adorno writes: "[Utopia], the consciousness of possibility, clings to both the concrete and the undisfigured. Utopia is blocked by what is possible, never by immediate actuality; that is why what is possible seems abstract in the midst of what exists. Inextinguishable colour comes from non-being. Thought, a piece of existence, serves non-being, which thought reaches, however negatively."[40] The apparent contradiction lies in the way utopia, which is supposed to be the consciousness of possibility, is also *blocked* by possibility. However, if we admit the "middle" possibility or the emphatic "ought" that we have been discussing, then the contradiction disappears. The passage can then be understood as follows: "[Utopia], the consciousness of [unsanctioned, unactualized] possibility … is blocked by [so-called real possibility], never by immediate actuality [which is contingent]; that is why [what ought to be] seems abstract in the midst of what exists." In other words, the real possibilities of the existing order are seen as total and exhaustive only because we are accustomed to regarding self-reproducing actuality as an absolute norm. But if we refuse this metaphysical prejudice and admit the category of *blocked* possibility situated between familiar real possibility and the formal possibility, then actuality opens itself up to the different, and thereby frees itself from the tyranny of the same, of self-reproducing actuality. In other words, blocked possibilities are both real and unreal (because blocked); but they are nevertheless not *merely* formal to the extent that they are really blocked. They lie between merely formal and fully real possibilities in the Hegelian sense.

A similar problem of interpretation arises at the end of Lecture 17 of *Einführung in die Dialektik:* "It is also part and parcel of the historical dialectic that what appears anachronistic may in some circumstances have greater actuality and relevance [*Aktualität*] than what may seem, on the surface of things, entitled to lay claim to greater actuality and relevance, in the sense of functioning within existing structures."[41]

This passage, like the previous one, at first seems difficult to decipher. But the difficulty is utterly dispelled just as soon as we see that there is a double modal structure in play, hinging on a special kind of "anachronism" (which Marx was probably the first to diagnose in the introduction to his critique of Hegel's *Philosophy of Right*[42]). Actuality is not reducible to what merely *appears* to possess actuality and relevance, namely, the administered world and its inherent, self-reproducing real possibilities; it can also be the manifestation of the *blocked possibility* of an *other* actuality, of another future, that has "greater actuality and relevance." In other words, actuality here again expresses an emphatic ought that is suppressed by what so-called real actuality makes possible. "Anachronism" names this difference or this gap: the time of actuality and its self-reproduction *versus* the time of blocked possibility and of an other future.

Other examples include Adorno's critique of popular psychology, which, he says, standardizes normal and abnormal behaviour and so reduces human possibility to schemata, thereby sacrificing the process of dialectical experience to "ready-made enlightenment,"[43] *i.e.*, illusory or reductive "real" possibilities of health and illness. A more substantial example would be the frequent criticisms of Eastern Bloc Marxism in Adorno's writings, which take aim at the metaphysical prejudice to which institutional Marxism's emphasis on determinate praxis often blinded it: the prejudice according to which present and future actuality form a closed whole defined by the objective and economically determined possibilities of the present. At root, this prejudice is just the social and political manifestation of what is taken to be the metaphysical nature of actuality, which Hegel's theory of possibility defines and defends.

Adorno, on the other hand, offers us an implicit philosophy of possibility that challenges the prevailing view. The possible is to be measured not merely positively in terms of what already exists, but also negatively – in terms of the *difference* from actuality that actuality itself emphatically suggests in the form of an "ought" that is not reducible to formal possibility. Perhaps the simplest example in Adorno's writings would be the recurrent observation "that no-one ought to [*soll*] go hungry anymore."[44] The technical means to eliminate hunger are available here and now, but at the same time the current arrangement of productive forces makes the demand seem impossible.

Response to an Objection and Concluding Remarks

Naturally, there is a Hegelian rejoinder to this Adornian line of reasoning. The problem seems to be that our *grasp* of possibility – what we merely *take to be* possible – is structured in such a way as to rule out certain possibilities as unreal, whereas those same possibilities are, in fact, actualizable. It is not the fault of spirit if I fail or refuse to grasp the real possibilities in play within a given actuality. And in any case, philosophically speaking, the dialectical identity of real actuality and real possibility is all that matters. For Hegel, that *I* should fail to grasp how actuality and possibility are concretely related to each other is almost certainly devoid of philosophical interest, for what mere *individual* consciousness takes to be the case or takes to be possible has little bearing on the structure of actuality and the real possibilities it contains. In fact, individual consciousness *often* finds itself on the wrong side of actuality:

It may certainly happen that the ideals of individuals are not realized. Individuals often have their own peculiar opinions of themselves, of their lofty intentions, of the splendid deeds they hope to perform, and of their own supposed importance from which the world, as they think, must assuredly benefit. Be that as it may, such ideas merit no further attention.[45]

The point is this: individual consciousness may be mistaken in what it takes to be really possible, in what it takes to be the true content of actuality. Indeed, such opinions – and the conservatism or radicalism that they may sometimes inform – can frequently be quite disconnected from dynamic historical actuality and world spirit, which plays itself out in history in spite of our beliefs. Of course, exceptional errors of judgment may be instructive and philosophically interesting – *e.g.*, Antigone or Macbeth –, but only as instances of the power of spirit over individual beliefs. But it is utterly unsurprising that we should sometimes find ourselves in a situation where we misrecognize what is possible (or actual or necessary). That is just the nature of individual consciousness's one-sidedness (*Einseitigkeit*).

There is no question that individuals are prone to misjudging possibility. However, from an Adornian perspective, the questions we should be asking are the following: why do such misjudgements occur and how is it that actuality itself seems currently to be organized so as to perpetuate these errors? The "real web of illusion" that Adorno seeks everywhere to undo is for him nothing other than this actuality's global tendency to promote the misrecognition of unsanctioned possibilities of emancipation as impossibilities. In this regard, the Hegelian rejoinder does not reach the core of the problem, which is that our society as a whole seems burdened by the metaphysical prejudice concerning the priority of actuality over possibility – a prejudice that cannot but affect our vision of the possible. Philosophically, and specifically, the fault lies with the extension of the formal relation of actuality to possibility into a critique of the "ought" that treats systematically unrealized possibilities of emancipation as vain. For Adorno, in at least some cases, if the "ought" remains unrealized, it is due to ideologies that depend, implicitly or explicitly, upon the claim that actuality is a totality exhaustive of possibility and complete in itself. Of course, Adorno accepts the claim that actuality is productive of possibility and that it is, in this way, self-productive. He is not a fantasist. But the Hegelian critique of the "ought" cuts too much away; consequently, only those possibilities that become actual are considered real. Yet among those which do not become real are some whose unreality is in fact the sign of a sham totality. There is, of course, a gap separating Hegel's view from the ideological affirmation that the reproduction of existing conditions is right and good because that is in fact what actuality produces.

However, bizarrely, it is made smaller by the relegation of the "ought" to the status of mere formal possibility. Against this relegation, Adorno effectively pleads for an intermediate category unrecognized by Hegel: an "ought" that reduces neither to the pre-sanctioned real possibilities of the status quo, nor to the fantastic unreal possibilities of the imagination gone wild.

Adorno's heterogeneous "more," or the "middle" possibility situated between Hegelian formal and real possibilities, is not utopian in the sense of demanding the impossible. It is utopian in the sense of demanding that the social whole *not refuse as impossible* what does not already exist and agree with actuality. He is not asking us to consider possibilities *outside* the social whole, but rather those *within* it – the "real" oughts – that are systematically obstructed by metaphysical (as well as other kinds of) prejudice. A just society would be one in which real possibilities of emancipation are not systematically blocked. This is the meaning of Adorno's "utopia of the whole truth."

NOTES

1 An earlier, and shorter, version of this essay first appeared in French as "Un utopisme modal ? Possibilité et actualité chez Hegel et Adorno," in *Les normes et le possible : héritage et perspectives de l'École de Francfort,* ed. Pierre-François Noppen, Gérard Raulet, and Iain Macdonald (Paris: Éditions de la Maison des sciences de l'homme, 2013). The present text is a revision of an English-language version of the essay first published in *Adorno Studies,* vol. 1, no. 1 (2017): 1–12. Parts of the text were subsequently incorporated into Iain Macdonald, *What Would Be Different: Figures of Possibility in Adorno* (Stanford: Stanford University Press, 2019).

2 Other lines of attack are to be found, for example, in the works of Herbert Marcuse and of Ernst Bloch, but also in those of Martin Heidegger.

3 Jay M. Bernstein, *Adorno: Disenchantment and Ethics* (Cambridge: Cambridge University Press, 2001), 418, 435. See too Deborah Cook, "From the Actual to the Possible: Nonidentity Thinking," *Constellations,* vol. 12, no. 1 (2005).

4 Theodor W. Adorno, *Negative Dialectics,* trans. E. B. Ashton (London: Routledge, 1973), 313; Theodor W. Adorno, *Gesammelte Schriften,* ed. Gretel Adorno, Susan Buck-Morss, and Klaus Schultz, 20 vols. (Frankfurt am Main: Suhrkamp Verlag, 1997), 6:308.

5 Theodor W. Adorno, "The Experiential Content of Hegel's Philosophy," in *Hegel: Three Studies,* trans. Shierry Weber Nicholsen (Cambridge, MA: The MIT Press, 1993), 83; Adorno, *GS,* 5:320.

6 Theodor W. Adorno, *Minima Moralia*, trans. E. F. N. Jephcott (London: Verso, 1978), §29, 50; Adorno, *GS*, 4:55.

7 G.W.F. Hegel, *The Science of Logic*, trans. George Di Giovanni (Cambridge: Cambridge University Press, 2010), 749; G.W.F. Hegel, *Werke*, 20 vols. (Frankfurt am Main: Suhrkamp Verlag, 1969–1971), 6:569.

8 Adorno, "The Experiential Content of Hegel's Philosophy," 87; Adorno, *GS*, 5:324.

9 Adorno, "The Experiential Content of Hegel's Philosophy," 87; Adorno, *GS*, 5:324.

10 Adorno, "The Experiential Content of Hegel's Philosophy," 88; Adorno, *GS*, 5:325.

11 Theodor W. Adorno, "The Actuality of Philosophy," in *The Adorno Reader*, ed. Brian O'Connor, trans. Benjamin Snow (Oxford: Blackwell, 2000), 31; Adorno, *GS*, 1:335.

12 Rainer Traub and Harald Wieser, eds., *Gespräche mit Ernst Bloch* (Frankfurt am Main: Suhrkamp Verlag, 1975), 61.

13 Max Horkheimer, "On the Problem of Truth," in *Between Philosophy and Social Sciences: Selected Early Writings*, ed. G. Frederick Hunter, Matthew S. Kramer, and John Torpey, trans. Maurice Goldbloom and G. Frederick Hunter (Cambridge, MA: The MIT Press, 1993), 189; Max Horkheimer, *Gesammelte Schriften*, 19 vols. (Frankfurt am Main: S. Fischer Verlag, 1988), 3:295, for example.

14 Horkheimer, "On the Problem of Truth," 189; Horkheimer, *Gesammelte Schriften*, 3:292.

15 Horkheimer, "On the Problem of Truth," 190; Horkheimer, *Gesammelte Schriften*, 3:293.

16 Horkheimer, "On the Problem of Truth," 192; Horkheimer, *Gesammelte Schriften*, 3:295.

17 In this sense, Horkheimer's view is consistent with that of Hegel in the introduction to the *Phenomenology of Spirit*, while remaining true to Marx's second thesis on Feuerbach: "The question whether human thinking can reach objective truth – is not a question of theory but a *practical* question. In practice human beings must prove the truth, that is, actuality and power [*Wirklichkeit und Macht*], this-sidedness of their thinking. The dispute about the actuality or non-actuality of thinking – thinking isolated from practice – is a purely *scholastic* question." (Karl Marx, "Theses on Feuerbach," in *Writings of the Young Marx on Philosophy and Society*, edited and translated by Loyd D. Easton and Kurt H. Guddat (Garden City: Doubleday, 1967; reprint, with corrections, Hackett, 1997), 401; Karl Marx and Friedrich Engels, *Werke*, 43 vols. (Berlin: Dietz-Verlag, 1956), 3:5, cf. 3:533.)

18 Adorno's many critical references to the first line of Wittgenstein's *Tractatus* – "The world is everything that is the case" (*Die Welt ist alles,*

was der Fall ist) – are meant precisely to adumbrate the openness of the dialectical view that he defends. See Ludwig Wittgenstein, *Tractatus Logico-Philosophicus*, trans. C. K. Ogden, Bilingual (London: Routledge & Kegan Paul, 1983), proposition 1.

19 Adorno, *Negative Dialectics*, 106; Adorno, *GS*, 6:112.

20 G.W.F. Hegel, *The Encyclopædia Logic: Part I of the Encyclopædia of Philosophical Sciences, with the Zusätze*, trans. T. F. Geraets, W. A. Suchting, and H. S. Harris (Indianapolis: Hackett, 1991), §143, Zusatz, 217; Hegel, *Werke*, 8:284. My emphasis.

21 Hegel, *Science of Logic*, 482; Hegel, *Werke*, 6:208.

22 Hegel, *Science of Logic*, 482; Hegel, *Werke*, 6:208.

23 Hegel, *Encyclopædia Logic*, §148, 224; Hegel, *Werke*, 8:292.

24 Hegel, *Science of Logic*, 484; Hegel, *Werke*, 6:210.

25 Hegel, *Science of Logic*, 484; Hegel, *Werke*, 6:210–211.

26 Hegel, *Science of Logic*, 484; Hegel, *Werke*, 6:211.

27 Hegel, *Science of Logic*, 481; Hegel, *Werke*, 6:206.

28 Whereas in the previous section of the greater *Logic* contingency is defined merely as that which may or may not be, it is here defined as dependence upon another, *i.e.*, non-self-sufficiency or dependence upon circumstances.

29 Hegel, *Science of Logic*, 486; Hegel, *Werke*, 6:214.

30 Hegel, *Science of Logic*, 418; Hegel, *Werke*, 6:124.

31 "Essence itself is only a moment and … has no truth without being." Hegel, *Science of Logic*, 479; Hegel, *Werke*, 6:204.

32 Hegel, *Encyclopædia Logic*, §145, Zusatz, 218; Hegel, *Werke*, 8:285.

33 Adorno, *Negative Dialectics*, 161; Adorno, *GS*, 6:164.

34 Compare Bernstein, *Adorno*, 418.

35 Hegel, *Encyclopædia Logic*, §143, Zusatz, 216; Hegel, *Werke*, 8:283.

36 Hegel, *Science of Logic*, 479; Hegel, *Werke*, 6:204.

37 Hegel, *Science of Logic*, 479; Hegel, *Werke*, 6:204.

38 Traub and Wieser, eds., *Gespräche mit Ernst Bloch*, 61.

39 Adorno, *Negative Dialectics*, 52; Adorno, *GS*, 6:62.

40 "[Utopie], das Bewußtsein der Möglichkeit, haftet am Konkreten als dem Unentstellten. Es ist das Mögliche, nie das unmittelbar Wirkliche, das der Utopie den Platz versperrt; inmitten des Bestehenden erscheint es darum als abstrakt. Die unauslöschliche Farbe kommt aus dem Nichtseienden. Ihm dient Denken, ein Stück Dasein, das, wie immer negativ, ans Nichtseiende heranreicht." Adorno, *Negative Dialectics*, 56–57; Adorno, *GS*, 6:66.

41 "Aber ich glaube, daß es zur geschichtlichen Dialektik auch hinzugehört, daß unter Umständen gerade das Anachronistische eine größere Aktualität hat als das, was seiner eigenen Oberfläche nach, nämlich im Sinn des Funktionierens innerhalb der gegebenen Apparaturen, die größere

Aktualität beanspruchen darf." Theodor W. Adorno, *Einführung in die Dialektik* (Frankfurt am Main: Suhrkamp Verlag, 2010), 261.

42 As Marx writes: "If we were to begin with the German *status quo* itself, even in the only appropriate way, which is negatively, the result would still be an anachronism. For even the negation of our political present is already a dusty fact in the historical junk room of modern nations. If I negate powdered wigs, I still have unpowdered wigs." Germany in 1843 is thus considered to be "beneath the level of history," *i.e.*, anachronistic, in the specific sense that its actuality and attendant possibilities of reform still leave it lagging behind the true actuality of world history. Karl Marx, *Critique of Hegel's "Philosophy of Right,"* trans. Annette Jolin and Joseph O'Malley (Cambridge: Cambridge University Press, 1970), 132, 133.

43 Adorno, *Minima Moralia*, §40, 65; Adorno, *GS*, 4:72.

44 Adorno, *Minima Moralia*, §100, 156; Adorno, *GS*, 4:178.

45 G.W.F. Hegel, *Lectures on the Philosophy of World History: Introduction*, trans. H.B. Nisbet (Cambridge: Cambridge University Press, 1975), 30; G.W.F. Hegel, *Vorlesungen über die Philosophie der Weltgeschichte*, 4 vols. (Hamburg: Felix Meiner Verlag, 1955), 1:76.

REFERENCES

Adorno, Theodor W. *Negative Dialectics*. Translated by E.B. Ashton. London: Routledge, 1973.

—— *Minima Moralia*. Translated by E.F.N. Jephcott. London: Verso, 1978.

—— "Aspects of Hegel's Philosophy." In *Hegel: Three Studies*, translated by Shierry Weber Nicholsen. Cambridge, MA: The MIT Press, 1993a.

—— "The Experiential Content of Hegel's Philosophy." In *Hegel: Three Studies*, translated by Shierry Weber Nicholsen. Cambridge, MA: The MIT Press, 1993b.

—— *Gesammelte Schriften*. Edited by Gretel Adorno, Susan Buck-Morss, and Klaus Schultz, 20 Vols. Frankfurt am Main: Suhrkamp Verlag, 1997.

—— "The Actuality of Philosophy." In *The Adorno Reader*, translated by Benjamin Snow and edited by Brian O'Connor. Oxford: Blackwell, 2000.

—— *Einführung in die Dialektik*. Frankfurt am Main: Suhrkamp Verlag, 2010.

Bernstein, Jay M. *Adorno: Disenchantment and Ethics*. Cambridge: Cambridge University Press, 2001.

Cook, Deborah. "From the Actual to the Possible: Nonidentity Thinking." *Constellations* 12, no. 1 (2005): 21–35.

Hegel, G.W.F. *Vorlesungen über die Philosophie der Weltgeschichte*, 4 Vols. Hamburg: Felix Meiner Verlag, 1955.

—— *Werke*, 20 Vols. Frankfurt am Main: Suhrkamp Verlag, 1969–1971.

—— *Lectures on the Philosophy of World History: Introduction.* Translated by H.B. Nisbet. Cambridge: Cambridge University Press, 1975.
—— *The Encyclopædia Logic: Part I of the Encyclopædia of Philosophical Sciences, with the Zusätze.* Translated by T.F. Geraets, W.A. Suchting, and H.S. Harris. Indianapolis: Hackett, 1991.
—— *The Science of Logic.* Translated by George Di Giovanni. Cambridge: Cambridge University Press, 2010.
Horkheimer, Max. *Gesammelte Schriften*, 19 Vols. Frankfurt am Main: S. Fischer Verlag, 1988.
—— "On the Problem of Truth." In *Between Philosophy and Social Sciences: Selected Early Writings*, Translated by Maurice Goldbloom and G. Frederick Hunter, edited by G. Frederick Hunter, Matthew S. Kramer, and John Torpey. Cambridge, MA: The MIT Press, 1993.
Macdonald, Iain. "Un utopisme modal ? Possibilité et actualité chez Hegel et Adorno." In *Les normes et le possible : héritage et perspectives de l'École de Francfort*, edited by Pierre-François Noppen, Gérard Raulet, and Iain Macdonald. Paris: Éditions de la Maison des sciences de l'homme, 2013.
—— *What Would Be Different: Figures of Possibility in Adorno.* Stanford: Stanford University Press, 2019.
Marx, Karl. *Critique of Hegel's 'Philosophy of Right'.* Translated by Annette Jolin and Joseph O'Malley. Cambridge: Cambridge University Press, 1970.
—— "Theses on Feuerbach." In *Writings of the Young Marx on Philosophy and Society*, translated by Loyd D. Easton and Kurt H. Guddat, edited by Loyd D. Easton and Kurt H. Guddat. Garden City: Doubleday, 1967. Reprint, with corrections, Hackett, 1997.
Marx, Karl, and Friedrich Engels. *Werke.* 43 Vols. Berlin: Dietz-Verlag, 1956.
—— *The Communist Manifesto.* Translated by Samuel Moore. Harmondsworth: Penguin (Pelican), 1967.
Traub, Rainer, and Harald Wieser, eds. *Gespräche mit Ernst Bloch.* Frankfurt am Main: Suhrkamp Verlag, 1975.
Wittgenstein, Ludwig. *Tractatus Logico-Philosophicus.* Translated by C.K. Ogden. Bilingual. London: Routledge & Kegan Paul, 1983.

5 Possibility Entails Itself in Actuality: Hegel's Theory of Conditions

NAHUM BROWN, MAHIDOL UNIVERSITY INTERNATIONAL COLLEGE, MAHIDOL UNIVERSITY

Introduction

The "Actuality" chapter of Hegel's *Science of Logic*[1] has received significant attention in recent years. The chapter's popularity comes partially from Hegel's provocative discussion of the relationship between necessity and contingency, leading commentators to conclude that contingency is a necessary category in Hegel's system.[2] The chapter's popularity also comes from its location at the end of the *Doctrine of Essence*. There are many clues to be found in the chapter to explain why the *Doctrine of the Concept* emerges from *Essence*. Yet another reason why the chapter has warranted so much attention in recent years is because it challenges us to revisit the common assumption that actuality is separate from and more primary than possibility. Hegel's catch phrase in the preface to the *Elements of the Philosophy of Right* – "what is rational is actual and what is actual is rational"[3] – supports a prevalent interpretation that Hegel is preoccupied, primarily, with actuality. This, along with other catch phrases – such as "the identity of identity and difference" (SL: 74) – has helped to fuel a long-standing view of Hegel as a philosopher who privileges identity over difference and who sees possibility as dependent on actuality. Critics as influential as Kierkegaard, Adorno, and Levinas have exposed Hegel as a thinker who cannot genuinely approach non-identity, alterity, and unactualized possibility. However, when we look closely at what Hegel really said about the modal categories in the chapter, we encounter a noticeably different view of Hegel. We see a philosopher whose preoccupation with actuality is also a preoccupation with possibility. We see a philosopher who views actuality and possibility as categories that pass over into each other. In what follows, I argue that Hegel's theory of conditions plays a major role in his conception of actuality and possibility as transitional categories.[4] By offering a rational explanation through his theory of conditions for how to think of actuality and possibility as one unity, Hegel thereby addresses one of the most fundamental problems of modal reality: how to actualize possible contraries without reducing these to contradiction.

Deleuze finds in Leibniz's theory of "incompossibility" a solution to this same modal problem of how to actualize possible contraries without reducing these to contradiction. It might seem to be the case, as Deleuze recognizes in the "Incompossibility" chapter of *The Fold*, that "Adam the sinner and Adam the nonsinner is a relation of contradiction."[5] Certainly, thought can attempt to avoid the conclusion that possibility is self-contradiction simply by dividing possibility into the dual relation of "actualized possibility" and "unactualized possibility" (i.e., if "Adam the sinner" is actualized possibility, then "Adam the nonsinner" is unactualized possibility). However, Deleuze proposes that "between the two worlds" thought discovers a new relation, i.e., "incompossibility." In this relation, the *contraries* of possibility become *differences* that coexist without being reduced to contradiction, but also without being divided into what is actual and what is merely possible.

In this study, I propose that Hegel has already found a solution to the problem that Deleuze articulates through Leibniz. While I recognize that a study of this kind might only appear after Deleuze's reading of Leibniz's incompossibility, my aim is to explore a version of this solution that one can already find in Hegel.[6] In the "Actuality" chapter of *the Science of Logic*, Hegel first explicates the formal problem by acknowledging that although what is actual is possible, nevertheless one cannot actualize the negativity of possibility (that what is possible can also *not be*). But Hegel then finds a solution to this problem in the "Real" and "Absolute" sub-chapters because he discovers a material version of actualization which mediates between contraries so that the actualization of possibility no longer succumbs to contradiction.[7] I argue that even though he de-emphasizes it in the chapter, Hegel's claim about conditions is the essential premise for this solution.

One of the more provocative statements Hegel makes in the "Actuality" chapter is that actuality and possibility are implicitly the same category. He writes: "When all of the conditions of something are completely present it enters into actuality; the completeness of the conditions is the totality as in the content, and *the something itself* is this content determined as being equally actual as possible" (SL, 548/WL, 209–10). This statement is provocative because it runs against a tradition that sees actuality and possibility as distinct categories. By the end of the chapter, Hegel proposes that actuality and possibility are the absolute conversion of each into the other. Does this mean that something is actual *if and only if* it is possible? While it might be intuitive enough to infer that if something is actual, then it is possible, does Hegel also mean that everything possible is actual? Does he mean that everything possible exists in the same way that everything actual exists?

Read out of context, the claim "everything possible is actual" must look quite paradoxical. But I will attempt to demonstrate, not only that Hegel has a rational explanation, but that by deducing the implicit transitional identity between actuality and possibility, Hegel presents an important solution to the initial formal problem of the chapter. I will begin by supplying a short explication of this formal problem, what Hegel describes as "the ought" between actuality and possibility (SL 543, WL 203–4; SL 547, WL 209). Then I will argue that Hegel's subsequent discussion of conditions plays a key role in the solution of this problem. Hegel claims that the only way to actualize contrary possibilities is if immediate actualities are at the same time the possibilities of other actuals. In as much as each thing is a condition for the possibility of others, each really has its possibility in others, and each is thus the other of itself as itself. This is why, in the sentence quoted above, Hegel says that the actuality that results from this process is not only a new determinateness of content, but becomes the same actuality throughout all possibilities. This is ultimately why Hegel turns to "substance," to an actuality that sustains itself in the contrariety of possibility.

Although commentators have had insights about the role that conditions play in the "Actuality" chapter, no one has examined this category in great detail. Lampert analyses how dispersion, transference, production, and various other movement-structures work in terms of multiplicity, and analyses the function of conditions at the same time. He argues that "a possibility is not about its own actualisation but about conferring on an actuality the power to produce another actuality." If each actuality is the possibility of other actuals, then "the truth of one thing is *in* a different thing."[8] Lampert develops this reading of the chapter from his recognition that, for Hegel, formal possibility is supposed to be the "totality of form" but also fails at this. "The function of a possibility," Lampert explains, "is to express the totality, but … no one possibility can express everything the totality expresses without generating contradictions. Each possibility thus fails to express all that it *itself* expresses."[9] My reading of the chapter develops these insights from Lampert by highlighting in more detail how Hegel's theory of conditions resolves Hegel's initial, formal problem that no actualization seems able to express the totality of possibility from one standpoint.

Houlgate also discusses the role of conditions briefly in his essay "Necessity and Contingency." He says that the reason why immediate actuality is contingency is because it harbours within this concept "the possibility of something else arising," i.e., the contingent actual is a condition.[10] The connection Houlgate draws between contingent actuality and conditions is extremely helpful, but he could have emphasized more explicitly why Hegel thinks that it is the unity of actuality and possibility that generates both of these categories. Burbidge presents the argument that conditions are always multiple, that no one condition can exist alone.[11] Longuenesse discusses Hegel's theory of conditions and Leibniz's "complete determination of a thing" in the same breath.[12] Ng claims that if Hegel's "conditions of possibility" are full of content (not empty and formal), the consequence is that there can be no real distinction, for Hegel, between the empirical and the *a priori*. Readers who are interested in Hegel's revision of Kant's "conditions for the possibility of experience" should turn to her essay.[13] Taylor defines real necessity as the necessity of conditions. But then the conditions themselves are contingent. "B follows from A, but A might not have happened."[14] Marcuse mentions conditions briefly in terms of "presuppositions."[15]

While developing these insights from others, I claim that at the heart of the matter is Hegel's definition of a "condition" as an immediate actuality that is equally itself and possibility. A condition is, for Hegel, a process concept that unifies actuality and possibility in a productively temporary and unstable way. It both grounds the possibility in the identity of the immediate actuality but also signals the further development of something, of the emergence of something, a new actuality, which is, at the same time, tacitly embedded in the immediate actuality from the start. A condition is, thus, an actuality that holds the opposite of the actuality – i.e., the negative possibility of its other – as the self-same actuality throughout. To analyse this concept, let's begin by looking at Hegel's articulation of the initial, formal problem that actuality does not seem to be able to hold within it the negativity of the possible as one actual.

Hegel's Exposition of the Formal Problem: There Is No Immediate Way to Actualize the Contrariety of Possibility As One Actuality

Hegel begins the "Actuality" chapter from the immediacy of actuality, which he says is the same as being or existence, with one noteworthy difference: what is actual has emerged into actuality from possibility.[16]

This process is then the immediacy of actualization, but what emerges from actualization, however, is not the simple one-to-one correspondence of actuality and possibility. What emerges is not at first what Hegel calls "the totality of form,"[17] the actual in the complete sense of the possible, but only some limited actuality of content. The reason he gives for this is that while possibility contains the form of any actuality whatsoever, actualization must limit in actuality the contraries that possibility projects of the actual. Hegel gives the principle of contradiction as the reason behind why this initial, immediate, and ultimately inadequate actuality cannot be the one-to-one correspondence of itself as possibility.[18] While everything is formally possible, actualization could never sustain the contraries that possibility projects. Certainly, what is merely possible can *and* can not be.[19] If becoming a musician is possible, then *both* becoming a musician *and* not becoming a musician are equally possible. But what is actually possible always expresses the compound of possibility as a disjunction instead of as a conjunction. If becoming a musician is possible, then *either* I become a musician *or* I do not become a musician. Although both are possible, it would be a logical contradiction if both being a musician and not being a musician were one actuality. Possibility is thus both what actuality actualizes and what exceeds actuality in every case. And actuality is thus only possibility in this limited sense, once the possibility of the contrary is removed.

In terms of traditional, non-dialectical conceptions of everyday modality, we normally think of actuality as one of many possibilities but not as the totality of possibility. While it is possible to live in different cities, if I decide to move to Berlin and actually take up life there, I cannot also in the same time, manner, and place, take up life in Hong Kong or anywhere else in the world. That whole variety of other possible outcomes cannot also come from this decision. The actual is, in this sense, only one of many possibilities. And the possible is that which can be actual but it is also that which can remain unactualized. It would seem, then, at least from the perspective of conventional thinking, that the categories actuality and possibility are not truly transitional, that although possibility is a necessary and minimum condition for the actual, the two do not truly pass over into each other because the actual cannot persist as mere possibility without negating its status as actual.

Robert Frost's 1916 poem "The Road Not Taken" is a good illustration of this division. The poem begins:

Two roads diverged in a yellow wood,
And sorry I could not travel both

> And be one traveler, long I stood
> And looked down one as long as I could
> To where it bent in the undergrowth[20]

Frost's traveller comes across a divergence of roads, sees both as possible, but must limit in actuality the possibility of going down both. Both roads are possible but only one or the other can become actual. The road not taken then stands against the traveller as unactualized possibility, that is, as possibility that exceeds actuality.[21]

Frost's remark is quite poignant: "And sorry I could not travel both." In the "Unhappy Consciousness" passages of *the Phenomenology of Spirit*, Hegel also explores this standpoint of remorse. Although he does not directly discuss unactualized possibility in these passages, Hegel's description of how self-consciousness attempts "to hold on to" its constantly vanishing individuality anticipates his exposition of the formal tension between actuality and possibility.[22] There is literally no way, at least not formally, to actualize possibility *qua* possibility. To act at all is to lose that which could have been. Every gain of some determinate actuality is the loss of its opposite. From this standpoint, I look back as I grow old at what I could have been and feel genuine remorse for the various possibilities and directions that my life could have taken. While this sentiment of remorse is one that Hegel ultimately rejects, just as he rejects the formal exposition of disjunction in the "Actuality" chapter, we can still see in the perversely remorseful, as in the formal impossibility of actualizing contrary possibilities in one actuality, the starting point for Hegel's further project of conditions and compulsive necessity.

While Frost's traveller might feel remorse for the road not taken, there is, of course, nothing good that could come from actualizing both roads as one traveller. This would either lead (1) to the actualization of death by contradiction, because the body would be torn apart by the actualization of too much possibility or (2) to the unactualized possible as a mere abstraction. Since the actualization of possible contraries would lead only to the contrary as the contradictory, we can barely even imagine (1), the traveller who literally, impossibly, goes down both roads as one traveller. This would be the actualization of the impossible, the traveller's body torn apart by possibility.[23] Death by possibility happens when a body attempts to actualize without further mediation both the possibility to be and the possibility not to be. Death is, in this modal sense, the actualization of contradictory possibilities without the further mediation of what Hegel will soon describe as conditional actualization. Death is the expression of an unmediated surplus of possibility in actuality, when conditions do not allow for this. But the latter – (2) the unactualized possible as a mere abstraction – fares no better and is equally unimaginable. As Burbidge explains in *Hegel's Systematic Contingency*, one finds the meaning of the possible from the supposition of the actual, and not the other way around.[24] One finds the meaning of "going down one road or another" from the supposition of actually going down one or the other road. If Frost's traveller were able to go down both roads and be one traveller, this would collapse the variations and meaning of the possible.

This tension between actuality and possibility amounts to a problem about multiplicity. Actualization cannot actualize the multiplicity of the possible because it is precisely this multiplicity that harbours those contraries which, if taken together, would lead to contradiction. This is why Hegel says that everything (i.e., any one thing) is possible, but everything (i.e., all things together) is equally impossible.[25] Possibility itself is an open boundless multiplicity, but since its only access to itself is by way of actualization, this boundless multiplicity is at the same time the impossibility of actualizing possibility itself.

Two inferences come of this. On the one hand, actualization cannot instantiate every possibility and therefore cannot grasp the "whole." To actualize possibility is to reduce the *many* possibles to one or another actual. There is no way to actualize the whole possibility because all contraries are latent in the multiplicity, and to actualize even two contraries at once would lead to contradiction. But on the other hand, it is only in terms of the one actual that the possible seems to be multiple in the first place.

The first inference exposes the contrary nature of the possible as the multiple. Actualization must reduce the multiplicity of the possible in order to actualize the possible. To actualize the possible is to create a limit in the face of the infinite variety of what could have been. If actuality were not to block off the multiplicity of the possible, the contrary that the possible harbours in the multiple would become full-blown contradiction, which would lead, not to the actuality of the multiple, but to the impossibility of everything.

The second inference then exposes the infinite and finite nature of possibility. It is not simply the case that the actualization of the possible removes the multiplicity from the possible. This multiplicity only appears in its unending variety *because the one becomes actual*. Frost's two roads only appear as a multiplicity of diverging sides because the one that will become actual must make the possible conform to this. Our recognition of there being "directions" at all, or of there being a "multiplicity of determinate possibilities," is one that appears because of actuality. The possible would be inconceivable, direction-less, and indeterminate if it were not always and already set down in the terms of the actual. This is the case because there is no way to think of the endless variety of possibility without thinking from the presupposition of the one that is actual. We might conclude from this that possibility *qua* possibility is in a certain important respect unac-tualizable, that there is really no way to grasp the "whole" possibility in one actuality.

We can also explain this problem in terms of entailment. While actu-ality necessarily entails possibility, possibility does not seem to entail actuality in the same way. On the one hand, if something is actual, it must have emerged into actuality from possibility. Aristotle notices this modal inference when he explains, in book 13 of *De Interpretatione*, that it would be impossible for something actual not to have been possible. "From being of necessity there follows capability of being."[26] It would seem, however, that this entailment does not work in both directions. Although the actual entails the possible, the possible does not recipro-cally entail the actual. Modal logicians call this the axiom of possibil-ity. "If p, then possible p" is an axiom of modal systems that include reflexivity (i.e., access to any possible world presupposes access to the actual world).[27] But from this it does not follow that "if possible p, then p." The reason why this is the case is because if something is merely possible, there is the equal possibility that what could become actual could not become actual.

For Hegel, however, this seemingly one-sided entailment is not the end of the story. If it is the emergence of being into actuality that is really of issue, then the contrary that actualization removes is equally the *content of being*, and this too ought-to-be the actuality of possi-bility. It is from these terms that Hegel deduces formal contingency. By formal contingency, he shows that even though what emerges in actualization is only some limited actuality of content, the contrary of this actuality equally could have been and equally does exist.[28] Hegel emphasizes that formal contingency is itself the immediacy of actual-ity, and that what is posited in contingency is the equal existence of non-actual possibility. When he claims, near the end of the "Formal Contingency" sub-chapter that "everything possible exists,"[29] he does not mean that every fantastical thought one might have, if it is pos-sible, is actual.[30] Just because I can think that a unicorn might exist does not mean that it actually exists. Hegel's point is rather that imme-diate actuality, precisely because it is the possible with all contraries removed, acts as a metaphysical gateway upon the existence of pos-sibility *qua* possibility.

Possibility appears through the limitation of immediate actuality. It appears in what Hegel calls the empty or superficial sense as the positive identity of the actual, that if something exists, then it can exist.[31] But it also appears in the negative sense, as the possibility of other actuals, and as the possibility of itself *qua* other. The contingent actual is thus grounded, not only in the possibility of its own identity, the positive sense, but also in the equal possibility of others, the negative sense. Hegel's solution to the formal problem (that there does not seem to be any way to actualize the "whole" possibility) begins precisely from this revision of immediate actuality as "contingent actuality."

Hegel's Solution to the Formal Problem: To Actualize Conditions Is to Actualize the Contrariety of Possibility As One Actuality

In the chapter titled "Actuality," the category of conditions does not obviously follow from immediate contingency.[32] Here, Hegel turns from contingency to formal necessity and from this to his theory of content-related modality. But in the "Actuality" passages of the *Encyclopedia Logic*,[33] we see Hegel directly deduce conditions from contingency. "[Contingency] is something-presupposed, whose immediate way of being is at the same time a possibility, and is destined to be sublated – i.e., to be the possibility of an other: the condition."[34] This step of his argument is particularly important, and it is misleading that Hegel does not emphasize it more. By turning from formal contingency to conditions, Hegel begins to explain how to think of an immediate actuality as itself and possibility. The transition begins from the initial recognition that in actuality something cannot both be and not be, but secures from this an actuality that is both itself and possibility, not in the limited sense of disjunction, but in the full sense, that something is both itself and its other.

Conditions are immediate actualities that get used up in the process of actualization. He states this in the addition of §146: "Immediate actuality as such is quite generally not what it ought to be; on the contrary, it is a finite actuality, inwardly fractured, and its destination is to be used up."[35] These actualities are not just themselves. They are the window onto other actuals. Material conditions are the medium from which something initial results in the actuality of something. This means that each condition is *both* actuality and possibility. Each is actuality in the sense that each is immediately given as the fact of existence. For example, a stone is a condition for something else, but it is also immediately actual and first appears as the earth itself. And yet each condition is also possibility in the sense that each has latent within it the result of further actualities. The stone is given as prior, yet carries within its content the further possibility of the statue (and of various other possibilities as well).[36]

Hegel sometimes describes conditions as "material" but Béatrice Longuenesse suggests that conditions can also be "spiritual." By "spiritual" she means historical, economic, social, geographic, and climatic conditions.[37] Hegel probably does not mean to exclude these strictly non-material versions of conditions. By "conditions" Hegel includes anything necessary for the mediated actualization of something initial into something actual, whether this is strictly "material" (e.g., stone, wood, blood, etc.) or "spiritual" (e.g., the disposition of mutual respect, the conditions for an economic boon, the deed to build a house, the license to drive a car, etc.). Prior to resolving themselves in actuality, each condition is similar to unformed (or semi-formed) matter, in the sense that unformed matter holds the possibilities of formed matter within it. Certainly, each condition is an immediate actuality on its own, and in this sense already contains order and form (e.g., the stone itself is form, not just the matter of the house), but in as much as each condition is the possibility of another, each appears first as materiality and then becomes the formation of others as the result of actuality.

There are also other complications that arise when we think of possibility as standing latent in the conditions. First of all, it would seem that not any possibility stands latent in the conditions, but only certain possibilities entailing certain actualities. The stone has its end in the resulting statue. It can also be "used up" in the actuality of the house or in the cobble of the street. But since the stone does not have within it the latent possibility of many other actualities (e.g., an elephant, a glass window, etc.), it would seem that the entailment from possibility to actuality can result in only certain actualities, only those which already exist latently in the conditions.[38]

Another complication arises from the multiplicity of conditions. Although each condition has a multiplicity of possibilities existing within it, it would be a contradiction to actualize everything that a condition could become.[39] While the log of wood has all sorts of possibilities latent within it, from the fire in the furnace to the shingles on the house, only one or the other of these can become actual. This is why Hegel emphasizes that conditions "go under" when the actuality "comes forth." If the fire were to become actual from the latent possibility in the wood, it would literally burn the wood to dust. While the shingles of the house still hold within them the real possibility of the fire, only one or the other of these can remain. If the fire takes the shingles, this is because it has burned the wood out of them and destroyed the form that they had become.[40]

Although these complications pose further issues for his theory, Hegel nevertheless finds the solution to the formal problematic in conditions because conditions are both actuality and possibility, and insofar as they are possibility, they entail other actuals. Formally, possibility does not entail actuality because actualization cannot take up the contraries of possibility into one actuality. But if immediate formal actualities are the conditions for the possibilities of others, these actualities are really possibility, and as possibility, they directly entail actuality. Hegel's point then stands in stark opposition to the axiom of possibility as modal logicians describe it. Certainly, actuality entails possibility in the sense that if something is actual, it must be possible, but possibility also entails actuality in the sense that what is immediately actual is the possibility of other actuals.

Hegel thus proposes a different model of actualization than the initial formal model, wherein one or another possibility becomes actual while all contrary possibilities are removed. In the conditions model of actualization, contrary possibilities are no longer removed but rather propel the immediate actuality to develop into the actuality of others. This propulsion is what Hegel calls relative necessity.[41] B must follow necessarily if we suppose the contingent content of A. While it might seem that a contingent actuality is only itself and not others, Hegel proposes that immediate actuality is only itself insofar as it is a condition for the possibility of others. The seed in the soil, after all, is just the seed. But because the seed is contingent, it is really the possibility of other actuals. Its existence is a material condition for the bird who eats it or for the tree that grows from it.

While the condition is the unit that mediates between actuality and possibility and entails each category in the other, this entailment is itself necessity. The process of mediation, where the possible equally entails the actual, requires the work of re-organizing the content so that something initial can become itself in others. In this sense, to be a "condition" is to be a "conditional." If there are conditions, then something initial *must conform* to the determinateness of other actuals, which at first remain stubbornly "outside" of the circle as raw exteriority, and only get "used up" if all conditions become present. This process of material actualization is the process by which something comes to adapt to the distinct circumstances with which it stands connected, on the one hand, turning itself into something that can accept the conditions, on the other hand, reshaping the conditions to make the parts harmonious at the point of actualization.

Hegel's theory would be uncontroversial enough if his conclusion were merely that these immediate actualities are really possibilities that necessarily entail *other* actuals. The developed actuality would be a new distinct actuality grown out of the conditions. One could then visualize from this a successive pattern of entailment. Immediate actualities would lead to further actuals, which in turn would be the conditions for the possibility of even further actuals, and on and on. While this result is interesting on its own, Hegel comes to a more controversial conclusion. He claims that when something makes its possibilities completely present, what emerges from this is not an entirely new actuality per se, but an actuality that is explicitly itself *and possibility*. This conclusion is quite unusual because it goes against that intuitive assumption, which forms the basis of most common-sense conceptual analyses of modality, that actualization must limit the contrary nature of possibility, where some limited actuality emerges at the expense of alternative possibilities. If Hegel's claim were only that something new results from the actualization of conditions, although this would lead to a more complex version of the formal problematic, it would not of itself be the solution to this problem. But Hegel is claiming that what results from conditional actualization is something that is *both* itself and its other. He is claiming that the actualization now sustains the "whole" possibility with the negative intact, that is, the possible *qua* the possible.

To understand how this process works, we will need to examine Hegel's theory of conditional actualization in more detail. In particular, we will need to explain his argument that what emerges from the actualization of conditions is not only a new distinct actuality, but also *the same actuality throughout*. What results from this process of actualization is the same actuality from which we began, but one that has digested the exteriority of its other, one that has, equally, become the other of itself.

In § 148 of *the Encyclopedia Logic*, Hegel divides conditions into three moments (in the *Lectures on Logic*, he calls these the three moments of necessity):[42] (1) conditions, (2) the thing, and (3) activity.[43] The conditions (*die Bedingung*) are the material requirements, the immediate actualities, that get used up in the process of the actualization. These actualities begin as external limitations that stand against the actualization, but if they are consumed, they contribute to the constitution of the developed actuality. The thing (*die Sache*[44]) is the initial possibility of what could become actuality. It represents the entire process that there is something initial which has the possibility, if it satisfies its conditions, of coming forth into actuality. And third, the activity (*die Tätigkeit*) is the agency or movement that uses up the passive conditions at the point of material actualization.[45] There is also, in a sense, a fourth moment, which Hegel describes in §147 as the developed actuality (*die entwickelte Wirklichkeit*). This is the final result, but also the complete reality, of the thing.[46]

Typical of Hegel, the definitions on their own do not adequately explain the dialectical movement of material actualization. From these definitions, we might assume a linear, distinct set of processes, from the possibilities in the seed, for example, to the actuality in the tree. But Hegel claims that these moments are not only distinct from each other, but each also posits all of the others as its own function in the process. Although each moment is itself an immediate actuality, each moment is also the complete process of the actualization. The water that happens to exist in the soil of the forest is on its own an immediate actuality. But it is equally a necessary condition for the possibility of the tree growing out of the seed. The thing in question also begins as a merely contingent possibility, which exists only in the hypothetical sense. But if all conditions were to come into play, the merely hypothetical thing in question would necessarily become actual. The hypothetical thing in question is equally the complete process of the actualization, not only the mere contingent starting point, but also the actualization that follows necessarily from this starting point. Hegel emphasizes that even the activity begins as an immediate, contingent actuality, e.g., a person, a character, or a disposition towards growth. But because the activity is also one of the conditions for the possibility of actualization, it is equally consumed in this process as the developed actuality emerges.

On the one hand, what emerges is the same actuality throughout. The thing in question has merely become itself. The tree has merely realized its possibility in the seed. The revolution has festered from social conditions that were already in place. But on the other hand, the developed actuality is something that none of the moments alone could complete, and which even the aggregate of the moments does not properly expose. The developed actuality is in this sense the actualization into an other, but this is equally the actualization into oneself. One indication of this is that the conditions vanish as the actuality develops from them. While they initially stand against the thing in question, as an external requirement that must be overcome, the conditions are consumed at the point of actualization; their possibility is released from their necessity; their exteriority becomes one with the interiority of the resulting actual.

This is not only a case of turning what is unlike into what is like. It is also a case of how to think of something as the other of itself. When the doe drinks the water from the forest, she digests the other. She makes it what she is. The water begins as an external contingent actuality. But it is not only this. It is also the possibility of the doe. And the doe is not only this. When she digests the water, not only does she turn this into what she is (i.e., the "water" turns into "doe"), but she also continues to be herself only in this transformation. She sustains herself in the contraries of possibility. By taking up the possibilities of her conditions, which exist dispersed in others, the doe becomes the other that she is.

This is why Hegel says that from the completion of the conditions, "the something is ... determined as being equally actual as possible." The actual that results from the actualization of conditions is not a new distinct actuality emerging against the background of many contrary possibilities. Nor is it an actuality that entirely succeeds the initial actuality of its conditions.

What results is rather an actuality that is both itself and possibility. Hegel calls this substance. "This *identity of being with itself* in its negation is now *substance*. It is this unity as *in its negation*."[47]

Substance requires us to think from the terms of a third model of actualization. From this model, what is actualized is the absolute conversion of actuality and possibility into each other, an actuality that completely sustains itself in possibility, one that turns its other into what it is, but only by becoming the other of itself.[48] Take again, for example, the doe drinking water in the forest. What the absolute model of actualization shows is that she is at one and the same time both existence and essence. She is *this* individual doe who is at *this* particular moment drinking water at the pond. But she is also *a* doe. She is the embodiment not only of her immediate existing actuality, but also of all possibilities of her essence. Since she is *a* doe, she is both always determinate (always in the forest, or on the hill, or in the pasture, always here or there) and yet also free from the limitations of her determinateness (her being in the forest does not exclude the possibilities of contraries in her essence.) She is free determinateness because her individual existence as *this* doe is at the same time the totality of her possibilities as her essence.

By the absolute conversion of actuality and possibility, Hegel means even more than the metaphor of a gateway between actuality and possibility. Whereas in the conditional model, the conversion of actuality and possibility into each other is only implicit since the possibilities of one thing exist only dispersed in the actualities of others, Hegel's subsequent discussion of absolute modality and his subsequent chapter "the Absolute Relation" presents the total, explicit conversion of actuality and possibility into each other, where the possibilities that seemed to be dispersed in others turn out to be one's own, and where the actualization turns out to be self-actualization. The absolute model of actualization goes further than the conditional model because it explains how to think the absolute conversion of actuality and possibility. Insofar as each individual substance is both existence and essence at the same time, each is the absolute conversion of actuality into possibility and of possibility into actuality. This model of actualization, which passes through the actualization of conditions, requires thought to recognize an actuality that is the "whole" possibility, and to establish from this the contrariety of possibility as irreducible to contradiction.

It is this irreducible relation that Deleuze also has in mind when he finds in Leibniz's theory of "incompossibility" a solution to the problem of how to actualize possible contraries without reducing these to contradiction. Deleuze proposes that the law of identity and the law of non-contradiction are merely derivative principles, derived from incompossibility, and that this origin prior to contradiction affirms difference and lets contraries coexist without exclusionary disjunction. He says this in *the Logic of Sense* when he writes: "The notion of Incompossibility is not reducible to the notion of contradiction. Rather, in a certain way, contradiction is derived from Incompossibility."[49] He also says this in *the Fold* when he describes the original relation as "vice-diction" rather than contradiction: "Between the two worlds there exists a relation other than one of contradiction ... It is vice-diction, not contradiction."[50] Hegel's theory of conditions initiates a similar relation. Conditional actualization exposes actuality and possibility as transitional categories. Actuality and possibility pass over into each other. This relation expands actuality, on the one hand, to include otherwise contrary possibilities, but also revises the category of unactualized possibility and lifts it to the status of concrete existence. While this relation remains implicit at the level of conditions, the same relation becomes explicit at the level of substance, as the absolute conversion of actuality and possibility into each other.

NOTES

1 Book 2, section 3, chapter 2 of G.W.F. Hegel, *Hegel's Science of Logic*, trans. A.V. Miller (Amherst, New York: Humanity Books, 1969), 542–53; Hegel, *Werke in zwanzig Bänden, 6: Wissenschaft der Logik II* (Frankfurt am Main: Suhrkamp Verlag, 1969), 202–17. Hereafter cited as SL/WL, followed by the English/German pagination. Unless otherwise noted, I have used Miller's translation of SL and Geraets, Suchting, and Harris' translation of *The Encyclopaedia Logic* throughout.

2 See, for example, John W. Burbidge's *Hegel's Systematic Contingency* (New York: Palgrave Macmillan, 2007).

3 G.W.F. Hegel, *Elements of the Philosophy of Right*, trans. H.B. Nisbet (Cambridge: Cambridge University Press, 1991), 20.

4 For a more complete analysis of Hegel's arguments in the "Actuality" chapter and their relation to Hegel's corpus generally, see my other work: Nahum Brown, *Hegel on Possibility: Dialectics, Contradiction, and Modality,* (London: Bloomsbury, 2020); Nahum Brown, *Hegel's Actuality Chapter of the* Science of Logic*: A Commentary,* (Lanham: Lexington Books, 2018); and Nahum Brown, "Indeterminacy, Modality, Dialectics: Hegel on the Possibility *Not to Be*" in *The Significance of Indeterminacy: Perspectives from Asian and Continental Philosophy,* eds. Robert Scott and Gregory S. Moss (London: Routledge, 2018).

5 Gilles Deleuze, *The Fold: Leibniz and the Baroque,* trans. Tom Conley (Minneapolis: University of Minnesota Press, 1993), 59.

6 For my related discussion of perfection in Leibniz and Hegel, see "Transcendent and Immanent Conceptions of Perfection in Leibniz and Hegel" in Nahum Brown and William Franke (eds.), *Transcendence, Immanence, and Intercultural Philosophy.* (Cham, Switzerland: Palgrave Macmillan, 2016), 183–205.

7 Excellent commentaries have been written about Hegel's "Actuality" chapter. For example, Herbert Marcuse's *Hegel's Ontology and the Theory of Historicity,* trans. Seyla Benhabib (Cambridge, Massachusetts: MIT Press, 1987) and Dieter Henrich's "Hegels Theorie über den Zufall" in *Hegel im Kontext* (Frankfurt: Suhrkamp, 1971) are pioneering contributions that have prompted further lines of investigation. The analyses of Hegel's argument that I have found most compelling include: Jay Lampert's "Hegel on Contingency, or, Fluidity And Multiplicity," *Bulletin of the Hegel Society of Great Britain* 51–2, (2005): 74–82; Burbidge's *Hegel's Systematic Contingency*; Stephen Houlgate's "Necessity and Contingency in Hegel's *Science of Logic,*" *The Owl of Minerva* 27.1, (1995): 37–49; George di Giovanni's "The Category of Contingency in the Hegelian Logic" in *Art and Logic in Hegel's Philosophy,* ed. Warren E. Steinkraus (New Jersey: Humanities Press, 1980); and Béatrice Longuenesse's *Hegel's Critique of Metaphysics,* trans. Nicole J. Simek (Cambridge, United Kingdom: Cambridge University Press, 2007), originally published in 1981 in French as *Hegel et la Critique de la Métaphysique.* I have also consulted more recent studies: Karen Ng's "Hegel's Logic of Actuality," *Review of Metaphysics* 63.1, (2009): 139–72; Christopher Yeomans's *Freedom and Reflection: Hegel and the Logic of Agency* (Oxford: Oxford University Press, 2012); and Franz Knappik's "Hegel's modal argument against Spinozism. An interpretation of the chapter 'Actuality' in the *Science of Logic,*" *Hegel Bulletin,* 36/1 (2015): 53–79.

8 Lampert, "Hegel on Contingency, or, Fluidity and Multiplicity," 77.

9 Lampert, "Hegel on Contingency, or, Fluidity and Multiplicity," 75.

10 Houlgate, "Necessity and Contingency," 43.

11 Burbidge, *Hegel's Systematic Contingency*, 34–7.

12 Longuenesse, *Hegel's Critique of Metaphysics*, 132.

13 Ng, "Hegel's Logic of Actuality," 11.

14 Taylor, *Hegel*, 284.

15 Marcuse, *Hegel's Ontology*, 96.

16 Burbidge explains this in "The Necessity of Contingency" chapter when he writes: "[t]hat the actual incorporates the possible specifies its difference from the apparently synonymous terms: 'being' and 'existence'." *Hegel's Systematic Contingency*, 17.

17 "[Actuality] is only in this form-determination but not as the totality of form." SL, 542/WL, 202.

18 "In the sense of this formal possibility *everything is possible that is not self-contradictory*." SL, 543/WL, 203.

19 It is important at this point in Hegel's argument not to conflate the negative moment of possibility with impossibility. Aristotle anticipates the conflation of the "can not be" and the "cannot be" in *De Interpretatione* when he explains that the opposite of "it is possible for something to be" is not "it is possible for something not to be," but rather "it is not possible (impossible) for something to be." Aristotle, *Complete Works of Aristotle: The Revised Oxford Translation*. Edited by J. Barnes. 2 vols. Bollingen Series (Princeton, New Jersey: Princeton University Press, 1983), 34–5 (21a34–22a12).

20 Robert Frost, *Mountain Interval* (New York: Henry Holt and Company, 1916), 9.

21 This might seem like a false disjunction in the sense that Frost could just as well not go down either road at all. But this objection is easily overcome when we remember that the negation of going down any road at all can also be an actuality that excludes other possibilities (i.e. going down a road at all). The point remains that actualization requires the simultaneous removal of excess possibility. This divergence and exclusion of the possible is part of the nature of modal reality.

22 "Consciousness … can only find as a present reality the *grave* [*das Grab*] of its life. But because this grave is itself an *actual experience* and it is contrary to the nature of what actually exists to afford a lasting possession, the presence of that grave, too, is merely the struggle of an enterprise doomed to failure. But having learned from experience that *the grave* of its *actual* unchangeable Being has *no actuality*, that the *vanished individuality*, because it has vanished, is not the true individuality, consciousness will abandon its quest for the unchangeable individuality as an *actual* existence, or will stop trying to hold on to what has vanished. Only then is it capable of finding individuality in its genuine or universal form." Hegel,

Phenomenology of Spirit, trans. A.V. Miller. (Oxford: Oxford University Press, 1977), 132; Hegel, *Phänomenologie des Geistes*, 126.

23 For an account of how contradiction can lead to death for Hegel, see Lampert, "Speed, Impact, and Fluidity at the Barrier between Life and Death," 145–56.

24 "Hegel is saying that conceptually, possibilities arise from actualities, and not vice versa." Burbidge, *Hegel's Systematic Contingency*, 17. We can anticipate from Burbidge's commentary why Hegel would begin his argument with the immediacy of actuality, and why he would reject Kant's starting point in the "Postulates" for beginning with possibility. For an explanation of why Hegel would reject Kant for beginning from possibility rather than actuality, see Longuenesse, *Hegel's Critique of Metaphysics*, 121. For Kant's theory of modality, see Immanuel Kant, *Critique of Pure Reason*, trans. Paul Guyer and Allen W. Wood (Cambridge, UK: Cambridge University Press, 1998), A218/B266- A235/B287.

25 "Everything is possible … Therefore everything is just as much something contradictory and therefore impossible." SL, 543/WL, 203. This is a paradoxical-looking passage from Hegel. However, many commentators have made reasonable sense of it. Burbidge distinguishes between particularity and universality: "The term 'everything' includes within its range a large number of distinct possibilities, some of which will contradict others. There is thus a sense in which *every*thing – stressing the universality of 'every' – is not possible." *Hegel's Systematic Contingency*, 19. Also see Longuenesse's claim that this controversy leads Hegel beyond the initial definition of possibility as the mere principle of identity to a definition of possibility that introduces contradiction. Longuenesse, *Critique of Metaphysics*, 123–4.

26 Aristotle, *The Complete Works*, 36 (23a18).

27 For an explanation of the "axiom of possibility," see Hughes and Cresswell. *An Introduction to Modal Logic* (London: Spottiswoode, Ballantyne and Co., 1968), 28. "If p, then possibly p" holds only in systems with reflexivity built into them, such as S4 and S5, but does not hold in systems such as K4, where the only frame condition is transitivity. Systems without reflexivity, such as K (no frame conditions), D (only the serial condition), and K4 (only the transitivity condition), cannot establish "if p, then possibly p" because there may not be access to the actual world. Fitting and Mendelsohn also discuss this in terms of the related necessity axiom, "if p is necessary, then p is actual." Fitting and Mendelsohn. *First-Order Modal Logic* (Dordrecht, Netherlands: Kluwer Academic Publishers, 1998), 9–10. "Once accessibility relations are brought in, this says that if P is true at every accessible possible world, then it is true at the real world. For this to remain valid, the real world must be accessible to itself … But

we could have defined the accessibility relation differently, so that the real world is not accessible to itself. In such a setting this formula is not valid."

28 "The contingent is an actual that at the same time is determined as merely possible, whose other or opposite equally is." SL, 545 / WL, 205.

29 "Everything possible has therefore in general a being or an existence." SL, 544 / WL, 205.

30 Hegel emphasizes how problematic it would be if every possibility *immediately entailed* itself in actuality: "any content, however absurd and nonsensical, can be viewed as possible. It is possible that the moon might fall upon the earth tonight; for the moon is a body separate from the earth – and may as well fall down upon it as a stone thrown into the air does. It is possible that the Sultan may become Pope; for, being a man, he may be converted to the Christian faith, may become a Catholic priest, and so on." *The Encyclopaedia Logic*, 216.

31 "[Actuality] immediately contains the in-itself or possibility. What is actual is possible." SL, 542 / WL, 202.

32 In the *Greater Logic*, Hegel has already discovered "Condition" as a division of the "Ground" chapter. See SL, 469–78 / WL, 113–23.

33 Hegel, *The Encyclopaedia Logic*, §142–8

34 Ibid., 219.

35 Hegel describes this process in the suggestive sense of "self-sacrifice." See Hegel, *The Encyclopaedia Logic*, 220.

36 For my related discussion of how Hegel's theory of conditions connects to the problem of incompossibility in Leibniz, see "Transcendent and Immanent Conceptions of Perfection in Leibniz and Hegel" in *Transcendence, Immanence, and Intercultural Philosophy*, 183–205.

37 See Longuenesse, *Hegel's Critique of Metaphysics*, 135.

38 Hegel acknowledges this complication when he discusses the problem of grounding conditions in prior causes. Although it would seem that each condition gives the reason for another, thought discovers from this the empty reflection that there is ultimately no reason why these conditions exist instead of others. Or thought falls into a vicious cycle of infinite regression, of reasons upon reasons upon reasons. We find Hegel's resolution of this complication in his argument that ultimately things supply their own sufficient reasons for the conditions from which they emerge. See SL, 552. For his discussion of infinite regress, see "The Determinate Relation of Causality," SL, 565.

39 Hegel acknowledges this complication in the real contradiction passages of the "Actuality" chapter. See SL, 548 / WL, 209.

40 There are of course various degrees of actualization. The shingles can become partly burned and remain partly intact.

41 SL, 549–50 / WL, 211.

42 G.W.F. Hegel, *Lectures on Logic*, trans. *Clark Butler* (Bloomington: Indiana University Press, 2008), 161.

43 Hegel, *The Encyclopaedia Logic*, 224–5.

44 Wallace translates *die Sache* as "the Fact," *The Logic of Hegel: Translated from the Enyclopedia of the Philosophical Sciences*, 272. Geraets, Suchting, and Harris translate this as "the matter [itself]," *The Encyclopeadia Logic*, 224. Butler, in *Lectures on Logic*, translates this as "the matter at hand," 162. I translate *die Sache* literally as "the thing" because I want to retain the connotation that when something emerges into actuality through the process of the conditions and the activity, this is nevertheless the same "thing" throughout.

45 Cf. Longuenesse, *Hegel's Critique of Metaphysics*, 151–2 and 160–2. She really emphasizes the role of "activity," dividing this into both agency (e.g., "a man, a character") but also the "movement" from conditions to the thing. She finds in this category the main point-of-transition from real necessity to absolute necessity, and from this into the concept. In her conclusion, she claims that "activity" is Hegel's development of the Kantian "I think."

46 Hegel, *The Encyclopaedia Logic*, 220–1.

47 SL, 553/ WL, 216.

48 In the subsequent section of the *Logic*, the "Relation of Substantiality," Hegel will call this relation of absolute conversion between actuality and possibility "actuosity" (*Actuosität*) (SL 556, WL, 220). Actuosity is a development upon the absolute conversion of actuality and possibility because it emphasizes not only the self-movement of substance, but also the tranquility of this movement.

49 Deleuze, *The Logic of Sense*, trans. Lester, Mark (New York: Columbia University Press, 1990), 111.

50 Deleuze, *The Fold*, 67.

REFERENCES

Aristotle. *Complete Works of Aristotle: The Revised Oxford Translation*. Edited by J. Barnes, 2 Vols. Bollingen Series. Princeton, NJ: Princeton University Press, 1983.

Brown, Nahum. "Transcendent and Immanent Conceptions of Perfection in Leibniz and Hegel." In *Transcendence, Immanence, and Intercultural Philosophy*, edited by Nahum Brown and William Franke. Cham, Switzerland: Palgrave Macmillan, 2016.

—— *Hegel's Actuality Chapter of the Science of Logic: A Commentary*. Lanham: Lexington Books, 2018a.

—— "Indeterminacy, Modality, Dialectics: Hegel on the Possibility Not to Be." In *The Significance of Indeterminacy: Perspectives From Asian and Continental*

Philosophy, edited by Robert Scott and Gregory S. Moss. London: Routledge, 2018b.

—— *Hegel on Possibility: Dialectics, Contradiction, and Modality*. London: Bloomsbury, 2020.

Burbidge, John W. *Hegel's Systematic Contingency*. New York: Palgrave Macmillan, 2007.

Deleuze, Gilles. *The Fold: Leibniz and the Baroque*. Translated by Tom Conley. Minneapolis: University of Minnesota Press, 1993.

—— *The Logic of Sense*. Translated by Mark Lester. New York: Columbia University Press, 1990.

Di Giovanni, George. "The Category of Contingency in the Hegelian Logic." In *Art and Logic in Hegel's Philosophy*, edited by Warren E. Steinkraus. New Jersey: Humanities Press, 1980.

Fitting, Melvin, and Richard L. Mendelsohn. *First-Order Modal Logic*. Dordrecht, Netherlands: Kluwer Academic Publishers, 1998.

Frost, Robert. *Mountain Interval*. New York: Henry Holt and Company, 1916.

Hegel, G.W.F. *The Logic of Hegel: Translated From the Enyclopedia of the Philosophical Sciences*. Translated by William Wallace. Oxford: The Clarendon Press, 1892.

—— *Science of Logic*. Translated by A.V. Miller. Amherst, New York: Humanity Books, 1969a.

—— *Werke in zwanzig Bänden, 6: Wissenschaft der Logik II*. Frankfurt am Main: Suhrkamp Verlag, 1969b.

—— *Phenomenology of Spirit*. Translated by A.V. Miller. Oxford: Oxford University Press, 1977.

—— *Elements of the Philosophy of Right*. Translated by H.B. Nisbet. Cambridge: Cambridge University Press, 1991a.

—— *The Encyclopeadia Logic*. Translated by T.F. Geraets, W.A. Suchting, and H.S. Harris. Indianapolis, Indiana: Hackett Publishing, 1991b.

—— *Lectures on Logic*. Translated by Clark Butler. Bloomington: Indiana University Press, 2008.

—— *The Science of Logic*. Translated by George Di Giovanni. Cambridge, United Kingdom: Cambridge University Press, 2010.

Henrich, Dieter. "Hegels Theorie über den Zufall." In *Hegel im Kontext*. Frankfurt: Suhrkamp, 1971.

Houlgate, Stephen. "Necessity and Contingency in Hegel's *Science of Logic*." *The Owl of Minerva* 27, no. 1 (1995): 37–49. DOI: 10.5840/owl199527122

Hughes, G.E., and M.J. Cresswell. *An Introduction to Modal Logic*. London: Spottiswoode, Ballantyne and Co., 1968.

Kant, Immanuel. *Critique of Pure Reason*. Translated by Paul Guyer and Allen W. Wood. Cambridge, UK: Cambridge University Press, 1998.

Knappik, Franz. "Hegel's Modal Argument Against Spinozism. An Interpretation of the Chapter 'Actuality' in the *Science of Logic*." *Hegel Bulletin* 36, no. 1 (2015): 53–79. DOI: 10.1017/hgl.2015.4

Lampert, Jay. "Hegel on Contingency, or, Fluidity and Multiplicity." *Bulletin of the Hegel Society of Great Britain* 51–52 (2005): 74–82. DOI: 10.1017/s0263523200002202

Longuenesse, Béatrice. *Hegel's Critique of Metaphysics*. Translated by Nicole J. Simek. Cambridge: Cambridge University Press, 2007.

Marcuse, Herbert. *Hegel's Ontology and the Theory of Historicity*. Translated by Seyla Benhabib. Cambridge, MA: MIT Press, 1987.

Ng, Karen. "Hegel's Logic of Actuality." *Review of Metaphysics* 63, no. 1 (2009): 139–72.

Taylor, Charles. *Hegel*. Cambridge, UK: Cambridge University Press, 1975.

Yeomans, Christopher. *Freedom and Reflection: Hegel and the Logic of Agency*. Oxford: Oxford University Press, 2012.

Phenomenological and Aesthetic Approaches to the Necessity of Freedom and Its History

6 Hegel on the Self-Fulfilment of Philosophy as the Opening of Human History

ALBERTO L. SIANI, UNIVERSITÀ DI PISA[1]

> Mortals can fathom many things once seen.
> But nobody, before he sees, can tell
> How he will fare in what is yet to come.
>   [Sophocles, *Ajax*, lines 1416–18]

The central thesis of this chapter, as the title suggests, is that, for Hegel, philosophy can and must, in his time, achieve self-fulfilment, and such fulfilment is the opening of human history. The chapter will unpack this claim in three parts. In the background of this claim are two famous sentences, dealt with closely in part 1 of this chapter. The sentences are found in the first pages of the preface to Hegel's *Phenomenology of Spirit*:

> "To help bring philosophy closer to the form of Science, to the goal where it can lay aside the title '*love* of knowing' and be *actual* knowing – that is what I have set myself to do [*vorgesetzt*]."[2]
>
> "Besides, it is not difficult to see that ours is a birth-time and a period of transition to a new era."[3]

These two sentences contain two very general statements. First, Hegel states his planned contribution to the self-fulfilment of philosophy – that is, to philosophy's becoming, in its scientific form, actual knowledge. Second, he identifies a transition to a new historical phase. As a first step, I give an interpretation of the former sentence that clarifies the sense of the latter (1.1). I then make explicit the link between them (1.2). In the two final sections of part 1, I critically address a widely accepted interpretation of the thesis of "the end of history"[4] and attempt to recover a viable version of it by investigating the task of scientific-actual, philosophical knowledge (1.3) and its impact on the conception of history (1.4).

After dealing with Hegel's programmatic formulation of the problem in the preface to the *Phenomenology* in part 1, I will, in part 2, summarize and systematize the results and raise some questions on the main conditions that a philosophy of history based on that program has to satisfy. In particular, I will maintain that such a philosophy of history has to leave substantial room for contingency and particularity, and at the same time has to enable the conceptual recognition of necessity (2). Based on this requirement, in the conclusive third part I will first comment on the transition from substance to subject in the *Science of Logic*, thereby outlining the space of contingency (3.1). Finally, I will substantiate the idea of this space by discussing a specific, yet emblematic case of how, in Hegel's philosophy of history, contingency is integrated into the knowledge of the actual (3.2).

1.1

The first sentence quoted above, in which Hegel expresses his general philosophical intention, can be read in at least two ways.[5] It could be interpreted as a mere polemical statement against contemporary anti-cognitivist[6] philosophers such as Jacobi and Schleiermacher, or as a more general and ambitious project of overcoming the erotic dimension that, from Socrates to Kant and beyond, is essential to philosophy – and therefore of finally transforming philosophy into "actual knowing" (*wirkliches Wissen*). These two interpretations are, in my opinion, not in conflict with each other, as I will now attempt to show.

As a starting point, I would like to focus on the cooperative dimension of the verb used by Hegel: "*Mitzuarbeiten*" (only partially translated by "to help" in the English edition). This immediately makes clear that Hegel is not willing to carry out an individualistic project, nor to develop a philosophical system based on a subjectively chosen principle (here we might see a polemical hint at Schelling's *Darstellung* meines *Systems der Philosophie* (my emphasis), or more generally at romantic, individualistically inspired projects). He is aiming, on the contrary, to participate in an epochal change of paradigm,[7] in a collective enterprise that does not depend on individual genius but on recognizing and seconding the need of the time. Hegel's philosophical intent responds to this need: a historical-spiritual necessity, a collective dimension in which the individual may take part only if he is first able to recognize it. Bringing the readers of the *Phenomenology* to this recognition is one of the goals of the work. The notorious obscurity of the *Phenomenology* is, then, not the result of arrogant linguistic and intellectual solipsism on Hegel's part; on the contrary, it stems from the necessity that the individual – the reader – come to recognize this necessity by himself, after passing through a "way of despair."[8] We could indeed call this an instance of Hegel's Socratic-maieutic method.

This brings us to a second consideration. For philosophy to be actual knowing it is necessary that it have the form of a scientific system: becoming such a system is the final goal of philosophy and, for Hegel, is a necessary process. He speaks of an external (historical-empirical) as well as of an internal (logical-systematic) necessity, which, he says, are bound to coincide in his own time, and through his own contribution.[9] This is not, however, a principle, a given starting point, of Hegel's reasoning, but rather its goal, the demonstration of which is the very task of the *Phenomenology*: "To show that now is the time for philosophy to be raised to the status of a Science would therefore be the only true justification of any effort that has this aim, for to do so would demonstrate the necessity of the aim, would indeed at the same time be the accomplishing of it."[10] It should also be noted that this does not imply that the previous philosophical systems were wrong in conceiving knowledge as an object of love and desire (this would be an utterly non-Hegelian thought); on the contrary, these systems led exactly to the point where the erotic conception of philosophy must surpass itself.

There is in Hegel's project, therefore, a continuity rather than a discontinuity with the former philosophical systems. The word *philo-sophia* houses a distancing between knowledge and its object, between knowledge and truth, and the pre-Hegelian philosophies have worked progressively at covering this distance, right up to the historical moment when – with Hegel – knowledge and truth are reconciled: the moment of absolute knowledge. Those philosophers, who at this moment refuse this reconciliation, understand this separation not as a coverable distance but as a structural rift that cannot be overcome by human reason. They therefore resort to different models (immediate intuition, religious representation, aesthetic experience, etc.). At this very moment, their conception of philosophy shows itself as non- or anti-cognitivist and, in Hegel's eyes, obsolete and anti-modern. For this reason, Hegel holds that they condemn philosophy to never become actual knowledge. Rather, the kind of knowledge, or the mental and spiritual attitude, reclaimed by the philosophers targeted by Hegel's polemic, are not able to effectively be in touch with the needs of the new era. Therefore, Hegel's goal of turning philosophy into actual knowledge, into *sophia*, entails not only this general philosophical intention, but also a critique of non-cognitivist positions: the coincidence of internal and external necessity shows that maintaining non-cognitivist positions is to be understood as a refusal to make the last step to the actuality of philosophical knowledge.[11]

A famous passage explains how that last step is to be taken according to Hegel: "In my view, which can be justified only by the exposition of the system itself, everything turns on grasping and expressing the True, not only as *Substance*, but equally as *Subject*."[12] In his use of the word *everything*, Hegel expresses both the plainness and the radicalness of his claim. In its plainness, it says: the True must be expressed as subject. This is all that is required to acknowledge the necessity of the transformation of philosophy into actual knowledge, and thereby to accomplish it. At the same time the radical claim is that there is no other way than this one. The claim of making philosophy actual, *wirklich*, can only be satisfied by showing that the time has come for understanding subjectivity as the very principle not only of philosophical investigation, but also of reality. Recognizing and accepting the necessity of the self-fulfilment of philosophy gives us the "*simple Concept* [*Begriff*]"[13] of the new time, but not yet its actuality. This is but the first stage of the development, which is then followed by a gradual "reconfiguration" of the living forms embedded in the new principle: "But the actuality of this simple whole consists in those various shapes and forms [*Gestaltungen*] which have become its moments, and which will now develop and take shape [*Gestaltung*] afresh, this time in their new element, in their newly acquired meaning."[14]

Science is not only the "the crown of a world of Spirit,"[15] but also the medium through which a new spiritual world becomes actual. Subjectivity is thus the principle that seeks itself in the time and space of modernity (taken in its broadest meaning, i.e., the European "Christian" world), then comes to itself when philosophy is able to recognize it (when inner and external necessity coincide), and eventually reconfigures itself in new shapes or embodiments. This is the core structure of Hegel's conception of the modern age.[16]

In these pages Hegel provides us with a sketch of the philosophy of history of the modern age that helps us to determine the task of science together with the actual need of the time. In the Middle Ages, "instead of dwelling in this world's presence, men looked beyond it, following this thread to an other-worldly presence, so to speak."[17] Afterwards, empirical philosophy (Francis Bacon, the scientific revolution, and the like) violently compelled the "spirit's eyes"[18] to the present world and kept it fixed there. Finally, in Hegel's time, "we seem to need just the opposite: sense is so fast rooted in earthly things that it requires just as much force to raise it."[19] If the Middle Ages acknowledged the divine and the universal contents to be in another world, and early modern empiricism focused only on the present world but did not concern itself with the divine, then the present task of philosophy and the great need of the time is to find and recognize the divine as immanent in the human world, and not as a transcendent essence. The task of the new era and of its science is, in other words, to actualize the universal. The self-fulfilment of philosophy as science – inseparable as it is from a diagnosis of the epoch, of its self-consciousness, and of its needs – is, thus, anything but a purely intellectual, time-independent enterprise.

1.2

Consequently, the fulfilment of philosophy and the birth of a new era come together. In this second step, the assumptions underlying this thesis must be made explicit. The core idea in this regard is that the True be conceived not as substance, but equally as subject. To be able to think the coincidence of subject and substance means nothing less than to be able to recognize that what was thought in the way of representation as a separate, transcendent divine essence is nothing but the inner core of human subjectivity. This is the central, decisive leitmotif of the rising new epoch.

The absolute as subject is the counterpart of the historical, political, spiritual need to take nothing that is positively given as absolutely valid. Overcoming the opposition of subject and substance implies thinking of the sphere of human practices, institutions, and history not as something independent of the subject as ruled or internally structured by transcendental forces, but as the field of action, knowledge, and decision of human subjectivity itself, with all of its power and limits – its contingent passions, its interests, its faults, and so on. A philosophy that takes nothing for granted and abandons any pre-determined certainty is the answer to the quest for freedom of the modern age. That is why human consciousness and self-consciousness are the starting point of the *Phenomenology*. This implies that "the True"[20] is no longer thought of as a static, immediately "posited," or original revelation, nor an absolute tautological identity, but as the dynamic result of a process of self-position, negation, and mediation – that is, as Spirit. (Incidentally, from this position there is no exegetical contradiction between "Science of the experience of consciousness" and "Phenomenology of spirit."[21] This point deserves, however, a much deeper discussion that there is room for here.)

The *Phenomenology* is needed in order to lead the non-philosophical consciousness to the point of absolute knowledge. Here, all the oppositions of natural consciousness and intellectual reasoning – subject/substance, subject/object, humanity/divinity, thinking/being – are overcome. In this way, the *Phenomenology* leads to the starting point of the *Science of Logic*. This process entails, as already noted, a radical act of scepticism and the inversion of natural beliefs. For us, readers of the work in our time, this may seem something foreseeable, even obvious, and not an inversion at all. But this was not the case for the readers of Hegel's own time to whom the work was directed. Of course, the Enlightenment, and especially Kant's Copernican revolution, had already put the subject in the foreground, but only at the high price of a dualistic conception that does not recognize the identity of subject and substance, but rather confines the latter to the realm of noumena: the thought of a being that cannot be part of our experience. On the contrary, the *Phenomenology* shows that all being is together also part of experience, and in order to do this elaborates a radically new notion of experience (*Erfahrung*), which allows the universal to be actualized.

The significance of the sentences quoted at the outset should now be clear: If philosophy remains only a *love* of knowledge and commits itself to a non-cognitivist approach, then the various dualisms of consciousness will not be overcome and, therefore, the quest for freedom that belongs to the new era cannot be satisfied. The principle of subjectivity, as the principle of the "new era," can find its fullest actuality only in and through philosophy as actual knowledge; in order to be true to its nature and to know itself, the spirit requires a scientific form.

1.3

Based on these results, I will now briefly work through two interconnected questions: First, what is the task of philosophical knowledge after it has come to its scientific configuration? And second, what are the implications of the fulfilment of philosophy for the conception of history? I address the first question in this section, and the second in 1.4.

In response to the first question, I suggest that, while Hegel clearly thought that he had, with his logic, given a definitive account of the pure form of thoughts and of the determination of beings, it does not follow that he thought he had given a definitive account of the empirical embodiments or shapes (*Gestaltungen*) in which subjective freedom is actualized. As many interpreters have already noted,[22] in Hegel's account there is nothing like a fixed human nature. Indeed, Hegel thought of history as the progress of freedom, which leads not to a fixed empirical human nature, but rather the opposite: it cannot be fixed, for human identity exists only as and in determining and constructing itself in different forms, and through giving accounts of why these particular forms count as authoritative. The peculiar form of modern European or Western identity lies in the necessity and capacity to give these accounts and in the commitment to them via reference to spiritual and cultural forms that owe their authoritativeness to their claim to be validated on the basis of a possible, but never certain, inter-subjective and rational reconstruction and recognition. If specific configurations of the actual cannot be conceptually and discursively reconstructed and defended, then they are not self-positions of the spirit-subject, and the destruction of untrue or obsolete configurations may be required. We may thus attribute to philosophy as actual knowledge the role of "controller" or "guarantor" of modernity.

In this regard, it is worth reminding that, of the four great works Hegel published in his life, only two are self-sufficient, namely the *Phenomenology* and the *Science of Logic*. Both the *Encyclopaedia* and the *Philosophy of Right* are lecture handbooks, intended to be explicated orally. Everyone familiar with Hegel's lectures is well acquainted with their work-in-progress character, and with the fact that they change from year to year as Hegel's knowledge and reflections on history, politics, religion, art and the rest also changed. The statement from the introduction to the *Science of Logic* denoting the content of logic as *"the exposition of God as he is in his eternal essence before the creation of nature and of a finite spirit"*[23] is not an exaltation of the pure power of eternal thought, but rather the assessment of its limitation, since a God without creation is not even able to know himself. The circular, closed nature of this system of logic does not exclude the linear, open character of history; rather they complement each other.[24]

More to my point, philosophy can never determine some ultimate characteristics of a fixed human or cultural nature, let alone prescriptively or deontologically set latter as a goal. The program of the *Phenomenology* is aimed at the dissolution of the claim to absoluteness of every given shape of the actuality. The principle of subjectivity remains actual only through the power to negate and reframe its own objective embodiments, not through the historical-empirical givenness of any of those individual embodiments, which are, in themselves, subject to contingency. To prevent a possible objection,[25] I must add that I am not claiming that the only era-appropriate form Hegel recognizes is a nihilist subjectivity constantly working at the destruction and transformation of objectivity. The subjectivity Hegel has in mind is and has to be concretized and embedded in the objective and cultural institutions of its time. The point is that those institutions are now to be understood as a product of subjective freedom; actuality is thus reconciled with human subjectivity. It would therefore be contradictory for subjectivity to constantly destroy its own embodiments in order to affirm its freedom. For modern subjectivity, this can only be the case when those embodiments *cannot* rationally be reconstructed as its own products anymore, or when they are latently or patently threatening the principle of subjective freedom. One may call this a pragmatist strategy or, more precisely, a "default and challenge model."[26] Subjective forms or attitudes nihilistically or narcissistically aiming at the pure destruction of the objectivity *qua* objectivity are just as much the target of philosophical critique as freedom-impairing objective forms, as Hegel's treatments of, for example, romantic irony, the beautiful soul, and abstract formalism both in the *Phenomenology* and the *Philosophy of Right* aptly show.

The dialectical nature of the relationship between forms of the subject and forms of the object becomes even clearer if we address a second possible objection, according to which Hegel's formulation of the embedment of the individual subject in the objective spirit leads to the irrelevance of the particularity of the former.[27] For Hegel, the embedment of the subject in specific objective forms does not imply the removal of difference. The very principle giving shape, actuality, and legitimation to those forms is the freedom of the subject, and Hegel's *Philosophy of Right* is very clear not only that the state has to respect the particular knowing and willing of the individuals, but also that it cannot achieve its universality without them. On the other hand, each particular individual has to recognize and act for the universal, through and beyond his own pursuit of particular goals: "The state is the actuality of concrete freedom ... The result is that the universal does not prevail or achieve completion except along with particular interests and through the cooperation of particular knowing and willing; and individuals likewise do not live as private persons for their own ends alone, but in the very act of willing these they will the universal for the sake of the universal, and their activity is consciously aimed at the universal end."[28] Individuals are not dissolved into the unity of the universal, and the unity of the universal is not dissolved into the infinite difference of the particular. On the contrary: "The principle of modern states has prodigious strength and depth because it allows the principle of subjectivity to progress to its culmination in the self-sufficient extreme of personal particularity, and yet at the same time brings it back to the substantial unity and so maintains this unity in the principle of subjectivity itself."[29]

There is hence a dialectical tension between forms of subjectivity and forms of objectivity, and between individual and universal, a tension that is healthy, unless it becomes extreme. There needs to be a balance, of which philosophy is, in the modern Western world, the central pillar, insofar as it works on reconciliation from both ends, with the awareness that the rationality of the actual is the result of free individual action within free universal institutions.

Herein lies the full actuality of philosophy as actual knowledge, based on the fact that "because ... substance is in itself or implicitly Subject, all content is its own reflection into itself."[30] This new form of knowledge does not impose from the outside some schema on the content, but goes deep into it, recognizing its inner necessity as a moment of the whole. The task of philosophy in its scientific form is, thus, to provide the space and the tools to reconcile subjective freedom with actuality, and to criticize the former and/or the latter insofar as they hinder the actualization of subjective freedom, and hence the possibility of reconciliation.

1.4

If this is the role of philosophy as actual knowledge, what are the implications for Hegel's philosophy of history, in particular insofar as the end of history is concerned? First of all, we must notice that there is, at least in this regard, a continuity between the view expressed in the *Phenomenology* and the one we find in the later Hegelian philosophy of history. Every reader of Hegel's lectures on the philosophy of history is aware that, for him, rationality plays but a small role in the actual decisions and actions of men: the making of history and the philosophical reading of it are situated on different levels that need to be kept well apart and not confused with each other. More precisely, rationality finds its place in the world, enabling us to interpret it beyond the heteronomy and heterogeneity of human behaviours, and, indeed, only by "exploiting" these behaviours (*List der Vernunft*). As a matter of fact, Hegel also speaks of *List* in the preface to the *Phenomenology*: "Science is not that idealism which replaced the dogmatism of assertion with a dogmatism of assurance, or a dogmatism of self-certainty. On the contrary, since [our] knowing sees the content return into its own inwardness, its activity is totally absorbed in the content, for it is the immanent self of the content; yet it has at the same time returned into itself, for it is pure self-identity in otherness. Thus it is the cunning [*List*] which, while seeming to abstain from activity, looks on and watches how determinateness, with its concrete life, just where it fancies it is pursuing its own self-preservation and particular interest, is in fact doing the very opposite, is an activity that results in its own dissolution, and makes itself a moment of the whole."[31]

Thus, the transition from substance to subject announced in the *Phenomenology* finds its actuality only in a process of coming-to-be, and never in a fixed form, which would imply the return to a static substantialist conception and the inhibition of the power of subjectivity. Scientific philosophical knowledge does not imply the end of history in the sense of the final, irrevocable triumph of certain objective forms and institutions, but rather the end of history's being subject to transcendent, not-fully-knowable forces. Of course, this means much more than a mere epistemic shift: it is nothing less than the actualization of the universal that we have seen to be need of the new era. The result is not the simple removal of contingency and of differences in reality, which would be Schelling's Absolute. As Hegel says, "the power of Spirit lies rather in remaining the self-same Spirit in its externalization [*Entäußerung*],"[32] and "knowing is this seeming inactivity which merely contemplates how what is differentiated spontaneously moves in its own self and returns into its unity."[33] The universal is actualized insofar as the subject finds himself in the otherness and is by himself within it: that is, is free. The subject is able to reconcile necessity and contingency by finding himself in otherness: the reconciliation is now immanent and not transcendent, the universal is actual, and not postponed to another world. Actual philosophical knowledge establishes the space and time of human history not by referring to some externally or individualistically given principle,[34] but by letting history be and by tracing the actualization of the "power of Spirit" within it. In the very moment in which it gives up the dualisms of subject and substance as well as of knowledge and truth, philosophy definitively renounces its claim to impose principles over history, because that would negate the absolute, infinite power of subjective freedom.

Thus, the end of philosophy, announced and carried out by the *Phenomenology*, does not have its counterpart in an end of history *à la* Fukuyama, but rather in the opening of truly human history – that is, history as the product of the freedom of the subject. At the same time, philosophy as actual knowledge provides us on the one hand with the insight that subjective freedom is not opposed to but in fact only actualized only through its becoming objective. On the other hand, philosophy provides us with the tools to criticize both subjective and objective forms that hinder freedom. Only such a form of knowledge is capable of recognizing and letting be the full value of contingency in human history, providing us with a dynamic view of the world in which no given "objective" shape is "absolute." (Here, one should take

Hegel's distinction of the two levels of spirit seriously). The admission and establishment of this space of contingency and the abdication of the claim to its philosophical determination is not the weakness, but the very strength of philosophy as actual knowledge. The change of paradigm of modernity, lying in grasping and expressing the substance always also as subject, is not accomplished once and for all together with the announcement and philosophical proof of its necessity. The latter makes up only the first stage of the new form of the world: its actuality consists in its embodiments or shapes, which are, however, not a philosophical product, but the playground of human agency.

2

My line of argument up to this point has shown:

1) That Hegel's general project of the self-fulfilment of philosophy is to be read as an answer to the actual need of the modern world, that is, the need to philosophically found and establish the principle of subjective freedom.
2) That the central idea of this project is an inversion of the common view of the True, which is now to be thought of and expressed not as substance, but also as subject.
3) That this idea implies the renunciation of every static and substantialist conception not only of philosophical knowledge, but also of the actual world and of human nature; therefore, this idea is incompatible with the assumption of a given form of reality as the ultimate actualization of freedom.

My aim in this section is quite modest. First, I will examine different patterns of conceiving history, showing why they are inadequate to the project of the *Phenomenology*. I will then outline what a pattern adequate to the latter should look like.

In order to draw a distinction between different patterns of conceiving history, I will start from the core issue of Hegel's project: the need to overcome the separation of subject and object and, subsequently, to overcome the separation of reality and idea. (I will henceforth refer to this separation with S).[35] Depending on how this core issue is dealt with, we may distinguish between three main patterns:

1) S has been overcome.
2) S has not yet been overcome, but can be overcome.
3) S cannot be (philosophically) overcome.

Based on inner differentiations, each of these patterns can then be further articulated in various sub-patterns, and identified with certain philosophical views, as I do below.[36] I use the non-Hegelian sub-patterns only as conceivable alternatives that are, nonetheless, bound to be ruled out as possible developments of Hegel's project. In presenting these alternatives, I do not, however, claim completeness or a precise historical reconstruction.

The alternatives I will deal with in this section, numbered according to the pattern they represent, are:

1.a)   Since S has been overcome, history has now ended, or at least it has ended in a particular geographical, cultural, and political context, in the sense that it has reached a stable, ultimate, objective shape (Kojève, Fukuyama).

1.b) S has been overcome, but this overcoming is only possible by thinking it dynamically and not statically. Even though, or more precisely, only because philosophy has come to its self-fulfilment, it is now possible to think of history as actual human history (Hegel).

2.a)   Hegel has provided the key for the overcoming of S, but he was not able to overcome S himself. Hence, we need to go past Hegel, radically reformulate his method, and project a conception that enables the material overcoming of S and of alienation (Young Hegelians, Marx, Marxists, partly the Frankfurt School).

2.b) S will be overcome in a final stage of history. A philosophically guided *Bildung*, and not the revolution of material conditions primarily, has to lead humanity to it. However, the overcoming of S is not conceived as a proper conciliation, but as a thorough, subject-based determination of the object. To this aim one should eventually resort to a complete "rational" determination of every aspect of the private and collective existence of human beings (e.g., Fichte's "closed state").

3.a) S is an essential feature of human existence. Human beings may only strive to the Idea or the Absolute in a movement of infinite approximation. The absolute cannot be reached philosophically and discursively, but only through other forms such as intellectual intuition, art and beauty, religious feeling, and so on. (Hölderlin, partly Schelling, partly the Romantic movement).

3.b)   The subject can never have full access to the object, neither theoretically nor practically. S is therefore to be thought of in the sense of a progressive, but never fully actualizable realization of a noumenal rational ideal. History can be thought of as an open progressive movement, but human beings can never achieve objective knowledge of its principle (Kant, the early Fichte).

Clearly, different conceptions of *S* imply different assumptions about the way history is to be conceived. It is thus useful to address these patterns (1.a and 1.b having already been dealt with) in order to clarify, *ex negativo*, which consequences are to be drawn from Hegel's assumptions about *S* with regard to his philosophy of history.

Pattern 2.a assumes that there exists an authentic human nature or essence but it is condemned to alienation, most remarkably under the conditions of the modern bourgeois state and capitalist economy. It also claims that (Hegelian) philosophy is not able to overcome alienation because it is in fact a product of the latter. Philosophy thus itself pleads for the overcoming of philosophy, or at least for its transformation into a more materially practical and effective form. Generally, this pattern assumes that *S* can be overcome, but in order to do so a revolution of the material-economic, political, and spiritual relations has to take place. Marx is a prominent example of this pattern, but not the only possible one: a religious eschatology might also have this form. Ultimately, though, this pattern is not adequate as a development of Hegel's project for a number of reasons, but especially because it: 1) refers to an essential human nature, of which the existent conditions in the modern era produce the alienated opposite; 2) assumes that alienation is not a structural component of modern life, but derives from precise material and spiritual conditions that have to be removed in order to reaffirm that essential human nature; and 3) declares modern philosophy a product of these alienated conditions, and thus something that needs to be overcome. To these, I suggest Hegel would refute: 1) there is no fixed human nature, and the modern world is the highest stage of freedom's actualization; 2) alienation is a structural component of modern life, at least in the practical-social sphere (in other words, objective spirit is *not* absolute spirit); and 3) only philosophy is fully able to deal with contradiction, even though this does not mean it can ultimately remove the latter from the empirical reality.

Pattern 2.b relies on a subjective ethical decisionism that may eventually justify a pedantic, closed, and authoritative state. This pattern is also incompatible with Hegel's project, as it both implies, at least in part, a predictive role for philosophy, and confounds the making of history with the philosophical reconstruction of it, thus resulting in a dogmatic view of the relation between reason and history.

Pattern 3, in both of its configurations, separates the levels of idea and reality. Even if this does not necessarily lead to that peculiar hypocritical inactivity described by Hegel towards the end of the Spirit chapter in the *Phenomenology*,[37] it still remains true that this pattern does not enable us to grasp the coincidence and overlapping of subject and substance but remains fundamentally dualistic. It is further inadequate in that it opens the way to a series of views that are simply incompatible with the principle of subjective freedom as the starting point of the new era and of philosophy together. Among these views, one can mention the attempt to avoid the limitations of discursive rationality by turning to a romantic genius – styled subjectivity, best embodied in non-philosophical forms and likely to result in nihilism, irrationalism, political and religious reactionism (as is partly the case in the Romantic movement and in Schelling). It is thus clear that a pattern claiming the insuperability of S is neither in itself nor in its results compatible with Hegel's idea of a rationally, cognitively, and intersubjectively founded and defensible, concrete free subjectivity. In other words, this pattern separates the finite subject and its knowledge from the objectivity of reason.

To summarize: there is, clearly, a close mutual dependence between Hegel's overall project to realize the self-fulfilment of philosophy, his view of modern subjectivity, and the fundamental features of his philosophy of history. His philosophy of history must rely on the principle of subjective freedom and satisfy the conditions posed by it. This is only possible if history is: 1) not thought of as concluded in a particular given empirical form, whatever this may be; 2) understood in terms of human activity, and not by referring to transcendent principles, independently of their origin (e.g., a transcendent god, a noumenal ideal of reason and so on); 3) conceived as a result of possibly conflicting human passions and interests, and not as a progression tending towards their complete removal and to a dogmatic over-determination of actuality through reason; and 4) conceived of in a way that leaves room for contingency and particularity, and at the same time enables the conceptual recognition of necessity (based on the overcoming of S and on the coincidence of the principle of reality and that of knowledge), in a sense that remains to be clarified.

These are therefore the main features of a philosophy of history based on the program of Hegel's *Phenomenology*. Whether and to what extent Hegel remained true to it in his later philosophy is an issue that cannot be exhaustively addressed within the limits of this chapter. However, I want, at least, to briefly touch upon two points related to this issue, especially in the context of point 4. First, in 3.1, I will comment on the transition from substance to subject in the *Science of Logic* in order to outline the space of contingency. Then, in 3.2, I will discuss a specific, yet emblematic case of how, in Hegel's philosophy of history, contingency is concretely integrated into the knowledge of the actual.[38]

3.1

In his groundbreaking study on Hegel's theory of contingency, Dieter Henrich strongly and convincingly contested a traditional view of Hegel's philosophy, according to which the latter, as a system of necessary determinations, did not leave any room for contingency, thus inevitably failing to deliver a satisfactory explanation of reality. Henrich showed, on the contrary, that the very systematic tendency to necessity does leave a fundamental space for a strong notion of contingency.[39] Further studies have developed this idea with different outcomes, but still defending the same core intuition: that contingency plays a fundamental role in Hegel's system, even though Hegel himself, admittedly, sometimes brings about the opposite impression. Defending the role of contingency in Hegel's philosophy further implies the claims that: 1) Hegel is not trying to logically deduce all particular aspects of reality; and that, therefore, 2) he does leave room for the contingency of the individual's planning and action within his philosophy of objective spirit.

The transition from substance to concept at the beginning of "Subjective Logic" is the systematic point in which the relationship between necessity and contingency, which up to that point had been implicit and abstract, becomes explicit and concrete. The core of this transition is the mediation of the concept with itself. This mediation is an immanent one – that is, it is not accomplished in an exterior way, but through the very power of negativity of the concept itself. Determinations thus become internalized: they are no longer something exterior, passively received by the substance, but rather are the positions of the concept itself. While determinations were something contingent for the substance, as they were not freely posited but were exterior to and limited by each other, in the concept they are now necessary. The concept does not disappear while positing the determinations, but "even when it posits itself in a determination, *remains* in it what it is. It is the *soul* of the concrete which it inhabits, unhindered and equal to itself in its manifoldness and diversity. It is not swept away in the *becoming* but *persists* undisturbed through it, endowed with the power of unalterable, undying self-preservation."[40]

In positing the determinations, the concept has to do only with itself: determinations are an immanent product of its freedom. The transition from the contingent to the necessary becomes "manifested." Necessity and freedom are bound together in the concept as the two perspectives of its immanent reflection: "In the *concept*, therefore, the kingdom of *freedom* is disclosed. The concept is free because the *identity that exists in and for itself* and constitutes the necessity of substance exists at the same time as sublated or as *positedness*, and this positedness, as self-referring, is that very identity."[41]

The becoming explicit or manifested of the determinations constitutes at the same time the genesis of the "I" – to be sure not the I of real philosophy, but the logical structure of subjectivity.[42] The concept, "when it has progressed to a concrete existence which is itself free, is none other than the 'I' or pure self-consciousness."[43] The subject, whose logical structure is engendered by the substance, is a result, not a presupposition. Hegel overcomes in this way both Spinoza's substantialism and Fichte's subjective voluntarism. Moreover, this genesis allows for the overcoming of two opposite points of view that would both compromise the strong role of contingency – namely, the views that everything is contingent (nominalism, or relativism) or necessary (hyperessentialism, or determinism). As a matter of fact, the conceptual structure is preserved in its position of the determinations: it identifies itself with them, but at the same time negates them. The concept is the source of the determinations, but at the same time it has the power to distance itself from them and be preserved as pure concept.

The sublation of contingency into necessity consists ultimately in the internalization and becoming-explicit or -manifest of the determinations through the free activity of the concept and of the subject. This does not mean, however, that the *Science of Logic* aims for a complete dissolution or sublation of nature's contingency into necessity. As a matter of fact, the contingency of nature is necessary for the freedom of the concept: "The concept is the absolute power precisely because it can let its difference go free in the shape of self-subsistent diversity, external necessity, accidentality, arbitrariness, opinion."[44] This passage is central for my argument. According to it, not only does the contingency of nature *not* contradict the freedom of the concept, but, on the contrary, it is the ground and the evidence of its absolute freedom and power. However, this is not because the concept imposes its determinations and necessity over the outer, accidental nature: "The universal is … *free* power; it is itself while reaching out to its other and embracing it, but without *doing violence* to it; on the contrary, it is at rest in its other as *in its own*. Just as it has been called free power, it could also be called *free love* and *boundless blessedness*, for it relates to *that which is distinct from it* as *to itself*; in it, it has returned to itself."[45]

The concept is free only insofar as it "exposes itself" and takes on the challenge of liberating its otherness as and into contingency, while preserving itself. Unlike Spinoza's substance (at least in Hegel's interpretation), the concept does not have any claim to self-sufficiency and to the complete correspondence of nature to its own determinations. The concept posits its own determinations, which are no longer exterior limitations to overcome and destroy. The concept is, therefore, free to act towards its other not in a violent, but in a free, loving way. At the real-philosophical level this means, according to my interpretation, that the freedom of the I respects, or even needs, contingency not only of nature but also of spiritual configurations insofar as they have a natural, exterior side. Moreover, it is only with the transition from the substance to the subject, required and prepared by the *Phenomenology of Spirit* and carried out in the *Science of Logic*, that an understanding of history that conciliates necessity and contingency becomes possible. As a result of this transition, contingency in its manifested form is shown to stem from the free activity of the subject, and not to disappear in it.

3.2

I now proceed to reflect on the shape taken by contingency in the philosophy of history. As I argued, contingency is not just an exterior substantial determination that disappears in the constitution of the subject, but an inherent determination of the free activity of the subject insofar as this is exercised in the external world. If the concept and the logical structure of subjectivity are to be understood as the negative power of both necessity and contingency, then, in a real-philosophical perspective, subjective freedom entails not only the faculty of sublating contingency into necessity but also its opposite. In a historical, no longer simply logical dimension, this means that something posited as necessary at a certain point in time can be recognized to be contingent at a later point of time.

To substantiate this thesis, I will make reference to a specific case in the philosophy of history: the relationship between state and (Christian) religion. I need to point out, first, that other examples could be made, and, second, that I am not interested in a discussion of this issue *qua* this issue, but only *qua* the real-philosophical instantiation of my argument on contingency. That is, I am not interested in either affirming or criticizing the plausibility of Hegel's argument in a historical or political-philosophical perspective, but only in showing the functioning of the logical structure of subjectivity (in which contingency plays a fundamental role) as it emerges in a specific case in the philosophy of history.

Christian religion is for Hegel, as it is known, a necessary moment of the historical progress of the consciousness and actualization of freedom, which has its most adequate embodiment in the modern state. However, the same solidly developed modern state, which is a result of this development including the necessity of Christian religion, can and should be so liberal as to consider a private and contingent matter the citizens' choice to belong to this or that institutionalized religion. Hegel claims that the state "should even require all its citizens to belong to a church – *any* [*irgendeiner*] church is all that can be said, since the state cannot interfere with the content of faith insofar as it depends on the inner realm of representation."[46]

Any is the keyword here. Christian religion, as we saw, makes up for Hegel the very transition point to modernity and to the establishment of the principle of subjective freedom and constitutes a necessary moment in world history. At a later point of time and from another perspective, however, this determination becomes accidental, based on the same principle that had made it necessary in the first place (subjective freedom), as it is no longer connected with a universal necessity, but with the private, contingent "inner realm of representation." It may be surprising at a first glance, but it is only consistent that Hegel's stance in this regard is a thoroughly liberal one: "A state which is strong because its organization is mature may be all the more liberal [*liberaler*] in this matter; it may entirely overlook individual details [of religious practice] which affect it, and may even tolerate communities (though, of course, all depends on their numbers) which on religious grounds decline to recognize even their direct duties to the state."[47] Affirming this contingency is an essential part of the modern conception of freedom: in modern societies, a specific religious belonging cannot be imposed. This case shows that, at the real-philosophical level, the ability to conceive and actualize the transition from necessity to contingency makes up a dimension as essential to subjective freedom as the ability to perform the opposite movement.

Freedom is thus grounded in the oscillation between self-reference and reference to other and between necessity and contingency. Subjective freedom as the power of negation is, indeed, this oscillation and not a unilateral progress from contingency to necessity. To be able to think as accidental what we assumed to be necessary also means to be able to question what currently exists and has a value, or what is "positive." The recognition of the necessity of contingency makes up a constitutive pillar of the individual right to critique. Thus, recognition of the role of contingency, subjective freedom, and individual right to critique belong together. As already remarked, one might believe that

Hegel only cares about the transition from the contingency of nature to the necessity of spiritual determinations and that he is not very eager to recognize the role of contingency (nor, for that matter, the right of individual critique). But I believe this has more to do with the specific – and contingent! – context of his philosophical-critical goals rather than with a fundamental incompatibility of his system with the recognition of the necessity of contingency.

In this regard, I want to close this section by quoting a largely neglected passage in which Hegel, while answering some observations by Göschel on the ineliminability of the representational dimension from religious experience and from philosophy of religion, matches "the transition in general *from the representation to the concept* and [the transition] *from the concept to the representation*." Science should not be indifferent to the "language of representation [*Sprache der Vorstellung*]" as this is "a different one from that of the concept, and men not only get to know things first of all with the names given by representation, but through these names they can in the first place feel alive and at home in the things." Strikingly enough, Hegel does not criticize this point of view; in fact, he explicitly apologizes for not having granted it a place in his works. By way of apology for the limits of his own work in this regard, he points out the fact that, especially in the beginning, a philosophical enterprise requires that we remain true to the pure concept in order to gain certainty about it. In this regard, the beginning (*Anfang*) of science requires that we "violently keep off the distractions provoked by the variety of representation and the form of contingency in the connection of its determination ... Once reached, the greater stability within the movement of the concept will allow to be less worried against the seduction of representation and to grant the latter more freedom under the dominion of the concept."[48]

This "liberal" attitude applies in parallel way to both the realms of knowledge and of politics. Once we are confident with the pure concept and able to deal with it scientifically, we might – and actually should – also perform the opposite movement, that is, from the concept and its necessity to the representation and its contingency, just like a solidly established rational state should be liberal with regard to the convictions (religious or other) of its citizens: it should be open to their contingency, and not impose a necessity.[49] The ability to perform this transition therefore makes up an essential component of the freedom of the subject, and of the (post-) philosophical opening of human history.

Patterns of the Separation (*S*) of Subject and Object and Its Overcoming in History (from section 2)

	A	B
1. *S* has been overcome	History has now ended, or at least it has in a particular geographical, cultural and political context (Kojève, Fukuyama).	S has been overcome, but this overcoming is only possible by thinking it dynamically and not statically. Right because philosophy has come to its self-fulfilment, it is now possible to think of history as actual human history (Hegel).
2. *S* has not been overcome yet, but can be overcome	Hegel has provided the key for the overcoming of *S*, but he was not able to overcome S himself. Hence we need to go past Hegel and to radically reformulate his method and project into a philosophical conception enabling the material overcoming of S and of alienation (Young Hegelians, Marx, Marxists, partly the Frankfurt School).	*S will* be overcome in a final stage of history. A philosophically guided *Bildung*, and not primarily the revolution of material conditions has to lead humanity to it. However, the overcoming of S is not conceived as a proper conciliation, but as a thorough subject-based determination of the object. To this aim one should eventually resort to a complete "rational" determination of every aspect of the human private and collective existence (Fichte's "closed state").
3. *S* cannot be overcome	S is an essential feature of human existence. Human beings may only strive to the Idea or the Absolute in a movement of infinite approximation. The absolute cannot be reached philosophically and discursively, but, under determinate conditions, only through other forms such as intellectual intuition, art and beauty, religious feeling etc. (Hölderlin, partly Schelling, partly the Romantic movement).	The subject can never have full access to the object, neither theoretically nor practically. Hence S is to be thought in the sense of a progressive, but never fully actualizable realization of a noumenal rational ideal. History can be thought of as an open progressive movement, but human beings can never achieve an objective knowledge of its principle (Kant, the early Fichte).

NOTES

1 This contribution grew out of my postdoctoral research project (2011–2013) at the Universität Münster, generously funded by the Alexander von Humboldt Stiftung to which I give thanks. I also thank Jim Devin

and Kay Rollans for the linguistic help, and Gianluca Garelli, Stephen Houlgate, Nadine Mooren, Michael Quante, Jeffrey Reid, Peter Rohs, Tim Rojek, and two anonymous reviewers for many precious comments. In the text body, I will give English translations of all quotations, referring the reader to the source of both the translation and the original German text (GW = *Gesammelte Werke*, in Verbindung mit der Deutschen Forschungsgemeinschaft herausgegeben von der Nordrhein-Westfälischen Akademie der Wissenschaften und der Künste. Hamburg: Meiner, 1968ff.) in the notes. In the twelve years passed between the first submission of this paper and its publication in this collected volume, I have presented some parts of it elsewhere, though never in this complete and systematic form. See, besides the works already quoted here, my chapters ""Freedom in the European sense": Hegel on Action, Heroes, and Europe's Philosophical Groundwork," in *Concepts of Normativity: Kant or Hegel?*, ed. Christian Krijnen (Leiden-Boston: Brill, 2019), 235–56; "Modern Philosophy and Philosophical Modernity: Hegel's Metaphilosophical Commitment," in *An Ethical Modernity? Hegel's Concept of Ethical Life Today*, ed. Jirí Chotaš and Tereza Matějčková (Leiden-Boston: Brill, 2020), pp. 191–203, and my book *Hegel and the Present of Art's Past Character* (New York: Routledge, 2024).

2 G.W.F. Hegel, *Phenomenology of Spirit*, ed. John Niemeyer, trans. Arnold V. Miller (Oxford: Oxford University Press, 1977), 3 / GW IX, 11.

3 Ibid., 6 / GW IX, 14.

4 See, paradigmatically, Francis Fukuyama, *The End of History and the Last Man* (New York: Free Press, 1992).

5 I have dealt more extensively with Hegel's *Vorsatz* in Alberto L. Siani, "Sapere, amore del sapere e fine della filosofia," in *Sostanza e soggetto. Studi sulla "Prefazione" alla* Fenomenologia dello spirito *di Hegel*, ed. Gianluca Garelli and Maurizio Pagano (Bologna: Pendragon, 2016), 133–53. There, I deepen the commentary presented here in sections 1.1 and 1.2, further clarifying Hegel's *Vorsatz* and his strategy to fulfil it, finally offering a deflationary reading of "absolute knowledge."

6 Cf. Michael Quante, *Einführung in die Allgemeine Ethik* (Darmstadt: Wissenschaftliche Buchgesellschaft, 2006), 40ff. See also Michael Quante, *Die Wirklichkeit des Geistes. Studien zu Hegel* (Frankfurt a. M.: Suhrkamp, 2011), 224f. I use the word *anti-cognitivist*, however, not in a primarily ethical sense, but with regard to the understanding of the way of access to the "absolute," the divine, and the highest principles.

7 Cf. Stephen Houlgate, *An Introduction to Hegel. Freedom, Truth and History* (Oxford: Blackwell, 2005), 7–8.

8 Hegel, *Phenomenology of Spirit*, 49 / GW IX, 56.

9 Cf. Ibid., 3 / GW IX, 11.

10 Ibid., 3–4 / GW IX, 11–12.

11 However, even these positions are, in Hegel's eyes, not to be considered
   as simple "mistakes" or regressions. Hegel's attitude towards Jacobi is
   particularly complex and multifaceted. As a matter of fact, Hegel does
   not only criticize Jacobi, but also credits him with the overcoming of
   Kantianism. See also Kenneth R. Westphal, "Hegel's Attitude toward
   Jacobi in the 'Third Attitude of Thought toward Objectivity' (Encyclopedia
   §§ 61–78)," *The Southern Journal of Philosophy* 27, no. 1 (1989): 135–56.
   I thank Jeffrey Reid for pointing out in a discussion the complexity of
   Hegel's attitude towards Jacobi.

12 Hegel, *Phenomenology of Spirit*, 9–10 / GW IX, 18. The translation here
   is quite problematic, as the word *only* is not to be found in the original
   Hegelian text.

13 Ibid., 7 / GW IX, 15, translation slightly modified.

14 Ibid.

15 Ibid.

16 With regard to this, see another famous Hegelian statement, this time
   from the *Philosophy of Right*, Annotation to §124: "The right of subjective
   freedom … is the pivot and centre of the difference between antiquity and
   modern times. This right in its infinity is given expression in Christianity
   and it has become the universal effective [*wirklichen*] principle of a new
   form of the world. Amongst the more specific shapes [*Gestaltungen*]
   which this right assumes are love, romanticism … moral convictions and
   conscience; and … the other forms, some of which come into prominence
   in what follows as the principle of civil society and as moments in the
   constitution of the state, while others appear in the course of history,
   particularly the history of art, science, and philosophy." (G.W.F. Hegel,
   Outlines of the Philosophy of Right, ed. Stephen Houlgate, trans. Thomas
   Malcolm Knox (Oxford: Oxford University Press, 2008), 122 / GW XIV.1,
   110.) Thus, the principle of subjectivity is announced in the world by
   Christianity and becomes the actual principle of the new world and the
   very core of all its shapes.

17 Hegel, *Phenomenology of Spirit*, 5 / GW IX, 13.

18 Ibid.

19 Ibid.

20 Ibid., 11 / GW IX, 19.

21 Cf. Werner Marx, *Hegels Phänomenologie des Geistes. Die Bestimmung ihrer
   Idee in "Vorrede" und "Einleitung"* (Frankfurt a. M.: Klostermann, 2006), 70.

22 Cf. esp. Terry Pinkard, *Hegel's Phenomenology. The Sociality of Reason*
   (Cambridge: Cambridge University Press, 1996), and Houlgate, *An
   Introduction to Hegel*, 12–18.

23 G.W.F. Hegel, *The Science of Logic*, ed. and trans. George di Giovanni
   (Cambridge: Cambridge University Press, 2010), 29 / GW XXI, 34.

24 See already Jean Hyppolite, "Anmerkungen zur Vorrede der
   Phänomenologie des Geistes und zum Thema: das Absolute ist Subjekt," in
   Materialien zu Hegels "Phänomenologie des Geistes," ed. Hans Friedrich Fulda
   and Dieter Henrich (Frankfurt a. M.: Suhrkamp, 1976), 47.

25 I thank Stephen Houlgate for pointing out this possible misreading of my
   thesis.

26 Cf. Quante, *Die Wirklichkeit des Geistes*, 295–7.

27 I thank an anonymous reviewer for suggesting this.

28 Hegel, *Outlines of the Philosophy of Right*, 235 / GW XIV.1, 208.

29 Ibid.

30 Hegel, *Phenomenology of Spirit*, 33 / GW IX, 39.

31 Ibid., 33 / GW IX, 39–40.

32 Ibid., 490 / GW IX, 431.

33 Ibid.

34 Hegel's philosophy is clearly anti-foundationalist and anti-individualistic
   in this sense. Cf. Dietmar H. Heidemann, "Substance, subject, system: the
   justification of science in Hegel's Phenomenology of Spirit," in *Hegel's
   Phenomenology of Spirit. A Critical Guide*, ed. Dean Moyar and Michael
   Quante (Cambridge: Cambridge University Press, 2008), 11–12.

35 Since I consider this distinction only according to Hegel's project itself, I
   will not need to deal with other patterns of the philosophy of history, as
   they are not relevant to my current topic.

36 See table at the end.

37 I thank Peter Rohs for making me notice the actual breadth of the
   Kantian presence, for example in the normative premises of the German
   Constitution and hence the factual falsity of the thesis of its ineffectuality.

38 In the first version of this paper, the conclusion was shorter, and the paper
   had a more interrogatory and preparatory character. I sketched the main
   lines of further research, thematizing the later development of the program
   of the *Phenomenology* in the *Logic* and the *Philosophy of History*, focusing on
   the issue of contingency. I have partly carried out that research in Alberto
   L. Siani, "Hegel's Logic and Narration of Contingency," *Revista Opinião
   Filosófica* 6, no.2 (2015): 8–27. The last part of the present version attempts
   to summarize some of the results presented in that article. See the article
   for further references.

39 See Dieter Henrich, "Hegels Theorie über den Zufall," in *Hegel im Kontext*
   (Frankfurt a. M.: Suhrkamp, 1971), 157–86.

40 Hegel, *The Science of Logic*, 531 / GW XII, 34.

41 Ibid., 513 / GW XII, 15–16.

42 See Christian Iber, "Hegels Konzeption des Begriffs," In *G.W.F. Hegel.
   Wissenschaft der Logik*, edited by Anton Friedrich Koch and Friedrike Schick
   (Berlin: Akademie, 2002), 184.

43 Hegel, *The Science of Logic*, 514 / GW XII, 17.
44 Ibid., 536 / GW XII, 39.
45 Ibid., 532 / GW XII, 35.
46 Hegel, *Outlines of the Philosophy of Right*, 246 / GW XIV.1, 216, translation slightly modified. See the whole Annotation to §270 in this regard.
47 Ibid. 246–7 / GW XIV.1, 216–17.
48 See the whole passage in G.W.F. Hegel, *Göschel-Rezension*, in GW XVI, 206–7.
49 It is clear, however, that for Hegel the relationship between concept and representation is not a symmetrical one, as philosophy can find its own form and contents in the form of religious representation, but not vice versa. In general, any attempt to outline a Hegelian standpoint on the reality that is alternative to the philosophical one has to acknowledge that, for Hegel, the truth of any alternative account is to be found in the philosophical concept, but not vice versa.

REFERENCES

Fukuyama, Francis. *The End of History and the Last Man*. New York: Free Press, 1992.

Hegel, G.W.F. *Phenomenology of Spirit*. Edited by John Niemeyer. Translated by Arnold V. Miller. Oxford: Oxford University Press, 1977.

—— *Outlines of the Philosophy of Right*. Edited by Stephen Houlgate. Translated by Thomas M. Knox. Oxford: Oxford University Press, 2008.

—— *The Science of Logic*. Translated by George di Giovanni. Cambridge: Cambridge University Press, 2010.

—— "Göschel-Rezension." In *Gesammelte Werke*, Band 16, edited by Christoph Jamme and Friedrich Hogemann, 188–215. Hamburg: Meiner, 2001.

Heidemann, Dietmar H. "Substance, Subject, System: The Justification of Science in Hegel's Phenomenology of Spirit." In *Hegel's Phenomenology of Spirit: A Critical Guide*, edited by Dean Moyar and Michael Quante, 1–20. Cambridge: Cambridge University Press, 2008.

Henrich, Dieter. "Hegels Theorie über den Zufall." In *Hegel im Kontext*, 157–86. Frankfurt a. M., 1971. First published in *Kant-Studien* 50 (1958/59).

Houlgate, Stephen. *An Introduction to Hegel: Freedom, Truth and History*. Oxford: Blackwell, 2005.

Hyppolite, Jean. "Anmerkungen zur Vorrede der Phänomenologie des Geistes und zum Thema: das Absolute ist Subjekt." In *Materialien zu Hegels "Phänomenologie des Geistes,"* edited by Hans Friedrich Fulda and Dieter Henrich, 45–53. Frankfurt a. M.: Suhrkamp, 1976.

Iber, Christian. "Hegels Konzeption des Begriffs." In *G.W.F. Hegel. Wissenschaft der Logik*, edited by Anton Friedrich Koch and Friedrike Schick, 181–201. Berlin: Akademie, 2002.

Marx, Werner. *Hegels Phänomenologie des Geistes. Die Bestimmung ihrer Idee in "Vorrede" und "Einleitung."* Frankfurt a. M.: Klostermann, 2006.

Pinkard, Terry. *Hegel's Phenomenology: The Sociality of Reason*. Cambridge: Cambridge University Press, 1996.

Quante, Michael. *Einführung in die Allgemeine Ethik*. Darmstadt: Wissenschaftliche Buchgesellschaft, 2006.

—— *Die Wirklichkeit des Geistes. Studien zu Hegel*. Frankfurt a. M.: Suhrkamp, 2011.

Siani, Alberto L. "Hegel's Logic and Narration of Contingency." *Revista Opinião Filosófica* 6, no. 2 (2015): 8–27.

—— "Sapere, amore del sapere e fine della filosofia." In *Sostanza e soggetto. Studi sulla "Prefazione" alla* Fenomenologia dello spirito *di Hegel*, edited by Gianluca Garelli and Maurizio Pagano, 133–53. Bologna: Pendragon, 2016.

Westphal, Kenneth R. "Hegel's Attitude toward Jacobi in the 'Third Attitude of Thought toward Objectivity' (Encyclopedia §§ 61–78)." *The Southern Journal of Philosophy* 27, no. 1 (1989): 135–56.

7 Organic Freedom: Hegel's Four-Way Dialectic

JENNIFER ANN BATES, DUQUESNE UNIVERSITY

Introduction

How are we to understand the frequent use of the word "organic" in Hegel's writings? For example, in the *Phenomenology of Spirit*, the "organic" development of moments over the history of philosophy is explained as the bud becoming the flower becoming the fruit;[1] and in the *Philosophy of Right*, Hegel refers to the organic nature of the State.[2] In what follows, I discuss what Hegel means by "organic," and then address how the "organic" is related to Hegel's conception of freedom.

I argue that we grasp Hegel's notion of organic freedom when we understanding his dialectic as a four-way dialectic of subject-object/unity-multiplicity; this dialectic shows how for Hegel the inorganic is part of the organic, and how Hegel's use the word "organic" – be it to describe philosophy or the State or even biological organisms – always exceeds merely literal and merely analogical meaning; accordingly, Hegel's organic freedom is a freedom from prosaic, mechanical language, for it engages in the liveliness of interpretation.

I. Organic Wholes

Let us begin with some examples of Hegelian "Organic" wholes that are not biological organisms in the normal sense.

Organic Wholes Are "Souls with Bodies," So to Speak

In the *Science of Logic*, Hegel explicitly states that the soul and body must be united, whether we are speaking of a human, or of the State, or of the Church, for when they are separated, we have inorganic, dead nature:

Wholes like the state and the church cease to exist when the unity of their Notion and their reality is dissolved; man, the living being, is dead when soul and body are parted in him; dead nature, the mechanical and chemical world – taking, that is, the dead world to mean the inorganic world, otherwise it would have no positive meaning at all – dead nature, then, if it is separated into its Notion and its reality, is nothing but the subjective abstraction of a thought form and a formless matter. *Spirit* that was not Idea, was not the unity of the Notion with its own self, or the Notion that did not have the Notion itself for its reality would be dead, spiritless spirit, a material object.[3]

If dead nature is the inorganic, then the unity of Notion and reality is the organic. Hegel writes:

That actual things are not congruous with the Idea is the side of their *finitude* and *untruth*, and in accordance with their various spheres and in the relationships of objectivity, either mechanically, chemically or by an external end … If an object, for example the state, *did not correspond at all* to its Idea, that is, if in fact it was not the Idea of the state at all, if its reality, which is the self-consciousness of individuals, did not correspond at all to the Notion, its soul and its body would have parted; the former would escape into the solitary regions of thought, the latter would have broken up into the single individualities. But because the Notion of the state so essentially constitutes the nature of these individualities, it is present in them as an urge so powerful that they are impelled to translate it into reality[.][4]

Finally, though obliquely, in Hegel's *Lectures on Aesthetics*:

the more Shakespeare proceeds to portray on the infinite breadth of his "world-stage" the extremes of evil and folly, all the more … does he precisely plunge his figures who dwell on these extremes into their restrictedness; of course he equips them with a wealth of poetry but he actually gives them spirit and imagination, and, by the picture in which they can contemplate and see themselves objectively like a work of art, he makes them free artists of their own selves.[5]

According to Hegel, the highest poetry is organic (and he considered Shakespearean drama an exemplary case[6]).

[T]he work of art confronts us in the form of something that appears in the real world, and therefore if the living reflection of the *actual* in the real is not to be jeopardized, the unity itself must be only the *inner* bond which holds the parts together, apparently unintentionally, and includes them in an organic whole. It is this soul-laden unity of an organic whole which alone, as contrasted with the prosaic category of means and end, can produce genuine poetry.[7]

Hegel's praise of how Shakespeare creates his characters highlights the relationship between "organic" and "free": for Hegel, something organic is a free, living *Gestalt*; it is not an abstract characterization. Accordingly, Hegel's project in the *Phenomenology of Spirit* is similar to what happens with Shakespearean dramatic characters. The *Phenomenology of Spirit* is a theatre of spirit. In the course of the book, Hegel is creating – educating, building (*bilden*) – his character; his character is the naïve natural consciousness of Sense-Certainty (and of his students), and his character's *Bildung* is to become a free artist of its own self. Consciousness (and his students) achieve this via its self-development in and through the way they mirror reality to themselves (thus Hegel, like Shakespeare "actually gives them spirit and imagination, and, by the picture in which they can contemplate and see themselves objectively like a work of art, he makes them free artists of their own selves"); the creation of 'absolute' character ("absolute knowing") occurs in and through *phenomenological* experience.

Admittedly, the sublating progress of that education is nonetheless different from Shakespeare's creation of his characters, by virtue of the variety of Shakespearean plots serving various dramatic ends; furthermore, unlike Hegel's students who plod through his book and experience each level, Shakespeare's characters do not all attain the same levels of self-awareness as Hegel's students, and most of Shakespeare's characters do not attain 'absolute knowing'.

But *in Shakespeare's art* in developing his characters, there is the same unifying, the same thinking-through, the same organicity that we see in Hegel's *Phenomenology*. Regardless of whether a naïve consciousness gets stuck in the "drama" of Sense-Certainty, or in the more advanced "stages" of spiritual contradiction (e.g., the Enlightenment's decline into Absolute Freedom and Terror), Hegel's book "character," like Shakespeare's characters, is *enacted*, embodied, alive.

The *final* freedom of Hegel's phenomenological character is the goal of conscious life in all of its phenomenological richness (artistic and otherwise). This is its real freedom. For Hegel, this freedom is organic, like the best in dramatic poetry. It is therefore not surprising that although the book is itself not a work of poetry, Hegel concludes it by citing a poem.[8]

With the exception of Prospero in his Epilogue[9] and a few others, Shakespeare's characters stay within the limits of their play. Hegel's conscious spirits, once they reach absolute knowing, exist on the world stage. True, they are inward turned in the sense that they recollect their dramas in a "gallery of images," comprehending the necessity of their prior "acts" while being liberated from them. But Hegel's consciousnesses' complete freedom takes place in nature and society: his readers, he tells us, release themselves into "the free play of contingency," assured of the continual birth and education of new generations in Spirit's "buildings."[10]

According to Hegel, a thus accomplished absolute knower can then return to the first "Act" of Sense-Certainty with the depth of the dialectical substance comprehended in the expression "I am here now," or she can move onto logical science (thoughts thinking, behind the "scenes"). In the latter case, what was organically developed in the *Phenomenology of Spirit* is freely released into the organic logical method of Speculative Science.

The Organic Method and Movement of Speculative Science: Not Merely Analogical

In the *Phenomenology of Spirit*, the *movement* of the Notion, and the *method* of philosophy which comprehends that movement are each organic: the former is the sublational process of consciousness' education (a process of revealing in ways not expected), the latter is the speculative logic of that education (it is sublational too, but in a way in which the alienation of externality and contradiction are expected). Hegel's accounts of the movement, and logical method, pitches "life" explicitly against death. For example, Hegel contrasts his philosophical method, which he calls organic, with mathematics, whose methods are inorganic and paralysing. Mathematical methods grasp "lifeless" quantities and cannot cope with the "sheer unrest of life and its absolute distinction."[11] By contrast, Hegel writes of the general movement of the dialectical method as follows: "This movement of pure essences constitutes the nature of scientific method in general. Regarded as the connectedness of their content it is the necessary expansion of that content into an organic whole."[12]

The logical centre of the organic *movement* of the Notion is contradiction (a point discussed by Songsuk Susan Hahn[13]). Hegel claims that "contradiction is the root of all movement and vitality;"[14] "[o]nly when the manifold terms have been driven to the point of contradiction do they become active and lively towards one another, receiving in contradiction the negativity which is the indwelling pulsation of self-movement and spontaneous activity [*Lebendigkeit*]."[15]

According to Hegel, Speculative Science is substance and subject in contradiction; it is a dialectical, vital, organic whole:

> *Noûs*, simplicity, is substance. On account of its simplicity or self-identity it appears fixed and enduring. But this self-identity is not less negativity; therefore its fixed existence passes over into its dissolution. The determinateness seems at first to be due entirely to the fact that it is related to an *other*, and its movement seems imposed on it by an alien power; but having its otherness within itself, and being self-moving, is just what is involved in the *simplicity* of thinking itself; for this simple thinking is the self-moving and self-differentiation of thought, it is its own inwardness, it is the pure Notion …
>
> It is in this nature of what is to be in its being its own Notion, that *logical necessity* in general consists. This alone is the rational element and the rhythm of the organic whole; it is as much knowledge of the content, as the content is the Notion and essence – in other words, it alone is *speculative philosophy*.[16]

Now, in all of these cases, Hegel is using the terms "soul" and "body" and "organic" in a way that we might want to say is analogical. But it is more complicated than this; it is *not merely analogical.* For contrast and to open up further elaboration, let us look at what Hegel takes to be biologically – and thus seemingly literally – organic.

The Biologically Organic: Not Merely Literal

In his *Philosophy of Nature*, Hegel distinguishes between inorganic and organic nature. The limit between them is chemistry. Cinzia Ferrini's careful examination of the transition from chemistry to life shows that not all identity is organic in the literal sense.[17] The literally organic concerns organisms. According to Hegel, "[t]he organism is the infinite self-stimulating and self-sustaining process."[18]

The wholes that I discussed above are also self-sustaining processes, but they are not "organic" members as living organisms, at least not in this apparently merely literal way. Now, in asserting here that these wholes are not "merely" literally organic, I imply that in some way, they *are* literally organic, just not *merely* so. I hope this becomes clear below. Another caveat: even organisms for Hegel cannot be *merely* literally organic, for they are organic and thus have life in part only because of the way in which they are determined by inorganic contradictions that are real and revealed in their logics.

The non-biological organic wholes are self-sustaining in historical, phenomenological, and social ways, ways that sublate (negate and yet preserve) whatever corporeality they have. But again, this externality *in bodies* and the *sublation of those bodies* is what makes these wholes not merely analogical, but partially literally organic as well. This needs further explanation.

To take a step back, given the distinctions thus far, it is tempting to just assert that Hegel uses the word "organic" in two ways: literally when referring to living thing possessing organs, e.g., a plant, and analogically when referring to a dialectic that operates like a living thing (i.e., self-sublating, living through its internal and external contradictions, for example, as self-consciousness does). But my claim is that we ought not give in to this temptation, for to do so would be to misunderstand Hegel. I claim this because, speculatively speaking, "organic" for Hegel, is always to be thought in terms of substance and subject, regardless of whether Hegel is using the word in what appears to be a traditionally literal or analogical way. This dialectic of substance and subject, I argue, is a four-way dialectic that includes the inorganic and the organic in a way that *complicates* the distinction between literal and analogical organicity. It makes unities such as self-consciousness and the State, *neither* merely literally organic, *nor* merely analogically organic. Let us walk through the reasons for this.

Four-Way Dialectical Organicity

On the surface, the dialectical nature of speculative philosophy seems to be an analogical, rather than a literal kind of "organic" process. But, this merely analogical organicity involves its inorganic other in a way that complicates the matter. Whether in the *Logic* or the *Phenomenology of Spirit* or the *Philosophies* of *Nature* or of *Right* – the Notion is equally organic and inorganic, and the Notion is equally substance and subject.[19] Indeed, Hegel's dialectic is a dialectic of the concept and reality, *in dialectical relation to*, the dialectic of subject and substance. And this changes the meaning of organic from being merely analogical or merely literal.

The key to understanding this lies in the *Science of Logic*: "the Idea has not merely the more general meaning of the *true being*, of the unity of *Notion* and *reality*, but the more specific one of the unity of *subjective Notion* and *objectivity*."[20] In other words, the "organic" whole of the Idea is a soul-body unity that is also a subject-object unity. It is a four-way dialectic. Let us investigate this further.

On one side, the dialectic is thought-being in the sense of beings that are thought of: "substance is in itself or implicitly Subject, all content is its own reflection into itself … Being is Thought."[21] Substance is the *what* that is speculatively realized; it is dialectical movements through formal constraints.

On the other side, the dialectic is subject, it is thought-being in the sense of the verb to be: it is a being which *is* speculative knowing at its most comprehensive level of *being* (as a verb). Thus in "Absolute Knowing," Spirit "displays the process of its becoming Spirit in the form of free contingent happening."[22] This is thought-*being* in the verb sense of to be. It is what gives consciousness the experience of the unexpected.

The highest unity of this substance-subject, this thought-being in both senses, is Absolute Spirit, the *I* that is a *We* that knows itself as Nature and as "comprehended history."[23]

In the *Science of Logic*, this thought-being seems to be literally organic when it is considered in terms of life. But the "Idea as Cognition" – (the next chapter in the *Logic*) – is a movement "beyond life," and the Absolute Idea – (the final chapter in the *Logic*) – while it unifies life and concept, is not literally organic life (in the sense that a bug is organic life as a determinate organism).[24]

The dialectic is the *what* determined by the thinking about it, *and* the thinking determined by the *what*. Each becomes in and through the other. In Hegel's language, each is, alternately, organic and inorganic. This dialectic of *thought*-being and thought-*being* in which the whole is just as much organic as inorganic, makes up what Hegel means by an "organic" method, movement or whole. This is true for both organisms and organic wholes of the kind we have been discussing. Thus, the Absolute Idea is not merely analogically organic.

To further explain this dialectic four-way dialectic, neither merely literally organic nor merely analogically organic, let look at some passages from the *Phenomenology of Spirit*.

The Dialectic of Organic and Inorganic in the Phenomenology of Spirit

Hegel refers to moments on the way up the dialectic as organic and alive: as "members" of the whole. But later, when we have read past these moments, he refers to them as *inorganic* or *abstract*: they are no longer organic in the way in which they appeared to be within their own logic. They have become inorganic members of a larger organic whole and only as parts of that whole do they have any claim to being called "organic."

Thus consciousness lives the "life" of consciousness in Sense-Certainty, Perception, and Understanding, and then the life of Self-consciousness, and then of Reason, but when we get to Spirit, we learn that *only* Spirit is actual and alive, and that it was Spirit which gave each of those prior moments their life: "Spirit … [j]ust because it is a being that is resolved in the self, it is not a dead essence, but is *actual* and *alive* … Spirit is thus self-supporting, absolute, real being. All previous shapes of consciousness are abstract forms of it."[25]

Hegel describes, in similar terms, how Speculative Science views its prior moments:

> [I]t [Speculative Science] is the cunning which, while seeming to abstain from activity, looks on and watches how determinateness, with its concrete life, just where it fancies it is pursuing its own self-preservation and particular interest, is in fact doing the very opposite, is an activity that results in its own dissolution, and makes itself a moment of the whole.[26]

Another instance is his discussion of past education:

> This past existence is the already acquired property of universal Spirit which constitutes the Substance of the individual, and hence appears externally to him as his inorganic nature. In this respect formative education, regarded from the side of the individual, consists in his acquiring what thus lies at hand, devouring his inorganic nature, and taking possession of it for himself. But, regarded from the side of universal Spirit as substance, this is nothing but its own acquisition of self-consciousness, the bringing-about of its own becoming and reflection into itself.[27]

The first education of consciousness is one in which one's sublation of contradictions has the unexpected outcome of learning something external (inorganic) that one didn't know by digesting that externality and making it into one's life (making it part of the organic); the second is speculative reflection on Spirit's life as the lives of people living it through their education and works and enjoyment. For these conscious individuals who are Spirit (the I's that are the We), the past events and things (an individual's memories, and historical individuals) are the inorganic elements, which, "digested" and "incorporated" into those consciousnesses, become members of the living, whole, Spirit.[28] It would seem, then, that the *Phenomenology of Spirit* is a book presenting Spirit as not merely literally organic nor merely analogically organic. But let us dig deeper.

The Life of the Idea Moving through the Dialectic

According to Hegel, abstract and inorganic moments of a greater whole which had been organic in their spheres, become members of a larger whole which re-members them as part of its organic being. One might therefore conclude that what moved through the earlier moments and gave them their actuality was the *life of the dialectic moving through the whole and that therefore the whole is fundamentally literally organic.*[29] Errol Harris has claimed that Hegel would endorse of the Gaia hypothesis that the earth is a living organism,[30] and Songsuk Hahn has claimed that "the concept Being" is structured as natural organic development. Songsuk Hahn calls this Hegel's "Negation Naturalized":

> Out of this organic process of self-repulsion, <u>Hegel naturalistically, not formally,</u> derives a principle of teleological development that orders the concept's inner progress. The principle of determinate negation reflects a naturalized process of thought that strenuously seeks to adapt itself to this natural tendency toward self-negation that Hegel thinks is present in every living thing. <u>Following nature's example, the concept Being exhibits an internally self-contradictory motion that develops precisely in the way that life appears in organisms.</u>[31]

I see no evidence in these passages by Harris and Hahn that they are using the word organic in a merely analogical way. (Note the expressions "naturalistically, not formally" and "develops precisely in the way" in the Hahn citation.) It is therefore at least *possible* to interpret Harris and Hahn to be claiming that Hegel is referring to the earth, and to Being, as literally organic. Even if in the end these two thinkers do not mean to assert that Hegel thinks of the earth or of Being as literally organic, this possible interpretation deserves investigation.

Let me begin with a counter to their ostensibly literal views. It would run as follows. Hegel cannot mean that the earth and/or Being are merely living organisms, because such an interpretation makes natural determinate being (where organic life actually *is* found) the ground of the earth or of Being pure Being; Hegel would not have allowed that *presupposition* into his system. Indeed, citing Hegel, Karin de Boer shows that we must rule out making the *determinate* define the absolute:

> "The forms of *determinate being* [*Dasein*] find no place in the series of those determinations which can be regarded as definitions of the absolute," for they are "posited only as determinate and finite forms" (L I, 149/137). The "forms of determinate being" seem to refer to conceptual determinations that can only be assigned to finite things: "Determinate being is therefore the sphere of difference, of dualism, the field of finitude … quality, otherness, limit – like reality, being-in-itself, the ought, and so on – are the imperfect guises of the negation of being." (174/157)[32]

If we make the earth or Being organic in a merely literal way, we are attributing to the earth or to Being the organic structure of a determinate being. This is not consistent with the beginning of Hegel's *Logic* in which the transition is from Being to Nothing to Becoming and *only then* to determinate Being.

Furthermore, (the argument would go), 'God's mind before creation'[33] is the becoming of the dialectic out of pure indeterminacy, an indeterminacy that cannot itself be referred to as literally organic: there is necessarily something more or outside of just the literal. According to this counter to Harris and Hahn, then, when Hegel calls its movement organic, it is, apparently by analogy only.

However, the merely analogical model does not work any better, as I will show below. Will this counter to the counter legitimize what we take to be Harris's literally organic Gaia hypothesis, or Hahn's literally organic Being hypothesis? No, but let us see why.

The merely analogical reading is not complete because there is a defence of the *literal* that draws on Hegel's *Lectures on the Philosophy of Religion* (1827).[34] In those lectures, Hegel refers to the development of religion in apparently literal, organic terms: he uses the language of the bud developing into the plant to describe spirit's developments in religion.

> God, the concept, judges or divides [*urteilt*]; *that is, God determines. Only now within this category of determination do we have existing religion – religion that at the same time* exists *determinately* ... [S]pirit is in principle not immediate – it is not [found] in the mode of immediacy. It is living, is active, is what it makes of itself. The living thing is this activity. Stone or metal is immediate, it is complete and remains just as it is. But anything alive is already this activity of mediation with itself. The plant is not yet complete when the bud is present, for this meager existence of the bud is just its abstract initial existence. [To exist] it must develop, must first bring itself forth. And finally, the plant recapitulates its unfolded self in the seed – this its beginning is also its final product ... It is the same for living things generally, for the fruit is something other than the initial seed. But because it is altogether alive, spirit is just like this. At first it is only implicitly, or is in its concept; then it enters into existence, unfolding itself, bringing itself forth, becoming mature, and bringing forth what it is in itself, the concept of its own self, so that what is implicit, its concept, may now be explicit.[35]

This accomplishment of the Divine seed's fruition from implicit to fully actualized seems to allow interpretation of the entire movement of God's creation as *literally* "organic."

However, one could counter that it is not necessarily the case that the *origin* of determinate religion is reducible to the necessary *developments* of determinate religion (i.e., to determinate religion's developments into its consummate form of revealed (Christian) religion); rather, *determinate*, *living Spirit* fulfils *its* concept; that is, according to this counter-interpretation, Hegel does not mean that God fulfils Himself through our community's (*Spirit's*) determinate fulfilling of itself. Spirit is I that is a We, the living community on earth: it is not the same as God; thus, Spirit's determinate fulfilling of itself is not God's fulfilment of His Being. It is only *Spirit* of humanity, not God, that is the seed which develops into its full fruition of knowing itself as God's creation. Accordingly, Spirit as seed is *determinate* religion, and determinate religion, even in its completely revealed form, is not an absolute organism, not the same as pure Being at the beginning of the *Logic* nor the Absolute Idea at the end of the Logic before it externalizes itself. The origin of the system (God or Being) is not literally organically related to its determinate moments (through which it would have had to live were it literally organically a whole only in and through them).

In this counter-reading, God's or Being's externalization would not be literally organic, even though the *created world* could be literally organic (in which case we could adopt the Gaia hypothesis but not the view that Gaia is God). This would mean that the *divine origin* of the whole is only organic in an analogical sense, not in a literal sense, even if the created moments are literally organic developments of organic (determinate) Spirit.[36]

However, keeping God separate from the movement of the concept as not literally organic but rather merely analogically organic is also problematic, for the following reasons.

In the chapter on Religion in the *Phenomenology of Spirit*, Hegel develops the Creation phenomenologically as God's self-othering.[37] Here in the *Phenomenology*, Hegel thereby explicitly makes God creator of and responsible for evil.[38] Following the seed imagery above, the implicit Truth of God's Self-Creation as Nature is actualized fully only when the self-knowing Spirit, the community, knows Creation to be its "own act," taking responsibility for and forgiving its own evil.[39]

In this interpretation, Christianity (as the religion of incarnate sublation of sin) is the *Vorstellung* of this divine (self-)knowledge rather than *philosophical* grasp of that truth.[40] Philosophically understood, the God or Being of religion is really "the Self's own act."[41] If we read the philosophical truth back into Christianity, Christian religion becomes a panentheism: God = all things being; Creation = beings *being*. "Being" is object and verb; the object and subject of the act of being.

Hegel's revealed Truth is thus literally true but not merely literal: it is not merely historical or pictured or a fixed concept; not just dead and *inorganic*. Nor is revealed truth merely analogical (as "Christianity" or as "Hegelian organic dialectic"). The nature of phenomenological representation, as philosophically *becoming*, cannot limit itself to its object or the act that makes it objectively actually be. Indeed, Hegel claims at the start of the *Phenomenology* that we kill the dialectic when we merely understand or picture it: "Of course, the *triadic form* must not be regarded as scientific when it is reduced to a lifeless schema, a mere shadow, when scientific organization is degraded into a table of terms. Kant rediscovered this triadic form by instinct, but in his work it was still lifeless and uncomprehended."[42])

Let us take as our final example the end of the *Phenomenology of Spirit*:

> The self-knowing Spirit knows not only itself but also the negative of itself, or its limit: to know one's limit is to know how to sacrifice oneself. This sacrifice is the externalization in which Spirit displays the process of its becoming Spirit in the form of *free contingent happening*, intuiting its pure Self as Time outside of it, and equally its Being as Space. This last becoming of Spirit, *Nature*, is its living immediate Becoming; Nature, the externalized Spirit, is in its existence nothing but this eternal externalization of the continuing existence and the movement which reinstates the Subject.[43]

The death of Absolute Spirit into/as Nature is clearly figured in this phenomenon, as well as a kind of resurrection ("reinstatement") of the Subject in and by Nature.

If the Subject that is being reborn at the end of the *Phenomenology of Spirit* is merely Absolute Spirit's self-comprehension in and through nature (and not itself God or Being), then we again have determinate being reinstating itself through its free act of sacrificing itself by knowing its limit and returning from that negation to know itself anew. This would be the phenomenological completion of ourselves as Spirit and our continuation as Spirit. It would thus be Spirit's double negation: its natural contingency in history negated as phenomenologically comprehended, and then that negated into the absolute "now" of that nature/reflection movement, the "Calvary of Absolute Spirit."[44] It would be the truth of Spirit as a kind of becoming, the becoming of a historical social organism, a spiritualized nature and naturalized spirit.

But, one could also interpret the "Subject" that gets reinstated to be "God" or "Being", and these as meaning "Absolute Spirit." In that case, the *Phenomenology of Spirit* is also a theodicy, and there is nothing outside its system of experience. On this reading, it makes sense to say, as

Hegel concludes the *Phenomenology*, that God would be "lifeless and alone" without Absolute Spirit's determinacies: for, "from the chalice of this realm of spirits/foams forth for Him his own infinitude."[45] (As Hegel articulates this in the "organic" poetry of Schiller.)

Or, one could conclude that it is only we, Spirit, that would be lifeless and alone without our memories, but that the real world of natural objects would remain even if Spirit became extinct. The danger of that metaphysical realism (which could also assert a Creator God of Nature for whom the natural world was wholly external), is that it introduces into Hegel's system two presuppositions – the existence of God, and the existence of God's created Nature (which Nature in turn gives rise to Spirit as self-conscious Nature); but these are presuppositions which Hegel was at pains to eliminate, since for him any metaphysical presupposition is dogmatic and necessarily one-sided.

If we accepted the externality of nature as a presupposition, we would ask: Is it God's externality that is at issue when we consider the externality of the Idea as nature (the move made at the end of the *Logic* and the start of the *Philosophy of Nature*)? If we stick to the merely analogical idea of organic, then the organicity of that externalization, that transition, that "decision" or release or death, remains an interpretive conundrum, the solution to which depends on whether one is a post-Kantian Hegelian or a metaphysical realist Hegelian. Either theory forces one into either a more literal organicity (ontology is what is known by the living knower – the post-Kantian Hegelianism) or the more analogical organicity (ontology as what is in existence independent of the knower and yet it is analogically organic because of how we living beings come to know it – the metaphysical realist Hegelianism).

I am of two minds about this. On the one hand, I have been swayed by Martin Krahn's argument in favour of a more metaphysical realist position as a result of his analysis of the role of externality in Hegel's *Philosophy of Nature*:[46] externality is not just the inorganic part of the Idea, it is really outside of thought.[47] The *Philosophy of Nature* is thus only organic after we reconstitute its content dialectically in thought; it is not literally organic in-itself, since in itself it is the place and time of externalities of its contents. In this view, only Spirit is organically fulfilling its implicit truth by filling itself up with its determinate moments and them self-consciously recollecting those moments. God and Nature remain distinct (from each other, even if as developed natural self-conscious beings we come to *know* God and God's Creation).

On the other hand, I tend away from this metaphysical realist position which (ironically) risks taking externality *literally* (i.e., there is really an outside to thought) and which thereby forces "organic" to be proper to determinate things only. I tend away from it because the *Phenomenology* passage cited above clearly indicates that spiritualized nature both enacts its own limit by sacrificing itself, and then as nature, reinstates the Subject, and that Subject could be the Idea ("God").

Nonetheless, it remains a *possible* reading of Hegel that Nature is literally external to the Idea. Therefore, in my view, it remains an unresolvable issue if we keep to these terms alone.

What we learn from this discussion is that it is problematic to interpret the adjective "organic" (like the adjective "external") only literally or only analogically.[48] My preference, therefore, is to do both a literal and analogical reading at once, or more specifically, to say that the truth is neither merely literal nor merely analogical. In my view, the key to reading Hegel is to get the dialectic to move through its four sides, as I indicated above: a vertical dialectic between subject and substance (subjective cognition-objectivity dialectic, or again act-deed dialectic or again subject-nature), crossed by a horizontal dialectic between unity and multiplicity (or again, necessity and contingency). In this way, we get the final, total show of the productive, revolutionary dialectic of absolute spirit and nature *as* self-knowing, self-enacting living and dying (in unities and externalities), as well as the reinstating of the subject (out of nature). For Hegel, all of this constitutes the science of experience without which we would be lifeless and alone.

"God," "the subject which is equally substance," "the community of interpreters" requires the inorganic for its organic revolutions; but this organicity is not merely that of an organism, nor is it merely analogically organic. For the semantic structure of the word "organic" is transformed by Hegel's four-way dialectic into meaning the double negation of literal and analogical in and through the other. Being literally thinks and in so doing it reflects itself out of itself and back into itself, thus becoming the organ of itself (a both literal and analogical reflection), an organ which is always in part inorganic because negated when sublated, but also always organic when preserved in that double negation. This is its freedom.

II. The Organic-Inorganic Dialectic of Freedom

The Idea's Organic Freedom

According to Hegel's *Science of Logic*, the moments of the notion in mechanism "remain external to one another in every combination."[49] This is the case for both "mechanism proper" and "Spiritual mechanism" (which Hegel describes as *"a mechanical style of thinking, a mechanical memory, habit, a mechanical way of acting*").[50] By contrast, "the Idea is the *process* of sundering itself into individuality and its inorganic nature, and again of bringing this inorganic nature under the power of the subject and returning to the first simple universality."[51] In other words, the Idea is the process of experiencing itself as moments, which it then re-members into wholes.[52]

Corporeality, considered in terms of mechanical and chemical relationships is a "*dead* thing";[53] by contrast, corporeal *life* has the inner Notion pervading the externality yet "remaining identical with itself"; corporeal things have *parts*, organisms have *members*:

> the Notion is immanent in it [corporeality], the *purposiveness* of the living being is to be grasped as *inner*; the Notion is in it as determinate Notion, distinct from its eternality, and in its distinguishing, pervading the externality and remaining identical with itself. This objectivity of the living being is the *organism*; it is the *means and instrument* of the end, perfect in its purposiveness since the Notion constitutes its substance; but for that very reason this means and instrument is itself the realized end, in which the subjective end is thus immediately brought into unity with itself. In respect of its externality the organism is a manifold, not of *parts* but of *members*.[54]

Living being is made of members and *re-members*. Re-membering happens at the level of digestion in substantive life (biological repetition), and at the level of cognition in self-consciousness. Complete freedom is for Hegel, remembering at both levels: the former is habitual; the latter, self-consciousness, re-members reflectively, but can also be mechanical by being merely habitual. The latter can escape being a mere mechanical spiritual habituation by reasoning about (and by means of) its members. Each level (biological repetition, cognitive recollection and cognition as reason) has its own level of freedom. The Idea as merely Life has a kind of biological freedom, but falls short of complete freedom because Life merely "has" the presupposition of an objective world, whereas cognition "*makes* for itself the presupposition of an objective world."[55] This latter, self-consciousness, is the movement from soul-body *to soul-body with subjective cognition of objectivity*:

> The *identity* of the Idea with itself is one with the *process*; the thought which liberates actuality from the illusory show of purposeless mutability and transfigures it into the Idea must not represent this truth of actuality as a dead repose, as a mere *picture*, lifeless, without impulse or movement,

as a genius or number, or an abstract thought; by virtue of the freedom which the Notion attains in the Idea, the Idea possesses within itself also the *most stubborn opposition*; its repose consists in the security and certainty with which it eternally creates and eternally overcomes that opposition, in its meeting with itself.[56]

He adds later:

The elevation of the Notion above life means that its reality is the Notion form liberated into universality. Through this judgment the Idea is duplicated into the subjective Notion whose reality is the Notion itself, and into the objective Notion that is in the form of life. *Thinking, spirit, self-consciousness*, are determinations of the Idea where it has itself for object, and its determinate being, that is, the determinateness of its being, is its own difference from itself.[57]

Hegel's universal is a *concrete* universal: it becomes, it is organic. The final shape of the Concept in the *Logic* is thus *not* merely subject as an *a priori* synthetic unity of apperception, nor Reason as an intellectual intuition, nor God as a merely subjective or merely objective One. The final shape of the Concept is "the subject [who] now exists as free, universal self-identity."[58]

The final shape is a *person*:

[In] [t]he absolute Idea, … [t]he Notion is not merely *soul*, but free subjective Notion that is for itself and therefore possesses *personality* – the practical, objective Notion determined in and for itself which, as person, is impenetrable atomic subjectivity – but which, none the less, is not exclusive individuality, but explicitly *universality* and *cognition*, and in its other has its *own* objectivity for its object. All else is error, confusion, opinion, endeavour, caprice and transitoriness; the absolute Idea alone is *being*, imperishable *life, self-knowing truth*, and is *all truth* … It is the sole subject matter and content of philosophy.[59]

Is the absolute person literally God? Or, is it only analogically God because literally, it is the self? My answer is that the absolute person is literally God and literally the self, but not merely literally so; it is also analogically God and analogically the self, but not merely analogically so. Why? Because the absolute assertion has two poles – subject and object, and each of their others creates that third and fourth pole through which the absolute reflects and is itself ("and in its other has its own objectivity for its object"). The *Phenomenology of Spirit* shows us that absolute organic freedom is the maturation of *Absolute Spirit* as Consciousness, Self-consciousness, Understanding, Reason, Spirit, Absolute Spirit, God, and Absolute Knowing (in and through the objects of those forms of knowing). Overall, it teaches us how to move through the four-way dialectic concretely. We learn how thinking can get stuck in the "members" of its whole, becoming mechanical, inorganic, losing self-conscious life and its becoming.

"Organic" Freedom in the Phenomenology of Spirit

In the *Phenomenology*, there are many ways in which human life is inorganic or encounters inorganicity as part of itself – in the murdered other (the "battle to the death"[60]), in the thing-ness of the bondsman, in the burial of the dead, in the self-reduction of the Unhappy Consciousness to a thing, in the theoretical *caput mortum* of phrenology or the real *caput mortum* of the guillotine, in the death of the god-man in religion, or finally, in Absolute Knowing's gallery of images.

The fear and work done by the bondsman are generative of his freedom: "work forms and shapes the thing … [and] in this way … consciousness, *qua* worker, comes to see in the independent being [of the object] its own independence."[61] In the development from the battle to the death to lordship and bondage, dialectical negation moves from killing to sustaining (even if what is sustained is an inadequate form of recognition); from making its other merely inorganic to incorporating the inorganicity of otherness in the economy of the organic productivity. From there onward in the *Phenomenology of Spirit*, we read of social forms which, in *negating, preserve.*

Thus, burial recollects, re-members, resurrects the inorganic, the dead person into the community. The person's death, her reduction to something inorganic, is sublated by her community: they reject "the wrong" of her having something merely happen to her.[62] This negation and preservation, this work of the organic-inorganic dialectic of spirit, is then repeated in more elaborate forms through the rest of the *Phenomenology*. The pinnacle of social spirit is forgiveness: the work of seeing the *inorganic* character of the deed – its deadness and completion – as a member of our *organic*, as something that needs to be interpreted.[63]

The sustaining spiritual form of Hegel's phenomenological person is the relation of organic and inorganic, not as desirous destruction of the other, but rather as communing with the other (however inadequate this communing is, especially in its early stages). The comprehensive end of these elaborations is the Calvary of Absolute Spirit: the 'burial' of each person in the natural, educational, cultural, and political experiences of spirit, and each person's self-recollection out of these structures of experience through speculative philosophy.

In the end, Absolute Knowing's "becoming Nature" and grasping comprehended history means knowing how moments in time and space become members of wholes. "In this, the moments of its movement no longer exhibit themselves as specific *shapes of consciousness*, but – since consciousness's difference has returned into the Self – as *specific Notions* and as their organic self-grounded movement."[64]

Conclusion

Hegel writes that "[t]he True is ... the Bacchanalian revel in which no member is not drunk."[65] Is this the ultimate expression of human freedom for Hegel? If it literally were, this would be strange, given that Hegel agrees with Heraclitus that "dry souls are best."[66] The Absolute Knower does not drown herself in recollected moments. She is re-membering, she *tastes* what froths forth from the chalice. She becomes in and through differences. There is no absolute replay in a merely literal sense.

If we are not to be mere moments in history – rendered inorganic through individual death or human extinction – we should *organ*ize absolutely. Poetically, our planet is the globe, 'the picture in which life can contemplate and see itself objectively like a work of art, making free artists of its own selves'. Thinking through Hegel's four-part dialectic is essential to such sustainable organization. Thinking and acting in this way is performing the Hegelian labour of the Notion. But we labour in order to play: by means of this dialectical living – Hegel's complete "organic" freedom – we can and should also enjoy to the fullest our membership in the Bacchanalian revel.

NOTES

1 G.W.F. Hegel, *Phenomenology of Spirit*, trans. A.V. Miller (Oxford: Oxford University Press, 1977), 2. Henceforth PoS.

2 E.g., the Ethical Substance is the Family, Civil Society and "the State as freedom ... (the) actual and organic mind (α) of a single nation." G.W.F. Hegel, *Philosophy of Right*, trans. T.M. Knox (Oxford: Oxford University Press, 1967), 36.

3 G.W.F. Hegel, *Science of Logic*, trans. A.V. Miller (Atlantic Highlands, NJ: Humanities Press, 1969), 757. Henceforth SL.

4 SL 757–58.

 5 Hegel's *Lectures on Aesthetics*, Vol. 1 + 2 translator T. M. Knox (Oxford: Clarendon Press, 1975), p. 1227–28. Henceforth *Aesthetics*.

 6 *Aesthetics* p. 1235–6. For more about Hegel's celebration of Shakespeare see my *Hegel and Shakespeare on Moral Imagination* (Albany: State University of New York Press, 2010), especially pp. 17–20.

 7 *Aesthetics* volume II p. 984. See also the run-up to this claim, pp. 982–4.

 8 PoS §808, 493; the *Phenomenology* ends with a line of poetry from Schiller's *Die Freundschaft, ad fin*. I argue elsewhere that something along the same lines as this final proper freedom is the goal of Shakespeare's final tragi-comic, Romance dramas: see *Hegel and Shakespeare* "Part III: The Romance Plays and Absolute Knowing."

 9 *Hegel and Shakespeare*, Chapter 11.

10 PoS §807–808, 492–3.

11 PoS §46, 27.

12 PoS §34, 20 my underline.

13 Songsuk Susan Hahn, *Contradiction in Motion: Hegel's Organic Concept of Life and Value* (Ithaca: Cornell University Press, 2007).

14 SL 439.

15 SL 442.

16 PoS §§55–6, 34.

17 Cinzia Ferrini, "The Transition to Organics: Hegel's Idea of Life," in *A Companion to Hegel*, eds. Stephen Houlgate and Michael Baur (West Sussex: Blackwell, 2011), 203–224.

18 G.W.F. Hegel, *Philosophy of Nature*, vol. 2, trans. and ed. Michael John Petry (London: George Allen and Unwin, 1970), §336, 220. Henceforth PoN.

19 PoS §17, 10.

20 SL 758.

21 PoS §54, 33.

22 PoS §807, 492.

23 Therefore, method and content are not, in the end, separate, nor have they ever been. But the way in which the word "organic" plays out is different depending on whether one is thinking about subject or substance as related to method or content.

24 Is the Absolute Idea therefor merely analogically organic? No. Is a bug's determinate life separate from the Notion? No. The Absolute Idea and the bug are each neither merely literally organic nor merely analogically organic. Is this to claim, weirdly, that a bug is itself the Absolute Idea? (And that the Absolute Idea is the bug?) More acutely, is the universe to be found in a grain of sand? I think that, actually, these conclusions are implied by Hegel's dialectic: Hegel's whole is panentheistic. This is not to say that the bug exhausts the Absolute Idea's complexity, because, for one

thing, the bug is not knowing itself. But the Idea is implicit in the bug as its completion, were the bug to be dialectically developed into the completion of the Notion. There is no radical departure in principle between one being and the whole of being. Even a mechanical, non-biological being like a grain of sand, is, at least in the *Phenomenology of Spirit* (where he discusses a grain of salt), a play of forces that gets developed through consciousness' thinking about it into Absolute Spirit's self-sacrifice into/as Nature. But these wild claims need to be worked out in another paper.

25 PoS §439–40, 264.

26 PoS §54, 33.

27 PoS §28, 16–17.

28 See too Hegel's discussion of Ethical life in terms of the necessary relation of its "organic" and "inorganic" sides. G.W.F. Hegel, *Natural Law: The Scientific Ways of Treating Natural Law, Its Place in Moral Philosophy, and Its Relation to the Positive Sciences of Law*, trans. T.M. Knox (Philadelphia: University of Pennsylvania Press, 1975), 98ff: "It remains a relation of organic to inorganic nature." (98)

29 Some Hegel scholars take the negative to be the heart of the dialectic. Citing Hegel's reference to the work of the negative in the *Logic* as the "simple life-pulse," de Boer writes:
This suggests that the *Logic* treats concepts as if they were living beings. In my view, Hegel's speculative science indeed requires that every given content be treated as a process impelled by the attempt at determining itself from within … as driven by the urge to resolve … The *Logic* deploys this pulse – that is, absolute negativity – to reconstruct the totality of the concepts generate in the actual history of thought. (de Boer, *On Hegel: The Sway of the Negative*, 43–4).

30 Errol E. Harris, "How Final Is Hegel's Rejection of Evolution?" in *Hegel and the Philosophy of Nature*, ed. Stephen Houlgate (Albany: State University of New York Press, 1998), 196–208.

31 Hahn, *Contradiction in Motion*, 26–27.

32 Karin de Boer, *On Hegel*, note 44, 221. The pages de Boer is citing are respectively from Hegel's *Wissenschaft der Logik* [1812–16, 1831]; Hegel's SL.

33 SL 50.

34 Hegel, *Lectures on the Philosophy of Religion One Volume Edition The Lectures of 1827*, edited by Peter C. Hodgson, translated by R.F. Brown, P.C. Hodgson, and J.M. Stewart with the assistance of H.S. Harris (Berkeley: University of California Press, 1988). Pp. 107–8. I thank the anonymous reviewer of my chapter for pointing out this passage and asking me to discuss it.

35 Hegel, *Lectures on the Philosophy of Religion*, p. 108.

36 In the *Phenomenology of Spirit*, Absolute Spirit in its final phenomenological *social* form is forgiveness: "God manifested in the midst of those who know themselves in the form of pure knowledge" (PoS §671, 409.) It is not evident from this alone that the created world is the substantial divine organism, the Absolute Spirit recognizing its divine organic self through forgiveness (i.e., God recognizing Himself through forgiveness as the substantial divine organism). For the alternate view is just as possible: one could think that Absolute Spirit, in knowing itself existentially, knows God, but that even in that knowledge, God and Absolute Spirit remain distinct (as would God and nature – Spirit being part of natural creation); sublation would therefore only be the movement of Spirit, not the movement of divine existing as Creation. However, as I go on to show below, both of these interpretations can be read into Hegel's works, and neither of them survives being contradicted by the other reading, so neither by itself can be right (neither *merely* one nor the other is right by itself).

37 PoS §§774–80, 467–8, and Findlay's analysis of §776 PoS p. 587.

38 Ibid., §780, 467–8.

39 In the *Phenomenology*, evil, philosophically understood, is the side of "self-sundering" (religiously called "Creation") which takes its own positing as final truth for itself, rather than as only one side of the dialectical movement of the in-itself. The other side of the for-itself is the oppositions of externality brought about by the sundering having become externalized act; the sublation of this opposition is the sublation of the positing and opposing into a whole that knows itself to be this whole process: "the pure knowledge of essence has in principle renounced its simple unity, for it is the self-sundering, or the negativity which the Notion is; so far as this self-sundering is the process of being *for itself*, it is evil; so far as it is the *in-itself*, it remains good" (PoS §796, 484).

40 "Spirit in religion *pictures* itself to itself, it is indeed consciousness, and the reality enclosed within religion is the shape and the guise of its picture-thinking. But, in this picture-thinking, reality does not receive its perfect due, viz. to be not merely a guise but an independent free existence," (PoS § 678).

41 PoS §797, 485.

42 PoS §50, 29.

43 PoS §807, 492.

44 PoS §808, 493.

45 PoS §808, 493.

46 See Martin Krahn's *Externality in Hegel's* Philosophy of Nature. (PhD Dissertation, Duquesne University, 2018).

47 See Ibid. "Conclusion," p. 287.

48 Similarly, it would be wrong to interpret the word "organic" as meaning
something merely *positive*, since as Hegel shows, what was organic can
become deathly *inorganic* despite the fact that it is a functioning moment
that within its own sphere appears to be organic. Slavoj Žižek's shows this:
he claims that Hegel's attribution of "organic" to the State is not always
as a positive attribute, that the temporal-historical nature of the dialectic
in Hegel is such that a merely literal interpretation of "organic" *as positive
determinateness or method* is nonsensical:

> According to the common perception, Hegel condemns the French Revolution
> as the immediate assertion of an abstract-universal Freedom which, as such,
> has to end in its opposite: a universal terror directed at all particular content.
> To this abstract freedom – so the story goes – Hegel opposes the "concrete
> Freedom" of the modern rational state in which one's individual freedom
> is grounded in assuming one's place within the articulated totality of the
> social order … The problem with this common perception is that it does
> not take into account the immanent temporal dimension of the dialectical
> process. A historical agent is never directly confronted with the choice: either
> revolutionary terror or organic rational state. On the eve of the revolution, the
> only choice is between the old "organic" order and revolution, inclusive of its
> terror. What tips the balance of choice towards revolution in this situation is
> the insight into how the organic harmony of the *ancient régime* is itself a fake,
> an illusion concealing the reality of brutal violence, division, and chaos
> (*Less than Nothing* [London; New York: Verso, 2013], pp. 69–70).

For the "organic" State defined by young Hegel vs. mature Hegel, see Slavoj Žižek,
In Defense of Lost Causes (2008–9 edition) pp. 129–31 of the 2008–9 edition;
for further discussion of organic in state see Žižek's *Tarrying with the Negative*,
pp. 180–1, and pp. 210–11. I thank Andrew Cutrofello and Emilia Angelova for
pointing out these passages to me.

49 SL 711.
50 SL 711.
51 SL 759.
52 SL 760.
53 SL 766.
54 SL 766.
55 SL 760.
56 SL 759.
57 SL 775.
58 SL 823.
59 SL 824.
60 PoS §188, 114.
61 PoS §195, 118.

62 PoS §462, 277–8.
63 As I discuss in an earlier article, "interpretation" is etymologically related to burial, since "Inter" means to "bury in the earth or a grave" (https://www.etymonline.com/word/inter, accessed August 7, 2025). (And in researching for that earlier article, it tantalizingly appeared that "pret" was related to Sanskrit "prath," which means "to unfold, disclose, reveal, show" (https://sanskritdictionary.com/?q=prath [accessed August 7, 2025]). However, the website that I used back then to connect pret and prath no longer exists, so that part of the etymological connection is uncertain. See Jennifer Ann Bates' "Absolute Knowing: Consternation and Preservation in Hegel's *Phenomenology of Spirit* and Shakespeare's *Troilus and Cressida*" in *Angelaki*, 21:3, 2016, 65–82, p. 70.)
64 PoS §805, 491.
65 PoS §47, 27.
66 PoN Addition to §336, 222.

REFERENCES

Bates, Jennifer Ann. *Hegel and Shakespeare on Moral Imagination*. Albany: State University of New York Press, 2010.

—— "Absolute Knowing: Consternation and Preservation in Hegel's *Phenomenology of Spirit* and Shakespeare's *Troilus and Cressida*." *Angelaki* 21, no. 3 (2018): 65–82. https://doi.org/10.1080/0969725X.2016.1205260

de Boer, Karin. "On Hegel: The Sway of the Negative." In *Renewing Philosophy*, edited by Gary Banham. New York: Palgrave Macmillan, 2010.

Ferrini, Cinzia. "The Transition to Organics: Hegel's Idea of Life." In *A Companion to Hegel*, edited by Stephen Houlgate and Michael Baur, 203–24. West Sussex: Blackwell, 2011.

Hahn, Songsuk Susan. *Contradiction in Motion: Hegel's Organic Concept of Life and Value*. Ithaca: Cornell University Press, 2007.

Harris, Errol E. "How Final is Hegel's Rejection of Evolution?" In *Hegel and the Philosophy of Nature*, edited by Stephen Houlgate, 196–208. Albany: State University of New York Press, 1998.

Hegel, G.W.F. *Philosophy of Right*. Translated by T.M. Knox. Oxford: Oxford University Press, 1967.

—— *Science of Logic*. Translated by A.V. Miller. Atlantic Highlands, NJ: Humanities Press, 1969.

—— *Philosophy of Nature*, Vol. 1. Translated and edited by Michael John Petry. London: George Allen and Unwin, 1970.

—— *Natural Law: The Scientific Ways of Treating Natural Law, Its Place in Moral Philosophy, and Its Relation to the Positive Sciences of Law*. Translated by T.M. Knox. Philadelphia: University of Pennsylvania Press, 1975.

—— *Phenomenology of Spirit*. Translated by A.V. Miller. Oxford: Oxford University Press, 1977.

Houlgate, Stephen, and Michael Baur, eds. *A Companion to Hegel*. West Sussex: Blackwell, 2011. http://www.etymonline.com/word/inter (accessed August 7, 2025)

https://sanskritdictionary.com/?q=prath (accessed August 7, 2025)

Petry, Michael John, trans. and ed. *Introduction to the Philosophy of Nature*, Vol. 1. Edited by G.W.F. Hegel. London: George Allen and Unwin, 1970. www.marxists.org/reference/archive/hegel/works/na/nature3.htm.

Žižek, Slavoj. *Tarrying with the Negative*. Durham: Duke University Press, 1993.

—— *In Defense of Lost Causes*. London: Verso, 2008.

—— *Less Than Nothing*. London, New York: Verso, 2013.

8 Hegel on Language and Freedom

JIM VERNON, YORK UNIVERSITY

The central tenet of Hegel's philosophy, of course, is that "the essence of humanity is freedom."[1] Coming to consciousness of the nature of that freedom, and actualizing it through the progressively developed forms of spirit, is thus the essential task of human history. However, since this task is grounded in an essence of which Hegel also claims that we have, for the most part, remained ignorant, our freedom must be determinately linked to a species-specific property, which both implies and makes possible our freedom, but which we can possess without necessarily either fully grasping or concretely actualizing it.[2] In the *Philosophy of Right*,[3] Hegel argues that the free will consists of two inextricable sides. On the one hand, freedom's actualization presupposes the will's concrete activity, or the "positing of itself as something determinate [or] the absolute moment of the finitude or particularization of the 'I'."[4] While this side of the will is uncontroversial, determinate decision or action alone – as Hegel knew well from Kant – is insufficient for demonstrating the existence of freedom, for it can always be credited to biological drive, physical forces, emotional affect, etc. Genuine freedom, Hegel therefore argues, also presupposes:

> the element of *pure indeterminacy* or of the "I"'s pure reflection into itself, in which every limitation, every content, whether present immediately through nature, through needs, through desires, and drives, or given in some other way, is dissolved; this is the limitless infinity of *absolute abstraction* or *universality*.[5]

Such abstract freedom is both universal, in that it would necessarily ground all possible free beings and actions, and infinite, in that it would make possible an immeasurable number of particularizations without being determined by any of them. It is thus the existence of this universal, infinite, self-determining freedom that Hegel is burdened to demonstrate. He helpfully informs us, however, that the "deduction *that* the will is free" is offered in the *Encyclopedia*,[6] where he argues that "*spirit* is initially *intelligence* and that the determinations through which it proceeds in its development, from *feeling* to *representational thinking* to *thought*, are the way by which it produces itself as [free] *will*."[7] This development, moreover, clarifies and deepens an argument sketched, more famously, in the 'Freedom of Self-consciousness' section of the *Phenomenology of Spirit*.[8] In what follows, I retrace this development – first in outline in the *Phenomenology*, then in more detail in the *Encyclopedia* – in order to determine the species-specific property that implicitly demonstrates our free essence. I close with some remarks on the import of his account for understanding freedom's historical actualization.

The *Phenomenology of Spirit*: Resolving the Unhappy Consciousness

Hegel's infamous account of the "unhappy consciousness" essentially rests upon the tension noted above: that between the concrete, empirical actions we can actually experience and the universal, infinite freedom upon which they rest, but which cannot simply be grasped through them. Coming out of the master/slave dialectic, Hegel argues that consciousness, just beginning to grasp itself as free, can only understand its activity in one of two ways: a) as the free agency that can rise above all given determinations and abstractly *think* of the actions it can perform (the slave's capacity to "rise above it all," whose affirmation Hegel identifies as the attitude of "stoicism"); or b) as the concrete works performed to alter given determinations in accordance with its thought (the slave's real negations of mere being into thought, whose affirmation Hegel identifies as the attitude of "skepticism"). On the one hand, grasping ourselves "stoically" means retreating from the finitude of particular actions into the infinite universality of pure thought; however, this leaves our freedom radically unproven, as it is merely "thought," but not experienced or acted. On the other hand, grasping our freedom "skeptically" allows us to experience its results, but the particular nature of our specific negations leaves it unclear as to how such finite particularities proceed from our universal, infinite thought. As H.S. Harris puts it, if it was the "Skeptics [who] realized the conceptual freedom of rational freedom recognized by the Stoics" they nevertheless thereby "set ... thought free from finite experience" by demonstrating that "pure 'thought' must be completely independent of sense-experience."[9] Self-consciousness, as the concrete application of

abstract freedom, is thus "unhappy" because "the unity of both is …
its essence [*Wesen*] [b]ut it is not as yet *for itself* this essence, not yet the
unity of both"[10] because it cannot grasp its universal, infinite freedom
through its particular, finite actions. Rather, Hegel claims, because our
infinite and finite "selves" seem radically incompossible, the more "natural" attitude is, in fact, to grasp them as "not the same, but *opposites*."[11]

Hegel explores three attempts to resolve this conflict by representing
it as the relation between a (finite, particular, determined) believing subject and a (infinite, universal, free) God, namely, the attempts expressed
by Judaism, Medieval Catholicism and contemporary Protestantism.[12]
These pages have produced a rich debate regarding the "transportabil-
ity" (or lack thereof) of the forms of attempted resolution.[13] My concern
here is not to enter into them, but merely to use the forms of religious
belief which Hegel uses as representative examples in order to articulate – in general form – the ultimately adequate solution to the problem
of freedom towards which they progress.

First, because nothing in our finitude reveals infinite freedom, and
because we can only "see" our activity through our concrete negations, self-consciousness takes itself to be constrained by finitude or to
be nothing more than the "Changeable consciousness" for whom the
universal and infinite, or "Unchangeable is … an alien Being [*ein Frem-
des*]."[14] In Hegel's *Vorstellung*, because the universal side of freedom
is unknowable to us, we project our essence into a radical outside, in
the form of a God unrelated to our empirical fetters. We are not free,
but God is, and thus particular finitude and universal infinitude are
essentially distinguished by a believer who posits a being in whom
abstract free thought can unchangeably exist without the contamination of changeable finitude.

The problem, of course, is that the tension between stoicism and
skepticism is only resolved in so far as the believer can and does posit
a God in whom the stoic "half" of itself can reside. No relation with the
alien Unchangeable is possible, and thus the only "evidence" for it is
the believer's consciousness itself. As such, the "elevation [of universality into the abstract Unchangeable] is itself this same consciousness.
It is, therefore, directly consciousness of the opposite, viz. of itself as
a particular individual."[15] This "Judaic" solution to the unhappy consciousness fails because the radical alterity of its unchangeable God
"that enters into consciousness is through this very fact at the same
time affected by individuality, [as it] is only present with the latter."[16]
Thus, this consciousness remains unhappy, because it remains the unactualized thought of the unity of the universal and the particular, now
merely transposed into the form of religious belief.

Having returned to the original tension, consciousness cannot simply rest within its contradictory knowledge. Consciousness now knows that the implicit knowledge of universal infinity by which it is troubled cannot be understood in mere distinction from particular finitude; any knowledge it can have of it must be tied somehow to the finitude it can experience. However, having grasped it as a distinct "Unchangeable," it equally cannot (yet) reconcile this essence with its own, changeable nature. Thus, consciousness once again posits the Unchangeable in another – no longer as "the pure *formless* Unchangeable [*ungestalteten Unwandelbaren*]" but as "the *Unchangeable in* [empirical] *form* [*gestalteten Unwandelbaren*]."[17] In other words, consciousness seeks to resolve the tension by positing the Unchangeable as somehow united with a finite individual – just not itself. Thus, the abstract God of Judaism gives way to the divine incarnation of Christ.

The difficulties with this attempt, however, are obvious: just as consciousness could not understand its own unity with the universal essence, neither can it grasp how any figure of incarnation can be unified with it. There is no rationality or necessity to this incarnation, as it simply satisfies a demand of consciousness, and thus "the fact that the Unchangeable receives the form of individuality is only a *contingent happening* [*ein* Geschehen]."[18] Thus, this does not resolve the tension within consciousness; to the contrary, it deepens it, "for if the [unchangeable] beyond seems to have been brought closer to the individual consciousness through the form of an actuality that is individual, it henceforth on the other hand confronts him as an opaque sensuous *unit* with all the obstinacy of what is *actual*."[19] Just as there is nothing in our mere finitude that reveals our infinite freedom, so there is nothing in any other finite particularity that demonstrates its presence either. Christ, as an empirical individual, cannot be concretely grasped as God, and thus our hope of unifying with the unchangeable through him "must remain a hope … without fulfillment of present fruition."[20] As Jean Hyppolite puts it, the "God who is dead is no more accessible than the God who never knew life,"[21] for the crucified Son brings the resolution of the "unhappy" tension between the Changeable and the Unchangeable no closer than the distant Father.

Hegel then details several methods consciousness might undertake to bring about the demonstrable unity of the Changeable and the Unchangeable through devotional works (prayer, service, etc.), but none, for obvious reasons, are actually convincing. What is required is a resolution of the original tension, or the demonstration that consciousness, in and through its finite particularity, nevertheless already possesses and exemplifies unchangeable infinity. The problem is not whether some random figure, ages ago, contingently happened to incarnate such a unity, or whether the world could somehow be transformed into an expression of it; the problem is grasping some form of our finitude – our concrete finite actions and expressions – as revelatory of our infinite, free essence. Somehow, we must be brought to grasp how we, in our particularity, partake of universality.

Because the two sides of the tension are still understood to be in opposition, the third attempt at resolving the unhappy consciousness takes the form of seeking some "middle term [*Mitte*]" between ourselves and the Unchangeable, or a mediator.[22] The Unchangeable is still distinct from empirical particularity, but the mediator (i.e. the priest) is tasked with the role of bringing particularity in line with universality, or turning consciousness into a vehicle for the Unchangeable. Because the priest is a finite, changeable personality no different than the consciousness who seeks mediation, their nature, unlike that of the incarnation of Christ, contains no mystery; they, like we, are merely changeable finitude. However, in taking this particular individual to be a mediator between oneself and the incarnate God, when we strive to be like the priest, we take ourselves to be striving to better actualize the unchangeable with which we seek unity. This third attempt at resolving our "unhappiness," then, takes the form of ceasing to will, think, or act as our own particular self, and doing only what the priest demands. Thus, this form of mediation demands "the *extinction* [*Vertilgung*] of [one's own] particular individuality,"[23] or the complete transformation of all of one's own habits, desires, and thoughts into those demanded by the priest. Through mediation, then, the unhappy consciousness *becomes some other particularity*, for its new empirical nature, "since it follows upon the decision of someone else, ceases, as regards the doing or *willing* of it, to be its own."[24]

Now, to be clear, the claim, here cannot be that the consciousness can judge the *validity* of the priest's mediation; given the failure of the positing of an incarnation to resolve the tension at the heart of consciousness, there is no ground upon which to suggest that what is at stake is the aligning of one's contingent willing and action with demonstrably universal aims or teachings. Rather, what appears to be at stake is the active elimination of all of the contingently given thoughts, actions and habits of consciousness seeking mediation through the rote, mechanical memorization of the *equally contingent* discourse of the priest, or what Hegel calls consciousness' "practicing of what it does not understand [*eines unverstandenen Geschäftes*]."[25] By effectively taking on the will, or mind, of the priest as its own, consciousness achieves the "certainty of having truly *divested* itself of its 'I' [*in Wahrheit seines* Ich *sich entäussert*]" nullifying its own particular capacity to think, act, and will on its own, and becoming the mere mechanical container, as it were, of a contingent discourse that is alien, to the point of it being nearly meaningless, to it.[26]

Once again, the true significance of this move cannot be that consciousness finally aligns itself with the universal; the remoteness of God or the mysteriousness of Christ cannot be overcome by simply deciding that one random priest is their true messenger. To the contrary, the positive aspect of this move – even if the individual consciousness fails to grasp it – lies in the fact that it has shown that *it can replace its empirical ego with a different, unrelated, even meaningless one*; consciousness, that is, can explicitly "posit[… its] will *as the will of another*"[27] and this can be achieved by positing its will as that of *any* other. By transforming one's own mind into the mind of some other individual, consciousness reveals that it can make its particular will the will of any particular other by simply memorizing a meaningless set of thoughts. Consciousness, in short, can become *any particular mind at all*, simply by mechanically internalizing any content at all, divesting itself of its own received particularity and effectively becoming an example of particularity in general.

Through this process, consciousness demonstrates to itself that it is not determined by its particular empirical actions and thoughts, for it can always empirically actualize itself in completely alien, even meaningless ways; consciousness, that is, can be any particular consciousness, and yet remain "itself" or its own "I," demonstrating that our particular, changeable self rests upon an infinite capacity for determining ourselves to be any such consciousness, or the general capacity for actualizing any and every empirical structure of consciousness whatsoever. In short, it reveals itself "not as a particular, but as a universal will,"[28] for, beyond its empirical individuality lies its universal capacity to become any other such individuality, even one which is completely meaningless to it as its empirical self, while always remaining "itself"; thus, this capacity to become any contingent particularity reveals that "the superseded single individual is the universal [*das aufgehobene Einzelne das Allgemeine ist*]."[29] Consciousness is always *some* particular consciousness, but because it can always become *any other* particular consciousness, it reveals itself, in and through its particularity, to be universal and infinite. As such, consciousness can – through its distinct particularities – grasp the universal, infinite essence that lies behind its finitude; thus the unhappy consciousness can be "resolved."

Of course, there is much within this proposed method of resolving "unhappiness" that remains problematic. As Hegel notes, while the particular individual, through self-supersession, "does indeed become

[the] universal and essential will," given the actual use of a priestly mediator taken to actually provide divine guidance in the exemplary case, it is inevitable that the believing "consciousness itself does not take itself to be this essential will."[30] Because consciousness only takes on the external discourse because they endow the priest with "universal" powers, whatever grasp of "the universal which comes to be for [consciousness], is not regarded as its *own doing*," but is credited to the mediator.[31] Moreover, because the priest mediates between the believer and the Unchangeable beyond, the universal essence itself is still held to be distinct from consciousness, and thus the long sought "overcoming [of unhappiness] remains a beyond."[32] As such, it remains unclear whether the unhappy consciousness is truly resolved through any form of religious representation.

Moreover, even if consciousness could come to explicit awareness of the implicit truth of this resolution through priestly mediation, the universal, infinite ground of its freedom still lacks explicit form. Thus, even if the argument above works, all that has been learned is that we have the general capacity for universal expression, thought and action; we have yet to discern what, within us, exactly grounds that capacity. In short, even if consciousness grasps *that* it is universally free, it does not know *how* it is so. In the "Psychology" section of the *Encyclopedia*, however, Hegel provides – not merely a "transported" version of the same argument lacking its religious *Vorstellungen* – but a more richly detailed and explicit account of the precise property that grounds human freedom.[33]

The Philosophy of Mind: The Linguistic Ground of Freedom[34]

Having – once again, through the master/slave dialectic–demonstrated that consciousness is, beyond the mind's "*phenomenal aspect* found in empirical representation, in thinking as well as in desire and will," something "above nature and natural determinacy [or] raised above the material" of its finite side into the "universal modes of activity of *mind as such* [*allgemeinen Tätigkeitsweisen des Geistes als solchen*]," Hegel tasks himself, in his discussion of "Psychology," with demonstrating mind's ability to "realize the concept of its freedom, i.e. to supersede [*aufzuheben*] the *form* of immediacy, with which it once again begins."[35] That is, on the one hand, Hegel once again asserts that consciousness "is *finite* in so far as … it has a particular determinateness [*eine Bestimmtheit*] to its knowledge, namely through immediacy and, what is the same thing, by being subjective";[36] on the other hand, mind is equally what he calls "reason," which is "infinite in so far as it is 'absolute' freedom,"[37] or the capacity to rise above all finite, merely subjective determinations. As in the "unhappy consciousness," the "finitude of mind lies in the fact that it cannot grasp the in-and-for-itself of its [infinite] reason, or equally, that it has not brought [its infinite reason] to full manifestation in [its finite] knowledge [*Die Endlichkeit des Geistes besteht daher darin, daß das Wissen das Anundfürsichsein seiner Vernunft nicht erfaßt, oder ebensosehr, daß diese sich nicht zur vollen Manifestation im Wissen gebracht hat*]."[38] Thus, the "Psychology" section opens with the same problem as the "freedom of Self-Consciousness" – the unresolved tension between universal, abstract freedom and its particular, concrete actualization, as grasped from the finite side of consciousness. And, once again, we find consciousness begin by "naturally" identifying itself with "its appearance [*ihr Schein*]," or its finite, empirical determination.[39] Thus, "Psychology" begins with an "[i]ntelligence [which] *finds* itself *determined*" by empirical externality.[40] Psychological mind, like the early stages of unhappy consciousness, begins by presupposing that it is not universally free, but is rather empirically determined by the given. However, deprived of the earlier religious *Vorstellungen*, Hegel's account of this affected, or "changeable," development of the mind takes a vastly different course, if only to arrive at much the same "solution."

An un-free mind whose content is empirically given is characterized by *affection*, or "*feeling*."[41] The passive determination of feeling, however, conceals an implicit activity. While the affective content is determined externally, its specific cognition tacitly presupposes the "diremption of this immediate finding"[42] by mind. While our perception of a table, e.g., arises from the presence of an affective field containing the relevant sensible content, in order to specifically experience the table as present, we must separate it from its background, or isolate it from all other present affective contents, on which we could equally well focus. Thus, the determinate content arising from seemingly passive affect in fact presupposes the subjective *act* of "*attention*, without which, nothing exists for [mind]."[43] Making explicit the foundational role of attention, Hegel claims, is mind's "awakening to itself ... its *recollection of itself* [*Erinnerung-in-sich*],"[44] in that it comes to see that it itself determines its experiences, rather than its experiences being determinative of it.

Realizing its experiences are determined by, rather than determining of, subjective activity, it then appears to mind that the "finding of content [is] no longer necessary,"[45] because mind is the real origin of cognition, which is, as it were, "freely" created through attention. However, this initial "freedom" is in fact severely limited, for objects can only be cognized in so far as the material to which we attend is affectively given to us (while we attend to the table, this is only insofar as a table is present in our affective field for our possible attention). Objects, thus, inevitably appear to us as though found, not founded, and thus mind experiences its cognition as both free and determined, and thus as self-contradictory, returning it to "unhappiness." This tension, Hegel now argues, can only be relieved if we can somehow transform found "external" content into something subjectively "internal"; and his account of "recollection" is intended to explain how mind "posits the content of [cognition] in its interiority" transforming it into something he calls an "image [*Bild*]."[46]

"Recollection," however, in many ways simply clarifies the process of attentive determination within an affective field. While objects initially appeared to be merely received with their own "objective" determinations, we have seen that they have no determinate existence outside of mind's attending to them. Comprehending this process, Hegel argues, deprives objects of "the complete determination that"[47] they had in affection, for a determinate cognition has only our "attention as its time as well as its place."[48] It is this attentive abstraction from affective immediacy that produces "images." Images thus do not *represent* external objects; they *produce* our determinate experiences of them. In attending to an object, I "interiorize" its "image" by retaining the abstract form of attention through which it was cognized. However, Hegel calls this process "recollection" because such forms, when not in use, do not simply disappear. Relying upon the common sense fact that we can and do recognize objects when we attend to appropriate fields, Hegel argues that such recognition presupposes that attentive images remain "within" mind when not in use, and therefore can be "recollected" for future use. Recollection, he thus argues, presupposes a "night-like pit in which a world of infinitely many images is kept ... yet without being in consciousness."[49] Attentive forms are called forth when we recognize objects ion our experience as identical or similar to others we have experienced, and are thus somehow "stored" when not in use. Recollection proper, then, is the "reference of an image to an intuition" in the form of recognition, or the "*subsumption* of the individual intuition under the form in accordance with the universal" image.[50]

However, because such images, when not in use, are sunk in the pit, recognition still requires affection. Thus, nothing in this process yet relieves the "unhappy" tension of attentive mind; it simply renders more explicit the structure that creates it. This tension can only be resolved if our images are somehow "posited simultaneously [as] distinguishable from the [recognized] intuition and [as] separable from the simple night in which [they were] at first sunk,"[51] and this self-presentation of recollected content is the work of the *"imagination."*[52] Hegel, unfortunately, offers little explanation of the nature of the imagination; his view, however, reflects common understanding: through the power of something called the imagination, formal images are linked with subjectively presented content, as when we represent food to ourselves in hunger-induced fantasies or dreams. Of course, the imagined meal, created by a subjective power, need not reflect the manner in which we normally "find" one within intuitive fields; imagined images can be associated with any others without the need for justification by affective content. Such creative association, free from external determination, "is thereby a subsumption of the particular under a *universal* which solidifies their connection," revealing consciousness to be the "power over the store of its dependent images and representations."[53]

Thus, the imagination (through both the representative reproduction of stored images and the creative association of them) allows consciousness to both determine and relate content independently of affection, removing all external determination from cognition. The images abstracted from affective fields, the imagined versions of them and the creative associations forged between them are all contingent to the "peculiar content [*eigentümlichen Inhalt*]"[54] of the experiencing subject, rather than any external input. Thus, it would appear that mind's drive towards freedom from the given, "in creative imagination's self-intuition [*Phantasie zur Selbstanschauung*] has come to its completion"[55] in that its cognitive content is entirely self-determined. Imagination, liberating cognition from external determination, would appear to render mind completely free.

However, while imagining mind is certainly less determined than affective or merely attentive consciousness, this self-determination as yet only occurs within its own imagination, out of its own history. There is no demonstration, as yet, of the *universality* and *infinity* requisite for human freedom, for the contents imagined are developed from the contingent experiences of individual subjects (and are thus *particular*) and are limited to imagined combinations of affectively received content (and are thus *finite*). Having begun with contingently "objective" determination from the outside, we have simply shifted to the contingently "subjective" manipulation of that content in imagination. As such, mind still remains with the "finite, particular" side of itself, lacking determinate universality and infinity, although – because it can raise itself from determination via attention, recollection and imagination – it implicitly knows itself to be equally the latter. Thus, once again, mind finds itself beset by the "unhappy" conflict between its implicit universality and experienced particularity.

In order to reconcile this tension, Hegel now argues, mind must thus somehow determine the universality of its forms of content-determination; that is, it must demonstrate that there are forms through which experienced content can be creatively re-arranged that are common to all other minds. Of course, we have no immediate access to other minds through which we can check for common possession, and therefore we require a *medium* that allows the exchange of attentive and imaginative forms between minds for the purpose of confirmation. Our forms of experience must be "made *to be*, and to be *a fact*"[56] that can be experienced by others, so that we can compare our ideas and associations with theirs. This can only be accomplished by somehow synthesizing the "objectively" given (affective intuitions) and the "subjectively" created (images and associations), forging what Hegel calls a "*sign.*"[57]

However, we have seen that merely affective experience leads intelligence to produce merely subjective abstract images. Signs are only possible, then, if "the proper [i.e. affective] content [*der eigene Inhalt*] of the intuition, and that [idea] whose sign the intuition is to be, never contaminate each other [*geht einander nichts an*]."[58] That is, the affective intuition through which ideas are expressed must be *arbitrary* in order to be cognized *as expressions*. A sign is thus first something given that "is deemed [by the signifying mind] in the identity [of the object and the image] not as positive or as itself, but as representing *something else*" or the sign's "meaning [*Bedeutung*]."[59] Obviously, few, if any, merely given affections will be readily experienced by others as meaningful. True signs must thus be intuitions that can be objectively recognized by all as expressing subjective ideas, or those which are experienced as "external, psychic determinac[ies], [or] posited being[s] arising from intelligence."[60] Signification, proper, Hegel thus argues, requires externalities that arise out of our "own anthropological naturalness" – specifically in the form of sounded "tone[s] [*Ton*]."[61]

Hegel argues that, prior to any determinate linguistic capability, we encounter the "voice in general"[62] as the primary vehicle of expressing internal states. Infants, after all, despite lacking determinate images and ideas, express general interior states through "speech, laughter, sighs and other particularizations" of voice, proving that vocalizations represent the "most familiar connections that link"[63] the internal and the external. However, what requires expression through signs are not vague affective states but the determinate forms of attention and connection forged by representational intelligence. Thus, Hegel argues, such vaguely expressive cries must be *refined* into clearly differentiable utterances, or "further articulated tone[s]."[64] Signs proper, then, consist of determinate ideas psychologically linked to articulated sounds, or what Hegel calls "words."[65]

Of course, these words will only be recognized as being those that indicate the specific meanings we seek to express if others also use them in the same way, and thus refining our articulation is not just a matter of making tones more determinate than cries; it marks the process through which we come to utter the specific words that others also use to communicate the particular images or associations whose objectivity we seek to test. While this process is not explicitly detailed by Hegel, his developmental logic of inter-subjective expression through refined articulation suggests that individuals come to articulate their meanings through signs appropriate to their community. Thus, the signs we articulate are subjective syntheses of arbitrary tone and specific meaning, our "acquisition" of them is driven by our need to communicate to others in a shared language.

It is for this reason that Hegel invokes *writing* as a "further progression"[66] in expression. The signs we use to speak to others, arising from a subjective source, are inevitably produced with peculiar accent and other linguistic contingencies, making *exact* replication of the words of others essentially impossible. "Roughly exact" mimicry no doubt works perfectly well in "ordinary" usage, but it is insufficient for the epistemic confirmation for which language was acquired. Spoken language becomes more universal in being explicitly posited as an externality in principle shared by all, and thus speech itself must be synthesized with a more universally perceivable, or more external, intuition. In short, speech, as the medium of objective communication, implicitly presupposes writing, which, due to its more "external," less "subjective" nature, is more universally communicable.

Of course, actual examples of writing are prey to the peculiarity of individual writers, so it is simply not plausible that "writing" in any standard sense eliminates the subjective particularity that haunts signs. It is thus appropriate to expand Hegel's concept of "writing" to signify more generally the presupposed standardization of signs within a community outside of all subjective peculiarity.[67] Such "written" signs would be the universal types of the spoken/scripted tokens, or generally articulated signs particular to no-one, but presupposed by subjective expression. Linguistic expression in general implies a communal, "external" set of signs that, while not identical to any actual expression, nonetheless receive expression in particular utterances or, as Hegel puts it, "the synthesis of the idea (as something internal) with the intuition (as something external), is itself external."[68] Thus, in order to test our images and associations against those of others through articulated tones, we must first internalize the external, generally articulated signs in use within our community. "The internalization of this externality," Hegel claims, "is *memory* [*Die Erinnerung dieser Äußerlickeit ist das* Gedächtnis]."[69]

The process of memory resembles the earlier stage of representation, in that it is marked by the formal abstraction of intuited particulars. What is new, here, is that these forms are specifically internalized as "names," or syntheses of articulated sound and subjective idea. Memory, then, is specifically linguistic and it is "through [memory's] internalization of each ... sign [that mind] raises the *particular* synthesis [i.e., the contingently subjective synthesis of meaning and tone] to a *universal*, permanent synthesis, in which name and meaning are objectively bound,"[70] that is, into an abstract, formal intention for hearing and expressing a generally articulated word. This first stage of memory "makes the intuition, which the name primarily is, into a *representation*, so that ... meaning and sign are identified as *one*."[71] We learn the lexicon of a communal language when memory creates permanent syntheses of sound and meaning as intentional forms for recognizing contingently expressed words as particular tokens of generally articulated types, through what Hegel calls "name-*retaining* memory."[72]

The work of linguistic memory, Hegel claims, fundamentally alters the content of mind. Formerly, we possessed a subjectively contingent stock of images called forth either by an appropriately constituted affective field, or through the subjective imagination of one; however, by permanently synthesizing subjective meanings with linguistic types, what is henceforth called forth from the pit in such recognition is the communally appropriate word. Thus, in memorized words, mind "has and recognizes the thing,"[73] insofar as it both recalls meanings synthesized with public words; and correlatively, in the recognition of an intuited content, the same synthesis is recalled, and thus "in the thing [one has and recognizes] the word."[74] As such, linguistic mind "has nothing more to do with an image which, as derived from intuition, is taken from an immediate, *ungeistigen* determination of intelligence."[75] The retention of a word allows us to forgo both external intuition and subjective fantasy and represent a meaning to ourselves as an objective, generally articulated but subjectively forged word, or "determinate being [*Dasein*] which is itself a product of intelligence."[76] While individual subjects create the syntheses for themselves, they create them in conformity with public signs that are peculiar to no-one, transforming the contents of consciousness from subjective peculiarities into objective determinacies; it would appear, then, that mind has satisfied its drive to verify the universality of its forms, finally becoming "happy."

Acquired words, however, are syntheses of external, public signs and internal, subjective meanings. These meanings, as we have seen, are already associated by the imagination, either habitually or creatively, and thus already determinately exist within linguistic mind in subjectively contingent relations; as Hegel puts it, the "association of the particular names [to each other] lies in the *meaning* of the determinations of the feeling, representing or thinking intelligence, the series of which [mind] runs through in so far as it feels, represents or thinks."[77] As such, the words we acquire are not yet *fully* objective, as their meanings are still associated in both contingently and subjectively meaningful senses. This, of course, also applies to the language use of others, and so simply imitating public expressions – e.g., memorizing and affirming the discourse of a contingent priest – will not determine their objectivity. Acquired public language is not yet universal enough to determine the validity of our experiential forms, as there still remains a difference between names (which are internalized as discreet, objective signs) and their meanings (which are related to each other in subjectively peculiar senses). The universality sought through language acquisition is only possible, Hegel claims, in "the sublation of every difference between meaning and name [*das Aufheben jenes Untershiedes der Bedeutung und des Namens*]."[78] Thus, in order to make its universality explicit, mind must divest its acquired, public words of their subjectively peculiar senses, or posit "itself [as] the universal space of names as such, i.e., of senseless words [*sinnloser Worte*]."[79]

Names as such are thus posited in order to eliminate the given connections contingently existing between words; they can only arise when a subject actively posits its acquired words as completely discreet or senseless. What requires elimination are not the subjective meanings of words (which, after all, have been permanently synthesized with tones),[80] but the associations or senses already forged by experience and imagination between the meanings. Names as such arise when we empty our acquired lexicon of all associative senses and simply retain words in some "stable order"[81] that is not determined by communal use or subjective particularity. Every mechanically memorized word, then, would be different from its others as a synthesis of tone and meaning (i.e., a *name* as such), but no more than different, lacking all relation to others (i.e., a name *as such*). Mechanical memory, then, deprives mind of all linguistic intentions and associations, transforming it into the "power over the different names as *totally abstract subjectivity*."[82] Having purged its content of the contingency of both the external determination of affection *and* the subjective particularity of associative sense, the mechanically memorizing subject could be *any linguistic mind at all,* holding *any linguistic content at all*. This represents both mind's "highest inwardization of representation," for it memorizes the most objective material, and also its "highest *divestment (Entäußerung)*," for it rids itself of all contingent particularity.[83] Implicitly, "intelligence is the universal" or "the simple truth of the *divestments* of its particularity [*die einfache Wahrheit ihrer besonderen Entäußerungen*],"[84] and it is mechanical memory that makes this explicit. Thus, as in the conclusion of the "unhappy consciousness" above, it is *by completely divesting itself of its own particularity*, ridding itself of subjectively meaningful discourse, thereby *revealing its universal, abstract subjectivity*, that mind can unite its seemingly opposed sides. However, here, this is accomplished *without the mediation of a specific other* – eliminating the possibility that we may not recognize our accomplishment due to the problems noted above – but individually, through *the generic linguistic contents any mind would need to relate to be an intentional subject*. Subjective mind, on its own, has become a mere *mind as such*.

Thus, if any relations can be shown to derive from the mere retention of discreet words within mechanical mind, they would be the objective and necessary forms through which any and all linguistic content would necessarily be determined. Because mechanical memory marks the shift from contingently related content (in all its forms: external affection, subjective attention, idiosyncratic creative association, priestly or communal sense, etc.) to the universal forms of determinate relation for *geistig* content in general, Hegel claims that "*memory* is … the transition to the activity of *thought*,"[85] or the objective and universal forms of linguistic content determination.

Thinking, then, is "universal in the dual meaning of universal as such," that is both the forms of content determination necessarily possessed by any and all linguistic minds "and identically as an immediacy or existence," the generic, *geistig* content that can be memorized by all such minds to be ordered by those forms.[86] In both content and form, then, mind is now free of both subjective and external contingency, and thus is "*in itself* the *universal*."[87] Mind no longer needs to look outside of itself – in either affection or mediating minds – for objective universality, as its internal content has now been purged of subjective peculiarity; in thinking *itself*, mind is objectively universal. Having revealed abstract universality in its own self through content particular to no-one, it would appear that mind is finally determinately, "happily" free.

However, two problems remain: first, as we saw from the start, abstract freedom is not simply universal; it is also infinite. The demonstration of our free essence demands, beyond mere necessity for all linguistic minds, the revelation of a limitless capacity for self-determining thought. Secondly, as Hegel notes, this universality is, as yet, merely *"formal*, [for] the universality and its being are simply the subjectivity of intelligence."[88] All mind has to think are whatever words it contingently memorized in the order in which it contingently holds them. Thus, thinking has no forms of its own, for the "thoughts [as yet] are not in and for themselves determinate and [thus] the representations inwardized to thinking are in this respect still the given content."[89] Mechanical mind, then, must determine–from its unrelated content alone–the universal, infinite forms of thought.

In determining its content, thinking mind (in Hegel's terse summation) *"explains* (a) ... the individual out of its universalities ... [then] (b) explains that same individual *as* a universal ... in judgment ... but it [then] (c) *determines content* out of itself in the *syllogism*";[90] this, of course, refers us to the account of the "Concept" in the *Logic*.[91] We lack the room here to completely explicate this determination, but recalling that the content at issue here is specifically linguistic, we can schematically indicate its nature.

Mind first seeks to categorically determine individuals. To preserve the universality of thought, we cannot presume the validity of any relations or categories (e.g., genus/species, etc.); within mechanical mind, all that can be determined of any individual name as such is that it is, *qua* specific synthesis of meaning and signifier, qualitatively discreet. Such qualitative discreetness, however, presupposes its qualitative difference from the other retained words, or that each name is distinct only in so far as it is distinguished from its others by the mind retaining them all. Names as such are thus never simply discreet, because their determination as distinct presupposes that they are qualitatively distinguished from their others within a mind that retains them all. As such, the form/content relation of mind/words is that of identity-in-difference, in that names are determined as distinct only through their distinguishing relation within mind, and thinking mind is determined only by distinguishing names from each other. This determining, yet distinguishing relationship of identity-in-difference is what Hegel calls *judgment*.

It is the form of judgment that posits the distinguishing relation as productive of its qualitative distinctness. The first word's determination *is*, in fact, the second word, and the judgment thus formally posits the distinguishing relation as an *identity*. The judgment, thus, relates a subject to a predicate, in that through it a word is determined as distinct only by being relationally identified with another that determines its distinctness. The form of judgment, as such, is the core structure of a truly universal grammar, or the objective, necessary form through which any and all linguistic content both can and must be related. In his Greater *Logic*, Hegel explicates a variety of forms this grammatical identity, moving from the mere identity-in-difference of any two distinct terms ("judgments of existence"), to the meaningful predication of some of the subject's qualitative determinations through specific, related predicates ("judgments of reflection"), to the categorial predication of the subject's essential characteristics ("judgments of necessity"), finally positing the predicating form itself as demanding a meaningful "fit" between subject and predicate ("judgments of the concept"). These forms of predication constitute the universal grammatical forms for formulating distinct determinate relations between terms, valid for every possible linguistic mind and all possible linguistic contents. They all are rooted, and therefore expressible, through the basic predicating form "S is P," which is the finite means through which an infinity of judgments can be made, from the most external (e.g., "the dream is furious") to the most essential (e.g., "God is being"). This relational grammar, of course, was already implicitly used prior to mechanical memory to make the habitual and creative predications that mind called into question; however, it has now been made explicit as the truly universal form of content relation, whose scope of application is unlimited, extending to all possible linguistic terms. It is thus the universal grammatical forms underlying all finite, particular expressions that demonstrate the abstract, infinite, universal freedom of humanity.

The only remaining problem is that it is unclear how they are to be applied. As it stands, "in these forms the *content* appears as given"[92] rather than fully determined by thought, for the forms of judgment do not themselves justify any particular predications. Thus, what is required is a new relational form that posits the universal forms of determinate correspondence between terms related via judgment. It is this that Hegel finds in the syllogism, wherein mind "*determines content* out of itself." Like the judgment, the syllogism progresses through rational forms for contingent, unreflective predications (the syllogisms of existence), more restrictive, sometimes meaningful predications (the syllogisms of reflection) and finally essential, invariably meaningful predications (the syllogisms of necessity). The result, however, is that mind comes to explicitly grasp its own forms of rational predication, through which terms and judgments may be determinately predicable of each other. Judgments are justified by other judgments, in strictly linguistic relations, as through subordinate clauses. Mind thus no longer needs to rely on its experiential habits or communal usage to determine its *geistig* content; it can now put its memorized names up to the test of syllogistic reasoning to see which predications are possible, yet merely contingent, which are reflective yet not essential, and finally which are categorially necessary for different terms. Words can now be related through their fit with rational forms of predication rather than the merely given contingencies of subjective and communal habit the rational forms of predication are themselves both universal to all thought and infinitely self-determining in their application. By grasping the rational forms of content relation, mind achieves the "last negation of immediacy" in that, henceforth, any possible linguistic "content is determined through" intelligence itself.[93] Because mind is no longer determined by contingency, either from within or without, but infinitely determines an objective, *geistig* content through its own universal forms of rational predication, its "thinking, as the free concept, is now also free in regard to *content*."[94] A thinking intelligence, grasping itself as the universal and infinite self-determiner of all of its possible content, is what Hegel rightly calls a free "*will*."[95]

Conclusion

For Hegel, the universal, infinite freedom of the will finds its ground in our linguistic capacity, or more precisely the species-specific property of a grammatically structured, rationally predicative language. This grammar, as demonstrated through mechanical memory, is not particular to a speaker, community, or even the contingently given collection of communities, but is necessary and universal for all possible speech and all possible speaking beings. Moreover, the universal forms of grammar also allow for an infinite number of self-determining predications from the most contingent and "nonsensical" to the most invariable and essential out of the communally objective meaning of words themselves. As such, the finite formal means of language, being both universal to all expression and infinitely self-determining in expressive application, ground the abstract side of the free will. While Hegel renders explicit these grammatical forms, they also structure unconscious, merely habitual language use, for they are required for meaningful speech of any kind. All language is necessarily structured through the basic forms of the rational judgment and, as such, the mere presence of a predicative linguistic capacity, resting on a universal and infinite grammar, is proof that we are implicitly free, even if we fail to grasp or actualize that freedom. In short, grasping the universality of grammar through mechanical memory demonstrates Hegel's assertion that "anyone can discover in himself an ability to abstract from anything whatsoever, and likewise to [freely] determine himself"[96] in thought and action; an ability that was implicitly present all along.

To be clear, rather than focusing merely on our general expressive capacity,[97] Hegel grounds our freedom in the determinate forms of grammatical predication, which are immanent to all expressions, but nevertheless distinct and abstractable from them. We are not free simply because we can and do express inner states, or merely because language allows us to consciously reflect upon our experience;[98] we are free because all of our possible and actual expressions are grounded in a rational, universal structure for relating all possible discreet linguistic materials in a self-determining manner. As such, Hegel finds himself closest, among his contemporaries, to Humboldt, and among recent theorists, to Noam Chomsky, in linking human freedom to a species-specific and inherently possessed linguistic capacity, which–as the infinite, self-determining use of determinate and limited, but universal means–is a rational "process of free creation; its laws and principles are fixed, but the manner in which the principles of [expressive] generation are used is free and infinite."[99] Thus, on Hegel's account, our freedom lies in our capacity, grounded in language, to both overcome adherence to merely given relations and rationally revise them in line with their own content and our rational essence.

From this we can infer that if the essence of humanity is freedom, then the historical actualization of that essence would be marked by emancipation from the contingently given relations received by consciousness (those of particular experience, subjective habits, communal mores, etc.) in and through the construction ones more fitting to the nature of the specific contents in and through which we must think and live. That is, grasping the nature of the language in which we must think teaches us that actualized freedom lies in our concrete emancipation from the naturally, habitually, and socially given, through the creation of structures that better reflect our innate capacity for rational self-determination. Our language capacity is what grounds our freedom, but – as the historical/religious narrative of the "unhappy consciousness" reveals – the "absolute determination or, if one prefers, absolute drive, of the free spirit … is to make its freedom into its object."[100] Our possession of language, then, merely demonstrates freedom to be our essence; its actualization remains the concrete, historical, and perpetual work of spirit.[101]

NOTES

1 G.W.F. Hegel, *The Philosophy of History*, trans. J. Sibree (New York: Dover Books, 1956), 99.

2 Of course, it is not uncommon to claim that freedom, in Hegel's
   philosophy, "is not … treated as an essential or really any other sort of
   property" (Robert Pippin, *Hegel's Practical Philosophy: Rational Agency as
   Ethical Life* (New York: Cambridge, 2008), 194). This paper aims to show
   that freedom – even if not itself a property – is essentially tied to one.

3 G.W.F. Hegel, *Elements of the Philosophy of Right*, ed. A. Wood, trans. H.B.
   Nisbet (Cambridge: Cambridge University Press, 1991); *Werke*, Bd. 7
   (Berlin, Suhrkamp: 1970-).

4 Ibid., §6

5 Ibid., §5

6 Hegel, *Werke*, Bd. 10. Hereafter cited by numbered paragraph, in the form
   Enc. §1. Hegel's own remarks will be noted by Anm. Translations are
   my own, although I have consulted *Hegel's Philosophy of Mind*, trans. A.
   Wallace and A.V. Miller (New York: Oxford, 1971).

7 *Philosophy of Right*, §4R

8 *Hegel's Phenomenology of Spirit*, trans. A.V. Miller (New York: Oxford,
   1977), cited by numbered paragraph.

9 H.S. Harris, *Hegel's Ladder I: The Pilgrimage of Reason* (Indianapolis:
   Hackett Publishing, 1997), 389.

10 *Phenomenology of Spirit*, §207, trans. mod.

11 Ibid., §208, my emphasis

12 As John Russon puts it in *Reading Hegel's Phenomenology* (Bloomington:
   Indiana University Press, 2004), "Hegel draws his illustrations of the
   phenomena of the unhappy consciousness from the world of religious
   devotion, for it is here that there is manifest a self-conscious self that
   distinguishes within itself an apparent and real self … recognizes that real
   self as what guides the self it apparently is" and seeks to determine the
   nature of that guidance (102). While freedom is extensively thematized in
   his book, it is interesting that Russon's discussion of this chapter hinges
   on the distinction between the "stoic [who] found freedom in an ability
   to assent" to determinations in thought and the "unhappy consciousness
   [which] finds truth in its ability *to have its assent compelled*" (103, emphasis
   added).

13 John Burbidge, "'Unhappy Consciousness' in Hegel: An Analysis of
   Medieval Catholicism?" in *Hegel on Logic and Religion: The Reasonableness
   of Christianity*, ed. J. Burbidge, 115–118 (Albany, NY: SUNY, 1992),
   provides both an excellent account of the case for limiting Hegel's case
   strictly to the context of his historical *Vorstellungen*, and a compelling
   argument for the 'transportable' nature of his logical moves. While
   certainly sympathetic with his view, I differ in reading this section as
   an argument primarily concerning human freedom, not "traditional
   epistemology" (118). See Bruce Baugh, *French Hegel: From Surrealism*

to Postmodernism (New York: Routledge, 2003) for a discussion of the
more ontological reception of these pivotal pages in French Continental
philosophy after the pioneering commentary of Jean Wahl, who "found
[in Hegel's account of the unhappy consciousness] a penetrating analysis
of an internally divided and self-alienated subject … that vainly strives
for synthesis but instead oscillates between self and not-self, between
being and nothingness" (5).

14 *Phenomenology of Spirit*, §208, trans. mod.
15 Ibid., §209
16 Ibid., §209
17 Ibid., §213, trans. mod.
18 Ibid., §212
19 Ibid., §212
20 Ibid., §212
21 *Genesis and Structure of Hegel's Phenomenology of Spirit* (Evanston, IL:
    Northwestern University Press, 1974), 202.
22 *Phenomenology of Spirit*, §227
23 Ibid., §227, my emphasis
24 Ibid., §228
25 Ibid., §229
26 Ibid., my emphasis.
27 Ibid., §230, my emphasis
28 Ibid., §230
29 Ibid., §231
30 Ibid., §230
31 Ibid., §230
32 Ibid., §230
33 Of course, because it comes immediately after the dialectic of "Self-
    consciousness," and immediately before the account of "Reason,"
    it is more natural to read the short section called "Universal Self-
    Consciousness" as the section of the Encyclopedia which corresponds to
    Chapter 4 of the *Phenomenology*. Because it lacks, however, any discussion
    of the Stoic and Skeptical forms of consciousness, or the tension
    produced between them, and because (as I aim to show presently) the
    "Psychology" section not only primarily concerns a similar "unhappy"
    tension within consciousness, but provides a similar resolution (down
    to very similar phrasing in the exposition), I think the latter can be read
    as providing a more precise and *Vortstellung*-free version of the same
    argument.
34 Much of the following draws upon work previously published in Jim
    Vernon, *Hegel's Philosophy of Language* (London: Continuum, 2007), esp.
    Chapters 2 & 3. At the time, I had neglected to notice the full connection

of these pages to development and resolution of the "Unhappy Consciousness" tension.

35 Enc., §440, Anm.
36 Ibid., §441
37 Ibid., §441
38 Ibid., §441
39 Ibid., §445
40 Ibid., §445
41 Ibid., §446
42 Ibid., §448
43 Ibid., §448
44 Ibid., §450
45   Ibid., §450
46 Ibid., §452
47 Ibid., §452
48 Ibid., §453
49 Ibid., §453
50 Ibid., §454
51 Ibid., §454
52 Ibid., §455
53 Ibid., §456
54 Ibid., §456
55 Ibid., §457
56 Ibid., §457
57 Ibid., §458
58 Ibid., §458, Anm.
59 Ibid., §458
60 Ibid., §459
61 Ibid., §459
62 Ibid., §401, Anm.
63 Ibid., §401, Anm.
64 Ibid., §459
65 Ibid., §459, Anm.
66 Ibid., §459, Anm.
67 Here, Hegel anticipates, at least in outline, the account of 'writing' as general articulation in Jacques Derrida, *Of Grammatology*, trans. G. Spivak (Baltimore: John's Hopkins, 1976) – *pace* Derrida's critique of Hegel in "The Pit and the Pyramid," *Margins of Philosophy*, trans. A. Bass. (Chicago: University of Chicago, 1982), 71–108.
68 Enc., §460
69 Ibid., §460
70 Ibid., §461, Hegel's emphasis

71 Ibid., §461
72 Ibid., §461
73 Ibid., §462
74 Ibid., §462
75 Ibid., §462
76 Ibid., §462 Anm.
77 Ibid., §462, my emphasis
78 Ibid., §463
79 Ibid., §463
80 This transition has been the site of considerable controversy. Some
    commentators – most notably Theodor Bodammer, *Hegels Deutung
    der Sprache* (Hamburg: Felix Meiner,1969), Werner Marx, *Absolute
    Reflexion und Sprache* (Frankfurt: Vittorio Klostermann, 1967) and John
    McCumber, *The Company of Words: Hegel, Language, and Systematic
    Philosophy* (Evanston: Northwestern University Press, 1993) – read this
    move as demanding the separation of meaning and name, leaving mere,
    'meaningless' words that thereafter can be objectively determined by
    thought. This contradicts not only Hegel's claim that linguistic memory
    creates "permanent syntheses," but his definition of a word as a synthesis
    of sound and meaning. My reading here is closer to Kathleen Dow
    Magnus, *Hegel and the Symbolic Mediation of Spirit* (New York: SUNY,
    2001) and Stephen Houlgate, "Hegel, Derrida and Restricted Economy:
    The Case of Mechanical Memory," *Journal of the History of Philosophy*
    34:1(1996): 79–94, although they credit the loss of connection between
    words to an *unconscious forgetting*, rather than a consciously posited *new
    form of memory*.
81 Enc., §463
82 Ibid., §463
83 Ibid., §463, my emphasis
84 Enc., §463, my emphasis
85 Ibid., §464
86 Ibid., §465
87 Ibid., §465
88 Ibid., §466
89 Ibid., §466
90 Ibid., §467
91 The account that follows is drawn from Hegel's *Science of Logic*, trans. A.V.
    Miller (New York: Humanity Books, 1969), 618–704.
92 Enc., §467
93 Ibid., §468
94 Ibid., §468
95 Ibid., §468

96 *Philosophy of Right*, §4R

97 As, e.g. Charles Taylor does in *Hegel and Modern Society* (Cambridge: Cambridge University Press, 1979).

98 As suggested by T.A. Lewis, "Speaking of Habits: The Role of Language in Moving from Habit to Freedom," *Owl of Minerva* 39 (2007–8): 25–53.

99 Noam Chomsky "Language and Freedom," in *The Essential Chomsky*, ed. A. Arnove, 75–91 (New York: The New Press, 2008), 88.

100 *Philosophy of Right*, §27

101 For a more complete defence of Hegelian freedom as actualized through concrete self-emancipation from the given, see my "Siding with Freedom: Towards a Prescriptive Hegelianism," *Critical Horizons* 12:1 (2011): 49–69 or "'Free Love': A Hegelian Defense of Same-Sex Marriage Rights," *The Southern Journal of Philosophy* 47:1 (Spring 2009): 69–89. For discussions of concrete social movements that exemplify the actualization of this essence, see my "'A Passion For Justice': Martin Luther King, Jr. and G.W.F. Hegel on 'World-Historical Individuals'," *Philosophy and Social Criticism* 43:2 (2017), 187–207 or "I Am We: Dialectics of Political Will in Huey P. Newton and the Black Panther Party", *Theory and Event* 17:4 (December 2014).

REFERENCES

Baugh, Bruce. *French Hegel: From Surrealism to Postmodernism*. New York: Routledge, 2003. DOI: 10.4324/9781315822051

Bodammer, Theodor. *Hegels Deutung der Sprache*. Hamburg: Felix Meiner, 1969. DOI: 10.1163/157007371X00252

Burbidge, John. "'Unhappy Consciousness' in Hegel: An Analysis of Medieval Catholicism?" In *Hegel on Logic and Religion: The Reasonableness of Christianity*, edited by J. Burbidge, 115–18. Albany, NY: SUNY, 1992. DOI: 10.2307/2185752

Chomsky, Noam. "Language and Freedom." In *The Essential Chomsky*, edited by A. Arnove, 75–81. New York: The New Press, 2008. DOI: 10.1604/9781595581891

Derrida, Jacques. *Of Grammatology*. Translated by G. Spivak. Baltimore: John's Hopkins, 1976. DOI: 10.56021/9781421419954.

—— *Margins of Philosophy*. Translated by A. Bass. Chicago: University of Chicago, 1982. DOI: 10.5840/intstudphil198820377

Dow Magnus, Kathleen. *Hegel and the Symbolic Mediation of Spirit*. Albany, NY: SUNY, 2001. DOI: 0.1017/S0263523200007977

Harris, H.S. *Hegel's Ladder I: The Pilgrimage of Reason*. Indianapolis: Hackett Publishing, 1997. DOI: 10.1604/9780872202788

Hegel, G.W.F. *The Philosophy of History*. Translated by J. Sibree. New York: Dover Books, 1956.

—— *Science of Logic*. Translated by A.V. Miller. New York: Humanity Books, 1969. 10.4324/9781315823546

—— *Werke*. Berlin: Suhrkamp, 1970.

—— *Philosophy of Mind*. Translated by W. Wallace and A.V. Miller. Oxford: Oxford University Press, 1971.

—— *Elements of the Philosophy of Right*. Edited by A. Wood and translated by H.B. Nisbet. Cambridge: Cambridge University Press, 1991. DOI: 10.1017/S0263523200005097

Houlgate, Stephen. "Hegel, Derrida and Restricted Economy: The Case of Mechanical Memory." *Journal of the History of Philosophy* 34, no. 1 (1996): 79–94. DOI: 10.1353/hph.1996.0012

Hyppolite, Jean. *Genesis and Structure of Hegel's Phenomenology of Spirit*. Evanston, IL: Northwestern University Press, 1974. DOI: 10.2307/2184282

Lewis, T.A., "Speaking of Habits: The Role of Language in Moving From Habit to Freedom." *Owl of Minerva* 39 (2007–2008): 25–53. DOI: 10.5840/owl2007/2008391/22

Marx, Werner. *Absolute Reflexion und Sprache*. Frankfurt: Vittorio Klostermann, 1967.McCumber, John. *The Company of Words: Hegel, Language, and Systematic Philosophy*. Evanston: Northwestern University Press, 1993.

Pippen, Robert. *Hegel's Practical Philosophy: Rational Agency as Ethical Life*. Cambridge: Cambridge University Press, 2008. DOI: 10.1017/CBO9780511808005

Russon, John. *Reading Hegel's Phenomenology*. Bloomington: Indiana University Press, 2004.

Taylor, Charles. *Hegel and Modern Society*. New York: Cambridge University Press, 1979. DOI: https://doi.org/10.1017/CBO9781139171489

Vernon, Jim. *Hegel's Philosophy of Language*. London: Continuum, 2007.

—— "'Free Love': A Hegelian Defense of Same-Sex Marriage Rights." *The Southern Journal of Philosophy* 47, no. 1 (Spring 2009): 69–89. DOI: 10.1111/j.2041-6962.2009.tb00132.x

—— "Siding with Freedom: Towards a Prescriptive Hegelianism." *Critical Horizons* 12, no. 1 (2011): 49–69. DOI: 10.1558/crit.v12i1.49

—— "I Am We: Dialectics of Political Will in Huey P. Newton and the Black Panther Party." *Theory and Event* 17, no. 4 (December 2014). DOI: https://doi.org/10.1177/02632764211039278

—— "'A Passion for Justice': Martin Luther King, Jr. and G.W.F. Hegel on 'World-Historical Individuals'." *Philosophy and Social Criticism* 43, no. 2 (2017): 187–207. DOI: 10.1177/0191453716680126

9 Re-presenting the Past: The Reason in Hegel's History[1]

JEFFREY REID, UNIVERSITY OF OTTAWA

The idea that Hegel does *a priori* speculative history has been largely put to rest, at least for those who care about the philosopher enough to have carefully read him or visited significant scholarship on the question of his philosophy of history.[2] It should now be clear that Hegel's philosophy of history is the history of consciousness and that forms of consciousness are tied to the spirit of the times and places in which they occur and can be witnessed. It should also be clear that Hegel respects the specificity of each epoch. True to the phenomenological method that he describes in the *Phenomenology of Spirit*, each historical moment must be allowed to present itself. The philosopher of history must not do violence to this historical content by imposing upon it anachronistic, formal, *a priori* categories.

However, the reassuring phenomenological aspect of Hegel's philosophy of history does not, of course, cancel out the metaphysical or speculative dimensions of his historical thought, represented in the use of such concepts as Reason, Spirit, the Idea, the Absolute and even God. The Hegel apologist defending him against the twin-fronted attacks of continental postmodernists and sober-minded analyticals might wish that their philosopher had avoided using such terms altogether. For it is difficult to maintain that a philosophy of history is anything but *a priori*, speculative, and metaphysical when the philosopher seems to assert that history is driven by Reason (*Vernunft*), that the events of world history follow the pre-established program of universal Reason itself and that history can therefore be understood according to the inherent dialectical principles of its internal logic. Although certain passages in the famous introduction to his *Lectures on the Philosophy of History*, posthumously published under the title of *Reason in History*,[3] seem to lend themselves to such misinterpretations, I believe that these are based on misunderstandings of what Hegel actually means by both Reason and history.

The best way to comprehend the role that Reason plays in history, and hence to grasp how Hegel actually conceives the philosophy of history, is by considering his epistemology of historiography, his theory of what makes the writing of history true and scientifically significant. It is this epistemology that is dealt with in the introduction to the *Lectures on the Philosophy of History*, a fact perhaps obscured by the usual English translation of the term *Geschichtsschreiber*, which occurs throughout the German text, as "historian" rather than as "historiographer." Here, in the introduction to his *Lectures*, Hegel is discussing nothing other than how the writing of history can be Scientific, in a way that is perfectly coherent with his definition of *Wissenschaft* as the systematic, actual articulation of the objective discourses of human knowledge. The question dealt with is, how can history itself come to form an objectively true discourse of Science?[4]

Exploring the historiographic dimension of what Hegel means by history reveals a different way of understanding its relation to Reason, one that is coherent with Hegel's phenomenological method and which attenuates some of the troubling metaphysical elements mentioned above.[5] In the historical context, Hegel's definition of "Reason" is either often taken for granted or simply thought to signify something like "logically determining" or even "reasonable." In fact, the term has a technical meaning which is best presented by referring to the eponymous chapter in the *Phenomenology of Spirit*: "Reason is the certainty of consciousness that it is all reality."[6] While this is not the place to develop a thorough Hegelian genealogy of *Vernunft*, I will present several important aspects that help us understand what is meant by this summary definition, in order to allow us to better grasp the relation between Reason, historiography and history itself.

Hegel's idea of *Vernunft* is, of course, tributary to Kant's idea of it as a legislative, universalizing, maximizing faculty, agent of the un-natural causality of moral freedom, autonomously determining the will to the good. However, there are other sources which can be said to inflect the concept of Reason in Hegel. First, perhaps, is the association, remarked upon by H.S. Harris, between Reason and love, through the early Frankfurt writings, where love is conceived as the fundamental conceptual power of *Vereinigung*.[7] Second, is Reason's commanding role in the historical narrative recounted in Lessing's influential essay on the *Education of the Human Race*, where *Vernunft* is presented as the true content of divine Revelation, whose pedagogical vocation is the reconciling constitution of the invisible church of all humanity. Along with these elements, it is important to stress the individualistic, even existentialist character of consciousness as it appears in the "Reason" chapter of the *Phenomenology*, for example, in the subchapters on "Pleasure and necessity," "The law of the heart and the frenzy of self-conceit" and "Virtue and the way of the world," all culminating in Kantian figures of legislative Reason. I believe that its specifically anthropological character demonstrates the limits of *Vernunft* in Hegel's mature thought, i.e. how Reason remains human, all too human, a conscious "certainty" weighted down by the immediacy of its embodied experience of knowing.[8] Briefly, this last aspect helps us see how *Vernunft*, while reflecting the conceptual movement of thought into otherness, does not enjoy the same *scientific* (in terms of systematic *Wissenschaft*) destiny as other absolute forms of Hegelian truth: Absolute Spirit (including art, religion and philosophy), the syllogism (the most accomplished form of the Concept) and the Absolute Idea.

What lessons might we draw from this all-too-brief sketch of Reason's Hegelian genealogy, which might then be applied to his historiography? We see that *Vernunft* is related to morality and thus to the human desire to realize the good, a quest that is indissociable from the idea of human freedom. "Reason in history" directly implies that the theme of historical narrative is the development of moral freedom. We also note that Reason, through its descendance from the notion of love, is deeply rooted in the idea of a unifying reconciliation. Hegel's definition of Reason as finding oneself in otherness is an expression of this aspiration for deep complicity. In a more modern vein, the inflection occasioned by Lessing, along with its Enlightenment echoes, adds to Reason a formative, educational dimension. Such a pedagogical project, as every effective teacher knows, can only be carried out by progressing gradually over (human) time. Learning takes place in stages. The Truth cannot be revealed all at once. While Reason, in its certainty, does share its absolute content with divine Revelation, the essentially human, individual aspect of consciousness means that it must take place historically. In fact, from a purely anthropological point of view, without any recourse to the conclusive syllogistic articulations of Science, Reason and its actuality (*Wirklichkeit*) are destined to the endless approximations of moral certainty. Scientific truth takes place behind Reason's back.[9]

Therefore, claiming that Hegel's historiography is grounded in his notion of Reason does not mean that history is somehow inherently logical or reasonable. Rather, historiographical science, which recounts the development of consciousness's certainty of being "all reality," recognizes that this reality is historical. In other words, as self-recognition in otherness, the unifying vocation of Reason means coming to know ourselves in the otherness of history, knowing that we are what we are through history and that history is what it is through us.[10] Such self-knowledge through historical otherness can only take place, educationally, through the various forms of historical writing that Hegel presents us with. These forms, taken together systematically, take place within the summative narrative of *Wissenschaft*.

It is thus crucial to see what Hegel means by *Vernunft* in the introduction to his *Lectures on History* and why he uses the term, with its inevitable anthropological limitations, rather than the terms "Spirit" or "Idea". For it is certainly faithful to Hegel's thought to say that history is the movement of Spirit or that it is the Idea's re-appropriation of itself in time. However, neither "Spirit" nor "Idea" captures the human selfness, the "we" of consciousness that Hegel ascribes to Reason and the essentially human determination inherent in history itself.[11] As the path of self-recognition, history necessarily takes the form of an apprenticeship, one that involves liberation both *through* history but also *from* history. For in recognizing ourselves in the past, we overcome its strange "otherness". It no longer appears to us something alien in which we have no stake nor play any part; it no longer appears as something that simply determines us heteronomously, whether we like it or not.

Only through Reason as self-knowledge in historical otherness does something as apparently arbitrary and senseless as history become part of Science. The epistemological question addressed in Hegelian historiography, which asks how history can become part of Science, must involve the recognition of what history truly is: the consciousness of present worldly reality as *having been*, where the past is seen as the story of human selfhood (of its freedom) and human selfhood is grasped as world-historical. The actuality of scientific comprehension, the embodiment of knowing and history, can only *take place* through the involvement of what Hegel defines as "original" and "reflective" historiography. These two elements form the content in which "philosophical" historiography acknowledges the play of Reason, as I have defined it above. Reference to such historiographical content helps us comprehend how its Scientific embodiment is essentially language, whether expressed in the *Lectures on the Philosophy of History*, in the *Philosophy of Right*, or in the *Objective Spirit* section of the *Encyclopedia of Philosophical Sciences*. History may be many things but unless it is language, it is nothing to Science.

In order to understand Hegel's epistemology of historiography, as he presents it in the first pages of the introduction to his *Lectures*, we must see Reason as a process taking place in the recognition between consciousness and its historical past, not as something static and immediate, but as a path of discovery. Hegel's historiography should thus be seen as a pedagogical process leading us to the *truth* of Reason, first in philosophical history and consequently in Science. The path itself is marked out as a progression in the writing of history, from original history through reflective history. These ways of *doing* history are not to be taken as alternative "methods" to philosophical history, which the invented subtitle in *Reason in History* ("Methods of Writing History") may lead us believe, nor as "Varieties of Historical Writing," as we find in another English translation.[12] Rather they must be taken as integral, constitutive moments. Original and reflective historiography are necessarily experienced and subsumed moments without which philosophical history would have no content and would therefore be abstract and *a priori*.

The different types of historiography outlined in the opening pages of the introduction to the *Lectures on the Philosophy of History* (or to *Reason in History*) correspond to the different levels of consciousness that are presented in the first four chapters of the *Phenomenology*. This is not surprising since, for Hegel, levels of consciousness represent different knowing relationships between subjectivity and objectivity. Historiography is a way of knowing the objectivity of history and is therefore an expression of consciousness. More specifically, original history, reflective history and philosophical history reflect the knowing relationships (forms of consciousness) that appear in the *Phenomenology*, as well as in the *Encyclopedia's Philosophy of Subjective Spirit*, under three main determinations: as sensible intuitions, as the reflective products of the understanding, and as realized in mutual recognition.[13] Just as all knowing must begin with and yet go on to subsume immediate (unreflected) empirical knowledge, historiography must begin with original history.

The intuitive, empirical dimension of original historiography is, in fact, double. First, the original historiographer is the eyewitness of the worldly events that he describes. Second, he presents, or represents, this world before the eyes of those reading his account. This is possible, because original historiographers "transform the events, actions, and situations that are present to them into a work of representation,"[14] which is essentially discourse, one which retains its features of empirical immediacy.

There are epistemological conditions governing this first level of historiographical content. In other words, there are conditions governing the scientific truth of these original narratives or, in more Hegelian terminology, conditions whereby certain original accounts may form the content of Science. Such truth conditions cannot be adequately grasped in terms of contemporary epistemological issues arising from the dilemma between historical realism and constructivism,[15] where the question is ultimately whether the truth of historical discourse is grounded in its correspondence to facts or in its narrative coherence within itself and to other accounts. As is typical when such unilateral options present themselves, as those offered by correspondence or coherence theories of historical truth, Hegel's solution involves both. There is a certain amount of constructivism in the original historiographer's narrative, which Hegel likens to that of the poet, and yet the immediate presence of the historian's witnessing guarantees a necessary realism.[16]

While the original historiographer's narrative work shares the poet's use of imagination (production of images) and *Phantasie* (production of linguistic signs), these instances must be understood in the technical, psychological sense that Hegel ascribes to them as central moments in the representing process (*Vorstellen*) itself, as described in the *Encyclopedia*'s *Subjective Spirit* section.[17] However, the content of the language produced by the historian is distinctively derived from witnessed "actions, events, and conditions,"[18] which are transformed into images by the imagination and then stored as memories in the mind's subconscious (*Schacht* – mine), to be remembered and represented in language. The fact that the images are derived through external, empirical perceptions makes them different from purely poetical constructions derived from inner emotions.[19] This is why Hegel protests against B.G. Niebuhr's idea that original (Roman) history is derived from popular folk tales and songs.[20] Such an origin would place original historiography in the realm of poetry and deprive it of any empirical grounding in reality. Since original historiography is the primary, fundamental content of history as it participates in Science, depriving it of its reality would deprive it of its specificity as (world) history. It would be (history of) art.

The original historiographer is immediately present in the epoch he describes and his participation in the events and conditions, combined with a certain degree of artistic *Phantasie* in the ability to represent this "second nature" in discourse, ensure that the writing is "*anschaulich*," a quality which may be translated as possessing "intuitive liveliness."[21] Indeed, this "intuitiveness" can be seen as Hegel's primary epistemological truth condition governing original historiographical accounts, a condition which we might say combines elements of both realism and constructivism in order to attain something higher. This "something higher," this artful intuitiveness reflects a deeper truth than either that which stems from pure correspondence to facts or truth involving the coherency of narrative. Intuitiveness means that the account captures the spirit (*Geist*) of its time. It does so because the original historiographer is an actual participant in the events that he describes. This immediate participation confers an immediate (non-mediated) actuality on his account, on his discourse, and ensures that his narrative is the spiritual embodiment of the epoch he is writing about.

It is necessary to emphasize the effectively actual nature of this discourse, which lies at the heart of what Hegel means by *"anschaulich."* Only by grasping the significance of this immediate narrative actuality can we grasp the *mediated* actuality of historical discourse as it re-occurs or takes place in systematic Science, through the presence of philosophical history. As we will see, this mediation is carried out in the second level of historiographical knowledge, reflective history. First, I want to say a word about the actuality of original historiography.

We must understand the actuality of original historiography as stemming from the mutual presence of the historiographer and his world. In other words, the immediate knowing relationship between the subject (historiographer) and the objectivity he is describing is

represented in the actual historical account. His narrative is thus itself an objective expression of the spirit of the age, so objective, in fact, that it must be seen as the existing, active embodiment of a certain form of spirit. Hegel expresses this powerfully in his comments on the original historiographer Thucydides, who re-presents the speech of Pericles. It makes little difference whether or not Thucydides provides a faithful account of Pericles' actual words, since the former is just as much a participant in the *Zeitgeist* of classical Greece as is the latter. Thucydides' narrative is therefore just as real, just as much an "action" (*Handlung*) as the event (e.g., the political speech) that it recounts.[22] It is discourse that is indistinct from the *Sittlichkeit*, the ethical life that it describes. The ethical (in the Hegelian sense) actuality of Thucydides' discourse is the immediate, effective expression of the participatory liveliness that scientific discourse should accomplish, and when Hegel writes, "[i]n these orations, these men expressed the maxims of their people, of their own personality, the consciousness of their political situation, and the principles of their ethical and spiritual nature, of their aims and actions,"[23] we may perhaps intuit the consummation Hegel reserves for (his own) Scientific discourse. I will return to this below.

Original historiography, the written, first-hand representations of participants in the spirit of their time, is the stuff (*Stoff*) of history. Although the Ancients provided some of the best models of this type of writing, it is important to see that original history is not exclusively ancient history. If it were, there would be no other history, and philosophical history would only have ancient Greece and Rome as subject matter. Original medieval historiography can be found in the chronicles of Bishops and humble monks, and more "contemporary" examples of original historiographers are Cardinal von Retz and Frederick the Great. Further, even "today" original history continues to be written in the form of "reports" or accounts, some of which are "excellent."[24] This ongoing writing of original history is significant because it means that there will always be enough of what we might call "primary source material" to reflect upon, even if this material has become principally journalistic, which Hegel seems to be indicating when he speaks of "reports" (*Berichte*), something that, as a former journalist, he could certainly value. As well, having original historiography to reflect upon is at least a necessary condition for any further philosophical history, an idea which impugns what might be referred to as the "strong version" of Hegel's "end of history" thesis.[25]

However, the account of original historiography does end with a reference to historians who, like Frederick the Great, because of their "high social position" have a synoptic, more general view of their times than do those who "peer up from below through a small opening."[26] The synthesizing of individual points of view into a more general perspective represents a typical Hegelian *Übergang*, a transition or passage where one moment is pushed to its maximum and thus moves into its dialectical "opposite." Here, the dialectical nature of the transition is another indication that we are meant to grasp the different ways of doing historiography, not as alternative methods but as levels of knowledge in an organic progression. Original history is not reflective; it is the immediate representation from an individual point of view. In a way, we can say that this individual point of view comes to contradict itself by becoming more general, leading to the subsequent, first level of reflective history, which is one of generalization.

The goal of historical science is to make history actual, to bring the past to the present in such a way that we may recognize ourselves in the past and the past in ourselves (Reason), so that the actuality of history may finally "take place" in the effective reality of Scientific discourse. In this way, we can say that historical discourse comes to rediscover the actuality that it first enjoyed as immediate "action" in the speeches of Pericles, as represented by Thucydides, but now enriched through mediation. The mediation takes place in reflective history, whose goal can thus be seen as a historiographical process, a way of writing history that takes the immediate representations of original history and re-presents them "for us."

In general (not universal) history, which is the first form of reflective history, historiographers work on the immediate "historical material," the primary sources that are provided by the original historiographers, in order to provide the synoptic or general view of a people or a country or the world. The general historiographer reflects on the material he is presented with and compiles it, synthesizes it or, in more Hegelian language, thinks it and sublates it into a newer, more thought-ful and therefore more spiritual representation. This reference to "spirit" is not gratuitous. Since the reflective, general historiographer is representing past accounts "for us," for a contemporary time that is *not* that of the original account, his work necessarily implies the investment of this newer time or spirit into the old material. Thus, "Livy makes his old Roman kings, consuls, and generals speak in the fashion of accomplished lawyers of the Livian era."[27] More succinctly, the generalizing compilations make the past "present" by re-presenting them in the spirit of a newer age. The best of these accounts are those that do not attempt to ape or imitate the particularities of the original epoch, only serving to give the writing a "stilted, hollowly solemn, pedantic character", but rather those like Livy's that allow the more reflective writer's spirit to penetrate the original material and thus make it actual for a new time. Once again, we see how Hegel's epistemological criterion of lively intuitiveness is directly related to spirit. Here, the *anschaulich* aspect of the reflective historiographical account is derived from the fact that its more contemporary spirit is represented, and made present to us, in its discourse.

Pragmatic history, the next form of reflection on original historical accounts (possibly reflecting on both original and general historiography) continues this work of "re-presenting the past." Although pragmatic history claims to use the past in order to teach us moral lessons about the present so that we may "learn from the past," in fact, as Hegel writes, the only thing we can really learn from past events is that the specificity of their conditions ensures that they can teach us nothing useful. Rather than using the past to inform the present as it claims to do, pragmatic history, in fact, does the exact opposite; it virtually does away with the past altogether. "It sublates the past and makes the given event present"[28] by interpreting past accounts in such a way as to make them supposedly relevant to the spirit of his times. Specifically, the pragmatic historian, carrying out the work of reflective history, seeks to impose on the rich chaos of past accounts his own universal, moral principles. In the best cases, where the writer is steeped in the spirit of his own epoch, he may do as the French do and "spiritedly create a present for [himself] and refer the past to the present state of affairs."[29] However, the fact that the liveliness of these accounts depends so directly on the "spirit of the writer" means that they tend to arbitrariness, where "each [writer] can think himself able to arrange and elaborate [the original histories] and inject his spirit into them as the spirit of the ages."[30] This subjective arbitrariness, which is, for Hegel, always present where morality is concerned, provides the dialectical *Übergang* or transition to the next form of reflective history, where personal arbitrariness appears to be given free reign: critical history.

I think it is possible to see Hegel's take on critical history as a kind of meta-critique, a critique of historical criticism. Doing so invites us to recognize the dialectical nature of this stage in his epistemology of historiography. Certainly, the criticism of criticism can be seen as negating its critical negativity, thus overcoming it and superseding it into the organic systematicity of Science itself. In this vein, critical history first appears as an external challenge to the philosophy of history and therefore to philosophy itself, as something oppositional that must either be ignored or taken into account. Of course, as Hegel explains in the introduction to the *Phenomenology of Spirit*, with regard to philosophy, such "errors" cannot be left outside absolute knowing but must rather be shown to be constitutive elements of its process. The same is true, here, in critical history.

To the extent that criticism is associated with Kantian idealism and more definitively and perhaps unjustly with Friedrich Schlegel's theory of irony, Hegel tends to see it as dangerously subjective and arbitrary. Indeed, the language Hegel uses in describing critical history, which produces "unhistorical monstrosities of pure imagination" and "subjective fancies – fancies which are held to be more excellent, the bolder they are" takes up expressions he uses elsewhere to qualify Fr. Schlegel's critical irony, and makes it probable that his historical works are Hegel's target here.[31] This is interesting because Fr. Schlegel would stand here accused of what Hegel is usually charged with: ignoring the "factual basis," the "definite facts of history." We must understand, however, that for Hegel, as I have been arguing, these "facts" are only meaningful to the extent that they are embodied in the narrative discourse of history. To the extent that the critical historian does not take these accounts (*Erzählungen*) "at their word," but seeks only to look at them, one might say, hermeneutically, there can no longer be any solid factual (i.e. textual) basis for historical science. The same result occurs as the one we witnessed with Niebuhr's idea that Livy's historiography is derived from popular folk songs rather than from the accounts of original historiographers: history's textual foundation loses its footing.[32]

Given Hegel's critical stance towards critical history and its "subjective fancies," how can it be part of the dialectical historiographical process that I am putting forward, one claiming that the different "methods" of historiography are different levels of historical knowing or consciousness, leading to Reason and Science? There are several answers to this and the first one can be stated as follows. For history to be actual, for it to be present to us, i.e., for us moderns (post-moderns?) to be able to recognize ourselves in it, it must also embody that which makes us who we are: individual agents of critical subjectivity. Critical history puts us in the story: *dubito ergo sum*. To express this another way, individual freedom and modern selfhood must be part of any historiographical process which is meant to lead to the actuality of recognition. In order for historical knowledge to become speculative, in the Hegelian sense of a systematic unity incorporating difference, it must integrate the difference between present consciousness and the past. This is the space of our critical freedom, the fact that we are neither absolutely crystallized in the present nor determined by the causal chains of the past. Critical history is a necessary spacing between our past and our present, the separation without which the recognition and reconciliation of Reason (self-knowledge through *otherness*) would be inoperable or meaningless.

On a more systematic level that I introduced above, criticism provides a necessary dose of negativity, one that is essential to the dialectical movement that the historiographical process follows. In past work, I have referred to this type of negativity as "cometary," drawing from Hegel's dialectical presentation of the solar system, in order to stress the evanescent, fluidifying character of the moment, as opposed to lunar "for-itselfness" that is found in the other, recalcitrant and exclusive moment of particularity. Here, the cometary negativity of critical history can be seen to dissolve the hard, dry "lunar" presentations of general and pragmatic history, i.e., the sort of dogmatic historical writing that we might find in school manuals and textbooks.[33]

As Reason, historical knowing is ultimately philosophical.[34] The final reflective form of historiography demonstrates this. To say there is Reason in history is to see it as the discursive process whereby consciousness comes to recognize itself in its past. We only come to know ourselves through knowledge of our history, and history is only something for us in that it is known. Furthermore, if historical knowledge is ultimately self-knowledge in otherness, and self-knowledge in otherness is the goal of philosophy, then history is necessarily philosophical. The final *Übergang* or dialectical transition that takes place in Hegel's epistemological historiography is found in the ultimate form of *reflective* history, i.e., in its maximized form, where it actually becomes something else: *philosophy* of history.[35] In fact, this final form of reflective history is already, in truth, philosophy.

Unfortunately, this fact is lost in translation when the final section of reflective history is referred to as "fragmentary."[36] A more appropriate title would be "conceptual history," to borrow the phrase from within Hegel's text itself. The point of the passage is to show how the specific histories dealt with in this type of historical account, e.g., the history of art, of law, of religion, when they are fully carried out must be grasped according to the movement of the concept. It is the same movement that we see played out in historical knowledge itself as it moves from the immediate intuitions of original history, through the mediating representations of reflective history, to their philosophical truth, incorporated into the system of Science. Thus, we can say that the history of art, as a discourse presenting (making present and indeed actual) the historical knowledge of art, becomes the *philosophy* of art in the same way that history, in general, becomes the philosophy of history. This is why Hegel's extensive *philosophies* of art, religion, and law (world history or history of State constitutions)[37] are all *histories*, philosophical histories of their subject matter. To these histories, of course, we must add that of philosophy itself: the history of philosophy is, above all, philosophy. As is the case with historiography in general and with the specific histories of art, religion, and law, the goal is ultimately the knowledge or recognition that "we are what we are through history,"[38] which also implies that history is what it is through us. Consciousness recognizes itself as historical and sees history as the path of consciousness, which is the most we can expect from Reason.

As Hegel writes in the introduction to the *Phenomenology*, there is no distance between the method of philosophical knowing, as it moves through phenomenological forms of consciousness, and the actual content of that knowledge. The form of knowing is always determined by what is known and *vice versa*. Similarly, we can see that the "method" of historiography that Hegel outlines in the introduction to the philosophy of history is not to be separated from the content of history. Since this method implies different ways of representing history in language, we must conclude that history is fundamentally historiographical, that it is meaningless unless it is written. It is through such re-presentation that history *presents* itself *to us* as actual.

If these affirmations have a postmodernist, constructivist flavour, it is not entirely because they refer to history as textual in nature. It is above all because joining together the epistemology of historical science (methods of knowing history) and historiography (methods of writing history) while conflating both with what we generally mean by history itself is a thoroughly postmodern way of doing history. Frank R. Ankersmit describes the postmodern relation between epistemology and history in these terms: "[e]pistemology is ... historicized in that the history of historical writing has now become the foundation of epistemology."[39] Such affirmations echo what Hegel says about critical history, which "is not history itself ... but rather history of historiography,"[40] which leads me to reaffirm the pivotal role of critical history in Hegel's philosophy of history. The fact that we do understand history as a historiographical process that is inherently epistemological provides support for my belief that the critical moment is a necessary element in *our* ability to recognize ourselves in history as it is represented for us.[41]

Since critical history re-reads, re-evaluates and even re-writes the representational content (i.e. the texts) through which philosophical history comes to see itself as the enactment of Reason, this ultimate historiographical form is not spared from the action of its own critical moment. This means that the "final" form of history, i.e., its philosophical embodiment is constantly negated, dissolved, fluidified and re-constituted by critical reflection, even as it is taken up within systematic Science. More concretely, both the content and form of Hegel's philosophical narrative, for example with its problematic depictions of the Orient, Africa and Native America, are open to revision, through the critical agency of its own epistemological historiography.

The fact that the content and form of philosophical history are open to critical revision has two crucial consequences. First, systematic philosophical history as the free reflection on constantly renewed historical content, remains epistemologically guaranteed. Second, the "we" who are invited to partake in self-recognition through historical narratives remains as open as does the narratives themselves. For example, women, who are conspicuously absent from original and reflective historical accounts may recognize themselves, through historical criticism, in that very absence and exclusion. Consequently, previously neglected or ignored accounts may form new historical content. Philosophical reflection upon such accounts, on both their exclusion and inclusion, might become the realization of what Hegel means by Reason in history.

In order to avoid falling into the spurious portrayal of a thoroughly postmodern Hegel,[42] however, we simply have to recall that critical history is only part of the story. It does not annihilate reflective history nor does it do away altogether with the empirical content requirements of original historiography as *anschaulich*. As well, we must recall that critical history is followed by history's integration into the systematic narrative of Science, where history has become philosophy (of history) and philosophy becomes Science.

I will conclude with several remarks on history as it is related to systematic Science. This relation is essential. For if indeed the epistemological dimension of Hegel's historiography is inseparable from its historical content, then reflection on such content necessarily implies its relation to Science. Further, in establishing how Reason in history involves its becoming *present* to us in such a way that we recognize ourselves in it, and it in us, as mutually constitutive, I am thereby implying that the actuality of such recognition takes place in systematic Science.

In the final section of reflective history, what I called "conceptual history," it becomes apparent that the specific histories of art, law, and religion, when pushed to their maximum, when thoroughly grasped or conceived, become philosophy, namely the philosophies of art, of law, and of religion. The end of art is the philosophy of art; the end of religion is the philosophy of religion; the end of law is the philosophy of law (right). This does not mean that there is no more art, religion, or law. It simply means that their histories necessarily end in a philosophical discourse that integrates immediate intuitions and further reflections into present recognition. The fact that all histories end in philosophy does not drown out their rich specificity in a night of black cows, and this is precisely because these "specialized" conceptual philosophies are integrated into the narrative of Science. Indeed, it is the systematic nature of fully articulated Science that preserves the specificity of the different historical contents. It is because the philosophies of art, religion, and law (world history) are part of the *Encyclopedia of Philosophical Sciences* that the specificity of their histories is actually maintained.

The historiographical trail we have followed, leading from original historiography, to reflective historiography, to the texts of philosophical history (of art, of religion, of law), includes the path's final embodiment in systematic Science. Indeed, this is the final locus of these conceptual historical/philosophical discourses. The *Encyclopedia of Philosophical Sciences* was conceived as a teaching manual and this reveals the true destination or vocation of Scientific actuality, and of the historical/philosophical discourses that are part of it. The fact that the content of Science was meant to be taught, and thus to really take place in the world, reveals the effective nature of historical/philosophical discourses within what Hegel calls ethical life. The actuality of Science is its pedagogical destiny and its ability to form the world in which it is read and pronounced. We must not forget that all Hegel's writings on history, his philosophical historiographies, are expressed either in lectures or in teaching manuals within the university setting. In this actual world of Science, historiography rediscovers the lively *Anschaulichkeit* of its original accounts. No longer immediate, but re-*presented* now through reflective mediation, historical discourse within Science becomes the performative language evoked above, in Thucydides' account of Pericles's discourse to the Athenians: "speeches that are actions among men."[43] However, this reference will only make sense if we have learned who Pericles was, and consider him to be part of our story.

Finally, Hegel's notion of Reason in history must be grasped in reference to his idea of *Vernunft* as a unifying, educational process of self-recognition in the past. The recognition of selfhood in otherness is only realized through a reciprocal act of liberation. The pedagogical actuality of historical science is the theatre where such freedom is played out. In recognizing ourselves in history, we free ourselves from the "otherness" of its heteronomous determinacy. It becomes "our" story. Of course, reciprocally, through such *self*-recognition, history is freed from "us." We recognize that its narrative does not belong to us, that there are and will always be other histories, other stories. We let it go.

NOTES

1 This is a reconsidered, revised, and augmented version of "Presenting the Past: Hegel's Epistemological Historiography," Chapter 5 in my book *Real Words: Language and System in Hegel* (Toronto: University of Toronto Press, 2007), 58–70.

2 For examples: Frederick C. Beiser writes, "Once we recognize that Hegel's method is phenomenological, we can quickly see what is wrong with those who accuse Hegel of following a 'speculative' or a priori method. The very opposite is the case, given that it was precisely Hegel's aim to avoid the problems of such methods. His own phenomenological method is more akin to the empirical method of the historian, who immerses himself into his subject matter." Frederick C. Beiser, ed., "Hegel's Historicism," in *The Cambridge Companion to Hegel* (Cambridge University Press, 1993), 287. Already more than thirty years ago George Dennis O'Brien wrote, "Hegel is universally regarded as a speculative philosopher of history, but it seems that from the standpoint of his own system no such philosophical enterprise can be derived." George Dennis O'Brien, *Hegel on Reason and History* (Chicago and London: University of Chicago Press, 1975) 13.

3 I will refer to Robert S. Hartman's translation of *Reason in History* (with occasional alterations) which is taken from the second German edition, edited by Hegel's son Karl and published in 1840. For the German text, I refer to *Werke in 20 Bänden*, edited by Eva Moldenhauer and Karl Markus Michel (Frankfurt am Main: Suhrkamp, 1970) vol. 12 (*Werke* 12) which is based on the Karl Hegel edition. I subscribe to Moldenhauer and Michel's affirmation that the Karl Hegel text is the most "authentic" of either Lasson's (1917–23) or Hoffmeister's (1955). This preference is particularly justified where the opening pages of the introduction, dealing with the

different forms of historiography, are concerned. For an explanation of this preference, see *Werke* 12, 566–8. Hegel gave his course on world history five times, at Berlin, between 1822 and 1830. The Karl Hegel edition is based on manuscripts from 1822 and 1828. Both these sets of manuscript notes have introductions that begin with the epistemological considerations that I am concerned with. It is true that the manuscript notes to the 1830 lectures begin differently but since that series was curtailed by Hegel's death, there is no way of knowing how or if he might have included remarks on original, reflective, and philosophical history. Since the opening remarks from the 1830 lectures do begin with a defence against doing a priori historiography, one might assume that Hegel's epistemological/historiographical remarks were forthcoming.

4 Capitalized "Science" or "Scientific" refers to Hegel's systematic notion of *Wissenschaft*.

5 I am certainly not saying Hegel's thought is not metaphysical. However, for Hegel, what is truly metaphysical cannot be what is commonly meant by the term: an abstract, transcendent, a priori ideal.

6 G.W.F. Hegel, *Phenomenology of Spirit*, trans. A.V. Miller (Oxford: Oxford University Press, 1977) §233. *Werke* 3, 179.

7 H.S. Harris, *Hegel's Development, toward the Sunlight 1770–1801* (Oxford: Oxford University Press, 1972), 294.

8 In my article, "Insight and the Enlightenment: Why Einsicht in Chapter Six of Hegel's Phenomenology of Spirit?", I show how reason in its opposition to faith is associated with the German Enlightenment. Hegel shows how both are expressions of immediate knowing. *Hegel Bulletin*, pp. 1–23. doi: 10.1017/hgl.2016.61.

9 In my article, "Reason and Revelation: Absolute Agency and the Limits of Actuality," *Symposium* 21, 1 (2017), 182–202, I argue that Hegel's systematic truth involves both human agency, as Reason, and the absolute agency of the Idea (God) as Revelation. Figures of actuality, in Hegel, are doomed to the endless approximations that he finds in morality, but also in world history (i.e., in the development of political constitutions) but also in the on-going practice of art. We must never expect perfection in what Emile Fackenheim despaired as "the Hegelian middle," i.e., actuality.

10 Andrew Buchwalter associates the self-recognition through reflection on the past, implied by Hegel's historiography, with his political theory of constitutionalism, in "Historiography and Constitutionalism in Hegel," *Hegel-Jahrbuch*, (1998), 175. Buchwalter rightly sees Hegel's historiography, in terms Buchwalter takes from the *Lectures on the History of Philosophy*, as not just "the becoming of things foreign to us, but the becoming of ourselves and of our own knowledge (175)." Cf. *Lectures on the History of Philosophy*, trans. E.S. Haldane and F.H. Simson (London, New York:

Routledge and Kegan Paul, the Humanities Press, 1955), 4. Buchwalter does not develop the true nature of the symmetry he notices between Hegel's historiography and his constitutionalism: their shared linguistic content. The original historiography recounts past constitutions (which are integral to history of States and therefore to world history) just as it recounts or represents past events. In other words, as laws and constitutions are linguistic or narrative contents of original historiography, they may also become part of reflective and philosophical historiography.

11 We can certainly view Reason and Spirit from the point of view of the Absolute or God or the Idea. We may say, for example, that Spirit is the historical realization of the self-consciousness of God or the Idea. However, this view is more suited to the perspective of the Logics and the Absolute Idea. Philosophical historiography sees Reason in terms of a relationship between human consciousness and historical objectivity. Thus Hegel writes that Reason, in the philosophy of history, "may be accepted here without closer examination of its relation to God" and that its relation to "the True, the Eternal, the Absolute Power ... is being presupposed here as proved." (*Reason in History*, 11 / *Werke* 12, 20–1)

12 G.W.F. Hegel, *Lectures on the Philosophy of World History, Introduction: Reason in History*, trans. H.B. Nisbet (Cambridge University Press: 1980), from the Hoffmeister edition.

13 Paul Redding sees this historical recognition (*Anerkennen*) "in the type of reflective history which treats the historical world as a spectacle of passions ... structurally analogous to that operative in civil society." Redding contrasts this "abstract recognition" with a more concrete recognition of one's actual personal identity as historical and constituted by other societies. "Absorbed in the Spectacle of the World: Hegel's Criticism of Romantic Historiography," *Clio* 16, 4 (1987), 306. For Redding, the recognition involved in reflective history is related to a devalued, Debordian world of the spectacle, opposed to a more authentic inter-subjectivity, *à la* Charles Taylor, engendered through philosophical history. In any case, I want to show how original and reflective narratives are integral to the ultimate philosophical recognition (Reason) between the self and its history.

14 *Reason in History*, 4. *Werke* 12, 12.

15 In fact, these questions stretch back (at least) to Hegel's time. Historical realism, as an epistemological position, can be traced back to the classical historicism of Leopold von Ranke (who was already critical of the speculative, perhaps overly narrative quality of Hegel's philosophy of history) and continues through the twentieth century with the *Annales* and Social Science schools. The constructivist or narrative trend is perhaps best represented by Hayden White.

16 *Reason in History*, 4. *Werke* 12, 11.

17 *Encyclopedia of Philosophical Sciences* §§455–60.

18 *Reason in History*, 4. *Werke* 12, 11. "Conditions" may include laws and constitutions, founding the possibility of history of law – an essential aspect of history of States and therefore of world history.

19 In the Introduction to his *Lectures*, Hegel refers to the poet's representations as based on emotion (*Empfindung*). The reference to emotion is dropped from the *Reason in History* text. *Werke* 12, 11.

20 Hegel's exclusion of "myths, folk songs, traditions" from original history and his affirmation that "The base of intuited or intuitive (*angeschauter oder anschaubarer*) reality provides a more solid foundation for history than those growing out of myths and epics" (*Werke* 12, 12) reflects his criticism of B. G. Niebuhr's hypothesis, presented in his *History of Rome*, that Livy's accounts of early Rome are based on folk tales and traditional songs. Indeed for Niebuhr there is an unbridgeable gulf between the marvellous in myth and the dryness of historical fact. It is an error to attempt to derive the latter from the former. See also Hegel's review of Solger's work, where Hegel aligns himself with A.W. Schlegel and Solger in their condemnation of Niebuhr's hypothesis. *Werke* 11, 233–234.

21 Hegel's term *"anschaulich"* may also be translated as "lively" (the French translation of the text gives "vivant" – See G.W.F. Hegel, *Leçons sur la philosophie de l'histoire*, trans. J. Gibelin (Paris: Vrin, 1987), 19 – or, apparently by "plastic," which is found in *Reason in History*, 6. Hegel uses the term to describe the immediate sensible intuitions experienced by the original historiographer (*Werke* 12, 12) but also to describe the best sort of reflective historiography, i.e., the one that reproduces in writing what is successful in original historiography. In both cases, the historiography represents the immediate knowing relationship between the original historiographer and his epoch, a knowing relationship which is not yet truly reflective or determined by understanding.

22 *"Reden aber sind Hundlungen unter Menschen, und zwar sehr wesentlish wirksame Handlungen."* *Werke* 12, 13.

23 *Werke* 12, 13. R.H. 4–5.

24 *Werke* 12, 14. R.H. 5.

25 Jere Paul O'Neill Surber puts the strong version as including "the 'end' of 'universal history' as a temporal sequence capable of 'rational comprehension'." "The 'End of History' Revisited" in David A. Duquette, ed., *Hegel's History of Philosophy: New Interpretations* (Albany: State University of New York Press, 2003), 212. The continued production of original historiography as the foundation of further reflective philosophical historiography would seem to contradict the idea of "the end of universal history as a temporal sequence."

26 *Werke* 12, 14. *Reason in History*, 5.

27 *Werke* 12, 15. *Reason in History*, 6.

28 *Werke* 12, 16. *Reason in History*, 7.

29 *Werke* 12, 18. *Reason in History*, 9.

30 Werke 12, 18. *Reason in History*, 8.

31 *Werke* 12, 18–19. *Reason in History*, 9. Terms such as *"höher Kritik"* as well as forms of *"Eitelkeit," "Kühnheit"* and *"Vortrefflichkeit,"* all found in this passage on critical historiography, are typical of Hegel's references to Fr. Schlegel. For example, in Hegel's *Lectures on Esthetics, Werke* 13 or in his review of K. W. F. Solger's work, *Werke* 11, 233–4. In the present passage on critical historiography, Hegel refers to critical philology and the history of literature, exactly the same areas where he criticizes Fr. Schlegel in the Solger review. Hegel seems to be referring to Fr. Schlegel's early philological writings and his later work *On the Language and Wisdom of the Indians* (1808). He is not referring to Fr. Schlegel's *Philosophy of History*, taken from his lectures in Vienna, published in 1828, which Hegel almost certainly hadn't read when he wrote the first part of *Reason in History* (1822 and 1828).

32 It is therefore probably not by accident that Niebuhr is generally considered the first critical historian and that the Hoffmeister edition refers to him.

33 In a paper presented at an earlier meeting of the Ontario Hegel Organization (Ottawa, 2012), I presented this idea of cometary negativity, inspired by the fluidifying, for-another/for-us action of the comets, over against the recalcitrant, dry "lunar" aspect of for-itself particularity, as illustrated in his dialectical presentation of the solar system, in the *Philosophy of Nature*. In the lengthy *Zusatz* to *Encyclopedia* §270 and again in §279, Hegel gives a conceptual reading of the solar system and the bodies within it. The same moment of negativity is played out in other Hegelian contexts: the negating freedom of scepticism dissolves and renders fluid the uncompromising substantiality of the stoic world, just as, we might also say, individual, moral freedom (*Moralität*) comes to break down the statuesque individuality of the Greek city-state.

34 "Pure self-recognition in absolute otherness … is the ground and soil of Science or knowledge in general." *Phenomenology of Spirit*, trans. Miller, §26.

35 Hegel is explicit about this. "The last kind of reflective history … forms a transition [*Übergang*] to philosophical world history." *Werke* 12, 19. *Reason in History*, 9.

36 This is the name that Hartman gives to the section, in his translation of *"Teilweise."* Nisbet chooses "specialized history."

37 Note from *Philosophy of Right*, §344.

38 *Lectures on the History of Philosophy* vol. 1, trans. E.S. Haldane, 2. *Werke* 18, 21.

39 "The Origins of Postmodern Historiography" in Jerzy Topolski, ed., *Historiography Between Modernism and Postmodernism* (Amsterdam – Atlanta, GA: Rodopi, 1994), 110.

40 *Werke* 12, 18. *Reason in History*, 9.

41 On the for-us in Hegel, see Kenley Royce Dove, "Hegel's Phenomenological Method", *Review of Metaphysics* 23 (1970), 615–41. See also: William F. Bristow's excellent discussion of the for-another and the "we" in *Hegel and the Transformation of Philosophical Critique* (Oxford: Clarendon Press, 2007), 218–241.

42 I use the term "postmodern" here, in a very specific sense, i.e. as defined by Lyotard in his *La Condition Postmodern*, where it is associated with the end of grand narratives.

43 *Werke* 12, 12. *Reason in History*, 4. Georg G. Iggers sees the newly created University of Berlin as the "embodied fusion of *Wissenschaft* and *Bildung*." Within this context, "History was to be both a scientific discipline and a source of culture." Leopold Ranke, who began teaching there in 1825 was motivated by this ideal, which he did share with Hegel, in spite of their different conceptions of science. Ranke wrote his thesis on Thucydides. George G. Iggers, *Historiography in the Twentieth Century: From Scientific Objectivity to the Postmodern Challenge* (Hanover, NH and London: University Press of New England, 1997), 24–5. On historical thought at the University of Berlin, see also T. Ziolkowski, *Clio, the Romantic Muse: Historicizing the Faculties* (Ithica and London: Cornell University Press, 2004) and my review of the book in *Clio* 34, 1–2 (2005), 199–206.

REFERENCES

Beiser, Frederick C. "Hegel's Historicism." In *The Cambridge Companion to Hegel*, edited by F.C. Beiser. Cambridge: Cambridge University Press, 1993.

Bristow, William F. *Hegel and the Transformation of Philosophical Critique*. Oxford: Clarendon Press, 2007.

Buchwalter, Andrew. "Historiography and Constitutionalism in Hegel." In *Hegel-Jahrbuch*. Berlin: Oldenbourg Akademieverlag, 1998. (*Hegel und die Geschichte der Philosophie, Zweiter Teil*.)

Dove, Kenley Royce. "Hegel's Phenomenological Method." *Review of Metaphysics* 23 (1970): 615–41.

Hegel, G.W.F. *Lectures on the History of Philosophy*. Translated by E.S. Haldane and F.H. Simson. London: Routledge and Kegan Paul, the Humanities Press, 1955.

—— *Die Vernunft in der Geschichte*, Vol. 12 of *Werke in 20 Bänden*. Edited by Eva Moldenhauer and Karl Markus Michel. Frankfurt am Main: Suhrkamp, 1970.

—— *Phenomenology of Spirit*. Translated by A.V. Miller. Oxford: Oxford University Press, 1977/*Werke* Vol. 3.

—— *Lectures on the Philosophy of World History, Introduction: Reason in History*. Translated by H.B. Nisbet. Cambridge: Cambridge University Press, 1980. (Hoffmeister edition.)

—— *Leçons sur la philosophie de l'histoire*. Translated by J. Gibelin. Paris: Vrin, 1987.

—— *Reason in History*. Translated by Robert S. Hartman. New York: Pearson, 1995/*Werke* Vol. 11.

Iggers, George G. *Historiography in the Twentieth Century: From Scientific Objectivity to the Postmodern Challenge*. Hanover, NH: University Press of New England, 1997.

O'Brien, George Dennis. *Hegel on Reason and History*. Chicago: University of Chicago Press, 1975.

Redding, Paul. "Absorbed in the Spectacle of the World: Hegel's Criticism of Romantic Historiography." *Clio* 16, no. 4 (Summer 1987): 297.

Reid, Jeffrey. "Review of *Clio, the Romantic Muse: Historicizing the Faculties*." *Clio* 34, nos. 1–2 (2005): 199–206.

—— "Presenting the Past: Hegel's Epistemological Historiography." In *Real Words: Language and System in Hegel*, edited by Jeffrey Reid, 58–70. Toronto: University of Toronto Press, 2007.

Schlegel, Fr. "On the Language and Wisdom of the Indians (1808)." *Philosophy of History* (1828).

Surber, Jere Paul O'Neill. "The 'End of History' Revisited." In *Hegel's History of Philosophy: New Interpretations*, edited by David A. Duquette. Albany: State University of New York Press, 2003.

Ziowlkowski, T. *Clio, the Romantic Muse: Historicizing the Faculties*. Ithaca: Cornell University Press, 2004.

10 Hegel on the Need for a Philosophy of Art: An Ethical Account[1]

TIMOTHY L. BROWNLEE, XAVIER UNIVERSITY

It is a curious fact that, while the concept of "history" receives little systematic articulation in his lectures on aesthetics, Hegel nonetheless understands the philosophy of art to be essentially historical. The implications of Hegel's historical approach to understanding art are far-reaching. No less an authority on the matter than Ernst Gombrich remarks that "Hegel is the father of art history."[2] On Gombrich's account, it is not an accident that we find in Hegel's philosophy of art the beginnings of "*Kunstgeschichte*." Instead, among the basic commitments of Hegel's philosophy of art is the claim that art is historical, that it embodies a development in time that marks it indelibly, and that art works and art worlds can only be understood in terms of their place within that development. While earlier thinkers took historical works and movements as their subject-matter, what distinguishes Hegel's approach to the history of art is that, while Hegel recognizes the achievement of the "the classical" form of art, he nonetheless understands it to be "only one transient mode of appearance of art, for art history can stand still just as little as history itself."[3]

It bears noting that implicit in this model for understanding the history of art there lies a deep tension. Even if "the Greeks remain unchallenged in the fame of having given sensuous beauty a classical form," their achievement remains a "transient" one. In identifying the classical form as the highest achievement of art, but one that passes away, Hegel's history of art eschews the model of linear historical progress that we seem to find in his conception of world history. Hegel is famous for first proposing that, in the modern age, art finds itself at an "end," having exhausted its capacity to achieve its highest aim. This tension animates Hegel's account of the art form that follows the classical, "romantic art," and it is particularly palpable in the conclusion of that account.

Starting in the 1826 lectures on aesthetics, Hegel concludes his treatment of the romantic form of art with an account of its "disintegration" (*Zerfallen*) into two apparently opposed strands.[4] These remarks are of interest, at least in part, because they concern the art of Hegel's own "present day," and therefore may be indicative of Hegel's view of the capacity of art to continue to address a vital need of the spirit. In its subjective strand, which Hegel claims culminates in humour, the work of art becomes an expression for the subjectivity of the artist, a symbolic sign of the artist's own wit.[5] In its objective strand, the work of art is held to a naturalistic standard, according to which its central task lies in imitating the "prosaic" conditions of bourgeois social life.[6] In both cases, Hegel suggests that the work ceases to be a work of *art*, in the former case because it does not present any objective content, and in the latter case because the merely objective presentation is free of anything "spiritual" (*geistig*).

Interpreters have dwelled on this specific disintegration of the romantic form of art to account for the puzzling idea, ascribed to Hegel, that art in general, not only in its romantic form, is somehow at an end in the modern age. On the one hand, these interpretations make significant progress in identifying that, for Hegel, if art is to continue to embody our highest aims and ideals, its content, what it conveys, must be *freedom*.[7] On the other hand, there is another tendency to identify freedom as a *problem* for modern works of art, in part responsible for the disintegration into subjective and objective that marks the end of romantic art.

Terry Pinkard argues that the central limitation of "modern art" consists in the fact that, in acknowledging the subjective side of freedom, it must also acknowledge the plurality and diversity of individual perspectives:

> The dissolution of modern art of which Hegel speaks is thus not the "end of art" in any real sense. It rather testifies to modern art's basic problem: there can be no form of art that is appropriate to the "spirit of the age" since "spirit" has become too fragmented for any aesthetic presentation to work as presenting the "truth" to us. Each of us has a life to lead, and there are simply too many different ways to lead those lives for any aesthetic exhibition of what that means to count; in fact, perhaps the greatest modern art must be that which conveys a sense of its own perspectivally limited view.[8]

To this extent, Pinkard focuses on one of the "sides" into which Hegel argues romantic art "falls apart" and exhausts itself. While Pinkard's remarks call to mind Hegel's characterization of the limitations of the modern novel,[9] their significance for the disintegration of romantic art should nonetheless be clear. If freedom depends essentially on subjectivity, and the subjectivity of different individuals is itself essentially different, there is no content that could be shared between them. Hegel stresses that primarily subjective works, those of humour, "can no longer be called artworks" since they can no longer express in an objective way what matters most to us, freedom.

By contrast, Robert Pippin argues that the prosaic nature of modern social life compromises the capacity of art to embody the truth for us. On Pippin's account, the changed status of art in modernity has to do with the unique character of the modern world itself, "a *prosaic*, unheroic world, not much of a subject for the divinizing or at least idealizing transformations of aesthetic portrayals at all." Art is *unnecessary* on this account:

> The "Idea" *need* not "sensibly shine" any longer because it can be grasped conceptually; norms get their grip on us without primary reliance on the sensual. But, said the other way around, it *cannot*; the sensible appearances of modern ethical life themselves are not fit vehicles for such "shining" because they and our very sensual lives have themselves been rationalized, transformed into practices, habits, and institutions with some sort of rational transparency to themselves ... *The modern social world itself may be rational, in other words, but it is, to say it all at once, just thereby not very beautiful, and its "meaning" is not very mysterious.*[10]

If modern bourgeois life need only be rational to be satisfying, and if it wears its rationality, we might say, on its sleeve, art ceases to address any vital need. Not only is the world of the modern bourgeois unsuited to artistic treatment, such treatment would be redundant. Presenting the prosaic world in all its prose in the absence of anything "spiritual" expresses a truth, but not one that is significant.

There is a question, however, as to whether this split is ultimate, or whether Hegel envisions the possibility of a reconciliation between these two apparently opposed subjective and objective poles. To be sure, we find frequent indictments throughout Hegel's writings of the dividedness of the modern world. From Hegel's early writings, through the Jena *Phenomenology*, and up to the mature Berlin system, we find a consistent account of modern life as riven by a set of divisions ultimately expressed in the "world-view" (*Weltanschauung*)[11] or "standpoint" (*Standpunkt*)[12] which Hegel calls "morality." According to Hegel this division between subject and object, reason and nature, freedom and necessity, whose quintessential formulation we find in Kant's critical philosophy, in fact pervades the entire culture, including even the fundaments of our conception of ourselves and our world. This division clearly informs the "disintegration" of romantic art: the domains of subjective inwardness indicated by humour and of a prosaic objective world devoid of spirit are mutually exclusive, and their splitting apart appears, from the standpoint of the present day, irreparable.

Of course, we also find consistent *criticisms* of the moral standpoint throughout Hegel's writings. Those criticisms aim to demonstrate that the domains that appear contradictory from the moral standpoint are not, in fact, mutually exclusive. Rather, the central aim of philosophy is to show that reason and nature, freedom and necessity, subject and object, can in fact be "reconciled." Indeed, this is the task that Hegel sets for the philosophy of art. Hence, my aim in what follows is to consider what Hegel has to say about the reconciliatory capacity of the philosophy of art, especially in the introductions to his lectures on aesthetics.[13] I begin with an account of the role that the "moral standpoint" plays in Hegel's account of art and aesthetics in the "present day" (§§1–3). I argue that Hegel ultimately offers an ethical criticism of the moral standpoint that parallels the one he presents in the *Philosophy of Right* (§4). Since that latter criticism is centrally concerned with demonstrating the possibility of a worldly freedom, a freedom that acknowledges the necessity of engagement in the central objective institutions and practices of modern ethicality (*Sittlichkeit*), it proves equally significant for understanding the way in which works of art can contribute to freedom, namely by presenting to us by sensible means what is substantial in modern social life (§5). In short, I aim to investigate the ways in which a philosophy of art can provide a helpful corrective to the "worldview" that Hegel believes predominates in his own "present-day," and to consider, if briefly, how that corrective might affect attitudes towards the capacity and achievement of art. I conclude by stressing that Hegel leaves open the possibility of an art of freedom which presents to our senses the experience of life within modern ethicality, but in a way that encourages our thought and reflection (§6).[14]

Among my aims here is to argue that the issues of freedom and history lie at the core Hegel's account of art, in particular the art of his "present day." Moreover, that account indicates the extent to which the apparent optimism of the lectures on world history, where Hegel famously argues that history has a rational shape because it embodies the actualization of our highest purpose, freedom,[15] remains open to challenge from within Hegel's own thinking. In contrast to the progressive picture that we find in the history lectures, the lectures on the philosophy of art seem to present a much more ambivalent perspective on modernity. However, I aim to argue here that this appearance of ambivalence is significantly weakened when we come to see the essential role that Hegel thinks philosophy can play in understanding art.

1

The claims that "Art is and remains according to the side of its highest determination something past for us," and that it "has lost genuine truth and liveliness for us," should be familiar to readers interested in the "end of art" thesis.[16] However, these claims leave open a significant question: According to Hegel, who are "we," for whom art is lost, a thing of the past? This question is a significant one for understanding a number of issues essential to Hegel's conception of the role of art in "the present day," and for its capacity for future revitalization.

Who, then, are "we"? We can achieve a better understanding of Hegel's view in this connection by attending to the immediate context of the claim that art is now "something past." This assertion appears for the first time in the 1826 lecture course.[17] In those lectures, Hegel traces the roots of this "pastness" to "our culture" (*Bildung*), claiming that "the *standpoint of the culture from which art has essential interest is no longer ours*."[18] In this connection, he points to the fact that "for the interest of art, we require more of a liveliness [*Lebendigkeit*]" than our insistence on adopting a "universal standpoint" admits. In contrast to the domain of intuition (*Anschauung*) in which works of art present themselves to us, "our interests lie more in the sphere of representation [*Vorstellung*]." By consequence, "The position of art is no longer so high in the liveliness of life; representation, reflection, thoughts are the preponderants, and our time is therefore principally provoked to reflections and thoughts about art."[19]

While Hegel does not assert directly, in 1823, that art is "past" for us, he stresses nonetheless that art is not the *highest* way of expressing the truth. Because of its "sensible material" art is limited in the content it can convey.[20] In particular, Hegel stresses that "the content of our religion [and] culture," which he identifies as "the deeper existence of the idea," does not admit of complete sensible expression: "our world, religion, and culture of reason [*Vernunftbildung*] has proceeded beyond art as the highest level for expressing the absolute to another level. The work of art therefore cannot fulfil [*ausfüllen*] our final absolute need, we worship [*beten … an*] works of art no longer, and our relation to works of art is of a more considerate [*besonnener*] kind."[21] In this connection too he insists that works of art now no longer convey their meaning directly to us, but instead "provoke our judgment," so that "we submit the content of the work of art and the suitability of its presentation to our thoughtful testing [*Prüfung*]."

In both cases, Hegel stresses that "our culture" insists that what is true is not accessible to sense alone, but must instead be an object of reflection and judgment, whose domains lie in representation and thought. This culturally rooted need is the source of a renewed demand for a "philosophy" or "science" of art, which takes up the cultural challenge of approaching art thoughtfully.[22] However, there is a significant ambiguity in the later account of what we might hope to achieve through this thoughtful consideration. In the 1823 lectures, Hegel offers a very modest assessment of the influence that we might expect philosophy or thinking to have on art itself: "we respect and have art, but we see it as no final thing [*Letztes*], but rather only meditate [*denken ... nach*] about it. This thinking cannot have the aim of again evoking [*hervorzurufen*] art, but rather [only that] of cognizing its accomplishment [*Leistung*]."[23] By contrast, in the 1826 lectures, Hegel suggests that the fruits of a philosophy of art may be more significant. Identifying this significance, however, requires that we first consider the diagnosis of contemporary thinking about aesthetics that he presents in the account of the possible "purposes" of art which immediately follows the assertion of art's pastness.

2

After claiming, in the 1826 lectures, that "we" are satisfied more by "representation" and "abstraction" than by artworks, which are lively objects of intuition, Hegel immediately turns to an assessment of the different "determinations" belonging to the "concept of art." What follows is an account of different philosophical conceptions of the "purpose" of art that should be, in large measure, familiar to readers of Hotho's text. The lectures, however, make the *dialectical* character of Hegel's account of imitative, emotive, and moral conceptions of the purpose of art easier to identify. While the *imitation* of "naturalness" is an "essential true moment of the artwork, and of the ideal" of art, imitation is not the sole aim of works of art. Rather, it is the "spiritual" and not the merely "natural" that is the "principal matter" of artworks.[24] Artworks communicate the spiritual by addressing themselves to the "mind" (*Gemüt*), making it possible for us "to feel more foundationally [*gründlicher*], more deeply" those familiar situations of common life. Artworks present otherwise prosaic objects, but address themselves to our "sentiment, inclinations, and passions," rather than our day-to-day practical concerns. However, while, this *evocation of passion and emotion* is an essential determination belonging to the concept of art, it is not alone art's "final purpose." Rather, the capacity to evoke emotion is a merely formal characteristic, indifferent to art's content. Hegel calls the fact that works of art can evoke all manner of emotions, even those which might prompt us to approve of evil and crime, the "sophistry of art."[25] We might distinguish between those passions which art should encourage and those it should not by saying that art's aim lies in the *purification* of the passions in the promotion of a *moral purpose*. Hegel approvingly suggests that art works can purify the passions of their "barbarism" by bringing them into the form of "representation." When the passion is thereby made objective, distinct from the subject, Hegel contends that "the concentration [of the passions] is broken" and "the mind comes thereby to a kind of freedom" from the "necessity" which the passion previously imposed on it.[26] Insofar as it contributes to submitting the passions to "something higher," Hegel contends that art promotes a "moral purpose."

In considering this "moral purpose," it is clear that Hegel means something very specific by "morality." Indeed, he goes on to argue that the "moral standpoint" (*der moralische Standpunkt*)[27] involves not only a specific conception of "the highest thing" (*das Höchste*), to which the passions ought to be subordinated, but also a particular understanding of the relation between this higher purpose and the passions, namely that of "opposition" (*Gegensatz*) or even "contradiction" (*Widerspruch*).[28] From the "moral standpoint," *freedom* is "the highest thing."[29] This freedom is achieved, however, only through a "struggle" (*Kampf*) with an "antagonizing force" (*Widerstrebenden*), which Hegel identifies most broadly as "nature."[30] As a result, the moral standpoint is essentially one of conflict and strife, constituted by "opposition" (*Gegensatz*): between freedom and necessity; the universal and particular; the dead concept and abstraction on the one hand, and liveliness on the other; thought and actuality; theory and experience; the spirit and the flesh.[31] These oppositions emerge in human beings as a "duality of worlds" of spirit and nature, so that "the human being finds themselves in the infinite contradiction between [on the one hand] earthly temporality, and material, sensible aims, but on the other hand, raises themselves to freedom, to the eternal idea existing in and for itself, divests the world of its lived [*belebten*] actuality and dissolves it to abstractions in thought."[32]

Perhaps unsurprisingly, Hegel claims that we find the highest articulation of this moral standpoint in "the Kantian philosophy." Echoing his critique of Kant's moral philosophy, Hegel suggests that while Kant identifies the "dissolution" (*Auflösung*) of the opposition which defines the moral standpoint as a "requirement" (*Forderung*), Kant is unable to articulate the "true" reconciliation between freedom and nature.[33] Even though Kant suggests, in the third *Critique*, that "artistic beauty" can play a significant role in overcoming this opposition, Hegel argues that the only resolution available from the "moral standpoint" is one in which "[f]eeling, mind, sense, inclination is subsumed, dominated [*subsumiert, beherrscht*] by a determination of right [*rechtliche Bestimmung*] which proceeds from the concept of freedom."[34] By contrast, a resolution through artistic beauty requires an approach according to which sense and particularity are not "dominated" by freedom and universality, but rather in which the former can be understood to be "inwardly adequate" to express the latter. However, this possibility is precisely that which the "moral standpoint" forecloses.

As should be clear, however, the oppositions which render an aesthetic solution to the "contradiction" between freedom and nature impossible are the very same as those which provide the foundation for "our culture." Because we identify primarily with the universal demands of thought, reason, and representation, we can allow no self-standing place for the intuition and sense by means of which art works might convey their content to us. In short, "our culture" *is* essentially that of "the moral standpoint," and our problems with art are essentially the same as those which stem from adopting just that standpoint. However, most importantly, in what follows, Hegel does not hesitate to offer a *criticism* of the aesthetics and philosophy of art of his contemporaries on the grounds that they present inadequate solutions to the challenges to the historical place of art which our culture and the "Kantian philosophy" which expresses it have introduced. Hegel's critique of his predecessors is aimed precisely at showing that the "contradiction" between freedom and nature can be reconciled, and that philosophy, in particular the philosophy of art, plays an essential role in achieving that reconciliation.

3

Hegel begins his account of his immediate predecessors by suggesting that "the Kantian viewpoint is the point of departure" for their aesthetic thinking. Not only does Hegel argue that the moral standpoint supplies a common groundwork, shared by thinkers as diverse as Schiller, Goethe, the Schlegels, Fichte, Winckelmann, Solger, and Tieck, but that their central problem (and his) is the one which Kant bequeathed to philosophy, namely how to understand "the higher [standpoint]" of "the unity of necessity and freedom – of the particular and universal, of the minded [*Gemütlichen*] and the understanding [*Verständigen*]."[35] The fact that Hegel treats his account of their views as explicitly "historical" is itself significant.[36] After all, he devotes some attention, in each of the prior accounts of the "purpose of art," to identify historical figures who endorsed each conception. By contrast, in the "historical" account, he is interested in identifying a range of "historical" trends that shape the aesthetic landscape within which we find his own philosophy of art. While Hegel refrains from excessive praise of any one figure, he does not hesitate to offer criticisms of elements of the views of his immediate predecessors and contemporaries. That critique focuses especially on the aesthetic of romantic irony.[37]

On Hegel's account, August and Friedrich Schlegel count "irony" as "the highest thing" which art promotes.[38] While their view is not itself philosophical (it "is not guided by foundational philosophical cognition"), he claims that their conception of irony is ultimately anchored in "the Fichtean philosophy," in particular Fichte's view that "the principle of knowing, of cognition in general is [the] *Ich* in its entire abstraction." Since this *Ich* is "that which is entirely simple, in which all difference is completely negated," Hegel argues that "all matters perish [*gehen alle Sachen unter*] in abstract freedom, I can demolish, negate [*vernichten, negieren*] all in myself," even those things which in fact "count" for me.[39] This Fichtean view retains the central characteristics of the Kantian "moral standpoint": "the highest thing" remains a kind of "freedom," and that freedom is sustained only through its opposition to and domination of an opposed term over which the individual is "lord and master."[40] This view is ultimately expressed in a sort of artistic conception of human life, according to which "the vocation of the human being, of life, of the individual, is to express [*auszusprechen*] their individuality, to bring themselves to appearance," and that expression is understood as the product of a kind of artistry. The primary implication on which Hegel dwells, however, is that ascribing such a "divine geniality" to myself entails a correlative undermining of that which I "posit," so that "right, bonds, religion, love are likewise for the individual only a shine, that is, the individual comports themselves in such relations only ironically against them. Everything ethical, true, right [*Rechtliche*] is only posited, the genius is not in such relations, but rather exists over and above them [*ist über sie hinaus*]."[41] Likewise, the *Ich* itself, if it is to be able to take on and then negate any content, must itself consist in a kind of "emptiness." This is not alone a problem for Hegel, who understands subjectivity itself to consist solely in a kind of "negativity." However, in rejecting any objective content as binding on oneself, the ironist undermines those factors which might shape and supply content to their "character." Instead, the ironist is condemned to being "characterless."[42]

Hegel's critique of the romantic aesthetic of irony is significant for a number of reasons. First, the fact that he even offers a criticism indicates that he believes that a philosophy of art is in fact justified in not merely chronicling near-contemporary developments, but also in pointing out when those developments are illegitimate.[43] To this end, he is clear that "the moral" and "irony" both "only indicate the true, what the idea is," each falling short of identifying "the idea, the divine [*das Göttliche*], the absolute," which Hegel recommends that we understand instead as "the spiritual [*das Geistige*]."[44] Put otherwise, Hegel is not only confident that the Kantian moral standpoint is not ultimate, but, in addition, he clearly also believes that he has at his disposal criteria for distinguishing good from bad responses to the oppositions and contradictions at its heart.

Second, because the specific criticism of the romantic response that he offers is ethical, he clearly believes that ethical considerations are not irrelevant to aesthetics and art. At this stage, however, the specific character of Hegel's critique is not immediately clear. It might first seem, as Judith Norman argues, that Hegel's criticism of the Schlegel of *Lucinde* is ultimately grounded in a prudish and regressive conception of the place of women in society. On Norman's account, Hegel rejects the "revaluation of values" that she finds in Schlegel on the grounds that Schlegel promotes the wrong set of values, destroying the idea of "female virtue" that she finds in Hegel, and "derid[ing] women's genuinely positive contribution to ethical life."[45] Is Hegel's rejection of romantic irony really simply an argument against the specific values that Schlegel and others aim to promote? This question bears significantly on the aesthetic one that has been our focus thus far. Is Hegel's critique of romantic art and aesthetics grounded ultimately on his disagreement with the romantics' avowedly progressive aims? Is it simply a disagreement over which moral values are the right ones to hold? We find an analogous criticism in the *Philosophy of Right* account of "Morality." There, Hegel's critique is aimed at a more fundamental set of ideas. That is, Hegel does not simply endorse the rejection of a specific set of moral values, but rather the overcoming of "the moral standpoint" itself, in favour of a theory of "ethicality" (*Sittlichkeit*).[46] His account of the transition from "morality" to "ethicality" in that text is instructive for understanding the critique of "the moral standpoint" that we find in his philosophy of art.

4

When Hegel takes up romanticism in the philosophy of objective spirit, his target again is positions that share the essential presuppositions of the "moral standpoint": the highest aim, the moral good, is a condition of freedom which we attain through the subordination of all other aims to that of duty.[47] However, since the moral standpoint identifies subjectivity alone as authoritative, it leaves us without any objective content for our duties,[48] and can ultimately appeal for such content only to the subject's "conscience," the "absolute certainty of itself in itself, that which posits particularity, that which is determinative and decisive [*das Besonderheit Setzende, das Bestimmende und Entscheidende*]."[49] Hegel ultimately argues that this moral conscience is just as much the possibility of being "evil." However, the evil of conscience does not simply consist in the denial or violation of existing ethical standards. Instead, for Hegel, evil consists in a specific subjective attitude towards those standards, those ethical "contents." Specifically, while the evil agent considers herself to be the ultimate moral authority – not only the judge, but also the source of all moral norms – she achieves and sustains that authority only by means of ironically playing with established ethical contents, those matters which in fact constitute the terms within which agents make sense of themselves, and which they in fact impose on themselves in their actions.[50] That is, the evil agent is a *hypocrite*.[51] She is able to achieve freedom, the condition in which she subordinates all objective contents to the majesty of her own will, only so long as there are such existent objective contents with which she can scandalously play. Or, her own freedom presupposes the existence of exactly those ethical standards from which she claims to stand apart. When no one takes seriously the values which she subverts through her action, the ironist loses the ground of her distinctive freedom.

When Hegel introduces the idea of "ethicality" (*Sittlichkeit*) in the *Philosophy of Right*, he points to precisely this fact. The problem with the ironist's evil lies not in the fact that the "ethics of conviction" to which she subscribes is just as likely to result in "moral" action as not.[52] Rather, the problem is that the ironist's standpoint, that of *"subjectivity that considers itself to be the absolute,"*[53] is actually grounded in and answerable to a set of objective ethical standards without which it would not be possible.[54] It is not just that the ironist's standpoint entails that certain actions that we might be inclined to think are wrong or unsavoury are not. Instead, the problem is that the ironist's standpoint itself is inherently contradictory. That is, freedom is not solely a "subjective" condition that arises from the domination of all objective contents. On the contrary, the argument that Hegel offers throughout the *Philosophy of Right*, and which culminates in the account of "ethicality," is that freedom, whose "concept" is that of right, and whose "subjective" form is that of morality, in fact *requires* participation in a set of objectively existing institutions and practices for its "actualization."

What does it mean to say that freedom is only "actual" (*wirklich*) within concrete forms of "ethicality"? The concept of "actuality" (*Wirklichkeit*) lies at the heart of Hegel's metaphysics, and it is among the key concepts in the *Philosophy of Right*. In the work's "Preface," Hegel famously argues that philosophy must not limit itself to merely subjective convictions or abstract ideals about right, but rather to demonstrate the rationality of what is "actual."[55] In the "Preface," Hegel stresses the methodological claim that the task of philosophy is to engage with "ethical actuality" in its concrete forms.[56] In the remainder of the text, Hegel's task is to consider not only the determinations of the concept of right, but the concrete, objective forms in which that concept is "actualized."[57] Since "right" is simply the "existence [*Dasein*] of the free will" or "freedom as idea,"[58] the philosophy of right will be concerned with the concrete shape of ethicality in which the idea of freedom is itself actualized.

On one account, Hegel's concept of actuality is basically Aristotelian: actuality is the realization of an inherent purpose (*Zweck*) or *telos*. Hegel's history lectures seem to construe actuality in this way.[59] However, it is unclear whether we ought to understand the relation between freedom, actuality, and ethicality in the *Philosophy of Right* in this way. We arrive at a different account if we follow those readers who have recently argued that we can understand the role of actuality within the text by considering it in terms of Hegel's account in the logic.[60] That account makes no substantive reference to the idea of a purpose. Instead, actuality unites ground and existence, so that when we say that something is actual, we mean both that it exists and takes on external form, and that it contains its ground within itself: "The actual is thus *manifestation* [Manifestation]; it is not drawn out into the sphere of *alteration* through its externality, nor is it a *shining* in *an other*, but rather it manifests itself, that is, it is *itself* in its externality, and is *itself* only in *it* [*this externality*], that is only as movement distinguishing and determining itself from itself."[61] On this account, ethicality is the actuality of freedom in the sense that freedom is something actual only insofar as it is embodied in the "laws and institutions" of an ethical world.[62] These objective and, in a sense, "external" determinations are not incidental to freedom. Instead, freedom, we might say, "is *itself* in" them, and it "is *itself* only in" them: They are constitutive of freedom as something actual.

Of course, these two accounts need not be incompatible. One can hold both that freedom exists as an ultimate end and purpose, and that it is actual only when realized in specific, concrete, "external" conditions.

However, rendering these two accounts compatible requires acknowledging that the objective institutional conditions that we find within ethicality do not simply exist as detachable means to the achievement of freedom. In place of such an instrumental conception of the relation between freedom and institutions, Hegel's concept of actuality entails a *constitutive* conception of their relation. When Hegel writes that "Ethicality is the *idea of freedom*, as the living good that has in self-consciousness its knowing and willing, and, through the action of self-consciousness, its actuality, just as self-consciousness has in the ethical being its foundation existing in and for itself and its motive purpose," he is pointing out that freedom exists as something actual only under specific concrete institutional conditions. The elevated and "ultimate purpose" of reason is actual only in specific, "prosaic" practices. Outside of the institutional framework provided by the family, civil society, and the state, freedom is an unreal abstraction, an empty ideal. Freedom is "actual" only within a specific ethical "world."[63]

At the same time, it is clear that Hegel acknowledges that, in making this argument for the necessary objective conditions for the realization of freedom, he must push against the prevailing intellectual and cultural trends of his own day, romanticism among them. This tension is clearest in the "Preface" to the *Philosophy of Right*, in which he indicts the "shallowness" (*Seichtigkeit*) of contemporary thought for refusing even to consider anything but subjectivity as the source of ethical content. He condemns as modern "sophistry" the conviction according to which "the principles" of right are based solely "on *subjective purposes and opinions*, on *subjective feeling* and *particular conviction*" on the grounds that such an approach entails "the destruction [*Zerstörung*] of inner ethicality and of the upright [*rechtschaffenen*] conscience, of love and right among private persons, and the destruction of the public order and the laws of the state."[64] In contrast, Hegel stresses the need for a thoughtful, concrete engagement with objective ethical institutions, with a view to demonstrating that what is actual in them is rational. According to Hegel, the resulting "rational insight" into those institutions, and into the ineliminable contribution that they make to a free life is just "*reconciliation* [*Versöhnung*] with actuality."[65]

Finally, Hegel stresses the need for *philosophy* to achieve this thoughtful engagement which results in reconciliation. Not only must philosophy challenge the excessive claims of subjectivity to know the truth and secure a free life solely on the basis of immediate feeling or knowledge, but it must also counteract a specific attitude towards the world according to which that which is "present and actual" in the world is of secondary importance in comparison to an ideal and better "beyond" posited by subjectivity. That is, in order for philosophy to bring about "reconciliation with actuality," it must demonstrate that those familiar or (as Hegel is fond of saying) "prosaic" institutions of ethicality are in fact necessary elements of a free life. To this end, philosophy plays a very important role in "contemporary life," both in defusing the excessive claims of subjectivity, but also in redeeming a prosaic world (whose institutions and practices we might be inclined to disregard) by demonstrating its essential contribution to the best life, one of freedom. In the *Philosophy of Right*, Hegel accomplishes this aim by providing a rational grounding for the demands of right and morality, dialectically demonstrating the inherent shortcomings of those standpoints, and then showing that the concept of right is ultimately only "actualized" in a shared ethical world. This requires, on the one hand, drawing out the specific purposes which the "prosaic" institutions and practices of the modern social world, the family, civil society, and the state, promote. On the other hand, however, it requires demonstrating that that world is one in which self-conscious subjectivity is in fact at home, in which we find the materials for the realization of our reflexively determined aims.

5

The ethical critique of "the moral standpoint" that Hegel offers in the *Philosophy of Right* is therefore essential to the central task of that work, namely showing that those "prosaic" institutions of modern bourgeois life that the romantic ironist aims to demonstrate as beneath her by subordinating them to the majesty of her divine will, are in fact essential conditions for a free life. While the ironist hypocritically depends on the existence of those institutions for the achievement of the unique "freedom" that comes from elevating herself above them, Hegel argues that a free life instead requires a good-faith, "earnest"[66] engagement in the world that they shape. Finally, *philosophy* is indispensable in drawing out the ineliminable contribution that those institutions make to a free life. The critique of "the moral standpoint" does not simply aim to show that the specific values that the romantics promoted are the wrong ones. Rather, it is aimed at the idea that the "objective" world of modern life is of secondary importance, a mere thing to be dominated and controlled by the majesty of the agent's subjectivity. Hegel takes issue with the central commitment of the moral standpoint, namely that we achieve a free life through that domination, and instead argues that the best life requires a good-faith engagement in a social world whose institutions make an essential contribution to our freedom. And that, of course, requires, to a great extent at least, shaping our own lives in accordance with that world's demands rather than understanding it to be a mere object to be subordinated to our wills.

I have taken so much time to stress the specific character of Hegel's critique of "the moral standpoint" in the *Philosophy of Right*, especially as it bears on the ethical views of his contemporaries, because I believe that we find essentially the same features in the account of art in the aesthetics lectures. First, in each case, whenever Hegel remarks on the condition of art and aesthetics in the present day, be it at the outset of the lectures when he points to its "pastness," or in his account of "the moral standpoint," he reasserts the need for a *philosophy* of art, stressing, in particular, the reconciliatory capacity of philosophy. Because the "satisfaction" of "our interests" lies more in the domain of "abstraction" than in the lively impressions of sense, "the science of art [*Wissenschaft der Kunst*] [has become] a greater need for us than in prior times."[67] Likewise, the contradictions endemic to the "moral standpoint" are not insurmountable. Instead, "philosophy" shows us that "[t]he truth is first the dissolved opposition [*der aufgelöste Gegensatz*], the reconciled contradiction": "the highest thing, the idea of the self-reconciling opposition, is the standpoint in which art finds itself, and this is the point of view from which we proceed in the following consideration [*Betrachtung*] of art."[68] That is, philosophy shows that the oppositions which underlie the moral standpoint are not necessarily contradictory.

In this connection, Hegel goes on to argue specifically that the *sensible form* of works of art need not compromise art's "final purpose," namely "[t]o unveil the truth, what moves itself in the human breast, and to do so in a pictorial [*bildlich*], concrete way."[69] Hegel therefore argues that a philosophy of art can help to reconcile us to the objective character of artworks, their sensible form, by showing that that objective form is one in which "the truth" can be presented. Against the denigration of the domain of sense that we find in "the moral standpoint," philosophy can show us that that objective domain is not an alien object to be dominated or coolly judged, but rather a venue for the expression of "the highest things": art "is the middle term [*Mittelglied*] between pure thought, the supersensible world, and the immediate, present sensation, the sensible regions, which is presented as a beyond by thought as such. Art reconciles [*versöhnt*] both extremes, and is the binding middle term of the concept and nature."[70]

In addition to vindicating art's sensible *form*, Hegel also offers a justification of art in light of its *content*. That is, Hegel stresses that the philosophy of art shows us that art constitutes one of the three forms of "absolute spirit." Since the genuine final purpose of art lies in "unveiling the truth," it shares a common content with religion and philosophy, namely "the true": "[a]rt is only as the intuiting consciousness of absolute spirit so that this is filled in an immediate, sensible manner, in a manner of immediate figuration."[71] In comparison with religion, whose domain is the inwardness of the subject's representations, art presents the true in the form of "objectivity."[72] What does it mean to say that art is one of three forms of absolute spirit? This raises a deep question concerning the basic character of absolute spirit itself. Angelica Nuzzo argues that, for Hegel, "absolute spirit" is not distinguished by being about a distinct object, "the absolute," but that Hegel instead employs "absolute" adjectivally: "the term 'absolute' is used as an *adjective* qualifying a stage of a *process* of development or realization ... Absoluteness, for Hegel, always has something to do with the *conclusion* or *end* of a process of development."[73] On this account, even if, in the lectures, Hegel identifies "God" as the object of religion and philosophy, the appeal to God does not identify an object completely separate from other forms of the expression of spirit. Instead, art, religion, and philosophy are forms of "absolute spirit" in the sense that they involve a kind of ultimacy, that they embody fundamental claims about what a people takes to be true: "Art has its highest vocation in common with religion and philosophy, to be able to express thought, and art is, like religion and philosophy, a way of expressing the divine, the highest requirements of the spirit and of bringing these to consciousness. In art, peoples have laid down their highest representations, and it [is] often the only key to knowing the religion of a people."[74] Against the "moral standpoint," according to which sensuous objects cannot express "the highest things," the philosophy of art vindicates a higher content for art, namely "the divine, the highest requirements of the spirit."

While art is a form of absolute spirit, Nuzzo's thesis entails that art can nonetheless concern itself with other subject matters, most importantly with finite spirit. However, its concern with these things will ultimately be with the extent to which they express the truth. In the account that Hegel offers in his mature systematic philosophy, the "highest thing" for us, that which we take most fundamentally to be true, is *freedom*.[75] To this extent, his view is consistent with that of "the moral standpoint." However, he again stresses that philosophy can show that what appeared to be a contradiction between the inward domain of freedom and the outward domain of sense in which we find art works is in fact not genuine. Instead, it is precisely the task of "romantic" art to present freedom sensuously. To be sure, the romantic work of art does not do this directly. Instead, in romantic art "the spiritual emerges as spiritual, the ideal is free and independent in itself.

Insofar as the spirit comes to be for itself, it is freed from the sensible form; the sensible is for it something indifferent and to be passed over, and the mind [*das Gemüt*], the spiritual as spiritual, becomes the significance [*Bedeutung*] of the sensible."[76] That is, while the romantic work of art does not bear its content in itself, it has its content, the highest thing, freedom, as its *significance*, so that the "contingent shine" of the sense object is in fact "guided [*gelenkt*] by something inward [*Innern*] in the interest of the mind."[77] Romantic works of art retain a content, but that content is one whose proper place is *not only* in the object, but in the mind, and the function of the work is to signify that inward content.

There is one additional way in which the philosophy of art can help to correct significant errors endemic to the moral standpoint. It does this by pointing to the ways in which the content of the work of art, which is, for us, freedom, can be presented sensuously, or *figured*. If the ultimate significance of the work of romantic art is something essentially *subjective*, we might worry about the capacity of sensuous *objects* to express that significance. Indeed, Hegel stresses that "Christianity" and "Protestantism" complicate the way in which works of art can be bearers of absolute content, insofar as both "return the content of divinity to its truth, spirituality, and have brought to a stronger consciousness the inappropriateness [*Unangemessenheit*] of the sensible element."[78] If freedom is an *exclusively* subjective condition, then no object would be completely adequate to it.

However, Hegel also argues that philosophy can lead us to a correct understanding of the sensuous form of objects, and that form's relation to subjectivity, in a way that *redeems* objective content. The passage that is most relevant for understanding this idea appears at the conclusion of the "historical" account of the purpose of art in the 1826 lectures, but is excised, edited, and moved in Hotho's text.[79] In the lectures, immediately after his account of romantic aesthetics, Hegel draws a distinction between the "chaos" of "sensuous reality" (*sinnliche Realität*), and the "actuality" (*Wirklichkeit*) that works of art present by means of "shine" (*Schein*).[80] While we are "accustomed" to encountering the objective world in its immediacy in the former mode, Hegel stresses that artistic shine is better able to show us what is true and actual in that world. Moreover, it is philosophy that shows us that "sensuous reality" is in fact lacking in genuine actuality, since it is not something that exists "in and for itself." By contrast, even though art works appear in the mode of "shine," and may seem pale copies of immediate "sensuous reality," they are in fact capable of bearing significance and expressing the truth more adequately.

Most importantly for our present purposes, he stresses the *ethical* character of art in this connection:

> What the true is in the sensible present [*sinnlichen Gegewart*] are the powers [*Mächte*] that we find therein, the spiritual, the ethical [*das Geistige, Sittliche*]; it is these eternal powers that are presented through art. What is called shine in art is the fact that common reality [*gewöhnliche Realität*] is sublated [*aufgehoben*]. And the shine in it is a much more true, higher form against the form in which we are accustomed [*gewohnt*] to see the ethical. The ethicality of the customary world [*der gewöhnlichen Welt*] we call customary reality. What we call reality is this chaos; the chaos is however only in shine, and it is the powers in the chaos that art brings to appearance ... That which is eternally in history art frees entirely from this sensible accessory being [*Beiwesen*], and so makes present for us the idea.[81]

That is, art animates the mere "sensuous reality" of the world of ethicality, the humdrum way in which we are accustomed to encountering it, and presents to us those "divine" powers which sustain it. To this extent, a philosophy of art can correct another tendency inherent to "the moral standpoint." For morality, ethicality appears as a second-best sort of life, as a "life in the state" that forces "the mind" to be "imprisoned in small [*kleinlichen*] interests, in the point of view of utility," so that "the universal mind has lost the freedom which belongs to living in the disinterested enjoyment of art."[82] Instead, Hegel insists that art can in fact present to us more directly those divine "powers" that animate ethicality, that we might otherwise be inclined to overlook and to consider *merely* prosaically when we approach art from the standpoint of morality. The aesthetic failure of the moral standpoint lies in the fact that the dominating attitude towards objectivity that seeks only to pass judgment and assert our own authority forecloses the possibility that art could convey a significance to us. "We" fail to experience art as enlivening not because of the objective or sensuous character of the artwork, but rather because we are unwilling to engage with it, to experience it as speaking to us, since that experience would require a kind of submission that morality deems unacceptable. To this end, philosophy can help to vindicate an ethical *subject matter* for art. If the content of art in modernity is freedom, and a free life actually requires engagement in objective ethical institutions and practices, an art which presents that engagement sensuously satisfies the high standards which Hegel has identified for art throughout its history.[83]

The reconciling aspect of art distinguishes the sort of "satisfaction" that it makes possible from that which is available from the practical standpoint. In the 1828/29 lectures, Hegel states that "satisfaction" (*Befriedigung*) is the condition in which "the subjective become[s] objective," so that, for example, eating "sublates" the one-sidedness of subjectivity in hunger, so that "I am then [something] affirmative" in the resulting satisfaction.[84] However, he thinks that there are distinctive kinds of satisfaction that are possible for us. He argues that one kind of satisfaction is possible through practice, for example when I obey laws that are rational, but that this satisfaction is only relative because it is finite and limited.[85] By contrast, "absolute" modes of knowing are not finite or relative in this way, and art is one of these modes: "Art therefore has the content of absolute truth, satisfaction of the spirit, beatific [*seligen*] sensations of spirit."[86] When Hegel claims that "The human being is an amphibian, a duality belongs to it [of freedom and natural necessity], and it is not able to satisfy itself in one or the other," he is not simply acknowledging a dividedness that is inescapable for us.[87] Instead, he is pointing to the distinctive role that art can play in showing us that satisfaction need not be of the either/or variety characteristic of the moral world-view, a point that even his practical philosophy and its theory of ethicality demonstrates is false. But, in addition, he is arguing that there is a higher satisfaction than the relative and limited one that we derive from action and practice, and that art is one of the sources from which it is derived.

On the account that I've offered here, in the modern age, there is an important sense in which art stands in need of philosophy. I've been arguing that the moral standpoint cannot ascribe a significant role to art in human life, because art and art works fall on the subjected side of the dichotomies comprising that standpoint. Since it is philosophy that shows us the limitations of that standpoint, the redemption of art requires the philosophy of art to demonstrate the ways in which art works can continue to embody our highest interests.[88]

6

I have been focusing on the ways in which Hegel presents his own philosophy of art as part of an ongoing conversation concerning the nature and purpose of art. In particular, I have been interested in pointing out the ways that Hegel's own conception of art entails the need to reject some "current" views about art's significance. First, Hegel stresses the reconciliatory capacity of philosophy to demonstrate the appropriateness of *art in general* for the expression of our highest concerns. If we give up the dualistic presuppositions underlying the "moral standpoint," the central idea is that we can come to see art as a *form* of absolute spirit. In this connection, art is not merely an idle plaything or a mere imitation of a reality which is more true, but a sensuous expression of our highest interest, freedom, the essential *content* of art in modernity. Second, art can play an essential role in "enlivening" and redeeming its *subject matter* insofar as it might be a spur to reflection on, and thoughtful consideration of the institutions and practices of modern ethicality.[89] To the extent that art portrays the "divine powers" that animate those ethical institutions and practices essential to a free life, institutions and practices which we are otherwise inclined to think are merely "prosaic," art can make manifest for us the essential contribution that ethicality itself makes to a free life. In this connection, Hegel is explicit in asserting that "the gods" are "the highest purpose of art," and this "not only according to its past temporality [*vergänglichen Zeitlichkeit*]," but just as much in the present day.[90] In this connection, Annemarie Gethmann-Siefert identifies an essential role for art in its contribution to "formal enculturation" (*formelle Bildung*) in the modern age: "through alternate intuitions of the world and representations of human action, art forms [*bildet*] toward critical reflection" on modern life.[91] In short, art can reconcile us to modern social life by showing us how engagement in its institutions and practices contributes to the realization of our highest purpose, freedom.[92]

The suggestion that art might continue to be a vital and significant part of our lives does not contradict any of the claims that Hegel makes concerning its changed status in the modern age. As we have seen, Hegel traces one such shift in art's status to the rise of Christianity, and to the increasing focus on subjectivity and inwardness within Protestantism. While Hegel is clear that art reaches a kind apogee in its classical form in ancient Greece, insofar as it achieves "the perfect adequacy of the idea and its figure," classical art is limited to portraying our highest concerns only bodily, in the absence of subjectivity and inwardness.[93] By contrast, it is precisely the achievement of romantic art to present that subjectivity and inwardness by making the objective work a sign of the mind. In so doing, romantic art gains a significant expressive capacity that classical art lacks, concerned as it can now be with subjectivity, the entire domain of the inward and human.

We have seen that Pinkard traces the central "problem" of modern art to precisely this fact, namely that art must take into account the subjectivity of the individual, and the differences between individual perspectives. However, Pinkard's account overlooks the central accomplishment that Hegel ascribes to the philosophy of art, namely of overcoming the limitations of subjectivity by reconciling it to the objective domain. In terms of art's ethical vocation, this means acknowledging the need for free subjects to be reflectively engaged in a shared ethical world. While Hegel does insist that such portrayals can only ever be "partial"[94] – they cannot hope to portray the ethical world as a whole, as did the founding efforts of the "heroes" in classical art[95] – conveying the "perspective" of a subject is not incompatible with presenting a meaning that can be *shared* on the basis of common engagement in the same world. That is, the philosophy of art shows the need to move beyond understanding freedom as merely subjective, and to consider subjectivity instead as expressed and engaged within an objective world.[96] Even though Christianity and Protestantism come to stress the significance of subjectivity for our understanding of freedom, Hegel points to the fact that Protestantism brings with a new understanding of *worldliness* too: "Through the self-introduction of the divine spirit into actuality, the freeing of actuality for this spirit becomes what should be called *holiness* [Heiligkeit] in the world, superseded [*verdrängt*] by ethicality ... The divine spirit must immanently permeate the worldly [*das Weltliche*], so that wisdom [*Weisheit*] is concrete therein and its justification [*Berechtigung*] is determined in itself."[97] Philosophy demonstrates the need to curb the excesses of subjectivity and understand freedom as objectively embodied, both in the shared ethical world of finite spirit and in art, the intuitive domain of absolute spirit. In all of its forms, absolute spirit points to the need to reject those rigid dualities inherent to the moral standpoint, and instead understand our highest interest, freedom, as essentially *worldly*.

Even if the changes in art entailed by the rise of Christianity, especially in its Protestant form, do not entail that art cannot remain vital and significant, we might be concerned that art's very sensible form entails a radical shift in its capacity to convey the truth. With respect to its "highest vocation," art *does* remain something past, insofar as we no longer consider it to be the sole or highest mode in which we are conscious of our highest interests. Indeed, we no longer worship art, as Hegel suggests we once did. If art is not an object of worship, how does it present "the divine actuality" of the ethical world to us? Representation and thought, the forms which predominate in religion and philosophy, are more adequate for completely expressing the truth, for identifying and grasping our highest value, freedom, and clarifying the objective conditions for its realization, and this fact poses a challenge for the capacity of art to continue to express what we take to matter. As Pippin stresses, from the standpoint of the senses, the modern world appears merely prosaic, and an art that concerns itself with that world seems condemned to being a merely external "naturalistic" portrayal of subject matters allergic to a higher content, and therefore to not really being art at all.[98]

However, Pippin's account overlooks the essential differences between objective and absolute spirit. From the practical standpoint, institutional life may very well present itself as merely prosaic, as inadequate to express or embody our highest interests. We found the roots of this attitude within "the moral standpoint," for which subjectivity alone is true and the objective world of nature is of secondary importance. At the same time, Hegel is equally emphatic in stating that art can help us to overcome this attitude, precisely by showing us that it is only the "sensuous reality" of ethicality that appears to be prosaic and insignificant. By contrast, as we have seen, he insists that art brings to appearance those "divine powers" that constitute the actuality of ethicality. To be sure, there is an important question about what it means to understand this "divinity" as "spirit." However, it would be rash to jump, as Pippin does, from the assertion that, for Hegel, divinity is human in the modern age, to the assertion that our practices include a complete understanding and rational grasp of that divinity. Hegel, after all, asserts the need for *absolute* spirit to supply us with a conviction of and justification for the *truth* of ethical institutions and practices.[99] For this reason, he stresses that "in contrast to abstract truths, we ascribe ethical truths [*sittliche Wahrheiten*] to art."[100] At the same time, it would be an equally great mistake to assume that the prosaic character of modern social life is insurmountable. After all, even in the 1826 lectures, Hegel identifies the unique capacity of the Dutch genre painters to portray "objects which themselves have no art interest, no great meaning [*Sinn*]" in such a way that they are expressions of the bourgeois freedoms for which the Dutch people fought.[101] Pippin dismisses the achievement of Dutch painters on the grounds that it does not "satisfy very lofty aesthetic ambitions."[102] However, Hegel's treatment of Dutch painting *does* indicate that an art concerned with portraying the divinity of modern ethicality, that is, with showing that modern ethicality is in fact indispensable for the realization of our "highest interests," *can* retain the "liveliness" (*Lebendigkeit*) which the interest in art presupposes, but which art seemed to have lost in modernity.[103] Being "alive" to that liveliness, however, requires that we reject the false dualism underlying the moral standpoint.

Indeed, elsewhere, Pippin argues that this changed, newly rational character of modern social life entails the need to give up the notion that beauty constitutes the highest aesthetic value, and instead replace it with an idea of "genuineness," a measure of the extent to which art actually "reflects the truth about norm, meaning, and human activity."[104] In this connection, Pippin stresses the role that the idea of "*Lebendigkeit*" or "liveliness" plays in Hegel's aesthetics, according to which "fine art is said to awaken in us an emotional and spirited responsiveness to everything which has a place in human spirit."[105] He suggests that "this ability, central to art's function, to help sustain (by expressing) the 'life' of the highest norms (when they can be so successfully affirmed) is said to be essential to the authority of such norms themselves."[106] He concludes that this task of "enlivening" the highest norms by presenting them sensuously ultimately inspires the cognitive activity of "criticism" which the critic should undertake "not as judge, as avatar of exemplary taste, but as interpreter."[107]

However, it is far from clear how these two conceptions of art and aesthetics fit together. If the modern world is one which is rational *on its own*, why does it require "enlivening"? If the world's meaning is not "mysterious," why would works of art require "interpretation" at all? If we generally understand institutional life to be both necessary for freedom but also fundamentally "prosaic," how can we expect an "enlivening" art actually to reflect what we take to be true? Most importantly, why cannot art "enliven" not just the highest norms, but also the shared ethical world in which they are realized? Instead, we should read Hegel as rejecting the idea that the prosaic character of modern social life prevents it from being an object of artistic treatment and, moreover, understand art to continue to play an irreplaceable role in showing how our highest interest, freedom, is expressed and embodied in the world. Such an art would *complement* philosophy insofar as it would be consistent with the commitment to a freedom that is essentially worldly. However, it would also contribute something that philosophy cannot, namely a directly sensuous presentation of that worldly freedom, a presentation that discloses itself to our intuition, emotion, and feeling, before it addresses itself to our consideration, reflection, and thought.

NOTES

1 Throughout, I employ the following abbreviations for works by Hegel:

> *VÄ* = G.W.F. Hegel, *Vorlesungen über die Ästhetik, I-III*, vols. 13–15 of *Theorie Werkausgabe*, ed. Eva Moldenhauer and Karl Markus Michel (Frankfurt am Main: Suhrkamp, 1970)
>
> *VphK* = Hegel, *Vorlesungen über die Philosophie der Kunst*, ed. Annemarie Gethmann-Siefert (Hamburg: Meiner, 2003)
>
> PhK1 = Hegel, *Philosophie der Kunst oder Ästhetik nach Hegel. Im Sommer 1826. Mitschrift Friedrich Carl Hermann Victor von Kehler*, ed. Gethmann-Siefert and Bernadette Collenberg-Plotnikov (München: Wilhelm Fink, 2004)

PhK2 = Hegel, *Philosophie der Kunst, Vorlesung von 1826,* ed. Gethmann-Siefert, Jeong-Im Kwon, and Karsten Barr (Frankfurt am Main: Suhrkamp, 2004)

VzÄ = Hegel, *Vorlesungen zur Ästhetik, Vorlesungsmitschrift Adolf Heimann (1828/1829),* ed. Alain Patrick Olivier and Gethmann-Siefert (Paderborn: Wilhelm Fink, 2017)

Note: all translations from the German are my own.

2 Ernst Gombrich, "Hegel und die Kunstgeschichte," in Gombrich, Dieter Henrich, and Manfred Rommel, *Hegel-Preis-Reden 1977* (Stuttgart: Belser, 1977), 7.

3 Gombrich, "Hegel und die Kunstgeschichte," 7–8.

4 *PhK 1* (1826), 151; *PhK 2* (1826), 170–1. In the 1823 lectures, as in Hotho's text, we find instead the "dissolution" (*Auflösung*) of the romantic form of art, which culminates in its "end" *(das Ende)*. *VPhK* 199, 198; *VÄ* II, 220.

5 *PhK 1* (1826), 153; *PhK 2* (1826), 172–3. See also *VPhK* (1823), 202; and *VÄ* II, 229–31.

6 *PhK 1* (1826), 151–2; *PhK 2* (1826), 171. See also *VÄ* II, 223–5.

7 See, for example, Terry Pinkard, "Symbolic, Classical, and Romantic Art," in *Hegel and the Arts,* ed. Stephen Houlgate (Evanston, Illinois: Northwestern University Press, 2007), 9; Robert B. Pippin, "What was abstract art? (From Hegel's point of view)," in *The Persistence of Subjectivity* (New York: Cambridge University Press, 2005), 285; Stephen Houlgate, "Hegel and the 'End' of Art," *The Owl of Minerva* 29, 1 (Fall 1997), 2; C. Allen Speight, "Hegel and the 'Historical Deduction' of the Concept of Art," in *A Companion to Hegel,* ed. Stephen Houlgate and Michael Baur (Malden, MA: Blackwell, 2011), 353.

8 Terry Pinkard, "Symbolic, Classical, and Romantic Art," 22.

9 See *VPhK* (1823), 197. See also the discussion in Benjamin Rutter, *Hegel on the Modern Arts* (New York: Cambridge University Press, 2010), 257–65.

10 Robert B. Pippin, "What was abstract art?" 295.

11 See G.W.F. Hegel, *Phänomenologie des Geistes,* Redaktion Hans-Friedrich Wessels und Heinrich Clairmont (Hamburg: Meiner, 1988), ¶599, 395.

12 See, for example, Hegel, *Grundlinien der Philosophy des Rechts,* vol. 7 of Theorie Werkausgabe, edited by E. Moldenhauer and K. Michel (Frankfurt/M: Suhrkamp, 1970), §105, 203; *VÄ* I, 79.

13 The introduction to the lectures on aesthetics does what Stern contends Hegel's prefaces and introductions generally do, namely to set out a specific conception of the task of philosophy in relation to the works' distinctive subject matters, in this case, art. See Robert Stern, "Hegel's *Doppelsatz*: A Neutral Reading," *Journal of the History of Philosophy,* 44, 2 (2006): 235–66.

14 Throughout, I rely heavily on the recently published manuscripts of Hegel's lectures, in particular Kehler's account of the 1826 lectures (*PhK*

1 [1826]). While I refer also to the text, initially assembled by Hotho and published in 1835 following Hegel's death, I rely exclusively on it only sparingly, instead working to establish the specific sources from which Hotho drew in putting together his edition. For a helpful account of the history of the publication of the text, see Annemarie Gethmann-Siefert, "Die systematische Bestimmung der Kunst und die Gechichtlichkeit der Künste, Hegels Vorlesung über 'Aestheticen sive philosophiam artis' von 1826," in *PhK 2* (1826), 9–39.

15 See Hegel, *Vorlesungen über die Philosophie der Geschichte, Theorie Werkausgabe* 12, 32–33.

16 *VÄ* I, 25. On the "end of art" thesis, see the still helpful discussion in Stephen Bungay, *Beauty and Truth, A Study in Hegel's Aesthetics* (New York: Oxford University Press, 1984), 71–89; Houlgate, "Hegel and the 'End' of Art"; Fred L. Rush, Jr., "Hegel's Conception of the End of Art," in *Encylopedia of Aesthetics*, vol. 2, 368–71 (New York: Oxford University Press, 1998); C. Allen Speight, "Hegel and Aesthetics: The Practice and 'Pastness' of Art," in *The Cambridge Companion to Hegel and Nineteenth-Century Philosophy*, ed. Frederick C. Beiser, 378–393 (New York: Cambridge University Press, 2008); and Rutter, *Hegel on the Modern Arts*, 6–62.

17 "The highest determination of art is on the whole for us something past [*ein Vergangenes*], has crossed over into representation for us, the proper representation of art no longer has the immediacy for us that it had during the time of its highest florescence." *PhK 1* (1826), 7–8. Compare *PhK 2* (1826), 54; *VÄ* I, 25.

18 *PhK 1* (1826), 8. Compare *VÄ* I, 24–5.

19 While I do not dwell much on it in what follows, the *difference* between "representation" and "thought" is, in this connection, significant. See the 1820/21 lectures' account of "absolute spirit," in Hegel, *Vorlesung über Ästhetik, Berlin 1820/21, Eine Nachschrift*, Redaktion Helmut Schneider (Frankfurt/M: Peter Lang, 1995), 34–5. On the redemption of "content" for philosophy and thinking from the excesses of subjective inwardness, see Hegel, *Enzyklopädie der philosophischen Wissenshaften III*, vol. 10 of Theorie Werkausgabe (Frankfurt am Main: Suhrkamp, 1970), §571R, 377–8.

20 *VPhK* (1823), 5. Compare *VÄ* I, 23–4.

21 *VPhK* (1823), 5, 6. Compare *VÄ* I, 24.

22 *VPhK* (1823), 6; *PhK 1* (1826), 7. Compare *VÄ* I, 25–6.

23 *VPhK* (1823), 6. Compare *VÄ* I, 26.

24 *PhK 1* (1826), 11. *PhK 2* (1826), 56.

25 *PhK 1* (1826), 12. *PhK 2* (1826), 56–7. Compare *VÄ* I, 70–2.

26 *PhK 1* (1826), 13. *PhK 2* (1826), 57. Compare *VÄ* I, 73–5.

27 "Der Standpunkt des Moralischen," *PhK 1* (1826), 14. "Diese[r] moralische … Standpunkt," *PhK 2* (1826), 58. Compare *VÄ I*, 79.

28 *PhK 1* (1826), 16. *PhK 2* (1826), 58. Compare *VÄ I*, 79–82.

29 *PhK 1* (1826), 15. *PhK 2* (1826), 59.

30 *PhK 1* (1826), 16. "The moral [*Das Moralische*] exists essentially in struggle against, in contradiction [*Widerspruch*] with the natural [*das Natürliche*]." *PhK 2* (1826), 58.

31 *PhK 1* (1826), 15. *PhK 2* (1826), 58–9.

32 *PhK 1* (1826), 15.

33 *PhK 1* (1826), 17. *PhK 2* (1826), 61. By contrast, we find no explicit mention of Kant in the account of morality in Hotho's text (he is first mentioned in the "Historical Deduction").

34 *PhK 1* (1826), 18. The claim that the moral standpoint entails not only a division between reason and sense, but the domination of reason over sense, is one that Hegel has made as early as the Jena-era *Differenzschrift*.

35 *PhK 1* (1826), 18. Compare *VÄ I*, 83.

36 He calls the initial remarks about Kant "[*eine*] *historische Bemerkung*," and the later account "*geschichtliche*." *PhK 1* (1826), 16, 18; *PhK 2* (1826), 61. On my account, the discussion of the "purpose" of art articulates more significantly the "true concept" of art than the "historical" remarks on recent art and aesthetics. Compare Speight, "Hegel on the 'Historical Deduction' of the Concept of Art," 362–5 especially.

37 There is an extensive literature on Hegel's relation to romanticism, and his views on romantic irony. See Otto Pöggeler, *Hegels Kritik der Romantik* (München: Fink, 1998); Jeffrey Reid, *The Anti-Romantic : Hegel Against Ironic Romanticism* (London : Bloomsbury, 2014); Fred Rush, *Irony and Idealism : Rereading Schlegel, Hegel, and Kierkegaard* (New York : Oxford University Press, 2016).

38 *PhK 1* (1826), 20. *PhK 2* (1826), 62. Compare *VÄ I*, 93.

39 Ibid.

40 *PhK 1* (1826), 20. *PhK 2* (1826), 62. Compare *VÄ I*, 94.

41 *PhK 1* (1826), 21. *PhK 2* (1826), 63. Compare *VÄ I*, 95.

42 "An individual has character only insofar as they are in earnest with the content [*Gehalt*] [that is supplied by ethical purposes]; their existence must be lost when they give up this determinacy – one thinks in this connection of Cato." *PhK 1* (1826), 23. Compare *VÄ I*, 97. An anonymous reviewer points out that Hegel's remarks, in the 'Ideal' of art, on character push against the model that we find in romantic irony. Since Hegel stresses the need for the individual in a work to retain a unity that they sustain even in spite of the plurality of powers that we find expressed in them. See *VPhK* (1823), 102–3.

43 For a thoughtful account of Hegel's critique of contemporary aesthetics, see Benjamin Rutter, *Hegel on the Modern Arts*, 20–4.

44 *PhK 1* (1826), 24. Hotho's "Historical Deduction" ends with the account of Tieck, and leaves out four paragraphs which, this one included. Those paragraphs are, I shall argue, essential for grasping the point of Hegel's historical account.

45 Judith Norman, "Hegel and German Romanticism," in *Hegel and the Arts*, ed. Stephen Houlgate (Evanston, Illinois: Northwestern University Press, 2007): 316.

46 See the account of Hegel's "ethical criticism of the arts" in Rutter, *Hegel on the Modern Arts*, 18.

47 Hegel, *Rechtsphilosophie*, §129, 243, §133, 250.

48 See Hegel, *Rechtsphilosophie*, §137, 255.

49 Hegel, *Rechtsphilosophie*, §136, 254.

50 The highest form of this evil consists in romantic irony. See Hegel, *Rechtsphilosophie*, §140R, 277–80.

51 Hegel, *Rechtsphilosophie*, §140, 265. See Timothy Brownlee, "Hegel's Moral Concept of Evil," *Dialogue* 52:1 (March 2013): 81–108.

52 See the concise account of this issue in Allen W. Wood, *Hegel's Ethical Thought* (New York: Cambridge University Press, 1989), 178–92.

53 Hegel, *Rechtsphilosophie*, §140, 265.

54 "The ethical" (*das Sittliche*) is "the bearer and foundation" of right and morality. Hegel, *Rechtsphilosophie*, §141A, 291.

55 Hegel, *Rechtsphilosophie*, 27.

56 See, again, Stern, "Hegel's *Doppelsatz*: A Neutral Reading."

57 Hegel, *Rechtsphilosophie*, §1, 29.

58 Hegel, *Rechtsphilosophie*, §29, 80.

59 See, again, Hegel, *Philosophie der Geschichte*, 32–3. On this note, see Robert B. Pippin, "In What Sense is Hegel's *Philosophy of Right* 'Based' on his *Science of Logic*?" *Hegel's Political Philosophy: On The Normative Significance of System and Method*, ed. Thom Brooks and Sebastian Stein (New York: Oxford University Press, 2017), 74. (Though compare also Paul Redding, "What Might it Mean to have a Systematic Idealist, but Anti-Platonist, Practical Philosophy?" in the same volume, 40.)

60 See, for example, Rocío Zambrana, *Hegel's Theory of Intelligibility* (Chicago: University of Chicago Press, 2015), 84ff.

61 Hegel, *Die Wissenschaft der Logik II, Theorie Werkausgabe* 6, 201.

62 Hegel, *Rechtsphilosophie*, §144, 294.

63 Ethicality is "the *concept of freedom that has become a world and has taken on the nature of self-consciousness*." Hegel, *Rechtsphilosophie*, §142, 292.

64 Hegel, *Rechtsphilosophie*, 21–22.

65 Hegel, *Rechtsphilosophie*, 27.

66 Hegel, *Rechtsphilosophie*, §140R, 279; §140A, 286; *VÄ* I, 13, 94, 95.

67 *PhK 2* (1826), 54; *VPhK* (1823), 6. Compare *VÄ* I, 25–6.

68 *PhK 1* (1826), 16; *PhK 2* (1826), 59. Compare *VÄ* I, 82–1.

69 *VPhK* (1823), 30. Compare *VÄ* I, 70.

70 *VPhK* (1823), 5. Compare *VÄ* I, 21.

71 *PhK 1* (1826), 32–33. *PhK 2* (1826), 71, 72–3. Compare *VÄ* I, 100.

72 *PhK 1* (1826), 34. *PhK 2* (1826), 73.

73 Angelica Nuzzo, "Hegel's 'Aesthetics' as Theory of Absolute Spirit," in *Internationales Jahrbuch des deutschen Idealismus* 4 (2006): 296.

74 *VPhK* (1823), 4. Compare *VÄ* I, 20–1.

75 I agree with Speight's assertion that, for Hegel, "Art may be said to be *free*, then, precisely because it serves no external purpose but manifests in its works the reconciliation of oppositions." Speight, "Hegel and the 'Historical Deduction' of the Concept of Art," 358. However, as I suggest in what follows, art can also play an emancipatory function in engaging us in a thoughtful consideration of those otherwise prosaic institutions and practices which he argues are necessary for a free life.

76 *PhK 1* (1826), 29. Compare *VÄ* I, 113.

77 *PhK 1* (1826), 29. Compare *VÄ* I, 114.

78 *PhK 1* (1826), 34. Compare *PhK 2* (1826), 74, which makes no explicit mention of "Christianity" or "Protestantism." Compare *VÄ* I, 142.

79 Hotho's edition obscures the importance of this account in two ways. First, Hotho moves it from the conclusion of the "historical" account of the purpose of art to the introductory discussion of the "worthiness" of art for a philosophical treatment. (See *VÄ* I, 22) In so doing, he undermines the clear contrast that Hegel intends to establish through it with the aesthetics of the "present day." Second, he excises mention of idea of *ethicality* from it, instead only mentioning "the common external and internal world."

80 *PhK 1* (1826), 25. *PhK 2* (1826), 64.

81 *PhK 1* (1826), 25. *PhK 2* (1826), 64–5.

82 *PhK 1* (1826), 8. Compare *VÄ* I, 24.

83 As an anonymous reviewer points out, this shift also opens up an entire new range of subject matters for romantic art, since it need not simply occupy itself with a specific set of established subject matters – the passion, Biblical scenes, etc. – but can instead pursue the diverse range of forms of life in which freedom might find expression and realization. Of course, this shift need not entail that art becomes propaganda for the existing state. Since modern art must address itself to us as reflective and thinking beings, it can equally engage with subject matters either outside of or even opposed to the predominant ones in the modern state, precisely to ask the question of whether and how a free life might be possible in them.

84 *VzÄ* (1828/29), 19.

85 *VzÄ* (1828/29), 20.

86 *VzÄ* (1828/29), 23. On this issue, see Mark Alznauer, "Hegel on Aesthetic Reconciliation," *Hegel's Political Aesthetics: Art In Modern Society*, ed. Stefan Bird-Pollan and Vladimir Marchenkov (New York: Bloomsbury, 2020), 11–30.

87 *VzÄ* (1828/29), 19.

88 Compare Danto's claim that art must, in some sense, become philosophy in Arthur C. Danto, "The End of Art," *The Philosophical Disenfranchisement of Art* (New York: Columbia University Press, 2005), 111. On the account that I am offering here, art need not *become* philosophy, to question its own character as a work of art, for example. Instead, art comes to depend on philosophy so that it can be understood as a site for the realization of our highest interests.

89 Validating the claim that art admits of this reflective engagement would require a fuller account than I offer here. At the same time, the claim is not inherently implausible. To take a very mundane example, book clubs gather not only to clarify what happened, but to reflect on and understand the book's meaning. Likewise, the idea that a work of art might present ethical meanings as questions which engage our thought and reflection just as much as they engage our sentiment and feeling should be familiar to any reader of Tolstoy, to mention just one author.

90 *PhK 2* (1826), 64. Hotho's rendering of this claim completely obscures its meaning. See *VÄ* I, 22. Hotho not only obscures the redeeming character of artistic *Schein* for which Hegel argues in the lectures, but he misconstrues the notion of the "past" that is Hegel's concern in this connection.

91 Gethmann-Siefert, "Die systematische Bestimmung der Kunst und die Gechichtlichkeit der Künste," in *PhK 2* (1826), 35–6. See also 32.

92 To this extent, Rutter's gloss of "objective humor," the living art of the present day as a "poetry of reconciliation" is appropriate. See Rutter, *Hegel on the Modern Arts*, 49. Of course, philosophy shows us that all art performs this reconciliatory role, so this expression does not distinguish modern art from its past appearances. The unique feature of modern art is not its reconciliatory capacity, but rather the fact that it addresses itself to our reflection and thought, not only to our senses.

93 *PhK 1* (1826), 28. Classical art presents "the most perfect beauty" (*die vollkommenste Schönheit*). *PhK 2* (1826), 68. Compare *VÄ* I, 109.

94 *VÄ* II, 240.

95 *PhK 1* (1826), 43–6. Compare *VÄ* I, 242–52. To this extent, even if we find a "political" component in an art of modern ethicality, it will not be the art of the classical world which constituted the *sole* and *unifying* ground for political life. On this score, see Dieter Henrich, "The Contemporary Relevance of Hegel's Aesthetics," *Hegel*, ed. Michael Inwood (New

York: Oxford University Press, 1985): 204–7; Terry Pinkard, "What is a 'Shape of Spirit'," in *Hegel's Phenomenology of Spirit: A Critical Guide*, ed. Dean Moyar and Michael Quante (New York: Cambridge University Press, 2008), 119; and the account of classical art in Gethmann-Siefert, "Die systematische Bestimmung der Kunst und die Gechichtlichkeit der Künste," in *PhK 2* (1826), 31–2 especially. Instead, it is religion (and perhaps philosophy) that constitute the "foundation" for modern political life, and philosophy which plays the unifying role. Art is no longer the exclusive founder, and it cannot hope to present a unified picture of modern ethicality.

96   It is in this light that we should approach the remarks concerning "objective humour." See *VÄ* II, 239–42.

97   Hegel, *Enzyklopädie* III, §552R, 358–9. On this issue, see Brownlee, "Conscience and Religion in Hegel's Later Political Philosophy," *Owl of Minerva* 43:1–2 (2011–2012): 41–72.

98   *PhK 1* (1826), 151. In the other lecture notes, he suggests that naturalistic imitation of the prosaic presents "a difficulty of saying what an artwork is." *PhK 2* (1826), 171.

99   Hegel most frequently puts this point in terms of the role of religion. See, e.g. Hegel, *Rechtsphilosophie*, §270R, 417–20; Hegel, *Enzyklopädie III*, §552R, 355; and Hegel, *Vorlesungen über die Philosophie der Geschichte I*, vol. 12 of Theorie Werkausgabe, edited by Eva Moldenhauer und Karl Markus Michel (Frankfurt/M: Suhrkamp, 1970), 70. Though here too he asserts that the content of art is nonetheless "the divine" and "the spiritual," presented to intuition and sense in a specific "figure." Hegel, *Philosophie der Geschichte*, 69. However, see also the discussion of the relation between objective and absolute spirit in the account of "the ideal" of art. *VÄ* I, 137.

100   *PhK 2* (1826), 65. In Kehler's text, Hegel states that "[w]e hold ethical, religious truths for the true, and express this [by saying] that such content should be for us in the form of universal thoughts," but then introduces a correction to our attitude, suggesting that art is one of "the different forms of the appearance [*Erscheinung*] of the universal," and that "[t]he shine of art is not to be discarded; it is a much higher way of appearing than common reality, against which it appears to be the inauthentic." *PhK 1* (1826), 25. This remark is, again, absent from Hotho's text.

101   *PhK 1* (1826), 152–3. Compare *PhK 2* (1826), 172, which mentions only that "[t]hese citizens [*Stadtbürger*] and farmers [*Bauern*] in Holland have asserted [*behauptet*] themselves against the strong power of Phillip II." The "ethical" character of Dutch painting is even more evident in *VÄ* II, 225–9.

102   Pippin, "What was abstract art?" 295.

103 See again *PhK 1* (1826), 8; *PhK 2* (1826), 54. Compare *VÄ* I, 25. See also
Speight's remark on the changed status of art as deriving specifically
from "the modern culture of *reflection*" in Speight, "Hegel and the
'Historical Deduction' of the Concept of Art," 364.

104 Robert Pippin, "The Absence of aesthetics in Hegel's aesthetics," *The
Cambridge Companion to Hegel and Nineteenth-Century Philosophy*, ed. F.
Beiser (Cambridge: Cambridge University Press, 2008), 412, 407.

105 Pippin, "Absence of aesthetics in Hegel's aesthetics," 400.

106 Pippin, "Absence of aesthetics in Hegel's aesthetics," 401.

107 Pippin, "Absence of aesthetics in Hegel's aesthetics," 402–3.

REFERENCES

Alznauer, Mark. "Hegel on Aesthetic Reconciliation." In *Hegel's Political
Aesthetics: Art in Modern Society*, edited by Stefan Bird-Pollan and Vladimir
Marchenkov, 11–30. New York: Bloomsbury, 2020.

Brownlee, Timothy. "Conscience and Religion in Hegel's Later Political
Philosophy." *Owl of Minerva* 43, nos. 1–2 (2011–2012): 41–72.

—— "Hegel's Moral Concept of Evil." *Dialogue* 52, no. 1 (March 2013): 81–108.

Bungay, Stephen. *Beauty and Truth, A Study in Hegel's Aesthetics*. New York:
Oxford University Press, 1984.

Danto, Arthur C. "The End of Art." In *The Philosophical Disenfranchisement of
Art*, 81–115. New York: Columbia University Press, 2005.

Gombrich, Ernst. "Hegel und die Kunstgeschichte." In *Hegel-Preis-Reden 1977*,
edited by Dieter Henrich Gombrich and Manfred Rommel, 7–28. Stuttgart:
Belser, 1977.

Hegel, G.W.F. *Grundlinien der Philosophie des Rechts*, Vol. 7 of *Theorie
Werkausgabe*. Edited by E. Moldenhauer and K. Michel. Frankfurt am Main:
Suhrkamp, 1970a.

—— *Vorlesungen über die Ästhetik, I–III*, Vols. 13–15 of *Theorie Werkausgabe*.
Edited by Eva Moldenhauer and Karl Markus Michel. Frankfurt am Main:
Suhrkamp, 1970b.

—— *Vorlesungen über die Philosophie der Geschichte I*, Vol. 12 of *Theorie
Werkausgabe*. Edited by Eva Moldenhauer and Karl Markus Michel.
Frankfurt am Main: Suhrkamp, 1970c.

—— *Die Wissenschaft der Logik, II*, Vol. 6 of *Theorie Werkausgabe*. Edited by E.
Moldenhauer and K. Michel. Frankfurt am Main: Suhrkamp, 1970d.

—— *Phänomenologie des Geistes*. Edited by Hans-Friedrich Wessels and
Heinrich Clairmont. Hamburg: Meiner, 1988.

—— *Vorlesung über Ästhetik, Berlin 1820/21, Eine Nachschrift*. Edited by Helmut
Schneider. Frankfurt am Main: Peter Lang, 1995.

—— *Vorlesungen über die Philosophie der Kunst*. Edited by Annemarie Gethmann-Siefert. Hamburg: Meiner, 2003.

—— *Philosophie der Kunst oder Ästhetik nach Hegel. Im Sommer 1826. Mitschrift Friedrich Carl Hermann Victor von Kehler*. Edited by Gethmann-Siefert and Bernadette Collenberg-Plotnikov. München: Wilhelm Fink, 2004a.

—— *Philosophie der Kunst, Vorlesung von 1826*. Edited by Gethmann-Siefert, Jeong-Im Kwon, and Karsten Barr. Frankfurt am Main: Suhrkamp, 2004b.

—— *Vorlesungen zur Ästhetik*. Edited by Alain Patrick Olivier and Gethmann-Siefert. Paderborn: Wilhelm Fink, 2017.

Henrich, Dieter. "The Contemporary Relevance of Hegel's Aesthetics." In *Hegel*, edited by Michael Inwood, 199–207. New York: Oxford University Press, 1985.

Houlgate, Stephen. "Hegel and the 'End' of Art." *The Owl of Minerva* 29, no. 1 (Fall 1997): 1–21.

Norman, Judith. "Hegel and German Romanticism." In *Hegel and the Arts*, edited by Stephen Houlgate, 310–36. Evanston, IL: Northwestern University Press, 2007.

Nuzzo, Angelica. "Hegel's 'Aesthetics' as Theory of Absolute Spirit." *Internationales Jahrbuch des* deutschen Idealismus 4 (2006): 291–310.

Pinkard, Terry. "Symbolic, Classical, and Romantic Art." In *Hegel and the Arts*, edited by Stephen Houlgate, 3–28. Evanston, IL: Northwestern University Press, 2007.

—— "What is a 'Shape of Spirit'." In *Hegel's Phenomenology of Spirit: A Critical Guide*, edited by Dean Moyar and Michael Quante, 112–29. New York: Cambridge University Press, 2008.

Pippin, Robert B. "What Was Abstract Art? (From Hegel's Point of View)." In *The Persistence of Subjectivity: On the Kantian Aftermath*, 279–306. New York: Cambridge University Press, 2005.

—— "The Absence of Aesthetics in Hegel's Aesthetics." In *The Cambridge Companion to Hegel and Nineteenth-Century Philosophy*, edited by Frederick C. Beiser, 394–418. Cambridge: Cambridge University Press, 2008.

—— "In What Sense is Hegel's Philosophy of Right 'Based' on His Science of Logic?" In *Hegel's Political Philosophy: On the Normative Significance of System and Method*, edited by Thom Brooks and Sebastian Stein, 67–81. New York: Oxford University Press, 2017.

Pöggeler, Otto. *Hegels Kritik der Romantik*. München: Fink, 1998.

Reid, Jeffrey. *The Anti-Romantic: Hegel Against Ironic Romanticism*. London: Bloomsbury, 2014.

Rush, Fred L., Jr. "Hegel's Conception of the End of Art." In *Encyclopedia of Aesthetics*, Vol. 2, 368–71. New York: Oxford University Press, 1998.

—— *Irony and Idealism: Rereading Schlegel, Hegel, and Kierkegaard*. New York: Oxford University Press, 2016.

Rutter, Benjamin. *Hegel on the Modern Arts*. New York: Cambridge University Press, 2010.

Speight, Allen C. "Hegel and Aesthetics: The Practice and 'Pastness' of Art." In *The Cambridge Companion to Hegel and Nineteenth-Century Philosophy*, edited by Frederick C. Beiser, 378–93. New York: Cambridge University Press, 2008.

—— "Hegel and the 'Historical Deduction' of the Concept of Art." In *A Companion to Hegel*, edited by Stephen Houlgate and Michael Baur, 353–68. Malden, MA: Blackwell, 2011.

Stern, Robert. "Hegel's *Doppelsatz*: A Neutral Reading." *Journal of the History of Philosophy* 44, no. 2 (2006): 235–66.

Zambrana, Rocío. *Hegel's Theory of Intelligibility*. Chicago: University of Chicago Press, 2015.

PART THREE

Hegel on the History of Freedom and the French Revolution – Symposium on Comay's *Mourning Sickness:* Hegel and the French Revolution

11 Introduction to Comay's Approach to History and Revolution in Hegel

EMILIA ANGELOVA

As noted in the introduction to this collection, Rebecca Comay's *Mourning Sickness* advances an innovative reading of Hegel's *Phenomenology*[1] that puts the French Revolution at its centre, in ways that complement Houlgate's systematicity interpretation and the efforts in his work, and the chapters collected here to connect history and logic across Hegel's work. Comay's contribution in this regard is her detailed argument that for Hegel, the Revolution is not simply an historical event that can be located within the *Phenomenology*'s dialectical study of experience, but is rather *the* concrete exemplar of what that dialectic is really about, namely, the self-structuring of freedom, which is not merely some movement of the Ego as cause, and cannot be captured by any sort of transcendental normativity, but is embedded in and develops through concrete history that articulates and founds its own systematic logic. This introduction to the themes of history and revolution of Comay's book draws out central points of her reading that pertain to the systematicity interpretation discussed in chapters above, and helps situate the two commentaries on her book, by McCumber and Balfour, and Comay's response.

Comay's reading strategically puts the question of welcoming the Other at the centre of Hegel's reaction to the French Revolution. I attend in particular to the importance of the Unhappy Consciousness to her strategy, since this deepens her perspective on the latency of the arrival and action of Consciousness. For Comay, this means that Consciousness is "untimely,"[2] that is, it is not a sequence in some sort of external time, but a self-structuring deformation that establishes its own necessity.[3] This point is at the core of her original approach to Hegel's philosophy of history, which connects it to the themes of this collection.

Hegel, according to Comay, does not suppress the force of violence that the Revolution inflicts upon the individual. The Revolution is not some systemically derived step needed on the way and subsumed into a successive purpose. Rather, Hegel studies and describes the Revolution as an exemplary case of concrete cultural work. For Comay, in the idea of the Revolution, Hegel addresses the very notion of Culture and its symbols, as well as alienated Self-consciousness head on. She draws from this more thorough consequences than others have explored in the *Phenomenology*. Her approach to these matters takes the chapter on the Revolution as sandwiched between the Unhappy Consciousness, on the one hand, and Morality's uncertain arrival, on the other. Morality's arrival is not guaranteed since the movement forward of the dialectic, for which the Revolution stands, is premised as promise, as securing something new. On the other hand, the Unhappy Consciousness is a juncture that readers of Hegel have identified as the turning point of the *Phenomenology* (e.g., Kojéve, Hyppolite and Adorno[4]). In a strict sense, the *not* of the negation of being, on which Houlgate's systematicity interpretation turns, begins at this juncture.[5] Here Comay astutely observes that the past or tradition, which the Revolution rejects, is that of the Unhappy Consciousness as past. This cultural gesture and disruption is the very centre of the Revolution, and Comay's insight lets us see how the *not* complicates itself in and through this disruption.

In other words, this turning point of consciousness cannot be understood in terms of metaphysics prior to Hegel, which introduces dogmatic premises, even at foundations of morality, notably Kant's apriority of the moral law. These premises suppress rather than fully integrate the alterity of the Other. For Hegel, the Revolution, ruthlessly turns against such isolationism, which again connects the logic of the Revolution to its own history.

Put otherwise, the roots of the enunciated ideals of the Revolution do not merely lie in the promise of progress of rationality, they are indebted to the tradition, to the medieval rule of titles and Monarchy of the past. For Hegel, the transition to Culture requires that this new shape of Self-consciousness translate its ends into objectivity, and yet remain with itself in objectivity, thus transitioning into Morality. But Hegel is also well aware that the pre-history of the battle between Faith and the Enlightenment is precondition of this succession. For Hegel, the question is twofold: articulating the ideals behind the transition to Morality; and this means as well, articulating what the program of Revolution bears as negation in its promise – establishing new ideals while abolishing old ones.[6] Again, the point here is that for Hegel the ideals that drive the system are not dogmatic premises or abstractions, but arise within historical dimensions and work.

It is this connection to the tradition, and the need to overturn it from within, that links Comay's reading to Houlgate's systematicity interpretation. For her, the clue to this reading of Hegel and to his novel method, lies in the sort of succession that the *Phenomenology* describes in the movement between Consciousness and Self-consciousness, through Unhappy Consciousness. Hegel recognizes in the Unhappy Consciousness a new form of individual, for whom thought is not an ideality, but a contingency, tied to the mortality of the body in the Stoic school and early Christianity. Unhappy Consciousness is that shape in which Self-Consciousness supersedes the object in claiming to comprehend it, yet realizes that the object still exceeds it, and that only a consciousness greater than its own would in fact secure such comprehension.[7] Unhappy Consciousness is thus the organism whose theoretical concept of itself splits itself up: it is at once a particular individual, yet it is an individual capable (so it claims) of grasping everything, and could not just be this particular, mortal individual, but must be able to apprehend itself as given in the object as comprehensible, and thereby as capable of universal judgment, as mind. Mind arrives at its only dignity in separating from the body.

To recall the framing of this collection, for Houlgate, Hegel's effort to begin from presuppositionless thinking is precisely an effort to undermine abstract or transcendentally ideal beginnings. This is precisely what Comay helps us identify in the Unhappy Consciousness: this is a form of consciousness that is Unhappy precisely because it cannot locate within itself what would make it be complete or happy, it splits itself between inside and outside, it separates from itself, its mind pitted against its body, and this gives a model of what Houlgate calls the *not* as a negation of being (as opposed to an ideal not).

In Comay's reading of Hegel on the Revolution, this splitting is the point of dignity, which, in Modernity, is the representative of the bourgeoisie. Dignity turns into detachment from beginnings and this becomes the mind's one and only fixed obsessive-compulsive idea, its death wish. This realization about the happiness of particularity, as possibility of detachment, leads to the further point that no detachment (e.g., theoretically abstract ideals) is free from the negativity and objectivity of its contradiction, namely that it is still a particularity bound to objects from which it must detach.[8] This is precisely the nexus where freedom arises in Hegel's system, and this means that freedom must secure its own logic from within an exposure to particularity. The program of freedom in Kant thus has to be turned on its head, since for Kant freedom would be calculative, utilitarian, a normative mandate of an Ego that is its own sovereignty.

I will conclude with naming three important advances over Kant which Comay secures through this research. First, Comay's main oppositional claim as regards Kant is that Hegel's theory of the Desire of Self-consciousness in the *Phenomenology* approaches a model closer to the scene of confession. Traditional readers of Hegel as "spiritual profiteer" suggest that Hegel understands the rationality of self-knowing spirit not as adapting to rationality (which is what Hegel actually argues for), but as a conformism of the Master, which Comay rejects. Second, for Comay, then, the traditional reading changes. Hegel's refrain that there is now left "no pure death," that is, no safe death (no work without death/ sacrifice, and no sacrifice without work) for Comay, needs to be read to the effect that Hegel does not have at his disposal a Master of the order of Kant's harshness of the Judge of conscience.[9] Critics err on this matter often but we must revise our misconception. Comay's main objection to the critic derives from a more fundamentally incomplete form of the figure of Consciousness. Recall that Hegel introduces it as that which becomes the object of Self-consciousness – so that it is the being of self-consciousness as having Consciousness as its own object (the objectivity of the object) which gets going the progressions in the *Phenomenology of Spirit*.

Third, Comay believes that Consciousness is the figure of the master not being at home. This reflects a function of the more thoroughgoing untimeliness of the being of this phenomenon (having being as Idea), called on stage too early or too late, which guides Comay's interpretation. The paper "Mirror Stage," 1949, by Lacan, which Comay follows, allows for the position that the Unhappy Consciousness functions in Hegel as the primal scene of writing, inscribing in and with the loss of the Other the laws of Consciousness as subject in the *Phenomenology*. Consciousness takes on being as basis of the self as symbol and reciprocal response in relation to the Other, as the "cause" of the Other's (or the Thing's) desire.[10] This scene allows it to become being "for itself" as a mode of being the site from which Consciousness looks in on itself from outside, for meaning, while simultaneously projecting itself into the inner heart and soul of totality, its experience. This view of the entailment of repetition, reflection, replay as expressing the more true and past essence of the relation of the experience of the "in itself" but as recurrence of (the Ideal of) being "for itself," leads Comay to an argument for a stronger thesis underscoring the temporality of Consciousness or mind, with direct consequences for the role the Revolution plays in Hegel.

What we know is that the slave (psyche, the negativity of the rejecting drive) has no other way to go – these are demands for articulation in language to which self-consciousness abides. Again, the point is to re-write the Culture of the Enlightenment as incomplete victory over the past, the battle of Faith and the Enlightenment.[11]

To conclude, this does justice as to why, according to Comay, we need to see that Kantian aprioricity – his reserve, his fear, shrinking back before the abyss of the Revolution, losing his nerve – is a foundation against which Hegel's own sense of being unravelled leads the latter to decisions, and demands for systematicity far more superior philosophically and politically more acute, as well.

NOTES

1 G.W.F. Hegel, *The Phenomenology of Spirit*, trans. A.V. Miller (Oxford: Oxford University Press, 1977). Henceforth cited as *PS* and indicating a paragraph number.

2 Comay, *Mourning Sickness*, 5.

3 On necessity and contingency and implications for inaugurating the Unhappy Consciousness in Hegel's *Phenomenology*, see the seminal work of John W. Burbidge, *Hegel's Systematic Contingency* (London: Palgrave, 2007), esp. 73, 153. He writes that contingency is a theme that far exceeds the religious content behind Unhappy Consciousness, specifically he reads the concept of Force in Force and the Understanding as key to how Spirit emerges and of what it is comprised. Comay follows Hegel's use of the notion of contingency (in that necessity becomes *what is* through repetition), and as well follows his use of force which in the *Science of Logic* becomes "relation." For Comay, Houlgate's *The Opening of Hegel's Logic*, esp. 290, 277–9, stands out in this context, since he problematizes the activity of vanishing in Hegel, he asks "How are we to understand this vanishing?" and "Why does it occur?," that is, in the process of vanishing, Consciousness retains *itself* as reality. If Consciousness is a shape that is marked by delayed action and deformation it is because it is posited more essentially through the activity of vanishing, denial, *Verleugnung*, as Comay's *Mourning Sickness*, suggests – she argues that this implies the "defensive apparatus of a subject," and thus a subject "bent on sustaining itself on what it gives up" (64).

4 Theodor W. Adorno, *History and Freedom*. Lectures 1964–65 (Cambridge: Polity, 2006), 302, cf. PS, M231.

5 Houlgate, *The Opening of Hegel's Logic*, 436.

6 Comay, *Mourning Sickness*, esp. 8–26, provides ample context of the concrete historical events.

7 Comay, *Mourning Sickness*, esp. 81–118, cf. 180 n45. Comay relates PS, M639 to Hegel's politically charged critique of the contemporaries, Jacobi and

Fichte, and why Hegel rightly opposes "aestheticism as ideology." Hegel anticipates the need for the moral initiative passing immediately into an aesthetic one. That is, in the Revolution's abandoning the "sovereign right to pardon," which is reserved for the prerogative of the Monarch, Hegel sees loyalties divided between a secular morality of freedom and a theology of grace. On this point Comay refers e.g., to H.S. Harris, *Hegel's Ladder*, 2 vols. (Indianapolis: Hackett, 1997), 2: 464.

8 Comay, *Mourning Sickness*, 89. The "essential reflexivity of Terror" is for Comay, Hegel's centre in the study of the violence of the Revolution. This drives his critique of the abstraction of the individual and the negativity of Consciousness. The true occasion for philosophical reflection is, as Comay puts it, the "philosophical significance of the revolution, the 9 Thermidor." "If Robespierre must die ... only this elimination can express the infinity of circularity of a freedom that must learn to operate even in the absence of objects on which to practice" (89). For Comay, the logic of the terror culminates in realizing that the "instantaneity and absolute freedom is here transformed into the distended slave time of deferral and delay" (90). The lesson to take away from the violence of the Revolution is Self-consciousness turned into witness suffering violence at its own hands, what it "learns" *PS*, M592: "Self-consciousness learns what absolute Freedom is in effect."

9 Hegel nevertheless understands this entire figure from the vantage point of the debt to History. Comay writes: "We can only regret or fear what is there for the loss." "To face death is to convert the *caput mortuum* of History into conceptual capital; to turn death mask into a cipher of remembrance." Furthermore for Hegel, forgiveness is incomplete without preserving and recognizing itself concretely in the symbols of its cultural and political institutions. So Comay: "Just as confession does not generate forgiveness, so too forgiveness does not of itself produce reconciliation" (136).

10 Jacques Lacan, *Écrits*. A Selection. Trans. Alan Sheridan (New York: W.W. Norton, 1977), 1–8, "The Mirror Stage as Formative of the Function of the *I*."

11 Comay notes that Hegel did not quite foresee in 1806 the revolutions of a generation 1848, etc., but he knew as of 1806 that no single death has been redeemed. He was already working to dissuade the Marx wing from The German Ideology. She writes that "Marx will famously accuse Hegel of the worst sort of *Entwirklichung*," a collapse of actualization into abstraction. But as Comay continues, "By 1820, Hegel is on the verge of thinking the paradox that Marx himself will make famous, even if surely enough at Hegel's own expense; Germany is the only country to suffer a restoration without having endured its own proper revolution; it tastes freedom only vicariously and only once, on the day of its funeral" (145).

12 Against A Literalist Account of Time in the *Phenomenology*: On Comay's *Mourning Sickness*

JOHN MCCUMBER, UNIVERSITY OF CALIFORNIA
LOS ANGELES

To all who work on it, the *Phenomenology of Spirit* is a beastly work. To Hegel also: in contrast to plant-like texts, in terms of his *Philosophy of Nature*, it has an inside as well as an outside. Where the interiority of the plant is "immediately a relation to the outside world,"[1] the animal's "inner process" is a "free time" which, removed from real externality, determines its place.[2] Since, we may say, time for Hegel is nothing other than the abstract becoming of natural beings,[3] its "liberating" removal from external givens must reside in their capacity to conduct their coming-to-be, so to speak, on their own terms – which for Hegel means to locate themselves in space, and so to move themselves. The temporal slippage, then, between an animal organism and its surroundings is what allows it to develop an internal structure of its own and is the first and emptiest manifestation of such structure.

The *Phenomenology* is obviously animalian, then, in that it has an internal structure; Hegel spends most of the "Introduction" explaining what that structure is. The very fact of internal structure means that the *Phenomenology* is at a temporal distance from its external surroundings, from the world on which it reflects. (It also means that the *Phenomenology* can never be one of those texts which claims, like so much of contemporary philosophy, to be merely a series of true statements.) It is inevitably distorted. Its reflection on the givens it treats is necessarily a *distortion* of them.

It is surprising how little this is recognized. Generations of Hegel commentators, for example, have in the wake of Marx criticized his account of Lordship and Bondage because it distorts the realities of oppression. J.N. Findlay's commentary on the *Phenomenology*, included in the Miller translation, similarly downplays the book's own narrative – its "inner process – "while identifying, brilliantly, many of the historical realities on which it is reflecting." But the result of such an approach must, inevitably, be broadly Marxian in result: over and over again Hegel is seen as bringing up some phenomenon from human reality – Judaism, the *Antigone*, Catholicism, the Crusades, guilds, the Enlightenment, the Terror – and getting it wrong.

The only remedy for this, it would seem, is to forget about doing justice to the external realities and focus on the *Phenomenology*'s internal dynamics. But then we wind up with a hermetic work, self-sealed against everything but itself – the meaningless "foaming" with which it ends.

Part of the importance of Rebecca Comay's *Mourning Sickness*, then, is the way in which it highlights the *Phenomenology*'s own reflection on the relation between its internal process and the external world through which it moves. The key to such reflection – but by no means the reflection itself, which comes later – is the book's treatment of the French Revolution. The French Revolution is something on which, as Comay's first two chapters show, is something on which Germans reflected at a distance – a painful one. German partisans of the Revolution, such as Marx, see the spatial distance between Germany and the Revolution as a sad indication of German impotence, an ideology which keeps the Germans from acting. On the other hand, French thinkers such as Michelet, Quinet, and Guizot, see Germany as having eluded the Revolution by anticipating it with the Reformation.[4]

Hegel, for his part, conducts a long encounter with the Revolution's most salient phase, the Terror. It follows that the key to the Revolution, for him, is the kind of death it brings forward. This particular form of death is prefigured, in the *Phenomenology*'s account of Enlightenment, by utility. In utility (or, as Kant called it in the *Critique of Judgment*, external teleology), the human community: "is reduced to a collective survival mechanisms regulated by a tepid principle dedicated to the rule of maximum reciprocal serviceability."[5] This principle sees any being as validated *later*, by its usefulness for other, subsequent beings. Something is validated, then, only when it is no longer there – when it is dead. Terror merely explicates this utilitarianism: "Terror replaces the minimal utilitarian aesthetic, the "as if" fiction of serviceability, with a negative aesthetic in which the object is conjured up only under erasure, that is, as if it were already dead or nonexistent."[6]

The collective lives by the deaths of individuals, as in Hegel's account of Rousseau's *volontés – générale* and *de tous*. This is as true of the sovereign as of anybody else: "the king is dead – long live the country."[7] The "banal death" of Louis Capet is thus the exposure of a pre-existing emptiness at the heart of the symbolic order:[8] the throne is empty, the King is (and has always been) as mortal as his subjects. The emptiness revealed here by the Revolution is too deep, too near the heart, to be remedied by political action. It is in particular not remedied, but only carried forward and generalized, by the Terror: "As of 1806, the conceptual problems raised by politics can no longer be addressed by directly political means. The French Revolution finds its sequel in translation as it passes over to the "unreal world" of German philosophy."[9] The emergence of philosophical reflection on the most "reflectable" of historical events, the French Revolution, is thus driven by the nothingness at the core of that historical given itself. The political Revolution is not so much the object of the philosophical reflection as it is what generates it.

The philosophical reflection in question, however, is not Hegel's, but (sort of) Kant's. Terror becomes *Moralität* through abstraction. The guillotine's abstracting, or subtracting, of the head from the body prefigures the abstraction or subtraction of morality from the world:[10] the noumenal head, we may say, becomes separated from the phenomenal body (which, as empirical, lies lifelessly in the realm of the Useful).

We thus come to a crucial question: is a philosophical reflection even possible which is not allied with terror – which does not depend on the death of what is being reflected upon? This is the question of whether post-Kantianism is possible. I will not discuss whether this question is alive today, or ask about the terroristic complicities of contemporary philosophy; the urgency was greater for Hegel.

The first thing we notice is that such philosophical reflection cannot reflect merely upon the Revolution/Terror, or solely on its philosophical progeny, *Moralität*; it must reflect on the *movement* from one to another, on the loss of the physical in the passage from the careful cleavages of the guillotine to the careful distinctions of critique. And it must seek to undo that movement, to recover the physical. Such reflection must, then, be (and I think in Comay's view is) the truly revolutionary act in the *Phenomenology*.

It comes about as confession. Comay discusses Hegel's rendition of "Evil and its Forgiveness" by bringing out its strange temporality. Acting consciousness confesses, owns up to, identifies with, and thus resuscitates its evil action – which, as we know, is any action at all, since all actions, as phenomenal, are particular as to nature and circumstance and are opposed to the noumenal realm in which universality and morality reside. But the consciousness *to* which acting consciousness confesses, judging consciousness, remains obdurate: it refuses *and refuses* to forgive until, suddenly – it forgives.

The point of the delay here is to force a particular kind of confession from acting consciousness: one which has no hope of forgiveness. As long as acting consciousness can hope that the judging consciousness will acknowledge their community and thereby forgive it, it is in quest of a "spiritual payback: it wants to be validated, if not as acting (which was evil), then as having admitted its action. Only when the possibility of such validation is foreclosed by the hard-heartedness of the judging consciousness does the confession become what it needs to be: an "absolute" recuperation of the physical, i.e., absolute knowing: "Absolute knowing is neither compensation for the redemption of a debt, nor fulfillment: the void is constitutive … The ultimate sacrifice is without payback in that it suspends every symbolic context in which it could even be recognized as a sacrifice; it voids every possible standard of evaluation."[11]

The final hopeless confession of acting consciousness, a confession made to no purpose, breaks the rules of the current encounter, because such consciousness no longer seeks forgiveness from its other. Confronted with this, there is no point in the judging consciousness's refusal to forgive – and no point in such consciousness altogether, since it was defined by that refusal. Judging consciousness can no longer be what it is; and the only way to become something other is to give up what defines it, its obduracy. It forgives the acting consciousness – too late.

At this point, the depth and radicality of Comay's reading come to the fore, for here she breaks beyond the all-too-standard views of Hegel as a "spiritual profiteer." Absolute knowing *is not* the triumphant consolidation of a subject which, in Heidegger's phrase, finally succeeds in "swallowing the world." *It is* the loss of everything which, from sense-certainty on, consciousness has aspired to be. Hegelian *Aufhebung* is, and has always been, not the enrichment of a subject through the trials and tribulations of *Erfahrung*, but the exposure of the emptiness at the core of those aspirations, and so of consciousness itself.

This, I think, is where Comay's reading of the *Phenomenology*, so powerful in its details, becomes a major advance in Hegel reception. We may put the case as follows: from the beginning of the *Phenomenology*, consciousness has been on a quest to find an enduring truth – a certainty beyond which it need not go. There are two ways such a quest can end. Traditionally, Hegel is thought to have ended it with success: in absolute knowing, consciousness achieves what it has been seeking for so long. But there is another way for a quest to end: the questor can give up. Comay clearly and persuasively takes this approach. What the *Phenomenology* so laboriously teaches is that the recovery of the physical is and has to be the abrogation of *everything* else, so that at the end we have only – foam. And a particular foam at that (*seine Unendlichkeit*, the last two words of the book).

Mourning Sickness shows us that we can come to this conclusion only by seeing the way in which the crucial event of modernity, the French Revolution, relates to German philosophy; for it is only when we see *Moralität* as the prolongation of terror that we see both that its abstraction must be overcome – and the monstrous stakes of that overcoming.

The gigantism of those stakes can be indicated by returning to the sad fact that Hegel's accounts of historical phenomena are one and all inaccurate: in Comay's words, they are "silhouettes," "abbreviations" (also Hegel's word), and "caricatures."[12] This, she points out, is true for Hegel of our encounters with history in general. What we now see is that Hegel's accounts are caricatures, we now see this to the extent that those historical phenomena were themselves caricatural – distorted attempts to deny the nothingness at the core of human reality.

The quest which has ended is not Hegel's, but all of ours.

At that point, for Comay, there appears to be nothing we can do except mourn the enterprise: the *Phenomenology* is the sorrowful record of a possibility unfulfilled because it was never a possibility in the first place. And here is where I have a question, because it seems that Hegel, somehow, saw things differently. For his work after the *Phenomenology* is not (merely) the mourning of what has happened, but claims to be the dawn of a new era: history comprehended by a new kind of philosophical system. Comay clearly thinks this is wrong: that Hegel's system is not the direction to go.

I would like to ask her why she thinks this. But I won't, because it just reawakens the oldest question we have about Hegel: what did he take his system to be?

What, again and always, is this man doing?

NOTES

1 G.W.F. Hegel, *Philosophy of Nature*, trans. and ed. M.J. Petry, vol. 1, (London: George Allen and Unwin, 1970), § 346a.

2 Ibid., § 351.

3 Ibid., § 258.

4 Rebecca Comay, *Mourning Sickness: Hegel and the French Revolution* (Stanford: Stanford University Press, 2010), 57.

5 Ibid., 67.

6 Ibid., 68.

7 Ibid., 78.

8 Ibid., 79.

9 Ibid., 85.

10 Ibid., 93.
11 Ibid., 125.
12 Ibid., 86f, 95.

REFERENCES

Comay, Rebecca. *Mourning Sickness: Hegel and the French Revolution*. Stanford, CA: Stanford University Press, 2010.

Hegel, G.W.F. *Philosophy of Nature*. Translated and edited by M.J. Petry. London: Allen and Unwin, 1970.

—— *Phenomenology of Spirit*. Translated by A.V. Miller. Oxford: Oxford University Press, 1979.

13 Hegel before Comay: *Mourning Sickness* and the Absoluteness of Freedom

IAN BALFOUR, YORK UNIVERSITY

There is no one way to read Hegel, *pace* one possible take on the title of Adorno's great essay, "*Skoteinos* oder wie zu lesen sei" ["*Skoteinos* or How to Read"]. There Adorno sketches out not so much the one true method of understanding Hegel, as the title might imply, but rather certain parameters that should pertain to any reading, given the peculiar texture of Hegel's thought, its real and putative obscurity, and the character of the corpus as systematic or not or somewhere in between. Readings of Hegel tend to gravitate to the poles of whole or part, or, what is not quite the same thing, to read with or against the grain. Rebecca Comay's landmark study of Hegel, steeped in decades of close reading and pedagogy devoted to making Hegel intelligible, including to undergraduates (not unlike Hegel himself, lest one forget), hones in on a moment of Hegel, or versions of a moment – the French Revolution – that is massively informed by Hegel's "theory" of history (explicitly an *ex post facto* theory) shadowed by some sense of the (changing) "system," on the one hand, and yet, on the other, in crucial respects something unparalleled. The French Revolution is embedded in the grand history of (the consciousness of) freedom but stands out as the extreme, singular instance of it: *absolute* freedom.

In the sometimes dusty, cramped corridors of Hegel studies, Comay's focused intervention is a breath of fresh air. There are, to be sure, numerous good analyses of "Hegel and the French Revolution," such as by Joachim Ritter, Jean Hyppolite, and the young Jürgen Habermas. Yet they all leave something to be desired when addressing this huge and still resonant topic. Moreover, a good many readers of Hegel who have written about him at length and whom one would suppose well positioned to think through Hegel on the revolution, on the order of a Herbert Marcuse or an Ernst Bloch, well disposed to revolution themselves, give this complex historical event – hardly one "event," indeed a good model of a "complex event," according to *The Philosophy of Right* – relatively short shrift. Dieter Henrich, in a compact essay on "German Idealism and the French Revolution," does not even so much as mention Hegel! Part of the problem with even many of the normally authoritative critics of Hegel is that they rest content with expounding his "ideas" about the revolution, articulating this or that position or telling a story about how the position shifts somewhat from one text to another.[1] These sorts of takes tend to fall short of what the texts demand, including in Hegel's own terms, Hegel being cognizant, in principle and often in practice, of the imperative to factor in language, representation, and the actual process and performance of thinking when confronting the subject in front of one. Thus, if Comay attends to the *ways* Hegel thinks and writes, that cannot simply be chalked up to a "deconstructive," much less a "literary" reading. That she scrutinizes Hegel's rhetoric, argumentation, and narratives with uncommon acuity makes the philosophical "content" – not separable from its articulation, as Hegel himself taught – all the more, well, philosophical.[2]

Comay's strategic, pointed insights can startle us by foregrounding what we hadn't sufficiently noticed, often by recalling a strikingly graphic figure or image that seems at odds with the textbook history-of-philosophy versions of Hegel, such as Bertrand Russell's or less dismissive ones, that abstractly characterize Hegel as impossibly abstract, lost in the ethereal clouds of "the idea" or some procrustean narrative of the idea's programmed, logical elaboration. Comay's Hegel is nittier and grittier than most, anchored – sometimes bogged down – in the world and not just the world-historical, even in daily and nightly life. Her readings can shock us into recognizing all this. The attention to figures and systems of figuration and even more the X-raying of structures of temporality and narrative, the prolepses and analepses, the future anteriors and subjunctive moodiness of the thinking, especially when the topic is the French Revolution, put us in a vastly better position to see what was and is actually happening in Hegel's thinking.

Perhaps somewhat controversial is the sustained reading in psychoanalytic terms, with texts, author, and history all laid out a bit like a patient (etherized?) upon a couch. From the title onward, *Mourning Sickness* posits psychoanalysis as a discourse that can elicit the investments in and stakes of Hegelian discourse, attending not just to the cunning of reason but the cunning of the unconscious, of what is not easily encompassed by reason, official or otherwise. This, I hope, could hardly be construed as anachronism, and not just because Comay finds so many signs of Hegel's anticipating, in terminological terms, as it were, any number of concepts that would later be codified as "Freudian":

splitting, disavowal, perversion and more. To have anticipated psycho-analysis is hardly a requirement to make a present-day psychoanalytic reading of Hegel viable, since the unconscious is just that: unconscious, and in full force long before Vienna around 1900, indeed, it stands to reason, from time immemorial.[3] In any event, we should not be surprised that there would be some such convergences between Freud and the Hegel who could survey the long march of world history and come away with a feeling of what he calls "the most hopeless sadness."[4] This last phrase should also alert us that one need not be a devotee of trauma studies to recognize Hegelian history as repeatedly and decisively traumatic, with some or perhaps all of the temporal and narrative consequences that this entails. Here too Comay wields a slightly non-Hegelian vocabulary to bring the actual structure and texture of Hegel's thinking into stark relief.

Mourning Sickness does an awful lot in its relatively small compass. If we were to probe a thing or two that either were elliptically addressed or left on the cutting room floor, it might make particular sense to prompt her to elaborate more pointedly on the status of freedom in and for her problematic, the freedom that is so famously absolute and then, in short order, *not*. Not absolute and not freedom. The preoccupation with absolute freedom might lead us in another direction or two towards some issues raised in *Mourning Sickness*: the character of the revolution as a peculiarly and constitutively philosophical one, together with the possible exemplarity – or singularity – of this revolution.

More than any philosopher before his time, Hegel committed himself to thinking together history and what we could only a little anachronistically call "theory," as if the reflection on one demanded the other. The lecture courses on religion, aesthetics, and even on philosophy as such all take the form of histories, and not just because his audience of undergraduates (and not a few famous or un-famous professors) needed background to get up speed for the present demands of any discipline or body of knowledge. What Hegel sometimes liked to call the "unfolding of truth" takes time and takes history.[5] In this conjuncture, freedom is hardly one topic among others in Hegel's thinking, for we read in the peroration of the *Lectures on the Philosophy of History* this ringing pronouncement: "The history of the world is nothing other than the progress of the consciousness of freedom."[6] All of human history does not lend itself very readily to summary in a single sentence but if it did, this last one, apparently, would be it. I take the point often made about the difference between the "authority" of the published Hegel *versus* the lectures but I would venture to say that if ever his students got a sentence of Hegel's right, this one would be a good candidate, since when, at the end of months of lecturing on history, Hegel is announcing that the history of the world is "nothing other than ...," surely ears would have perked up and especially those of the note-takers.

Hegel's story of world history, to be sure, is not one of the simple, linear progress of freedom as such. That would be violently at odds with the empirical facts and Hegel does say in those same lectures: "We must proceed historically, empirically."[7] The empirical record shows, for example, that, in Hegel's terms, as Comay recalls for us, for the rabble, "freedom has no existence." Hegel's singular pronouncement. "History is nothing other than," is not about freedom as such, then, but the history of the progress of the consciousness of freedom. One can be conscious of freedom in its absence, in the thrall of un-freedom, as spirit so often is. All of the dynamics of Hegelian consciousness – split, unhappy, and more – that Hegel so magisterially charted can be thought of as encapsulated in this phrase "the progress of the consciousness of freedom," the story that is one with what we just saw is the cause of infinite sadness, "counterbalanced," Hegel adds, "by no consolatory result."[8]

Hegel's onetime roommate and friend Friedrich Hölderlin has his hero Hyperion lament at one point: "Freedom! who understands it? it's a profound word, Diotima."[9] Hegel himself is a little more expansive on this indispensable word/concept: "the term freedom, without further qualification, is indefinite and infinitely ambiguous, being the highest concept, it is liable to an infinity of misunderstandings, confusions, and errors and may give rise to all possible kinds of extravagance."[10] Hegel is often attuned to and anxious to point out matters of ambiguity (*Zweideutigkeit*] but he pulls out several rhetorical stops to stress the extremity of freedom's equivocality: "infinitely ambiguous" and "infinite misunderstanding."[11] Presumably we would need to qualify, in order to avoid such infinite ambiguity, any given configuration of freedom. Perhaps we should even say we need to "historicize" freedom but in the era of the French Revolution history is in one respect not cooperating, since the form freedom takes is qualifiedly unqualified: *absolute* freedom. If this freedom is still recognizably historical, it is, in another sense, via its absolute character, potentially off the historical charts. The way Hegel writes about this absolute freedom allows for both readings.

The absolute freedom constitutive of what looks for all the world like the French Revolution, despite not being named as such in the famous account in the *Phenomenology of Spirit*, is not only informed by its pointed other, absolute un-freedom but it *becomes* its other, its opposite in the form of terror, perhaps *the* Terror, and perhaps "absolute terror" at that, though Hegel, as far as I know, does not use precisely such a formulation. (Comay seems justified, nonetheless, in invoking "absolute Terror" as a formulation to get at what Hegel is diagnosing.) Absolute freedom, one might have imagined, could have come across as the very culmination of spirit's millennia-long quest to realize the idea of freedom. And history never had any other occupation. Do not virtually all Hegelian narratives, following as they do the thrust of history itself as Hegel understands it, tend towards some version of the absolute as their culmination? But this absolute freedom, the product in part of Rousseau's "philosophy" of the will that lurched without mediation between individual and general, turns out in its very abstractedness, its absolute abstraction, as it were, to have cut itself off from "the Idea" of which it might have been supposed to be the high point and goal. It could sound odd to non-Hegelians that the sign of a formation's abstraction, such as that of absolute freedom, is to have not been articulated with or not to have articulated itself properly "the Idea," a concept that, outside Hegelian parameters, could easily be taken as the very height of abstraction. "Who thinks abstractly?" Hegel asked in his great little essay by that title, an essay curiously neglected, even though Heidegger could call it the best introduction to German Idealism. One of the answers to Hegel's arch but also serious question is: the French. It is they, it turns out, the French of the land of Descartes and Pascal, who thought abstractly, a little too abstractly, as say, Rousseau and all the more so the French revolutionaries who invoked him in writings and on the floor of the National Assembly. The full splendour and misery of the Idea entails its actualization and so in the modern state that means the realization of freedom, not just, despite the best "will" in the world, their proclamations as, say, in the "Declaration of the Rights of Man and of the Citizen."

One of the things I find puzzling in trying to make sense of Hegel's account(s) of the French Revolution is what unfolds as a matter of necessity and what happens as contingency or even chance, as *Zufall* (whose problematic importance for Hegel, Dieter Henrich long ago analysed[12]), or simply as one among other possibilities. Even if we recognize the limits of "the rational is the real" as a slogan for how history works in Hegel,[13] there is a pervasive sense that it does operate as a process of reason and perhaps all the more so at the level of the world-historical, for what really counts, for what remains. I find it hard to tell, in Hegel's rendition of the French revolution, whether absolute freedom absolutely had to issue into what he calls "its negation," "the death that is without meaning, the sheer negative of the terror that contains nothing positive," much less the more specific scenario of heads guillotined like so many cabbages. Readers disposed to Hegelian dialectics will have become accustomed by the point of the section of the *Phenomenology* on "Absolute Freedom and the Terror" to recognize how any number of entities tend to pass over into or turn into their others, even their opposites. Such dynamics might indeed be traced back to Hegel's earliest extended text, his *Life of Jesus*, his synthetic retelling of the Gospels, texts where we encounter numerous formulations of such reversals: "the last shall be first" and so on.[14] But how exactly, and how necessarily, does this change occur in the case of absolute freedom in the French revolution? Is Hegel generalizing from the Terror with a capital "T" and the specific modes of its death-dealing to the negative of [the] terror *sans* capital "T" and marking it as a necessary movement, paradoxically a necessary movement of freedom, and not just any freedom but *absolute* freedom?[15] It is, of course, at the extremes that limits are reached and, one might say, all the more so when the entity in question is (the) absolute. Glossing "the universal will" Hegel remarks that "it is the pure positive *because* it is the pure negative."[16] If Hegel is narrating the (un-named) French revolution, it is not hard to say, after the fact, that something like absolute freedom gave way to terror or the Terror. That is what the historical record shows. But did it have to be that way? Absolutely? It is true that in the Jena *Realphilosophie* Hegel characterizes the regime of Robespierre as one of *"reine entsetzliche Herrschaft,"* "pure disgusting domination." I trust Rebecca Comay to understand the force of the odd, charged term *entsetzlich* here better than I but I want to underscore rather the word "pure": the pure domination that emerges as the flip side of pure, absolute freedom. The more extreme, the purer an entity is, the likelier it is it will pass over into its utter, but not necessarily absolute, other.

Universal freedom, Hegel tells us, can produce "neither a work nor a deed: there is left for it only *negative* action: it is merely the fury of destruction."[17] But was this fury of destruction the only possible negative action? The fury of destruction was considerable in empirical terms but hardly "absolute." Or is the fear and the spectre of death in effect absolutely generalized by the considerable numbers of actual arrests and actual deaths, together with the pervasiveness of suspicion, as if the *citoyen* has done the math and multiplied from many to all? The empirical configurations of what Comay diagnoses as paranoia – producing an immense number of usual and unusual suspects – correspond perfectly to the totalizing possibilities of an absolute, absolutist logic.[18]

In the very next paragraph Hegel provides an answer of sorts to the question of necessity/contingency by positing that the universality "that does not let itself advance to the reality of organic articulation" will "by virtue of its own abstraction" "divide itself into extremes."[19]

There is no denying that, on the spectrum of historical events, the French Revolution could easily count as one that goes to extremes, in its force, effects, and its very self-conception. Yet it does sometimes sound as if Hegel is mapping something of a logical schema onto a messier historical dynamic that need not have been as extreme as posited or judged as just that extreme.

One of enigmatic features of Hegel's account of the French Revolution, as in so many sections of *Geist's* history, is that in what looks in many respects like a narrative of what happened in a specific historical event, all proper names and dates and locales are tellingly left out or undetermined – there are loads of circumlocutions and allusions – and the tense is almost always the present. We know that the texture of what is said is massively dictated by what happened in the French Revolution and yet what we get is a present-tense rendition of the dynamics of "absolute freedom and terror" abstracted from that historical moment that was nothing if not, in some important respects, abstract.[20] The absence of what might have been the past tense makes things tense in the present. It is this schema that at least partly helps render the revolution as if it were the logical, necessary unfolding of a dynamic already set in motion and so not pertinently dependent on contingencies – on the price of bread or a necklace, say, much less what someone happened to say, or not, about eating cake. Nonetheless, the passing over of absolute freedom into something like its absolute other looks as if it comes rather out of the blue (as Hölderlin's phrase has it, elsewhere). It's perhaps not unusual for Hegel that history (or is it the logic of culture, of *Geist*, what Jameson proposes we translate as "collectivity"?) should take itself to the extreme(s).[21] But was it necessary for it to entail just this dynamic of one absolute becoming its other?

Hegel is under no imperative to give a full account of even every key moment in or aspect of the French Revolution but some lacunae stand out. Comay notes, for one, "the aching absence of explicit political discussion following his analysis of the breakdown of revolutionary freedom."[22] Since freedom, in order for us to understand it, in order for it not to be infinitely ambiguous, needs to be qualified, a fuller account of *this* absolute might have shed some light on the passage from absolute freedom to the Terror and to the distinctly different aftermaths in France and Germany.

One way the arguably necessary movement is charted, as Comay recalls for us, comes via the solar trajectory of history, from the *Morgenland*, the morning land, of Asia to the *Abendland*, the evening land of modern Europe, more precisely mapping his version of the *translation imperii* from Asia to Greece to Rome to France and then, awkwardly, to the somewhat amorphously German present. Though Hegel does also speak of the French Revolution in terms of a "sunrise," "a glorious mental dawn," if history were just to "follow the sun," as it were, the next stop should have been something like the British Isles. But no. History's mobile centre of gravitas lurches back in the other direction, the sort of movement that fascinated Hölderlin in the course some rivers, figures, for him, for the founding and movement of history. The post-revolutionary moment is a kind of violent daylight savings time, springing forward by falling back, just as it's getting rather late in the day of history. Perhaps it's a world-historical case of *reculer pour mieux sauter*?

In his massive study, *Less Than Nothing: Hegel and the Shadow of Dialectical Materialism*, Slavoj Zizek,[23] whose understanding of Hegel on the French Revolution is in dialogue with and has learned from Comay's analysis, contends that for Hegel: the aim of the analysis of the French Revolution is not to unearth the "historical necessity" of the passage from 1789 to the Jacobin Terror and then to Thermidor and Empire, but "rather *to reconstruct this succession in terms of a series of (to use this anachronistic term) existential decisions made by agents who, caught up in a whirlwind of action, had to invent the way out of a deadlock*."[24] This makes history seem rather less inexorable than Hegel is usually thought to profess, though it would be in keeping with Hegel's insistence on the primacy of freedom and its multiple possibilities. Zizek maintains that "*dialectical analysis reinserts possibility into the necessity of the past*,"[25] a notion that perhaps has some basis in the odd way that Hegel sometimes recounts historical events in the present, as in the section of the *Phenomenology* that so clearly is about the French revolution without naming it as such. The present not yet turned past presents the prospect of freedom rather more than does the past written in the stone of the past tense. Such a rhetorical mode can still present historical agents as rational actors without conveying the sense that history is always already written in advance, as if just biding its time for people to go through the (logical) motions.

The movement from France in the era of the French Revolution to Germany in its immediate aftermath makes a kind of sense, even if history is moving geographically backwards, because the revolution was a peculiarly philosophical one and it would give way to a more-philosophical-than-not discourse of morality thriving in the loose amalgam of small states, principalities, and the like known as "Germany" but not yet constituted as a nation-state. The migration of history's centre of gravity to Germany allows it to reprise the earlier German revolution (spiritual, not so violent) in a setting that could hardly be more conducive for philosophical thought, in general, and for the concrete task of freedom's actualization in a nation to come, when the real would be all the more rational and the rational real.

The abstraction of the French revolution, still bent on its realization, is even more at home away from its temporary home in France. Hegel is far from alone in thinking the French Revolution, in its origins and some of its protocols, a decidedly philosophical one. Rousseau's thought, as suggested above, was explicitly invoked, quoted, and celebrated now and then by Girondists and Jacobins alike. Rousseau would be praised for having formulated what would become some of the Revolution's loftiest ideals and castigated for his supposed part in leading to what Lady Bracknell in *The Importance of Being Earnest* calls "the worst excesses of the French Revolution," adding that that she presumes [we] "know what that unfortunate movement led to."[26] Hegel, indeed, knew what it led to. The peculiarly philosophical character of the revolution was apparent to many intellectuals just beyond the borders of France. Coleridge wrote in one version of his lay sermon called *The Statesman's Manual* that "it would not be difficult, by an unbroken chain of historical facts, to demonstrate that the most important changes in the political relations of the world [another version gave the phrase as "commercial relations"] had their origin in the closets or lonely walks of uninterested theorists" ["closets" sounds like Locke; "lonely walks" like Rousseau].[27] Coleridge goes on to say that "all the epoch-forming Revolutions of the Christian world, the revolutions of religion and with them the civil, social and domestic habits of the nations concerned, have coincided with the rise and fall of metaphysical systems." If this was correct in general, it was often thought to be true in spades of the French Revolution. Its abstract, philosophical texture was decisive for the revolution in Edmund Burke's view, though his position does not often overlap with Hegel's. Burke certainly coincided with Hegel in discerning in the discourse of the French Revolution not just philosophy but heightened abstraction on the part of those whom Burke, in not the last British attack on French theory, called "upstart theorists," a charge the older Wordsworth would happily repeat. But one can probably not imagine Hegel subscribing to Burke's assertion that: "The pretended rights of these theorists are all extremes; and in proportion as they are metaphysically true, they are morally and politically false."[28]

In Burke's view, the failure of abstract theory among the French revolutionists could be chalked up to a rejection and a misrecognition of one's own history. Politics, for Burke, was not supposed to ask: what is the most rational form of government? Rather, the question should have been: given France's history (absolute monarchy, Catholic hierarchy, structural inequality), what is the best sort of reform to undertake? The specificity of France had little to do with the histories of its closest neighbours, England and Germany, at least insofar as the structures of government and religion were concerned. For Burke, the French revolutionaries had wilfully imposed a crazed version of Cartesian, geometric rationalism on a geography and a history that could not possibly accommodate it, as if overnight. In Burke's influential view, it was this precise texture of abstraction, as performed in history, that contributed to the excesses and the downfall of the Revolution.

I wonder if Comay thinks that the *philosophical* character of the revolution, whatever one's position on it, has much or anything to do with Hegel's sense that this movement of history makes sense, makes peculiar sense, that it is eminently rational, even though Comay notes that on occasion, from the Jena writings onward, we see how for Hegel history, especially revolutionary history, can take on a dark, blind, elemental texture (to invoke some of Hegel's explicit terms for historical movement). Perhaps this revolution was more rational than most (explicit, self-conscious, universalizing) if faultily so, not rational enough by being too merely rational, too abstract in its oscillating extremities.

I wonder too if this philosophical, perhaps hyper-philosophical character of the revolution has something to do with its peculiar exemplarity. Let me recall for you a suggestive passage from *Mourning Sickness* on the paradigmatic status of the revolution: "Schlegel pronounces it both 'the model of revolutions' (*das Urbild der Revolutionen*) and 'the Revolution' (*die Revolution schlechthin*), both exemplary prototype and inimitable exception – a class that seeks to embrace everything and yet ultimately admits only itself as its sole member. The Revolution provokes repetition even while it exhausts its own concept, rendering subsequent renditions at once mandatory, superfluous, and insufficient."[29] Comay goes on to note how, in the conception of thinkers contemporaneous with the revolution and its aftermath, this revolution is paradoxically oriented to both past and future beyond the so-called immediate future:

> The unprecedented strangeness of the French Revolution – its novelty, its contingency, its shocking incongruity – is exaggerated and denied as Germany seeks to absorb this "peculiar crisis" (Herder) within a prior and future upheaval of thought.
>
> Note the paradoxical temporality. The new is the déjà vu is the perpetually not yet. Always familiar and yet forever awaited, the present unfolds into both a memory and a promise. The Revolution plays out simultaneously toward past and future.[30]

The time of this revolution seems in and out of joint, rather as Hegel's own account of it is. This revolution that begins, as Hegel remarks in both the *Lectures on the Philosophy of History* and the *Philosophy of Right*, "in thought" hardly remains a thing of the past. Not simply "history," the revolution, in Hegel's account of the *Phenomenology*, unfolding in the present tense could also be unfolding "now."[31] Is the revolution, some version of this revolution, begun in thought, embracing absolute freedom, but not yet fully articulated in the idea, also the revolution to come, such that it will have made sense to do away with, originally, all those names and dates, all the better so that they can be named later?

NOTES

1 *Contra* those scholars who like to contrast the various positions Hegel takes on the revolution to line up with various received ideas about Hegel as youthful sympathizer to old reactionary apologist for the state, Comay helpfully highlights the constancy of how Hegel is almost systematically divided on the revolution. Cf. Rebecca Comay, *Mourning Sickness: Hegel and the French Revolution* (Stanford University Press, 2010): 76.

2 Related to this I might note that Comay seems as good as anyone at getting at the *tone* of what Hegel says. Has anyone else ever paused to notice the force of a rare exclamation mark in Hegel? Ernst Bloch went so far as to contend, perhaps a little archly, that if we really want to understand Hegel's language we have to hear its Swabian undertones – which would mean we have to hear and think, for example, in terms of *"Geisht,"* not *Geist*. Too often we imagine Hegel to be droning on in an Olympian monotony, with an even-handed distance towards the vast array of subjects and objects across the spectrum of the encyclopaedia, literally and otherwise. But Comay attends to the voice of the writing, as it were, and the results are revelatory.

3 For one significant precursor to Comay on this front, see Jean Hyppolite, *"Phénomenologie* de Hegel et psychanalyse," in his *Figure de la pensée philosophique*, Vol. 1 (Paris: Presses universitaires de France, 1991): 213–30.

4 Hegel, Georg W.F. *The Philosophy of History*. Trans. J. Sibree. (New York: Prometheus Books, 1991): 21.

5 Adorno in his studies of Hegel calls attention to the importance of this phrase for Hegel. "Unfolding" (*Entfaltung*) implies that truth is there *in nuce* from the start and only requires its elaboration over time.

6 Theodor W. Adorno, *Gesammelte Schriften*, Ed. Rolf Tiedemann (Frankfurt am Main: Suhrkamp, 1970-), Vol. 12: 538.

7 Hegel, Georg W.F. *The Philosophy of History*. Trans. J. Sibree. (New York: Prometheus Books, 1991), 17. The fuller sentence in German reads: "Die Geschichte aber haben wir zu nehmen, wie sie ist; wir haben historisch, empirisch zu verfahren." (G.W.F. Hegel, *Vorlesungen über die Philosophie der Geschichte* in Hegel, *Werke* (Frankfurt am Main: Suhrkamp, 1986), Vol. 12: 22.

8 Hegel, Georg W. F. *The Philosophy of History*. Trans. J. Sibree. (New York: Prometheus Books, 1991), 19. On the absence of a counterbalance, see 24.

9 Friedrich Hölderlin, *Hyperion and Selected Poems*. Ed. by Eric L. Santner. New York: Continuum, 2002), 168–178, "Menon's Lament for Diotima."

10 Hegel, Georg W. F. *The Philosophy of History*. Trans. J. Sibree. (New York: Prometheus Books, 1991), 19.

11 Ambiguity is not necessarily, in Hegel, a bad thing.

12 Dieter Henrich, "Hegel's Theorie über den Zufall," in *Hegel im Context* (Frankfurt am Main: Suhrkamp, 1971), 157–86.

13 Hegel, a little less famously, maintained that in history "nothing great is accomplished without passion" and was attentive to any number of operative factors that could not easily be ascribed to reason. See Slavoj Zizek's interesting essay along these lines: "Discipline between Two Freedoms – Madness and Habit in German Idealism," in Markus Gabriel and Slavoj Zizek, *Mythology, Madness, and Laughter: Subjectivity in German Idealism* (London and New York: Continuum, 2009), 95–121.

14 Indeed, a good many aspects of the Hegelian narrative machine (*Aufhebung*, negation of the negation) can be traced back to discursive configurations in the Gospels, texts that he knew, from his training in the Tübingen *Stift*, as well as any, not least from his study of them in order to write *das Leben Jesu*.

15 One of the virtues of Comay's analysis, applauded by Zizek in *Less Than Nothing*, is to show how absolute freedom turned into terror long before The (official) Terror, indeed, how it is built in from the start of the Revolution in 1789. Comay observes pithily of the pithy situation: "Absolute freedom *is* terror" (68). Recent works on our topic include the French Revolution chapter of Richard Bourke, *Hegel's World Revolutions* (Princeton, 2023) and Borna Radnik, *Freedom in Context: Time, History, and Necessity in Hegel* (London 2024). The former is concerned to contextualize and to chart the specificity of Hegel's account comparison with his other pertinent treatments and the latter works systematically with its announced categories occasionally with attention to the French Revolution. Few studies, however, query the argumentation for the absoluteness of absolute freedom (as Comay does) or the necessity for a certain terror, which is that of the French Revolution but perhaps not only, to be absolute.

16 Hegel, *Phenomenology of Spirit*, M594.

17 Hegel, *Phenomenology of Spirit*, M589.

18 Comay, *Mourning Sickness*, 69.
19 Hegel, *Phenomenology of Spirit*, M590.
20 One notes the absence of the definite article that might have preceded "terror," already capitalized in the German.
21 See Fredric Jameson, *The Hegel Variations* (Verso, 2010), Chapter 8, "Spirit as Collectivity (*Antigone*, or the One into Two)," 75–79.
22 Comay, *Mourning Sickness*, 138.
23 Slavoj Zizek, *Less Than Nothing: Hegel and the Shadow of Dialectical Materialism* (Verso, 2012).
24 Zizek, *Less Than Nothing*, 285.
25 Zizek, *Less Than Nothing*, 285.
26 Oscar Wilde, *The Importance of Being Earnest* (1895)
27 Samuel Taylor Coleridge, *The Statesman's Manual* (1816) in *Lay Sermons*, ed. R.J. White in *The Collected Works of Samuel Taylor Coleridge*, Vol. 6 (Princeton: Princeton University Press, 1972), 14.
28 Edmund Burke, *Reflections on the Revolution in France* (1790; Harmondsworth: Penguin, 1969). Cf. Comay, 95ff.
29 Comay, *Mourning Sickness*, 22.
30 Comay, *Mourning Sickness*, 22.
31 In Stephen Spielberg's *Minority Report*, one of the precogs, gifted people who can see the future before it happens, is brought out in the world from her "think tank" and asks of the social spectacle in front of her: "Is it now?"

REFERENCES

Adorno, Theodor W. *Gesammelte Schriften*, Vol. 12. Edited by Rolf Tiedemann. Frankfurt am Main: Suhrkamp, 1970.
Burke, Edmund. *Reflections on the Revolution in France*. Harmondsworth: Penguin Books, 1969.
Comay, Rebecca. *Mourning Sickness: Hegel and the French Revolution*. Stanford University Press, 2010.
Hegel, G.W.F. *Phenomenology of Spirit*. Translated by A.V. Miller. Oxford: Oxford University Press, 1977.
—— *The Philosophy of History*. Translated by J. Sibree. New York: Prometheus Books, 1991.
Hölderlin, Friedrich. *Hyperion and Selected Poems*. Edited by Eric L. Santner. New York: Continuum, 2002.
Markus, Gabriel, and Zizek Slavoj. *Mythology, Madness, and Laughter: Subjectivity in German Idealism*. London and New York: Continuum, 2009.
Zizek, Slavoj. *Less Than Nothing: Hegel and the Shadow of Dialectical Materialism*. Verso, 2012.

14 The Actuality of Anachronism, or, Absolute-Freedom-and-Terror Today (Response to Balfour and McCumber)

REBECCA COMAY, UNIVERSITY OF TORONTO

Ian Balfour and John McCumber raise compelling questions that highlight the exegetical and philosophical challenges of reading Hegel today: first of all, my profound thanks. Their excellent essays spill over into each other, so rather than parcelling out my responses I'm going to try to weave them together, touching on themes raised by each along the way. Both authors bring into relief the uncomfortable contemporaneity of Hegel's thought. They also both draw attention to some awkward issues that I tend to skirt around. Because I don't have final answers (and believe the central questions to be largely unanswerable), I'm going to try to elaborate a few of these questions a little further, and add one or two of my own. Here are some key issues, in order of decreasing generality.

First: a couple of hermeneutic questions. *Why does Hegel exaggerate so much*? Readers are always struck by his use of caricature generally and by his specific harshness towards Kant and company in the last part of the Spirit chapter: why the cruelty? And does this very belligerence not reveal and prolong his enmeshment in the whole Kantian apparatus? A completely separate question: *is there violence in my own reading*? Violence need not be a matter of overt aggression; there can also be something abusive in acts of sympathy or approval. (I hate you and prove my enduring attachment; I love you and kill you with devotion.) This pertains to the question of anachronism (in the ordinary sense): what does it mean to read a historical author through a contemporary theoretical prism? Do we smother Hegel by welcoming him as our neighbour; why in any case introduce the psychoanalytic vocabulary of mourning, melancholia, and so on; and why specifically an overheated term like trauma? These two sets of questions are prompted by passing comments by McCumber and Balfour, respectively, neither of whom actually intended anything critical in such remarks, I don't think, on the contrary, but the questions are nonetheless always hovering, at least in my own mind.

Second: speaking of anachronism (in the special sense that I take Hegel to be elaborating): *do the clocks ever get calibrated*? My argument in *Mourning Sickness* is that, for Hegel (and he's right), the untimeliness of experience is structural. It is the contribution of modernity to make this structure explicit. The delay that defines the "German" experience of the "French" Revolution is an extreme and therefore exemplary case of the temporal non-synchronicity or slippage that structures all experience and accounts for its latencies, omissions, regressions, blind spots. Hegel spends half the introduction to the *Phenomenology* explicating this slippage; he spends the first part of the book demonstrating its epistemological mechanics, and the second half drawing out its historical repercussions. He gestures towards the inescapability of this slippage in the forgiveness scene, which – belatedly, all too belatedly – concludes the Spirit chapter. The details are variable, but the non-synchronicity itself is axiomatic or structural – a kind of "constitutive lack," to use current parlance. It arises from the founding split in subjectivity itself. Consciousness is doomed to be forever overreaching itself (it "suffers violence at its *own* hands") while at the same time constantly lagging behind or recoiling from its own insights (its anxiety makes it "retreat and strive to hold onto what it is in danger of losing"): it's both too early and too late for its own experience (§80). This strange blend of precocity and retardation accounts for the *Phenomenology*'s uneven narrative rhythm, its endless lurching and backsliding (surely the most inefficient story ever told). Is this arrhythmia corrected when Spirit traverses the "unreal land" of Kantian moral philosophy to enter the Elysium of science? In other words: is absolute knowing traumatic? McCumber gestures towards this question at the end of his essay when he raises the issue of closure: does the *Phenomenology* ever come to an end, what would be the measure of its interminability, and what are the stakes?

Third: *does Hegel provide an alternative to the "German ideology"* or does he end up prolonging its errors? Hegel demonstrates that in the (philosophical) aftermath[1] of Absolute Freedom, revolutionary terror is simultaneously overcome, comprehended, embellished, disavowed – and of course prolonged. (There is in this sense, as I've suggested, something vaguely "Thermidorian" about the whole exercise. The morality squad arrives to restore order, to provide an

account of the events, and to settle the score with the terrorists –
and ends up reproducing their bloodiest tactics.) Arriving on the
scene the day after the Revolution, German philosophy reinterprets
freedom as moral autonomy and sublimates terror as pre-emptive
anxiety; a *conceptual* guillotine now separates thought and world.
(The details of this transaction are described in the fourth chapter
of *Mourning Sickness*.) If Kant is the successor to the Revolution,
and Hegel the successor to Kant, does this mean that the problems bequeathed by this Revolution are henceforth addressed on
a virtual terrain? By emphasizing the *necessity* of the passage from
politics to philosophy,[2] is Hegel dishing up a sophisticated version
of the German *misère* (Marx's well-known accusation), or does he
provide a diagnosis, critique, and even an alternative? This question
of necessity – the necessity of the passage to, through, and beyond
revolutionary terror – runs throughout Balfour's essay, and brings
us directly to the question of philosophy itself.

The "Spirit" chapter concludes with an anticipation of *The German Ideology*. Does Hegel forget to write himself into the book as its prime
suspect? The "Morality" section will deliver a scorching exposé
and refutation of every form of spectatorial disengagement. The
transition from politics to morality, from "Revolution" to "Kant,"
is shown to be a botched transition; the German Idealist solution
to the antinomies of absolute freedom, a false solution, will in turn
have to be surpassed, its premises redefined – but in which direction? There is not a whiff of politics once Spirit relocates to the
"unreal land" of morality; the last two chapters of the *Phenomenology* unfold within the rarified sphere of (what Hegel will later call)
"absolute spirit." Any return to the categories of objective spirit –
the world of concrete social institutions – seems to be blocked in
advance, as if all *political* options, after the Revolution, had been
exhausted. Forced to choose between the deadlock of Terror or
the various dead-ends of a defunct tradition, Spirit would now be
forced to seek its answers, and even to articulate its questions, on a
non-political, or post-political, "cultural" terrain. Does the beautiful
soul's final acceptance of its own ineluctable fallibility – its "evil"
particularity –enable and even require a return to political engagement? Or is this very concession, because of its easy universality,
also an empty one – an alibi for even more inventive forms of voyeurism? In short: is ascetic ideology overcome? This is McCumber's
central question: is the entanglement with Kant interminable?
(This question resonates with the central concerns of contemporary Hegel scholarship, where discussion tends to focus on Hegel's

"non-metaphysical" proclivities: is Hegel a pre-critical dinosaur or
has he absorbed the transcendental-critical lesson; has he made the
transition from substance to subject or does he remain mired down
in some kind of rationalist substance monism? Or is there some
other way of articulating the post-Kantian problematic – an articulation that would take the discussion beyond the narrowly epistemological framework in which things tend to get reduced these days?)
Finally: Why today, why now? (It would take another book to develop
this question, so I'll be very brief.)

1 Silhouettes and Ether: A Little Hermeneutic Violence

Two images mentioned in passing by McCumber and Balfour are
arresting. They pertain to the peculiar hermeneutic strategies followed
respectively by Hegel (when reading others) and by me (when reading Hegel). Despite their differences, both details have something in
common, and despite their morbidity, both should be embraced. Or so
I'd like to argue. This might seem like a peculiar starting point, and to
require an annoying amount of over-reading, so I'll need to press the
point a little. Bear with me for a few pages (or skip ahead to the next
section if you find this kind of approach too irritating).

One is the image of the *silhouette*: this is Hegel's own word – *Schat-
tenriss*. McCumber mentions it towards the beginning of his essay
when pointing to Hegel's peculiar style of portraiture: stunningly
subtle in his mode of argumentation, Hegel can be so clumsy in his
actual descriptions. As everybody knows, his philosophical-histor-
ical narrative can be rude and reductive. His depictions, especially
of other thinkers, can lack finesse (think of Kant), can be one-sided
(Spinoza), or blatantly incorrect (Rousseau). Hegel has a disarmingly
simple answer to this criticism: this is (truly) how things *appear*. And
it is moreover just how the appearances themselves explode: only by
"profiling" the object, by magnifying its most singular, most stupidly
idiosyncratic, feature, can I detonate its most devastating truth – an
explosion which will inevitably include consciousness itself among its
casualties. Exaggeration breaks the spell of both object and subject.
In overshooting the thing, I simultaneously irritate it to the point of
counter-attack and end up embarrassing myself by my own grandi-
osity. This discomfort can lead to greater argumentative precision, it
can provoke further rhetorical grandstanding, and it can become an
excuse for philosophical backpedalling – "things aren't *that* bad." In
other words exaggeration leads in all possible directions. We tend to
underestimate its subtlety.[3]

Hegel introduces the image of the silhouette in an under-read passage in the Preface to the *Phenomenology*.[4] He's describing how moments of the past present themselves in the twilight of philosophical retrospection: abbreviated, monochromatic, two-dimensional.[5] Each figure is etched flatly against a blank background – a *ritratto* momentarily torn out of context as a new environment is being forged. Stripped of colour and reduced to pure outline, the bygone object appears in temporary isolation and abstraction. "Its entire existence falls into *one* determinateness" (§28). We observe the avatars of the past in profile, viewed sideways, a discontinuous parade of transitory figures, each shape distilled into a single defining feature, a kind of *trait unaire* in Lacan's sense – the isolated detail that looms larger than life and comes to crystallize the object's entire being.[6] Adorno was thinking of something similar when he asserted, in his usual overstated fashion, that in psychoanalysis (he's really thinking about his own writing), nothing is true but the exaggerations.[7] It's not by "appreciating" or "understanding" (in the ordinary sense) things, not by tending to their endless subtleties and niceties, that we honour their intellectual vibrancy. It's precisely by vulgarizing them by magnifying their foibles to the point of absurdity – that we detonate their force. The reverse is equally true: it's only in losing traction that an object shows its most pervasive grip; it's at the point of dissolution that its edges become clear. We see things sideways: we "get" them only once they're already on the way out, and we recognize them only when they can't return the gaze.

This is why the silhouette is such a provocative image. It presents a visual analogue of the logic of determinate negation and offers a snapshot of the dialectical method: *reductio ad absurdum*. It is at its most extreme limit – on the verge of impossibility – that the object releases its truth. The image also hints at the dark side of enlightenment. The silhouette is created by a blockage of illumination, at the borderline between darkness and light. As an image of pure edge, the silhouette also works against the organicist cliché of experience as a process of continuous accretion or growth. This discontinuity (which works against the usual caricature of dialectical "development" as the gradual ripening of an oak, or rather forces us to rethink this image, since it is, after all, Hegel's own[8]) is captured perfectly in Hegel's surprising encomium to the mortifying power of *Verstand*. Hegel pauses for a moment to sing its praises: "the most astonishing and mightiest of powers, or rather the *absolute* power" (I'll return to this question of absolutism) – that is, the analytic power to pulverize the organic immediacy of appearances into a scatter of isolated *disjecta membra*.[9] This amounts to a confrontation with "the most terrifying, *das Furchtbarste*, of all things" – that is, death itself (§32). The famous Bacchanalian revel – that swirl of disappearing body parts – turns out to be a *Totentanz*, a dance of death (§47).

This perfectly captures Hegel's methodological brinksmanship. The shapes of Spirit appear in their most abstract or exaggerated (we might say *misshapen*) form, and nowhere more so than where Hegel is writing the history of the most recent past. The last half of the "Spirit" chapter is both captivating and exasperating in its crudeness; its bombast irritates Kantians especially. If Hegel is painting with particularly wide brush-strokes in these sections, it's because he's shooting at a moving target (to mix metaphors slightly). The caricatures accumulate as the narrative surges forward to catch up to the actual moment of writing: absolute monarchy is reduced to a pile of shiny ornaments clustered around a throne; the guillotine to a machine for decapitating cabbage-heads; Kant to a monkish hypocrite obsessing about a desire he doesn't even have the heart to desire; the Romantics all and sundry to a country club for unemployed tubercular psychotics. Such caricatures, and these are just a handful, seem designed for instant consumption, and no doubt contribute to the familiar cartoon image of Hegel himself as intellectual omnivore, master of the one-liner – a "belly turned mind."[10] (That last slogan is Adorno's, and underscores hyperbole's own metastatic tendency to proliferate: Hegel himself seems at times almost to invite, to want to provoke, caricature. I'll return to this point in the next section, when discussing his ambiguous relationship to formalism.)

McCumber rightly stresses the temporal dissonance: the frozen imprint of a passing moment, the silhouette marks the abrasion of two distinct temporal orders. I've already alluded to a mortuary dimension; the silhouette is a kind of death-mask. It offers a way to take leave of the past without quite having to relinquish it; we idealize, vulgarize, reduce, abbreviate, digest. Legend links the silhouette to the origin of painting: grief-stricken by the imminent departure of her lover, the Corinthian maiden Dibutades had tried to freeze time, to immobilize the image of the departed by tracing the outline of his shadow cast by candlelight on the wall.[11] By the late eighteenth century, the silhouette had become a popular parlour game and a commercial practice (under the influence of Lavater, portable machines had been invented), anticipating photography as an inexpensive technique of portraiture. It also anticipated some of photography's mortuary predilections.[12] Contemporary observers were quick to note its ghoulish aspect: in pre-empting loss, in forestalling death, the silhouette inexorably hastened its arrival. With its sharp efficiency and its uncanny ability to sever heads from bodies, the machine seemed also to bear an uncanny resemblance to the guillotine.[13]

The other image is of *ether*. That's another one of Hegel's words. In his own hands it has a quaintly consoling ring: ether (or rather, *aether*) is the elixir of absolute knowing – the exalted atmosphere in which consciousness is "able to *live* with science, and to *live* in science, and *for that matter to be able to live at all*" (§26, emphases mine).[14] Balfour uses the same word too but with exactly the opposite inflection – the lugubrious, Prufrockian sense more familiar to our modern disenchanted ears. Balfour introduces Eliot's famous image when pausing at the flagrant anachronism of my own approach to Hegel in *Mourning Sickness* – my repeated recourse to contemporary critical theory and specifically to psychoanalysis. Anachronistic readings can be violent; Balfour's too gracious to complain about this, but the surgical metaphor nonetheless awakens (in me at least) a discomfort that once registered is impossible to shrug off. The more "relevant" or "living" we find a writer, the more we threaten to reduce him to conceptual fodder: we risk numbing him (and ourselves) with the promise of conviviality. Can we read Hegel through the theoretical prism of the present without dismembering his corpus and tranquillizing his thought?

Every anachronistic approach to any author of course risks etherizing the patient, but when the apparatus happens to be psychoanalysis (and the table a couch) the challenges multiply.

In addition to the usual issues there's the specific hazard of psychologism: can we introduce the vocabulary of psychoanalysis without psychological overkill, that is, without personifying Spirit (or perhaps just the *Zeitgeist*) as if it were a gigantic corporate personality – suffering, toiling, remembering, mourning – a cosmic soul? The question lurks everywhere in the air these days and not just in Hegel scholarship, where the issue is usually broached in terms of Hegel's Kantian credentials (that is, whether we can even dare talking about a thing called Spirit without regressing to some kind of pre-critical substance monism or even theism). The more pressing "metaphysical" danger to be avoided, however, in my opinion, would be some kind of naturalism: does psychoanalysis (in the expanded field) risk reinstating the "natural attitude" by reifying the terms of subjectivity itself whether individual or social? The question extends beyond the terms of Hegel scholarship. It pertains to a much broader discussion surrounding the terms of collective memory, cultural identity, and collective agency, and there are concrete political and institutional implications. In Hegel, the question applies in the reverse direction as well, that is at a microcosmic level: can we isolate a "shape," aspect, or function of consciousness (sense-certainty, perception, etc.)–can we put it on stage, invite it to respond, to write down its answers, force it Socratically to account for itself, can we even simply "look on" dispassionately while it unwittingly self-destructs – without turning it into some kind of walking, talking homunculus?

The relevance of psychoanalysis to Hegel is intense and complicated. It's not just a matter of overlapping lexicons – projection, introjection, negation, disavowal, identification, loss, repression, memory, forgetting and so on – although the coincidences are startling: they all point to the *drive*, or the *drivenness*, of thinking itself – what Hegel calls *der Trieb der Idee*.[15] The most exciting point of contact is also the most awkward: in drawing attention to the porous membrane of the self, both Freud and Hegel reveal every individual to be an unstable amalgam of desires and insights bequeathed, borrowed, or somehow acquired from elsewhere, and every present a shifting precipitate of unworked residues of the past. In demonstrating the essential untimeliness of this inheritance both thinkers point to the unfinished condition of sociability as such. They force us to parse the frayed copula and the knotty conjunction of the "'I' that is 'We' and the 'We' that is 'I'" (§177). This fraying, and this knotting, is why we must risk using a somewhat bloated word like trauma, and why, despite recent overexposure, this category must retain or regain its conceptual verve. It's not for its pathos that I've chosen to foreground this term.

2 The Persistence of Anachronism

So: any engagement with Hegel must involve more than an antiquarian reconstruction of his intentions. It demands the special kind of fidelity demanded by Hegel himself: we must start by confronting his fundamental insight regarding the inextricable entanglement between thought and object. Every reading comes from *somewhere*. This doesn't imply a kind of "presentism," at least not in any vulgar sense; for one thing, Hegel's account of experience punctures every fantasy of a coherent or stable present. If all experience is afflicted by an essential untimeliness, if it comes either too early or too late (actually, both: this is the basic argument of *Mourning Sickness*), this anachronism works in both directions. The past becomes legible only belatedly, only through the prism of the present, but this present is precipitated into the future by the most recalcitrant remnants of the past. Balfour gestures towards this structure when he remarks on the peculiar tense and aspect of Hegel's grammar. "Absolute freedom"–unidentified by dates, place names, and personal names – is described as if the Revolution were happening right here and now. This is true of every shape of Spirit (Sophocles isn't named either, nor Louis XIV, nor Diderot): each episode is recounted in a kind of historical present, as if the stakes were immediate and ongoing, but the impact of this grammar is different with each throw of the dice. This is neither simply a rhetorical ploy on Hegel's part, to create an effect of vividness, nor the signpost of a timeless present in which the narrative were unfolding *sub specie aeternitatis*. Hegel's present tense expresses rather the intermittency of a past that continues, unpredictably, to intrude. These pockets of tangled or discordant temporality – Ernst Bloch spoke of non-synchronicity, *Ungleichzeitigkeit* – are precisely the point where irrecuperable obsolescence forges the most intransigent futurity.[16] Benjamin spoke of the "revolutionary energies of the out-of-date."[17]

In other words: if meaning is retrospective (the infamous owl of Minerva), it is also unfinished. This is what makes the Hegelian logic of retroactivity strictly traumatic (rather than blandly teleological or conciliatory). That is to say, the "distortion," if this is the right word for it, is reciprocal and unstable. The *Phenomenology*, like every human product, is not only "beastly" (McCumber's wonderful term is perhaps still a little too tame for what's at stake here): its metabolism is human, all too human. Thinking does not simply consume the world: it transforms it. Which is why its topics – its objects of consumption – are continually changing, along with the very terms of desire as such: unlike animal hunger, human desire cannot be satisfied, even momentarily, with any object, because desire itself, like everything else, is under scrutiny. Philosophy's enjoyment of everything, including its own legitimacy, is always inhibited, indirect, deferred. And this delay is transmitted to the reader: there's no royal road to science; comprehension is belated and short-lived: it comes either too early or too late (usually both); every claim to mastery is inherently self-defeating.

And yet such claims are irresistible: without leaping ahead of itself, without attempting to consume the unripened fruit (or, which amounts to the same thing, the shrivelled remnants) of the tree of knowledge – without making an untimely bid for mastery, that is, without pistol shots –experience wouldn't be possible in the first place: like the Revolution, thinking can't arrive on time, it is always ahead of or behind itself, and the very attempt to evade this distension or distortion – to overcome time itself – only reproduces this distortion. (This is the hard lesson of the Terror: the very attempt to reinvent clock and calendar, to start time again, to achieve synchronicity in a moment of perfect, unadulterated originality, ends up reactivating the most retrograde features of the past.)

This is perhaps why, in the last chapter of the *Phenomenology*, Hegel does exactly what he had disqualified as perfectly unphilosophical in the Preface: he shamelessly reproduces the error he has been diagnosing from the very beginning of the book – "surveys, tables of contents, overviews" (§53). He produces a breakneck summary of the entire preceding volume – several hundred pages condensed into a few killingly elliptical paragraphs, as abbreviated as "a skeleton with scraps of paper stuck all over it, or like the rows of closed and labeled boxes in a grocer's stall" (§51). This last phrase is another famous quotable; Hegel is here ridiculing the "monotonous formalism" of the post-Kantians: they keep reducing the fruits of wisdom to an array of consumer items. In the following paragraph he will pre-emptively concede the inevitability of such formalism, including perhaps his own. "The excellent [*das Vortreffliche*] cannot escape the fate of being thus deprived of life and Spirit, of being flayed and then seeing its skin wrapped around a lifeless knowledge and its conceit" (§52). This is Hegel's update of Spinoza's peroration to the *Ethics*.[18] And this is also perhaps why Hegel's final synopsis is not entirely convincing: the précis has the flimsy appearance of a "secondary revision" (Freud's description of the attempt, upon awakening, to impose some kind of minimal narrative scaffolding on the welter of the dream-work). Selective in its details, arbitrary in its arrangement, Hegel's recapitulation seems almost designed to demonstrate the fragility of all memory, including his own.

All this points to a severe limitation on the claims of Absolute Knowing: Hegel's final move is to demonstrate that the logic of distortion brooks no exception. This is the final lesson of the Spirit chapter; the miraculous achievement of forgiveness is to display to its own intractable corruption: it arrives only at the last minute, as if grudgingly, and only at gunpoint, and only when it's too late to make a difference. Like Kafka's Messiah (who arrives only on the "day after" the Day of Judgment (*nicht am letzten Tag, sondern am allerletzten*), forgiveness comes when it's no longer necessary, or no longer possible, or both.[19] And even this concession is not quite the end of the story. Part of the surprise of the "final" (the *really* final, for it's a staggered process) ending of the *Phenomenology*, part of its shock value, is that even Absolute Knowing, which concedes its own fallibility (thus earning title to that slipperiest of all monikers, "absolute"), even absolute knowing is not immune from the abstractness that this very concession should have overcome. If the wounds of spirit, infamously, heal and leave no scars (a surgical metaphor if there ever was one), there's no way of telling whether this represents a real healing or another retraumatization – an erasure, effacement, or scotomization – that is, whether this represents an act of productive mourning or a melancholic repetition of the abstract negativity that had reduced death to a meaningless pile of cabbage heads – unmarked, uncommemorated, unmourned.

Hegel's ultimate gamble is to leave this last question irresolvable.[20] McCumber hints that the image of the foaming chalice, Hegel's final image (lifted silently from Schiller), points in this direction, although he also suggests that the risk in this case would be sheer meaninglessness – an ultimate evaporation of determinacy and traction: thought would then disintegrate into a "frictionless spinning in a void" (to borrow McDowell's provocative if somewhat blackmailing phrase).[21] Foam, an image of proliferating formlessness, would seem, in this case, to undo the entire process of progressive determination that had structured the entire "series of *Gestalten*" – a conclusion that would threaten to throw the entire project into the abyss of scepticism (cf. § 808). McCumber and I have different readings of this strange foam, but this would take us into the most impenetrable heartland of Absolute Knowing, so I'll have to defer this discussion to another day.[22]

3 "German ideology," Then …

Nowhere are the challenges of reading Hegel more compelling than when we try to think, today, about the significance of Hegel's fraught relationship to the French Revolution. The challenges are multiple, not least because Hegel's actual position is almost impossible to decipher. He celebrates the Revolution as a "glorious mental dawn," even while characterizing it as "the most disgusting and drastic thing to have ever happened."[23] (This kind of discrepancy is ubiquitous in Hegel and cannot be dismissed as inconsistency, chalked up to ambivalence, or explained away as a function of disillusionment or disappointment, as if Hegel somehow changed his mind, grew old, or lost conviction: these words are pronounced in the same text and in virtually the same breath, and one can find similar juxtapositions in all phases of Hegel's career.) More puzzling yet is Hegel's intransigence: he refuses every effort either to domesticate the event or to demonize it. He dismisses the liberal attempt to gentrify the revolution, to siphon off its violence, even while he refuses to leap to counterrevolutionary conclusions. That's an almost impossible tightrope to walk.

Hegel is almost unique among his contemporaries to take "absolute-freedom-and-terror" as a package (the conjunction in this case designates a strict apposition) *without* drawing reactionary inferences. For Hegel, the revolution is a bloc. The Terror is not a contingent deviation or distraction: it can be neither peeled away from the revolution as a regrettable but inessential excrescence nor explained away as an emergency measure –a temporary response to exceptional circumstances (bread shortages, threat of popular insurrection, etc.). Terror is not a contingent epiphenomenon of revolution but expresses its inner logic. This relates to the question of necessity raised by Balfour, and I'll come back to this issue in just a moment. No 1789 without 1793. But this doesn't push Hegel in the direction of Burke, Taine, or de Maistre. And yet it doesn't push him in the direction of Saint-Just, either. And that's just the first puzzle.

But, and this is the second enigma, Hegel also resists the voyeuristic temptation, from Kant onwards, to soften the traumatic impact of the French Revolution by retrieving from the carnage an opportunity for moral uplift. That's a simple two-step operation but the variations can be subtle (I've rehearsed the various intricacies in *Mourning Sickness*): first, you distance yourself from the event by turning it into theatre, then you divert attention to the enthralled spectators; the real drama turns out to be the sublime enthusiasm of the viewing public.[24] And, hardest of all, because closest to home, Hegel resists the specifically German conceit that underwrites this kind of voyeurism. The standard version goes something like this: Germany is positioned to bypass the perils of political revolution, it can safely watch without fear of contamination because it's already had a bigger, better, in every way more thrilling one of its own. (The medical metaphor is ubiquitous throughout this period: infection, contagion, inoculation.) And because of its special viewing privileges, Germany is uniquely positioned for a more grandiose revolution on its own soil. That's a two-step procedure as well: first, you show that you've already been there, done that, then you argue that an even more splendid rendition is still in the works. Having already undergone its own Reformation, having achieved secularization in the right way and at the right place and time, Germany has acquired a cultural immunity to political revolution. It can thus advance calmly to modernity while extracting from the spectacle of the French Revolution the opportunity of a still more radical upheaval in the cultural sphere.

Hegel's own distance from this pre-emptive position can be sometimes hard to discern, if only because he's probably the one who's done most to formalize its logic. This is why he's usually singled out as the chief mouthpiece of the German ideology: he seems to settle for interpreting the world instead of changing it. The final section of the "Spirit" chapter in the *Phenomenology* is given over to a detailed analysis of the philosophical aftermath of the Terror.[25] Hegel devotes this last section to tracing the forcible migration of freedom from the slaughter-bench of Paris to the "unreal world" (*unwirkliche Welt*) of German moral philosophy – the alternative universe in which Kant and his followers set out to transcribe the political events in France into viable philosophical currency. This world is "unreal" in at least three distinct senses: Germany lacks the self-determination of a state (it will take a few more decades, and considerable military force, to achieve this); German morality, by which Hegel means in the first instance Kant, traffics in *irrealia* (it needs to negate the natural order of bodily particularity in order to affirm itself); finally, more subtly and sinisterly, it reproduces the mortifying operation of the guillotine (in derealizing the object, it forcibly traffics in death itself, the ultimate *Unwirklichkeit*, cf. §32).

Hegel not only describes this migration from politics to philosophy; he also insists on its *necessity*. He even calls this progress. The torch of freedom passes from revolutionary France to philosophical Germany with the inexorability of a cosmologically ordained event. This pertains to the modal question raised by Balfour, and I'll come back to this shortly: the "must" has the force of both an indicative and an imperative; it expresses both an "is" and an "ought." The paradox of necessarily relocating freedom relates to Hegel's version of compatibilism, although this latter term is far too bland to describe the intricacy of what's at stake: the whole debate with Kant – the antinomy of freedom/nature –hangs in the balance. This is Hegel's adaptation of the medieval theological-political story of the *translatio imperii*: the Idea *travels*. It rolls forward with the unstoppable force of planetary motion. Hegel will describe this movement as the "the great day's work of spirit" in the *Philosophy of History* – elsewhere, notoriously, as "the march of God." (*Der Gang Gottes* might be less tendentiously translated as "God's way," but that other rendition has been imprinted for several decades and is by now part of the baggages).[26] History follows the path of the sun from east to west (according to a curiously "pre-Copernican" perspective, but never mind). The hegemonic centre keeps relocating: it moves from Asia to Greece to Rome to France before settling at day's end in (northern) Germany, where the occidental movement grinds to a halt.

The racist baggage is too intractable to deal with here, and the philosophical yield too meagre,[27] so I just want to pause for a moment to consider a little glitch that Balfour seems to have been the only one to notice: Königsberg's east of Paris. Were we to take Hegel's solar figure literally, Spirit would have to just keep on rolling, eventually landing smack in America (why stop in England), and even beyond, ending up back at its starting point: the "westward course of Empire" would then regress into a "worst ward-ho" of endless, meaningless repetition, and freedom into the empty "freedom of a turnspit."[28] The rotary movement has to be contained, its circular trajectory scaled back to the swing of an arc whose fixed termini are Asia and Europe – what Hegel calls, provocatively, the "absolute East" and the "absolute West," respectively.[29] (The earth flattens.) That last little backstep across the Rhine thus functions as a kind of brake or *katechon*: it reins in the occidental course of Spirit, arresting the sun in its track, stopping the clock, like Joshua stopping the day. History would thus freeze in an eternal twilight – an infinitely protracted moment of occidentalization that will supply the backdrop for philosophy to paint its final grey on grey. This would seem the speculative-philosophical version of the epic *imperium sine fine* (Virgil). The Empire lasts forever, it survives its ultimate ruination, because the last stop, strictly speaking, is nowhere and everywhere: the *Abendland* becomes "absolute," a non-relative locality, because it is absolved from spatial-temporal determinacy – an "unreal world."

This is not quite the story the *Phenomenology* tells. And it's not quite the story that even the *Philosophy of Right* will tell, that most infamous of Hegel's texts, the work usually singled out, even in Hegel's own lifetime, for its bad politics. *Mourning Sickness* tries to demonstrate just *why* this isn't exactly Hegel's story, or at least why, if Hegel partly succumbs to this ideology, he is also for this reason uniquely positioned to analyse it. He spends the last section of the "Spirit" chapter trying to show just how and why German freedom, as elaborated to date, is a failure: its worldly promise has aborted. The whole "Morality" section reads as a catalogue of bad faith: Hegel is running through the various ruses with which German idealism keeps trying to peddle impotence as strength. It consoles itself for its own lack of revolutionary agency by generating elaborate theories of sublime spectatorship. Despite or because of its distance from the event, Germany wants to enjoy a vicarious share of the excitement. Having already long established itself as an expert in matters of freedom it claims a special intimacy with the revolutionary project. While Hegel decisively explodes this fantasy, he goes one step further: he acknowledges its appeal. He insists that we traverse the fantasy rather than simply refute it. This means extracting from this fantasy something beyond its usual pacifying effect. If the spectatorial, "German," solution is a non-solution, this doesn't mean that the immediacy of pure action is an option: like every other claim to immediacy, revolutionary "sense-certainty" is blind to its own deferrals, mediations, representational redoubling. Whatever shape freedom henceforth takes, it has to take account of this circuitry. Hegel's depiction of the Germany ideology is in this respect even more provocative than that of Marx and Engels, in that he tries not only to demystify or unveil ideology, but also to account for the tenacity of its grip. Why does Germany consistently miss the moment of revolution, and how does this lapse of experience get registered, embellished, and occluded? Hegel also demonstrates that far from bypassing the moment of terror, such fantasies generate secret terrors of their own. In taking on the German ideology, Hegel is of course also taking on his own lingering Kantianism, and this is what gives his polemic its special bite.

Balfour asks a modal question: solar business aside, what's the logical force of the necessity that binds absolute freedom to terror, and terror in turn to its *philosophical* sequel? Why, in claiming absoluteness, does freedom precipitate into terror, and what accounts for the apparent absorption and sublimation of this terrifying freedom into the more cerebral modes of freedom we know as Kantian autonomy and its various offshoots? If the *necessity* of this transition is vexing for so many of Hegel's readers, this is not simply because it's one of the places in the *Phenomenology* where the *contingent* force of circumstances seems to impinge most directly. The events are so raw and the stakes so urgent that historical events almost seem to be mobilized just because they're *there*, as if the cost of Hegel's formalism were a secret concession to positivism. The suspicion arises also because the dialectical machinery seems to be particularly magical at this juncture. The breathtaking transition from the "meaningless monosyllable" –the flat death on the French scaffold –to the speculative heights of German idealist philosophy takes place with the lightning flash of a conversion, a turnaround, *Umschwung*, in which the magnitude of the loss supplies the measure of Spirit's most prodigious powers of absorption.[30] "It is the pure positive *because* it is the pure negative" (§594). Having relinquished all content, having lost everything, including even the means to symbolize this loss, the subject is forced to confront its own emptiness: negativity is no longer to be located outside the self (every outside having been eliminated), but has now invaded the precinct of subjectivity itself. In forcibly identifying with its own nullity, the subject comes to redefine the terms of freedom, and, at least for a moment, to pacify its violence.

This is not the first time "absolute" appears in the *Phenomenology*, but it's the only time, apart from the final chapter, that the adjective is highlighted as either a title or a subtitle: two hundred pages before the book is finished, Spirit is already explicitly identifying with its own absoluteness. It's staking an explicit claim to an absoluteness to which, strictly speaking, it has not yet earned the title, social or "spiritual" conditions not yet having been established, even if it is also the case that the absolute is Spirit's own birthright and thus in some crucial, non-trivial sense always already attained. Timing is everything. Despite the fact that "the absolute is with us from the start" (the fundamental premise of the *Phenomenology*) it is also the case that it can (and even must) appear too early, or too late, or in the wrong place or way. A premature claim to absolute freedom – to absolute *anything* – not only backfires but can lead to directly opposite results. If revolutionary freedom, in its absoluteness (and is the idea of a *relative* freedom coherent or even thinkable?), exposes this logic of prematurity at its starkest, this is only the most exemplary instance of the bad timing that plagues every episode to the very end.

Terror is in this sense not the exception but the rule: it registers the violence – the "shot from a pistol"–that initiates every venture of Spirit (cf. §27). Hegel's warning is ineffective or too late: every significant experiment makes an illegitimate claim to an absoluteness that it unfailingly betrays. Revolutionary terror–"*the* Terror"–is the hyperbolic form of the ineluctable fear or "anxiety" (*Angst*) that afflicts every modification of consciousness: the mark of its persistent unpreparedness and the cue for its perpetual regression. If Terror steps on stage, for a brief moment, nominalized like an allegorical persona –forged into a visible "shape" – this is because fear in this instance is not simply the symptom of Spirit's chronic arrhythmia but its explicit topic. Revolution forces this arrhythmia to the surface. If every revolution is too early (were conditions prepared there would be no need of one), it is equally too late (no revolution can keep up with its own initiative). It's an extreme case but it only makes explicit the propulsive energy of experience as such – the price of its improvisatory daring. This is why the conjunction in "Absolute-freedom-and-Terror" signals not a contingent coupling but a strict identity: it marks the unconditional claim of freedom itself.

Here the "philosophical" character of the French Revolution – what Burke (as Balfour notes) called "upstart theory"–is paramount. Philosophy borders Terror at both edges. If the Revolution is like the filling in a sandwich whose crusts are the "white bread" of the French Enlightenment, on one side, and the "black bread" of German idealism, on the other, this does not guarantee that philosophy will be able to contain, or corral, or quarantine the Terror.[31] For one thing philosophy itself is responsible for generating this terror: by Hegel's own reckoning, the absolutism of absolute freedom is inseparable from its excessive (or rather ill-timed, premature) philosophicality. It is Enlightenment's "unenlightened" attitude towards the world (§565), towards its adversaries, and towards itself that precipitates its headlong rush into the vulgar pursuit of utility and the violent regime of death. For another thing, the philosophical activity that succeeds and tries to domesticate this terror also prolongs it. This is the gist of the "Morality" section: Hegel spends the whole time flushing out the inquisitorial energy that fuels the whole idealist project. Philosophy, like the Revolution itself, comes both too early and too late. Its blinding excess is just the exorbitant – and betrayed – promise of freedom itself.

The ambiguity of Absolute Knowing is breathtaking: on the one hand it is the unflinching disclosure of the untimeliness that afflicts every shape of consciousness, including the act of disclosure itself. On the other hand, it suggests that this very lateness can be the occasion of a radical futurity –even a revolutionary new beginning. (This ambiguity explains the title of my book). The whole relationship to Kant yet again opens up: is there a sliver of irreality that is not reducible to the *Sollen*? This would exert, in the present, a counterfactual pressure that is no longer located in the realm of securely unavailable regulative ideals: the future is rather to be found in the persistence of undischarged possibilities – the missed or squandered opportunities, in short the unrealized futures, of the past. This transforms the whole temporal horizon. Change is no longer restricted to the "next step" along the continuum of the existent (this is essentially Adorno's rebuke to pragmatism: it is shortsighted and narrow, reducing every future to the perpetuation of the present day)[32] nor postponed to the remote mists of an unachievable beyond. There's something of a conversion moment: time seems to turn around. Call it hope in the past, call it dialectic at a standstill, call it trauma – I would venture to say it remains the revolutionary kernel in the carapace of the dialectical method.

4 ... And Now

A short postscript (2013). The challenge is also because the relevance of this whole discussion is less obvious and more urgent than it might seem. To say that the crisis of German philosophy c. 1800 is *also* our crisis, that the virtual-vicarious-vicious circle continues, is not to equate the two. Of course everything has changed: the geo-political situation, the institutional-ideological apparatus, the cultural-technological conditions of spectatorship itself. Apart from anything else, recent transformations of the media have transformed the public sphere – on the one hand, expanding the opportunities for vicarious consumption, both reinforcing and disguising the split between spectator and actor (along with all the other classic divisions of intellectual and manual labour); on the other hand, suggesting that the classic Marxist formulation of this split may be misleading or incomplete. The recent cycling of revolutionary upheaval and counterrevolutionary repression, with their strange synchronicities, unpredictabilities, and planetary ubiquities, have demonstrated that the border between reportage and participation can be porous, that the line between consuming and producing, between reading about and making the news may be uncertain, and that the global *translatio* moves more quickly and in more directions (including backwards) than ever before imaginable. The technologies that facilitate the spread of consumer capitalism also contribute to its interruption, while of course, at a political level, these very interruptions manage simultaneously to sustain it. There's also the dizzying effect introduced by repetition itself. Marx's mordant comment about Germany c. 1840–it's managed to experience counterrevolution without even having had its own proper revolution: it is the only country to have tasted freedom only once, on the day of freedom's own funeral – has a depressing resonance in the interminable Waterloo of the present day. Hegel might harbour unexpected resources.

NOTES

1 Not the chronological aftermath. See n. 25 below.
2 And conversely, from philosophy to politics: Hegel insists on the Revolution's pedigree in the Enlightenment, as the legacy of a utilitarianism gone berserk.
3 For a notable exception, see Alexander García Düttmann, *Philosophy of Exaggeration*, (London: Continuum, 2007).
4 Hegel, *Phenomenology of Spirit*, §28. I discuss Hegel's use of the image of the silhouette in *Mourning Sickness*, pp. 86f and, in relation to his reading of Kant at pp. 95f. Henceforth all references to the *Phenomenology* will be given in the text by paragraph numbers, using Miller's translation (modified or adapted occasionally). References to *Mourning Sickness* will be indicated by MS, followed by page number.
5 Speculative skiagraphy in this sense comes perilously close to the "monochromatic formalism" that Hegel never stops ridiculing in his immediate predecessors (§51) – which immediately raises the question of Hegel's own potential formalism, which I will explore in the next section.
6 Jacques Lacan, *Seminaire* VIII, *Le Transfert*, 413f. Lacan is adapting Freud's discussion of *der einzige Zug* in his discussion of identification in his 1921 essay on *Group Psychology and the Analysis of the Ego* (*Standard Edition* 18: 107). In Lacan's version the "trait" is the primordial term of symbolic identification – the undifferentiated or "unbroken" signifier which the subject introjects in the construction of the ego ideal. Abbreviation thus tends, in Lacan, towards embellishment or improvement (rather than reduction or denigration, as in Hegel) but the result is similar: it allows for the efficient transmission or transfer of symbolic capital to the next "generation."

7 Adorno, *Minima Moralia*, §29. Lacan and Adorno are not the only ones to have taken Hegel's observation to heart. As many have observed (this is usually meant as an insult), Heidegger was also at his most Hegelian when he formulated his infamous pronouncement: "every thinker thinks only *one* thought" (see Heidegger, *Was heißt Denken?*, 20; the point is even more forcefully stated in *Nietzsche* I, 475 (trans. *Nietzsche* vol. 3: 6): "Each thinker things only one *single* thought."). Or, which amounts to more or less the same thing: each epoch is dominated by a *single* interpretation of Being. (See Heidegger, "Die Zeit des Weltbildes," GA 5:75; *Question concerning Technology*, 115; or again, in *Aus der Erfahrung des Denkens*, GA 13:76: "To think is to confine oneself to a *single* thought that one day stands still like a star in the night sky.") This is the precondition for writing something like a history-of-Being: every author can be reduced to a single leitmotif, every epoch to a single metaphysical world view, and history in its entirety to a single sweep of accumulating *Seinsvergessenheit*. The whole past condenses into a series of monadic abbreviations – *ousia*, ens realissimum, cogito, I=I, Spirit, Will-to-Power, and so on – a list of proper names which in their mnemotechnic efficiency impart unity, meaning, and direction to a history which might otherwise display none. (For an extreme example of this abbreviating historiography, see Heidegger, *Nietzsche* IV, 136–138, cf. 97–135.)

8 Hegel corrects the implicit gradualism of the developmental model at §11, 12.

9 Slavoj Zizek has frequently emphasized the significance of Hegel's celebration of the disintegrative powers of *Verstand* (which Zizek at times associates with a "presynthetic" tendency in the Kantian productive imagination). For his most sustained comments see *Tarrying with the Negative* (Durham: Duke Univeristy Press, 1993), 38–9; 140–146; and *Less than Nothing: Hegel and the Shadow of Dialectical Materialism* (2012), 285–87. Robert Sinnerbrink has a fine discussion of this in "The Uses of Disenchantment: Remarks on Rebecca Comay's Mourning Sickness: Hegel and the French Revolution," in *Parrhesia* (2013) 17: 41–9.

10 Adorno, *Negative Dialectics*, trans. E.B. Ashton (New York: Routledge, 2004), 23.

11 The primal scene is described by Pliny the elder in *Natural History*, Book XXXV, chap. 15, and becomes the subject of numerous allegorical paintings in the eighteenth century when, under the influence of Lavater's physiognomic theory, the silhouette became a popular medium of portraiture. There is thus an unmistakable irony in Hegel's decision to assign speculative significance to this figure in the preface to a work in which he will express his most virulent antipathy to everything Lavater represents (see §§309–346 for Hegel's attack on physiognomy

and phrenology). Hegel's museal description of Absolute Knowing as a "gallery of pictures" (§808) can in this light also be seen as a kind of shadow-theatre – a Platonic cave in which the relative positions of spectator, spectacle and dramaturge (or puppet-master) are constantly subject to renegotiation, and from which there is neither the possibility nor the necessity of exit. (Hegel's famous image of the "ladder," in the Preface – "the individual has the right to demand that science provide him at least with the ladder to reach this standpoint" (§26) is in this sense deeply misleading.)

12 Cf. Roland Barthes, *Camera Lucida*: Reflections on Photography. Trans. By Richard Howard (New York: Hill and Wang, 1982)

13 These associations are noted in Wendy Bellion, "Heads of State: Profiles and Politics in Jeffersonian America," in *New Media, 1740–1915*, ed. Lisa Gitelman and Geoffrey Pingere (Cambridge, MA: MIT Press, 2003): 42. On the relationship between the guillotine and the art of portraiture, see Daniel Arasse, *La guillotine et l'imaginaire de la Terreur* (Paris: Flammarion, 1987) and Patrick Wald Lasowski, *Les échafauds du romanesque* (Lille: Presses universitaire de Lille, 1991).

14 (General anaesthetic had not yet been invented.) On aether and natural science, in the eighteenth century, cf. Enz II., §§188.

15 Hegel, *Wissenschaft der Logik*, Bd. II, S. 471, 481.

16 Cf. Ernst Bloch, *Heritage of Our Times*, trans. Neville and Stephen Plaice (Berkeley: University of California Press, 1991).

17 Cf. Walter Benjamin, "Surrealism: The Last Snapshot of the European Intelligentsia," in *Selected Writings* (Cambridge Mass.: Harvard University Press, 1999), 2:210.

18 "But all things excellent are as difficult as they are rare." Spinoza, *Ethics* V, 42n.

19 I explore the ambiguities of this transaction in the fifth chapter of *Mourning Sickness*. The allusion is to Kafka's short parable, "Das Kommen des Messias," in Kafka, Parables and Paradoxes (New York: Schocken Books, 1961), 80–1.

20 See MS, esp. the fifth chapter, "Terrors of the Tabula Rasa."

21 John McDowell, *Mind and World* (Cambridge: Harvard University Press, 1996), passim.

22 John McCumber, "Writing Up (Down) the Truth: Hegel and Schiller at the end of *The Phenomenology of Spirit*," in eds. Richard A. Block, Peter David Fenves, Géza von Molnár, *The Spirit of Poesy: Essays on Jewish and German Literature and Thought* (Evanston: Northwestern University Press, 2000), 47–60. This fine essay came to my attention too late to discuss in my reading of the "foaming chalice" passage in my essay "Hegel's Last Words: Mourning and Melancholia at the End of the *Phenomenology*," in

Amy Swiffen and Joshua Nichols, eds., *The End of History* (New York: Routledge, 2012). I further develop this reading in *The Dash*, co-authored with Frank Ruda, which centres on the problem of Absolute Knowing and the transition from the *Phenomenology* to the *Logic*. See Frank Ruda and Rebecca Comay, *The Dash: The Other Side of Absolute Knowledge* (MIT Press, 2018).

23 Hegel, *The Philosophy of History*, trans. J. Sibree (New York: Dover, 1956), 447.

24 The *locus classicus* of this argument is of course Kant's *Conflict of the Faculties, in Religion and Rational Theology*, trans. and ed. Allen W. Wood and George di Giovanni (Cambridge: Cambridge University Press, 1996), 301–2; 307n.

25 This should not be confused with the *chronological* aftermath (Kant's second *Critique* was published in 1788). The "calendar of facts" does not synchronize with the "calendar of experience," to rephrase Proust slightly. If "morality" follows the Revolution in the order of experience, if it presents itself as the event's *phenomenological* successor, this is because Kantian practical philosophy attains legibility only retroactively as a result of the Revolution it chronologically preceded: the precursor becomes the successor to its own successor. And conversely: the Revolution also becomes legible retroactively: it attains its historical significance in the light of the philosophical articulation that (phenomenologically) succeeds it (thus also becoming successor to *its* own successor). Both Kant and the Revolution thus reciprocally subject each other to a "posthumous shock." This is why the last part of the Spirit chapter is less concerned with the philosophical "responses" to the Terror (Hegel ignores the *Conflict of the Faculties*, for example, or Fichte's *Zurückforderung*) than with the practical attitudes enabling such response, which is why the dates start to flow backwards at this point (just like geography shifts eastward, as we'll see in a moment). See MS, chapter two, "The Kantian Theater," for further discussion.

26 Hegel, *Philosophy of History*, esp. 78–9; *Philosophy of Right* §258 (*Gang des Gottes*), 275–81.

27 Although the theological details are interesting, see MS, chapter three, "The Corpse of Faith."

28 These three phrases allude to, respectively, George Berkeley, *A Treatise Concerning the Principles of Human Knowledge, in The Works of George Berkeley*, eds. A.A. Luce and T.E. Jessop (London: Thomas Nelson, 1949) 42, 72–3; Samuel Beckett, *Worstward Ho* (1983) (e.g., the phrase "circus colors" on the philosophical significance of grey in Beckett's plays, is borrowed by Theodor Adorno, *Aesthetic Theory* (Minneapolis: University of Minnesota Press, 1997), 81; and Kant, *Critique of Practical Reason*. Also see, MS, 142–5.

29 Hegel, *Philosophy of History*, 99.
30 A "total sacrifice," writes Hegel: "it has nothing positive and thus can give nothing in return for the sacrifice." ((§594).
31 See Thomas Saine, *Black Bread – White Bread: German Intellectuals and the French Revolution* (Columbia, SC: Camden House, 1988)
32 "Hence the contrast between dialectics and pragmatism, like every distinction in philosophy, is reduced to a nuance, namely, to the conception of that 'next step.' The pragmatist, however, defines it as adjustment, and this perpetuates the domination of what is always the same. Were dialectics to sanction this, it would renounce itself in renouncing the idea of potentiality. But how is potentiality to be conceived if it is not to be abstract and arbitrary, like the utopias dialectical philosophers proscribed? Conversely, how can the next step assume direction and aim without the subject knowing more than what is already given? If one chose to reformulate Kant's question, one could ask today: *how is anything new possible at all?*" Adorno, Veblen's Attack on Culture," *Prisms*, trans. Samuel and Shierry Weber (Cambridge: MIT Press, 1983), 91.

REFERENCES

Adorno, Theodor W. *Negative Dialectics*. Translated by E.B. Ashton. New York: Routledge, 2004.
—— *Minima Moralia: Reflections on a Damaged Life*. Translated by E.F.N. Jephcott. New York: Verso, 2005.
Comay, Rebecca. *Mourning Sickness: Hegel and the French Revolution*. Stanford University Press, 2010, 2011.
Hegel, G.W.F. *Vorlesungen über die Philosophie die Geschichte (1822–1831)/ Lectures on the Philosophy of History*. Translated by J. Sibree. New York: Dover, 1956.
—— *Enzyklopädie der philosophischen Wissenschaften im Grundrisse II (1830)/ Hegel's Philosophy of Nature*. Edited and translated by M.J. Petry. London/ New York: Humanities Press, 1970.
—— *Phänomenologie des Geistes (1806)*. Edited by H.-F. Wessels and H. Clairmont. Hamburg: Felix Meiner Verlag, 1988/Phenomenology of Spirit. Translated by A.V. Miller. Oxford: Oxford University Press, 1977.
—— *The Elements of the Philosophy of Right*. Edited by Allen Wood and translated by H.B. Niesbet. Cambridge: Cambridge University Press, 1991.
—— *Wissenschaft der Logik (2 Bände) (1812–16)/Hegel's Science of Logic*. Translated by A.V. Miller. Amherst, NY: Prometheus Books, 1997.

Notes on Contributors

Emilia Angelova is Associate Professor of Philosophy at Concordia University, Montreal, Canada. She holds a PhD in philosophy from the University of Toronto. Her research is in nineteenth- and twentieth-century continental philosophy and Kant. Her work has been directed to study of themes raised by Kant and transformed by Heidegger, e.g., selfhood, temporality, freedom, and the imagination. She has published mainly on Heidegger and Kant; other articles are on Hegel, Deleuze, and Nancy, and French feminist philosopher Julia Kristeva. She is the editor of an anthology on Kristeva, *Revolution in Poetic Language Fifty Years Later: New Directions in Kristeva Studies* (State University of New York Press: 2024).

Ian Balfour is Professor Emeritus of English at York University, where he also taught in the Graduate Program in Social & Political Thought. He is the author of *Northrop Frye* and *The Rhetoric of Romantic Prophecy*. He edited with Atom Egoyan *Subtitles: On the Foreignness of Film* and with Eduardo Cadava a double-issue of *South Atlantic Quarterly* on human rights, and was the sole editor of a *South Atlantic Quarterly* issue on *Late Derrida*. He was a co-translator of Walter Benjamin's dissertation for the Harvard edition. He has taught at Cornell as the M.H. Abrams Distinguished Visiting Professor of English and held visiting professorships at Williams College, Rice University, and the Johann Wolfgang Goethe University in Frankfurt, among others. He is currently completing a book on the sublime.

Jennifer Ann Bates is Professor of Philosophy at Duquesne University (PhD University of Toronto, 1997). She specializes in nineteenth-century German philosophy with an emphasis on Hegel. She is author of three books: *Over-Measure in Kant, Hegel, and Shakespeare: Putting the*

Principles Into Play (Bloomsbury, 2025), *Hegel's Theory of Imagination* (SUNY, 2004) and *Hegel and Shakespeare on Moral Imagination* (SUNY, 2010), and co-editor with Richard Wilson of *Shakespeare and Continental Philosophy* (Edinburgh University Press, 2014). She has published articles in *Philosophy Compass* and *Environmental Ethics*, as well as in literary journals (*Criticism, Memoria di Shakespeare*, and *The Wallace Stevens Journal*). She also published many book chapters. Since 2018 she is the editor-in-chief of *Idealistic Studies: An Interdisciplinary Journal of Philosophy*. Her research and teaching interests include philosophy and literature, philosophy of nature, environmental ethics, and Buddhist philosophy.

Nahum Brown is Assistant Professor in the philosophy and religious studies department at Mahidol International College, Mahidol University. He is the author of two books about Hegel: *Hegel on Possibility: Dialectics, Contradiction, and Modality* (Bloomsbury, 2020) and Hegel's Actuality Chapter of the *Science of Logic*: A Commentary (Lexington Books, 2018). He is also the main editor of two volumes on the philosophy of religion and intercultural philosophy: *Contemporary Debates in Negative Theology and Philosophy* (edited with J. Aaron Simmons, Palgrave Macmillan, 2017) and *Transcendence, Immanence, and Intercultural Philosophy* (edited with William Franke, Palgrave Macmillan, 2016). In addition, he has published numerous articles and book chapters on German idealism and contemporary continental philosophy.

Timothy L. Brownlee is Professor of Philosophy at Xavier University in Cincinnati, Ohio, where he also directs the Philosophy, Politics, and the Public Honors Program. He is the author of numerous articles on Hegel and German Idealism, and of the monograph *Recognition and the Self in Hegel's Phenomenology of Spirit* (Cambridge University Press, 2023).

Rebecca Comay is Professor of Philosophy and Comparative Literature at the University of Toronto, where she is also co-director of the Program in Literary Studies. She is the author of *Mourning Sickness: Hegel and the French Revolution* (Stanford: Stanford University Press, 2010) and co-editor (with John McCumber) of *Endings: Questions of Memory in Hegel and Heidegger* (Northwestern University Press, 1999). Her work engages the intersection of philosophy, literature, and psychoanalysis. Recent articles include: "Resistance and Repetition: Freud and Hegel," in *Research in Phenomenology* (2015) and "Hegel's Last Words: Mourning and Melancholia at the end of the *Phenomenology*," in Joshua Nichols and Amy Swiffen, eds., *The Ends of History* (Routledge, 2012). She developed a reading of mourning and melancholia in a monograph *The

Dash-The Other Side of Absolute Knowing, co-authored with Frank Ruda (MIT Press, 2018) and co-edited with Bart Zantvoort, *Hegel and Resistance: History, Politics and Dialectics* (Bloomsbury, 2019). In 2024, on recommendation of the University of Copenhagen's Faculty of Theology, she was awarded an Honorary Doctorate, including for her pioneering examination of the work of G. W. F. Hegel.

Niels Feuerhahn has translated several texts from German and French into English. Most recently he is the co-translator of the first English translation of Martin Heidegger's *Hegel* (Indiana University Press, 2015). He holds a BA in German philology from the University of Münster, Germany, an MA in philosophy from Concordia University, and a PhD in philosophy from the University of Guelph, Canada. His dissertation, "Nostalgia and the Displacement of Identity: A Time-Based Analysis of the Unheimlichkeit of Nostalgia," engages with the ideas of Søren Kierkegaard, Martin Heidegger and Paul Ricoeur, to develop a novel account of nostalgia. His main areas of research are metaphysics, ethics, and the interdisciplinary field of critical animal studies.

Stephen Houlgate is Professor of Philosophy at the University of Warwick. He is the author of *Hegel, Nietzsche and the Criticism of Metaphysics* (1986), *An Introduction to Hegel: Freedom, Truth and History* (1991, 2nd ed. 2005), *The Opening of Hegel's Logic* (2006), *Hegel's Phenomenology of Spirit* (2013), and *Hegel on Being*, 2 vols., of which volume 1 is *Quality and the Birth of Quantity in Hegel's* Science of Logic (2021) and volume 2 is *Quantity and Measure in Hegel's'* Science of Logic (2022) and he has also published numerous articles on Hegel, as well as on Kant, Schiller, Schelling, Nietzsche, Derrida, Danto, Rawls, Brandom and McDowell. He is the editor of *Hegel and the Philosophy of Nature* and *The Hegel Reader* (both 1998), *Hegel and the Arts* (2007) and *G.W.F. Hegel: Elements of the Philosophy of Right* (2008), and co-editor with Michael Baur of *A Companion to Hegel* (2011). He served as Vice-president and President of the Hegel Society of America and was editor of the *Bulletin of the Hegel Society of Great Britain* from 1998 to 2006. He is currently President of the Hegel Society of Great Britain.

Iain Macdonald is Professor of Philosophy at Université de Montréal. His publications include work on Hegel, Adorno, Heidegger, metaphysics, and aesthetics, among other topics. His most recent book is *What Would Be Different: Figures of Possibility in Adorno* (Stanford: Stanford University Press, 2019). He was the holder of the Leibniz Chair at the

University of Leipzig in 2021–2 and is a former fellow of the *Bad Homburg Forschungskolleg Humanwissenschaften*.

John McCumber is Professor Emeritus and was Distinguished Research Professor and Chair of Germanic Languages at UCLA. He received his doctorate from the University of Toronto, and has taught there and at the University of Michigan – Dearborn, the Graduate Faculty of the New School for Social Research, Northwestern University, John Carroll University, and UCLA. He was professor of Germanic Studies at UCLA. He is the author of numerous books and articles, including *Metaphysics and Oppression: Heidegger's Challenge to Western Philosophy* (Indiana University Press, 2000); *Time in the Ditch: American Philosophy and the McCarthy Era* (Northwestern University Press, 2001); *Time and Philosophy: A History of Continental Thought* (Acumen, 2011); *On Philosophy: Notes From a Crisis* (Stanford University Press, 2013); and *Understanding Hegel's Mature Critique of Kant* (Stanford University Press, 2014). He held the Koldyke Distinguished Teaching Professorship at Northwestern 1994–1996, and three of his books have won CHOICE Outstanding Title awards.

Angelica Nuzzo is Professor of Philosophy at the Graduate Center and Brooklyn College (City University of New York). She is the author of: *Approaching Hegel's Logic, Obliquely. Melville, Molière, Beckett* (SUNY, 2018); *History, Memory, Justice in Hegel* (Macmillan, 2012); *Ideal Embodiment. Kant's Theory of Sensibility* (Indiana University Press, 2008); and *Kant and the Unity of Reason* (Purdue University Press, 2005). And she is the editor of several collected volumes: *Hegel on Religion and Politics* (2013); *Hegel and the Analytic Tradition* (2009). She has written two books in Italian on Hegel, *Rappresentazione e concetto nella logica della Filosofia del diritto* and *Logica e sistema*.

Jeffrey Reid is Full Professor of Philosophy at the University of Ottawa. He has published books and articles on Hegel and German Idealism in both French and English, including *Real Words: Language and System in Hegel* (2007); and *The Anti-Romantic: Hegel Against Ironic Romanticism* (2014), and *Reason and Revelation in Hegel: Metaphysical Dimensions of the Absolute* (University of Toronto Press, 2025).

Michael Quante is Professor of Practical Philosophy in the Department of Philosophy at the University of Münster and Vice-Rector for Internationalization, Transfer, and Sustainability. He is Speaker of the *Centrum für Bioethik* and principal investigator of the Exzellenzcluster *Religion* *und Politik*. His areas of specialization include German idealism, theory of action, personal identity, ethics and biomedical ethics. He is author and co-author of 15 monographs, editor and co-editor of more than 30 volumes and has published more than 300 papers. His research has been translated into more than ten languages. He has been president of the German Philosophical Association (2012–14). Since 10/2017 he is both Chairman of the International Marx-Engels-Foundation [Internationale Marx-Engels-Stiftung; IMES] and Head of the Commission for the Marx-Engels Complete Edition of the Berlin-Brandenburg Academy of Science and Humanities. Monographs (in English): *Hegel's Concept of Action* (Cambridge University Press 2004, pbk. 2007), *Enabling Social Europe* (Springer 2005; co-authored with Bernd v. Maydell et al.), *Discovering, Reflecting and Balancing Values: Ethical Management in Vocational Education Training* (Hampp 2014; co-authored with Martin Büscher), Interdisciplinary Research and Trans-disciplinary Validity Claims. Berlin: Springer 2014 (co-authored with Carl F. Gethmann et al.), *Personal Identity as a principle of biomedical ethics* (Springer 2017), *Pragmatistic Anthropology* (Mentis 2018), *Spirit's Actuality* (Mentis 2018) and *Human Persons* (Mentis 2020).

Alberto L. Siani is an Associate Professor of Aesthetics in the Department of Civilizations and Forms of Knowledge at the University of Pisa. He studied philosophy in Italy and Germany and received his PhD through a joint program of the Scuola Normale Superiore di Pisa and the FernUniversität Hagen, with a dissertation on art and politics in Hegel (2010). After two years as an Alexander von Humboldt postdoctoral research fellow and temporary lecturer at the Universität Münster, he was an associate professor in the Department of Philosophy of Yeditepe University, Istanbul, before returning to Italy in 2016. He has done research mostly on the aesthetics of Hegel and German Idealism and, more recently, on landscape aesthetics. Among his publications, the books *Landscape Aesthetics: Toward an Engaged Ecology* (Columbia University Press, 2024) and *Hegel and the Present of Art's Past Character* (Routledge, 2024), as well as the co-edited volume *Women Philosophers on Autonomy. Historical and Contemporary Perspectives* (with S. Bergès, Routledge, 2018).

Jim Vernon is Professor of Philosophy at York University, where he teaches nineteenth- and twentieth-century continental philosophy. His recent work concerns resonances between Hegel's political philosophy and the emancipatory social movements of the 1960s and 1970s. He is the author of *Hegel's Philosophy of Language* (Continuum, 2007), *Sampling,*

Biting, and The Postmodern Subversion of Hip Hop (Palgrave MacMillan, 2021), and co-editor of several books: *Hegel and Deleuze: Together Again for the First Time* (Northwestern, 2013; with Karen Houle); *Intensities and Lines of Flight: Deleuze/Guattari and the Arts* (Rowman & Littlefield, 2014; with Antonio Calcagno and Steve G. Lofts); and *Badiou and Hegel: Infinity, Dialectics, Subjectivity* (Lexington, 2015; with Antonio Calcagno).

Index